ISLAMIC MODERNITIES IN WORLD SOCIETY

Edinburgh Studies of the Globalised Muslim World

Series Editor: **Frédéric Volpi**, Director, Prince Alwaleed Bin Talal Centre for the Study of Contemporary Islam, University of Edinburgh

This innovative series investigates the dynamics of Muslim societies in a globalised world. It considers the boundaries of the contemporary Muslim world, their construction, their artificiality or durability. It sheds new light on what it means to be part of the Muslim world today, for both those individuals and communities who live in Muslim-majority countries and those who reside outside and are part of a globalised ummah. Its analysis encompasses the micro and the macro level, exploring the discourses and practices of individuals, communities, states and transnational actors who create these dynamics. It offers a multidisciplinary perspective on the salient contemporary issues and interactions that shape the internal and external relations of the Muslim world.

Forthcoming and available titles

Salafi Social and Political Movements: National and Transnational Contexts
Masooda Bano

A Political Theory of Muslim Democracy
Ravza Altuntaş-Çakır

Literary Neo-Orientalism and the Arab Uprisings: Tensions in English, French and German Language Fiction
Julia Wurr

Why Islamists Go Green
Emmanuel Karagiannis

Islamic Modernities in World Society: The Rise, Spread, and Fragmentation of a Hegemonic Idea
Dietrich Jung

edinburghuniversitypress.com/series/esgmw

ISLAMIC MODERNITIES IN WORLD SOCIETY

The Rise, Spread, and Fragmentation of a Hegemonic Idea

Dietrich Jung

EDINBURGH
University Press

Edinburgh University Press is one of the leading university presses in the UK. We publish academic books and journals in our selected subject areas across the humanities and social sciences, combining cutting-edge scholarship with high editorial and production values to produce academic works of lasting importance. For more information visit our website: edinburghuniversitypress.com

© Dietrich Jung, 2023, 2025

Edinburgh University Press Ltd
13 Infirmary Street
Edinburgh EH1 1LT

First published in hardback by Edinburgh University Press 2023

Typeset in 11/15pt EB Garamond by
Cheshire Typesetting Ltd, Cuddington, Cheshire

A CIP record for this book is available from the British Library

ISBN 978 1 4744 9263 8 (hardback)
ISBN 978 1 4744 9264 5 (paperback)
ISBN 978 1 4744 9265 2 (webready PDF)
ISBN 978 1 4744 9266 9 (epub)

The right of Dietrich Jung to be identified as author of this work has been asserted in accordance with the Copyright, Designs and Patents Act 1988 and the Copyright and Related Rights Regulations 2003 (SI No. 2498).

CONTENTS

Acknowledgments	vii
Series Editor's Foreword	ix
Introduction: Why this Book and What Is its Argument?	1

PART I STATE OF THE ART AND THEORETICAL FRAMEWORK

1 Islam and Modernity: A Brief Discussion of the State of the Art — 13
2 The Emergence of World Society: Projects of Modernity in Global Social Contexts — 34

PART II MODERN STATE FORMATION AND THE ISLAMIC DISCOURSE OF MODERNITY

3 From Empire to National States: Modernization in the Ottoman Empire — 71
4 Making Modernity Islamic: The Quest for Religious, Political and Social Reform — 98
5 Diverging Directions: "Islamist" and "Secularist" Projects of Muslim Modernities — 128

PART III SCIENCE, ECONOMICS, AND AGENCY IN THE ISLAMIC DISCOURSE OF MODERNITY

6 Boundary Negotiations between Islam and Science: The Islamization of Knowledge and the Idea of an Islamic University 157

7 Boundary Negotiations between Islam and Economics: Islamic Finance, Halal Markets, and the Muslim Entrepreneur 196

8 Multiple Jihads: Modern Social Actorhood in the Name of Islam 231

Conclusions: The Mosaic of Islamic Modernities 258

Bibliography 275
Index 312

ACKNOWLEDGMENTS

This book is a kind of synthesis of about three decades of academic work. Consequently, to mention all of my colleagues, students, and other interlocutors who contributed to this book would be an elusive attempt. This is also not the place for academic name-dropping, so here I only acknowledge those who were directly involved in the writing and production of this book. The contributions of the many others who do not appear by name, however, are not forgotten.

In terms of institutions, I would like to thank the Centre for Advanced Studies in the Humanities and Social Sciences (CASHSS) "Multiple Secularities—Beyond the West, Beyond Modernities" at Leipzig University. The centre granted me two fellowships for four months in the fall of 2021 and the fall of 2022. I wrote large parts of the book at CASHSS. Together with their team, the directors of the centre, Monika Wohlrab-Sahr and Christoph Kleine, have shaped a scholarly and social environment which was enormously conducive to the writing of this book. Moreover, discussions with the international group of junior and senior fellows at the centre contributed remarkably to the development of my thoughts.

Equally important for the work on this book was the monograph fellowship that the Carlsberg Foundation gave me for the year of 2022. The foundation covered my salary expenses, thus giving me the opportunity to focus entirely on this book. In light of the current situation at Danish universities—caused by a combination of budget cuts with a chain of shifting, almost erratic political directives and government interventions in the conditions for teaching and research—the monograph fellowship was indispensable for this book getting written in such a short period of time. It liberated me from the daily administrative nightmares of handling the abovementioned situation.

As a third institution, I would like to thank Edinburgh University Press and their anonymous reviewers for the strong support of this book. In particular, in Frédéric Volpi I found an engaged and always accessible series editor who perfectly facilitated the publication of this monograph.

Turning to a group of individuals who directly contributed to this book, I am grateful for the critique and comments that the following colleagues and friends gave me after reading through one or more of its chapters: Neslihan Çevik, Sari Hanafi, Yee Lak Elliot Lee, Kirstine Sinclair, Monika Wohlrab-Sahr, Stephan Stetter, Ahmed Abou El Zalaf, and Florian Zemmin. Thanks to all of you for spending hours of your precious time on helping me develop my work further. In addition, my thanks also go to Catherine Schwerin, an old friend who nevertheless has been a strict language proofreader of my publications since the 1990s.

Finally, I am privileged for the support of my family in being able to do this kind of work. My wife Marianne and my son Oskar have often been confronted with not only my physical but also my mental absence while walking through our house with the analysis of Islamic modernities in mind. Thank you so much for enduring this over so many years. I dedicate this book to my mother Margarete Jung, who always encouraged me in my, for her often puzzling, endeavors. Sadly, she was no longer able to relate to the work on this book due to the ravages of progressive dementia, but the spirit of her support remains with me.

SERIES EDITOR'S FOREWORD

The Edinburgh Studies in the Globalised Muslim World is a series that focuses on the contemporary transformations of Muslim societies. "Globalization" is meant here to denote that although the Muslim world has always interacted with other societal, religious, imperial, or national forces over the centuries, the evolution of these interconnections constantly reshapes Muslim societies. The second half of the twentieth century has been characterised by the increasing number and diversity of exchanges on a global scale bringing people and societies "closer," for better and for worse. The beginning of the twenty-first century confirmed the increasingly glocalized nature of these interactions and the challenges and opportunities that they bring to existing institutional, social and cultural orders.

The series is not a statement that everything is different in today's brave new world. Indeed, many "old" ideas and practices still have much currency in the present, and undoubtedly will continue to in the future. Rather the series emphasizes how our current globalized condition shapes and mediates how past worldviews and modes of being are transmitted between people and institutions. The contemporary Muslim world is not merely a reflection of past histories, but it is also a living process of creating a new order on the basis of what people want, desire, fear and hope. This creative endeavor can transform existing relations for the better, for example by reconsidering the relations between society and the environment. They can equally fan violence and hatred as illustrated in the reignition of cycles of conflicts over sovereignties, ideologies, or resources across the globe.

The Globalised Muslim World series arrives at a challenging time for any inquiry into Muslim societies. The new millennium began inauspiciously with a noticeable spike in transnational and international violence framed in "civilizational" terms. A decade of "war of terror" contributed to the entrenching of negative mutual perceptions across the globe while also reinforcing essentialist views. The ensuing decade hardly improved this situation, with political and territorial conflicts multiplying in different parts of the Muslim world, and some of the most violent groups laying claim to the idea of a global caliphate to justify themselves. Yet, a focus on trajectories of violence gives a distorted picture of the evolution of Muslim societies and their relations with the rest of the world. This series is very much about the "what else" is happening as we move further into the twenty-first century.

Dietrich Jung's *Islamic Modernities in World Society: The Rise, Spread, and Fragmentation of a Hegemonic Idea* is an important contribution to the debate over the place of Islamic ideas and practices in the contemporary world. The book challenges common representations of modernity grounded in the notion that new western views and practices were foisted upon traditional Muslim societies. Instead, Jung outlines the multiple and varied occurrences of modernist thoughts and actions having their roots in multifaceted Muslim communities that laid the foundations for contemporary ways of being Muslim in an ever more globalized social order. By locating this more complex Muslim world within the main theoretical approaches to world society, the book provides new ways of understanding how the Islamic tradition constitute an active part of our shared global modernities.

The empirical evidence presented in this book illustrates Jung's argument from both a historical perspective and in connection to pressing contemporary issues. Starting with the emergence of the modern state system in the Ottoman context, the book provides an insightful account of the socio-religious and political modernization dynamics that underpinned the process of state formation and the emergence of a reform-oriented Islamic discourse. Jung then completes this account of a rather standard process of modernization in this socio-historical context by analyzing the creative impulse given by Islamic reformers who did not simply oppose or adopt western social perspectives on state and society, but instead opened new possibilities that transformed Muslim communities from within. These historical reflections conclude with the case of the secularization and Islamization of society by highlighting similarities between the processes of constructing modern citizens and modern Muslim actors in the nationalist and Islamic discourses that gained prominence within national and transnational communities.

In the final part of the book, Jung considers three crucial contemporary dimensions of Islamic modernities: the scientific positioning of Islamic knowledge, the economic implications of Islamic worldviews, and the discursive articulation of an elusive notion of Jihad as a form of agency. He illustrates how the growing visibility of new Islamic centers of knowledge in the academic world since the turn of the century indicates not only the interpenetration of multiple modernities but also the synergies that Muslim intellectuals create within and across social and educational systems. These endeavors are but one of the many economic dimensions of the expression of Islamic beliefs in globalized economy where both "older" and "newer" ways of being Muslim have tangible financial embodiments that shape both individual consumerism and institutional choices. Finally, the ever-evolving debate about the meaning and significance of jihad is used to provide a useful evaluation of the type of agency that is exercised of Muslim actors in such changing socio-historical circumstances.

Jung's contribution is a most welcome addition to the literature on both sociological approaches to global modernity and the studies of the Muslim world, one that will undoubtedly be influential in changing the way in which scholars conceive "east–west" interconnectivity.

Professor Frédéric Volpi
Chair in the Politics of the Muslim World
The University of Edinburgh

INTRODUCTION: WHY THIS BOOK AND WHAT IS ITS ARGUMENT?

This book is one of my last acts after having spent almost two decades of research on Islam and modernity. Even more important, it is also a personal account of more than 40 years of participant observations among Muslim peoples. Since a first trip to North Africa in summer 1978, I have studied, traveled, worked, and lectured in countries from Morocco in the west to Indonesia in the east. To be sure, personally I never really did research as an anthropologist. I made my—methodologically speaking, admittedly not very sophisticated—participant observations as a lorry driver, a construction worker, a language student, a tourist, and later as a research fellow, guest professor, and lecturer in countries such as Algeria, Egypt, India, Indonesia, Iran, Israel, Jordan, Kyrgyzstan, Lebanon, Malaysia, Morocco, Singapore, Sudan, Syria, Tunisia, Turkey, the United Arab Emirates, and Yemen. The inspiration to conduct the empirical case studies in this book is closely linked to the vast amount of anecdotal data from these years of participant observations. I have combined these data with the intense study of primary and secondary sources. Center stage of this book is the probably elusive purpose of putting an end to the meanwhile utterly fruitless debate about the (in)compatibility of Islam and modernity. What else are contemporary Muslims if not modern?

While the answer to this question seems so obvious, generations of scholars have dedicated their life and work to endless discussions about the relationship between Islam and modernity—and so did I. In more than a century of scholarship on Islam, this has seemingly been the central puzzle to solve.[1] In dealing with this relationship, scholars employed—more often implicitly than explicitly—sociological concepts of modernity, thereby representing different streams of social thought. In the end, these theoretical set pieces of social thought determined the way in which they attempted to solve the puzzle. In this book, I will by and large do the same. However, as far as I am concerned, my final answer to the question about Islam *in* modernity builds on an explicit and reflected-upon theoretical perspective.[2] The case studies in this book are written within a framework of global modernity that is based on a distinct and non-normative concept of modernity as world society.[3] This book is therefore about Islam in world society; it is about the various ways in which Muslims have imagined and practiced living modern lives in a globally shared social context. In the following chapters, I will explore these multiple Islamic modernities as inherent parts of a world society.

On my first visit to Cairo in 1980, Islam did not play the same visible role in the everyday life of the Egyptian capital as it does today. Of course, when dusk fell, the city resounded with echoes of the call to prayer from thousands of minarets. Yet when I was walking by the dilapidated facades of Cairo's city center from Tahrir Square toward Talaat Harb in August 1980, religious body politics expressed by head scarfs, abayas, Salafi outfits, and prophetic beards were not the dominant sight. A couple of years later, I took my first lessons in colloquial Arabic in Cairo. On a taxi ride from *waṣt al-balad* (city center) back to the quarter of Mouhandiseen, my "ethical soundscape" was still not that of the cassette sermons of an Islamic revival as described in Charles Hirschkind's book.[4] On the contrary, it was the Egyptian-born French singer and actress Dalida singing *Helwa Ya Baladi* (how sweet are you, my motherland) that prevented me from practicing my Arabic with the man behind the steering wheel.[5] Since then, things have changed. For instance, compare the public appearance of President Gamal Abdel Nasser and his wife, Tahia Kazzem, with that of the incumbent President Abdel Fatah al-Sisi and his wife, Entisar Amer. While the outfit of the two presidents largely remains the same, this does not apply to the first ladies. Kazzem did not appear in public with a headscarf or in pious dress. By contrast, Amer accompanies her husband in accordance with a demonstratively modest Islamic dress code. How should this change be understood?

Conventional answers to this question normally refer to the "resurgence of Islam" or to an "Islamic revival." Scholars and public opinion makers often associate this revival of religion with a reaction to historical developments such as the subsequent defeats of Arab states in the series of Arab–Israeli wars, the Soviet occupation of Afghanistan, the Islamic Revolution in Iran, the people's dissatisfaction with authoritarian secular Arab regimes, the rise of Saudi Arabia as a global sponsor of purist Islamic theologies, or the alleged failure of proper political and socioeconomic integration of Muslim immigrants in Europe and North America. Without any doubt, these events and political developments may have contributed to the search for specifically Islamic forms of modernity in the contemporary imaginations of Muslim peoples. Yet, I agree with Abdeslam Maghraoui that the narrative of "Islamic resurgence" somehow excludes "the possibility of modern, legitimate politics within Islamic discursive traditions."[6] In my own terminology, this narrative has a blind eye for the social legitimacy of specifically Islamic projects of modernity. Furthermore, the terms of "revival" and "resurgence" tend to imply a previous disappearance of Islam in the modernization of the Muslim parts of the world. Yet, from a historical perspective, such is my argument, Islam as a key marker of Muslim approaches to modernity has played an—at times more or less—constant and often significant role throughout the past two centuries. Islamic modernists in the nineteenth century once launched a reform program that has resulted in an "Islamization" of the Muslim discourse of modernity in which the very concept of Islamic reform attained a highly contested nature.[7] Therefore, my book will give a complementary answer to this question of historical change, so often labeled in terms of a religious revival. Contrary to the narratives of a resurgence of Islam, I put my focus on the historical continuity behind the Islamic character of Muslim projects of modernity. It is only at a first glance that the increasing public visibility of Islamic symbols appears to be a kind of fundamental change.[8]

I will interpret the visible dominance of Islam in Muslim public life as the historically specific answer of many Muslims to the question of how one is "authentically" modern. The book selectively investigates the multiplicity of answers that Muslims have provided to this question of modern authenticity since the nineteenth century. In so doing, its focus is on those answers that combined the quest for modern authenticity with Islamic traditions. Through six historical and thematic case studies, I examine the history of specifically Islamic projects of modernity. These projects relate to ideas of citizenship, educational and moral cultivation, economic entrepreneurship, political institutions, scientific knowledge, bodily performances, and forms of consumerist and creative self-made identities. Combining sociological theory with Islamic studies, I argue that throughout the twentieth century we can observe the rise, spread, and fragmentation of a relatively hegemonic idea according to which the attachment to Islamic traditions bestows projects of Muslim modernities with cultural authenticity. It is the continuation and broad dissemination of this specifically Islamic discourse of modernity that I discern behind the current dominance of religion in the discursive environments among Muslim peoples. Drawing on various strands of social theory, I interpret this specifically Islamic discourse of modernity as an inherent part of global modernity, in conceptual terms understood as the emergence of world society. The heuristically guiding research question of this book lies, then, at the interface of the rise of projects of Islamic modernities and the emergence of modern world society. In what ways do the multiple modernities of Islam represent inherent parts of world society?[9]

In answering this question, my intention is to provide a sociological approach to complement more recent and inspiring writings of global history such as by C. A. Bayly, Sebastian Conrad, and Jürgen Osterhammel. Conceptualizing global modernity in terms of world society can deliver a sociological fundament for the attempt to understand "local, national, or regional histories" in a framework of global history. The theoretical framework of global modernity as world society put forward in this book shares the same purpose as Conrad claimed for global history: "It is a historical [sociological, D.J.] device that allows the historian [sociologist, D.J.] to pose questions and generate answers that are different from those created by other approaches."[10] Like Bayly in his *Birth of the Modern World*, I argue in this book against the deeply entrenched narrative of "Western exceptionalism" that still characterizes contemporary works of both sociologies of modernity and Islamic history. Consequently, in my work I turn against arguments such as those of Wael Hallaq that the modern state—and therewith modernity as such—is "historically, substantively, and conceptually" purely a European and North American social invention.[11] Throughout this book, I try to underpin my conceptualization of modernity as an emerging world society with the search for indigenous traces of modernity in precolonial Islamic history. In contradistinction to Hallaq, I propose that we can find various traces of an emerging modernity in precolonial Muslim history.

I combine this proposal with an analysis of the factual multiplicity of faces that Islamic projects of modernity have attained. Even more important, the search for authenticity in specifically Islamic projects of modernity evolved into a rather hegemonic discourse in the course of the twentieth century. The thrust of my argument regarding these multiple Islamic modernities and their relative hegemony among Muslim projects of modernity runs as follows:[12] Beginning with the formation of the early modern Ottoman state and the rather elitist nineteenth-century Islamic reform movement associated with figures such as the Egyptian Muhammad Abduh (1849–1905), the Indian Sayyid Ahmad Khan (1817–98), and the Ottoman Namık Kemal (1840–88), through the establishment of modern national states and organized Islamist mass movements such as the Muslim Brotherhood (1928), and beyond to contemporary Islamic networks, a broad variety of imaginations of Islamic modernities and modern Muslim identities have appeared. In the course of this continuing historical development, we can observe the emergence of the almost hegemonic idea prevalent today that only the relationship with Islamic traditions bestows projects of Muslim modernities with cultural authenticity.[13] This historically and socially constructed idea of a specifically Islamic kind of modernity, however, represents in its contemporary forms a mosaic that is assembled from a multiplicity of imaginations of the Islamic modern. We do not observe one form of Islamic modernity, but multiple modernities within Islam, of which the empirical chapters of my book will give an account.

I will substantiate this argument throughout this book's eight chapters in three parts. Following this introduction, the first part of the book presents my theoretical approach in light of the state of the art. Chapter One offers a brief and focused discussion of the ways in which contemporary scholarship in Islamic studies addresses questions of Islam in modernity. This chapter does not claim to give any kind of comprehensive overview of the current state of scholarship. Instead, it serves to indicate the transformation of the field in the past decades. I will take up some issues related to the discipline's major themes, fields of research, and core questions, situating my own study in this disciplinary setting. This current set of problems, then, leads me to the second chapter, in which I will present my specific theoretical framework for addressing the puzzling relationship of Islam in modernity. This theoretical chapter builds on a variety of sociologies of modernity such as Max Weber's concept of formal rationality, Shmuel Eisenstadt's theory of "multiple modernities," and Niklas Luhmann's Modern Systems Theory. The recourse to meta-theoretical reflections on theories of "social emergence" will help me to put these components from different social theories together in a meaningful multi-leveled framework of global modernity as world society. In this second chapter, the reader should not expect a classical discussion of my theoretical arguments in light of possible alternatives. There is simply no room to engage in broader theoretical debates. The purpose of this second chapter is to make the reader familiar with my specific take on concepts of social theory and the way in which I combine them in my own heuristic and analytical approach to questions of Islamic modernity.[14]

The second and third parts of this book comprise three case studies each. The chapters are written in a way that the readers do not necessarily have to follow their chronology. While they are connected to each other, they are nevertheless readable as single case studies. The three chapters of the second part are guided by a historical perspective on the emergence of modern patterns of statehood in Muslim regions of the world. In this part, the focus is mainly on modern boundary negotiations between the social realms of religion and politics. On the one hand, this means there is an emphasis on the formation of the modern state. The chapters discuss this historical process from the pre-modern Ottoman Empire until the establishment of national states after the First World War. On the other hand, these three chapters address the rise of the Islamic discourse of modernity as a historical process that is closely interrelated to the institutionalization of global politics in the modern state. The nineteenth-century reform efforts in the Ottoman Empire and the concomitant modernist movement of Islamic reform, as well as its fragmentation in secularist and Islamist versions of modern nationalist thought, are thus topics of the chapters in this part. In the third part of the book, I then turn to three thematically different case studies. The first addresses modern boundary negotiations between religion and science, in particular ideas about the Islamization of knowledge and the institutionalization of Islamic universities. The second case study is about the relationship between Islam and modern economics, briefly engaging in discussions about Islamic economics and the ideal type of a Muslim entrepreneur. Finally, I take a look at the multiple forms of contemporary jihad and the ways in which this classical institution of Islam has been transformed into a multifaceted religious justification for modern social actorhood. I introduce each case study with a brief conceptual discussion with respect to my general framework, providing the necessary additional analytical terms that I apply in the following chapter. Moreover, the cases are presented in a historical perspective, beginning with premodern times. Given the diverse themes and historical periods covered by these six case studies, illustrating my central argument from different angles, the readers should not expect these chapters to provide intense discussions of the state of scholarship for each case. The necessarily wide empirical scope of this book would render such an undertaking obsolete anyway. Consequently, I do not claim to be an expert in every field touched upon in this book. Yet in developing its synthetic argument, I strove to do so on a sound scholarly basis. Whether this endeavor was successful or not I must leave to the judgment of my readers.

Notes

1. For an excellent overview on this debate, see: Masud, Muhammad K., Salvatore, Armando, and van Bruinessen, Martin (eds.). 2009. *Islam and Modernity: Key Issues and Debates*. Edinburgh: Edinburgh University Press.
2. Already posing the question of Islam *and* modernity puts them in opposition to each other and is therefore wrong.
3. This is to say that I do not associate world society with cosmopolitical notions such as those of Ulrich Beck and Jürgen Habermas or projects of "world ethos" such as that once launched by Hans Küng. In my theoretical framework, world society is instead synonymous with modern society as a global unit of the social. I will elaborate more on this in Chapter Two. See: Beck, Ulrich and Nathan Sznaider. 2006. Unpacking Cosmopolitanism for the Social Sciences: A Research Agenda. *British Journal of Sociology* 57 (1): 1–23. Habermas, Jürgen. 2005. *Zwischen Naturalismus und Religion: Philosophische Aufsätze*. Frankfurt am Main: Suhrkamp. Küng, Hans. 2010. *Projekt Weltethos*. Munich: Piper.
4. Hirschkind, Charles. 2006. *The Ethical Soundscape: Cassette-Sermons and Islamic Counterpublics*. New York: Columbia University Press.
5. For the transliteration of terms from Arabic, I follow the IJMES transliteration

chart and the journal's wordlist. The only exception is my use of the term Shiite instead of Shi'i (Shi'a). When it comes to names, I normally apply the mainstream usage in English without any diacritical marks. Turkish names are written according to the Turkish alphabet. In the references, I apply the wording of the publications.

6. Maghraoui, Abdeslam M. 2006. *Liberalism without Democracy: Nationhood and Citizenship in Egypt, 1922–1936.* Durham, NC and London: Duke University Press, 144.
7. Cf. Tayob, Abdulkader. 2021. Reform in the Discourse of Islam and the Making of Muslim Subjects. *Handbook of Islam in Africa*: 223–235.
8. In the course of Muslim history, we can frequently observe the emergence of revivalist movements. This applies equally to the modern history of Islam, in which a series of revolutionary and/or reformist movements and organizations have appeared since the nineteenth century. In this sense, Islam cannot be said to have come back in the late twentieth century but follows a continuity of more or less visible revivalist activities that aim at solving problems of social order as well as answering questions of individual and collective identity constructions in the course of the past two hundred years. For a brief overview of these revivalist movements in Sunni Islam, see: Rock-Singer, Aron. 2021. The Sunni Islamic Revival. In: *The Oxford Handbook of the Sociology of the Middle East.* Edited by Armando Salvatore, Sari Hanafi, and Kieko Obuse (online publication).
9. Bayly, Christopher A. 2004. *The Birth of the Modern World 1780–1914.* London: Blackwell Publishing, 2; Conrad, Sebastian. 2016. *What is Global History?* Princeton: Princeton University Press; Osterhammel, Jürgen. 2009. *Die Verwandlung der Welt: Eine Geschichte des 19. Jahrhunderts.* Munich: C. H. Beck.
10. Conrad 2016, 11.
11. Hallaq, Wael B. 2013. *The Impossible State: Islam, Politics and Modernity's Moral Predicament:* New York: Columbia University Press, 156. I will take up my critique of Hallaq's book in the conclusions, as it implies knowledge of both my theoretical perspective and the way in which I interpret Islamic history throught it.
12. We briefly presented this argument for the first time in a journal article: Jung, Dietrich and Sinclair, Kirstine. 2015. Multiple Modernities, Modern Subjectivities and Social Order: Unity and Difference in the Rise of Islamic Modernities. *Thesis Eleven* 130 (1): 22–42.
13. There is no doubt that the rise of this discourse of Islamic modernity to a posi-

tion of cultural hegemony has witnessed non-religious challengers, most notably the state-building project of Turkey under Mustafa Kemal Atatürk (1923–38) and İsmet İnönü (1938–50) and the policies of Tunisia's first President Habib Bourguiba (1957–87). Hegemonies always exist against challenging alternatives. In this book, however, the focus is predominantly on the discourse of Islamic modernity, although in Chapter Five I will also look at Turkish secularism in comparison to the Islamist project of the Muslim Brotherhood in Egypt.

14. Since the end of the 1990s, I have developed this theoretical position and discussed it in numerous articles and in a number of books (documented in the references in Chapter Two). I will therefore refrain from reprising the tiresome enterprise of explaining it again. In this book, this would prevent me from actually making my point. While I consider theoretical debates as an important part of scholarly work, on the flip side, they often become self-referential circles of cross-citing writings without delivering any added value. When necessary, I will refer to my engagement in these debates over the past decades in the endnotes.

PART I

STATE OF THE ART AND THEORETICAL FRAMEWORK

1

ISLAM AND MODERNITY: A BRIEF DISCUSSION OF THE STATE OF THE ART

In the mid-1980s, I began my university education in political science and Islamic studies. Topics and course literature in Islamic studies still reflected the Orientalist tradition of German university teaching on the Middle East and Islam. This should not have come as a surprise. Most of our professors had forged their careers in a period of time when the hegemony of Anglophone academia, in particular of the American university, had yet to take hold. Their paths toward professorship had normally been laid in the national confines of the German academic environment. Consequently, their careers were still predicated on their mastery of philological techniques and methods of historical criticism. My professors generated most of their knowledge through the critical reading of classical texts. The thematic focus of our curriculum was thus on the Qur'an, the interpretation of the Qur'an (*tafsīr*), Islamic jurisprudence (*fiqh*), the life of the Prophet (*al-sīra al-nabawiyya*), the relationship of the early Muslims to monotheistic religious minorities (*'ahl al-kitāb*), and the early period of territorial expansion after Muhammad's death (*futūḥ*). In terms of literature, authors such as Ignaz Goldziher (1850–1921), Rudi Paret (1901–83), Joseph Schacht (1902–69), Robert Bertram Serjeant 1915–93), Julius Wellhausen (1844–1918), and Jan Arent Wensinck (1882–1939) represented an essential part of the core readings of our curriculum. In short, I enjoyed a German version of the traditional path of Islamic studies that Frédéric Volpi identified as being in a semantic and a historical continuity: the focus on legal and theological texts and the understanding of the present in continuity from a very distant past.¹

Despite its "German bias," my Islamic studies program matched almost precisely the form of Western research on Islam criticized by the late Albert Hourani (1915–93). The Oxford historian once pointed to the fact that this research tradition put all-too-much emphasis on politics, law, and Muslim unity at the expense of Islam's plurality of religious belief and practices.² Indeed, our studies treated Islam as a systematic normative order, with its foundation in the life of the Prophet and its further elaboration in Islamic law. Consequently, my MA examinations precisely reflected this classical focus. I wrote a paper about jihad in traditional Islamic jurisprudence that I based on texts from the "book of jihad" (*kitāb al-jihād*) by the Hanafi jurist Ahmad al-Sarakhsi (1009–1090). In my oral examination, I translated and interpreted the so-called "Constitution of Medina," an agreement apparently made between the clans of Medina and Muhammad after his flight from Mecca, the *hijra* in the year 622. My task was to put this document into the context of later discussions about minorities in Islamic law. Writing this book in the first part of the twenty-first century, it's evident that the curriculum of my studies did not represent anything close to the contemporary state of the art in scholarship on Islam. So, what is this contemporary state of the art in Islamic studies?

In this chapter, I will give a brief but also quite selective answer to this question. Furthermore, I situate my own research within a set of pertinent questions of current discussions in Islamic studies. I will first give a quick and selective look at four introductory volumes on Islam. In a way, these introductions perfectly mirror the broad range of methods and themes that characterize the field today. They make their readers familiar with ongoing scholarly and public debates on Islam and the life of Muslims. These four introductions to Islamic studies clearly demonstrate the transformation of the discipline from studying Islam as a systemic unity to exploring "lived Islam" in terms of religious practices.³ In a second step, I zoom in on a specific branch of recent anthropological research which focuses in on pious activists among Muslim women in the Middle East and Europe. At first glance, this research agenda looks rather narrow. Upon closer inspection, however, this kind of research informs us about a number of more general questions in contemporary studies on Islam. Consequently, the focus on pietistic Islamic movements is not the core subject here. Rather this strand of literature serves me as an analytical prism for discerning the essential theoretical puzzle in current research on Islam. Finally, I take this puzzle as the starting point for the elaboration of my own theoretical framework, which follows in Chapter Two.

From Systemic Unity to Pluralistic Practices: The Transformation of Islamic Studies

In his *Islam: Eine Ideengeschichte* (Islam: A History of Ideas), Rüdiger Lohlker avoids any precise definition of his object.[4] Lohlker, who is Professor of Islamic studies at the University of Vienna, rejects the idea of a holistic Islam and wishes instead to introduce his readers to a history of multiple relationships and historical breaks.[5] Lohlker's book does not follow a historical chronology, but he organizes his history of Islamic ideas in thematic terms, discussing topics such as law, minorities, natural sciences, new media, philosophy, politics, and Sufism. He aims to give his readers an insight into the plurality of beliefs, ideas, religious practices, and organizations that have characterized the history of Islam. He underscores his departure from the classical Orientalist representation of Islam by categorically dismissing the "talk of the Prophets' theocratic rule" as a late ideological reconstruction by Muslims and non-Muslims alike.[6] Sensitive to the anachronistic use of terms, Lohlker historicizes his description of Islamic jurisprudence and warns against the utterly wrong but rather convenient equation of the shariʿa with modern law.[7]

Another good example of contemporary work on Islam is the book *Lifeworlds of Islam* by the American sociologist Mohammed A. Bamyeh. Like Lohlker, Bamyeh does not associate Islam with a total holistic structure. In his eyes, the lasting relevance of religious traditions for the life of generations of Muslims is due to the unsystematic plurality of expression of Islam. In this way, Bamyeh clearly rejects the basic assumptions of the Orientalist curriculum of my own university education. Even in premodern times, according to Bamyeh, the world of Islam (*dār al-islām*) represented an interactive global space of relatively free intellectual exchange. Numerous social movements have articulated the concerns of their times by resorting to the discursive potential of Islamic traditions. This global Islamic system, however, was not characterized by the hermetically closed structure of a normative social order. Rather the *dār al-islām* gave a home to a cacophony of different voices. The world of Islam in Bamyeh's analysis represented a communicative space in which mutually intelligible but highly diverse political, juridical, and moralistic discourses intersected. Addressing first and foremost a general, educated readership, Bamyeh introduces them to Islamic traditions in terms of a huge reservoir of the guidance they offer for many Muslims without determining anyone's behavior in a specific way. From this perspective, Islam represents a powerful social practice that over the centuries has been animated by the daily experiences of ordinary people.[8]

In *Contemporary Issues in Islam*, Asma Afsaruddin also takes her point of departure from the claim to the factual diversity and evolutionary nature of Islamic thought.[9] Afsaruddin, a Professor of Islamic studies at Indiana University, Bloomington, organizes her issues in Islam quite similarly to the thematic chapters of Lohlker's book. Attentive to Shmuel Eisenstadt's theory of multiple modernities, Afsaruddin looks at the multiplicity of ways in which Muslims have reimagined Islamic traditions while "grappling with modernity."[10] She observes these multiple Muslim modernities with respect to themes such as American Muslims, gender and feminisms, interfaith dialogues, the shariʿa, and questions about war and peace in Islamic history. With reference to the anthropologist Talal Asad and quoting the Turkish sociologist Nilüfer Göle, Afsaruddin looks at her own book in terms of the observation of processes of an "indigenization of modernity in non-Western contexts."[11] Modernization thus becomes disentangled from Westernization, and at least those with positive attitudes toward Islam consider these processes as expressions of the "internal pluralism of the Islamic tradition."[12]

Finally, I would like to mention Ron Geaves' *Islam Today*.[13] Geaves is Professor of the Comparative Study of Religion at Liverpool Hope University in the United Kingdom. He too seeks to make the reader familiar with contemporary issues in Islam. Briefly presenting an overview of the core beliefs, as well as the mythological and historical origins, of Islam, Geaves also organizes the subsequent chapters of his book thematically, examining Muslim diversity, ethics and morality, gender questions, fundamentalism, and the relationship between Islam and the West. The latter, relations between Islam and the West, forms something like the red thread running through all of the chapters of his book. In contradistinction to Asma Afsaruddin's focus on the United States, Geaves deals with Muslim minorities in Western Europe, in particular in Great

Britain, and with discussions around the concept of a "European Islam." In his concluding chapter on the future of Islam, Geaves therefore predominantly raises questions of religious and political bridge-building between different faiths and society. In so doing, he stresses the need to go beyond the problem of religious violence and terrorism to engage in an intensive debate with "the larger questions of civil life, governance and justice."[14]

It seems, therefore, that Albert Hourani's criticism has left an imprint on current research into Islam. The four authors of these introductions describe the contemporary state of the art in Islamic studies in sharp contrast to my German curriculum of the 1980s. Their common theme is Islam's historical pluralism. The life of the Prophet and early Islam are placed at the margins, and classical texts no longer play a central role as primary sources. These introductions represent Islam not as a holistic normative system, but as a point of reference for a plurality of discourses and social practices. In this sense, they confirm Shahab Ahmed's argument for the enormous historical diversity of Islam and the problem of defining its unity "in the face of *outright contradiction*."[15] Contemporary issues in Islam deal with the interlacement of Islamic traditions with social phenomena such as consumerism, gender roles, interfaith dialogues, migration, new media, or the relationship between Islam and the West. In today's Islamic studies, the rather narrow preoccupation with the holy scriptures and the classical volumes of Islamic jurisprudence has been replaced by a new focus on religion as "faith and practice in everyday life." In this way, scholarship on Islam seemingly follows the rise of the concept of "lived religion" in the study of religion at the expense of the previous engagement with religious institutions and belief systems.[16] The classical methods of philology have been superseded by the methodological approaches of anthropology, comparative religion, and sociology, a methodological shift that is also reflected in the different disciplinary backgrounds of the abovementioned authors.[17] In short, the limited traditional confines of Islamic studies have given way to a pluralistic fragmentation of analytical perspectives, methods, and themes. In this sense, Islam has become "an insider of the debates about religion and culture" with respect to a variety of disciplines.[18] How did this change occur?

According to Thomas Kuhn's groundbreaking work *The Structure of Scientific Revolutions*, we must take factors external to academic research seriously in order to understand shifts in scientific paradigms.[19] This also applies without doubt to the transformation in Islamic studies. Historical developments such as the decolonialization of the Muslim parts of the world, the migration of millions of Muslims to Europe and North America, or the rise of Islamist movements and jihadist ideologies with a transnational appeal have all contributed to the radical changes in the state of the art in Islamic studies. To a certain extent, Edward Said's seminal book *Orientalism* played the role of a catalyst in this transformation and combined both the abovementioned external factors with internal developments in the social sciences and the humanities.[20] To be sure, Said's argument was not entirely new, having had several predecessors.[21] However, in the specific historical context in which *Orientalism* appeared,[22] the book quickly became a bestseller, with translations into more than 36 languages. I read *Orientalism* first in a German translation during my undergraduate studies. The book appeared on a reading list for a class I attended on the developmental theory of political science. Said's book stood in sharp contrast to the readings in my curriculum in Islamic studies and the apparently orientalist bias in representing Islam upheld by many of its authors. Moreover, I discovered my own "romanticist leanings," which in the end could have brought me into the field of Middle Eastern and Islamic studies. My first journeys across the Mediterranean were presumably triggered by what Said would have called a romanticist search for difference and otherness. In this sense, his book gave me an important wake-up call to reflect upon both my own academic motivations and the representation of Islam with which I had become familiarized through my courses in Islamic studies. Generally speaking, Said's book enhanced a process of critical self-reflection in academic research on the global South, rather than defining a new research agenda on Islam.

In declaring himself an "Oriental," Said stressed that writing *Orientalism* was for him not "an exclusively academic matter."[23] He emphasized that he has written "a partisan book" and not a "theoretical machine."[24] In academic terms, *Orientalism* contributed to both the dissemination of poststructuralist thought, most notably the work of Michel Foucault, and the rise of postcolonial studies in the humanities and social sciences.[25] Edward Said's radical critique of orientalist scholarship provided a significant source for the development of the conceptual tools of postcolonial theories such as ambivalence, identity, representation, resistance, and the relationship between knowledge and power.[26] The normative message of *Orientalism* undoubtedly attracted me as a student. Like many of my fellow students, I was extremely receptive to his wholesale critique of the so-called Western academy. However, in the course of my career, I increasingly became aware of the scholarly flaws in *Orientalism* and their linkage to Said's aim of delivering what was once called an "overzealous" and "prosecutorial" argumentation.[27] Serious flaws in *Orientalism* relate to the ways in which Said applied the theory of Foucault, uncritically confused colonialist policies with orientalist scholarship, and asserted the transhistorical nature of European representations of the Orient. Furthermore, his critics have pointed to the very selective choice of sources and Said's failure to take into consideration the phenomenon of "Orientalism in reverse," that is to say, the equally stereotypical representation of the so-called West by Arab nationalist and Islamist thinkers.[28] These scholarly weaknesses of his book have been discussed for decades, and I do not see any need to recapitulate them here.[29] It is not the scholarly credentials or shortcomings of *Orientalism* that count for me here, so much as how the book became a catalyst in the transformation of the study of Islam. Edward Said contributed to the liberation of Islamic studies from the shackles of a scholarly tradition rather narrow in methods, themes, and disciplinary backgrounds.

This process of liberation, however, did not come without a price. The transformation of Islamic studies, at the same time, led to an increasing fragmentation of the field, as reflected in the introductory volumes mentioned here. In a German publication, *Das Unbehagen in der Islamwissenschaft* (The Malaise in Islamic Studies), the editors speak of a "feeling of disorientation" in a discipline that once found its "genuine method" in philology.[30] The plurality of contemporary scholars doing research on Islam can hardly be said to represent a scientific community in the sense of Thomas Kuhn. He defined a scientific community as a group of "practitioners of a scientific speciality" who have "undergone similar educations" and "absorbed the same technical literature."[31] If a scientific paradigm rests on what the "members of a scientific community share," it appears questionable whether such a paradigm exists in contemporary Islamic studies at all.[32] The study of Islam was transformed from being the scientific specialty of a relatively exclusive community of scholars into an object of academic scholarship meanwhile discussed across the disciplinary boundaries of the social sciences and humanities. A case in point is the volume *Colonial and Post-Colonial Governance of Islam*, for which the editors define three different fields of research alone: Islam in the light of colonial history; the legacy of the colonial governance of Islam in postcolonial societies; and contemporary forms of the governance of Islam by Western European states.[33] Consequently, it would be an elusive ambition to present the current state of the art in studies on Islam in a comprehensive way. Instead of attempting the impossible, in this book I take my point of departure in a much more narrowly defined discussion on Islam and modernity which nevertheless reflects the major changes in the field described so far. In addition, the set of problems associated with this discussion provide an excellent background for my own theoretical vantage point in observing the rise of the multiple modernities of Islam.

The Anthropology of Islam: Piety, Women's Movements, and the Battle against Secular Liberalism

Since the publication of Saba Mahmood's path breaking *Politics of Piety* in 2005, a series of studies on "hybrid and/or alternative forms of Muslim modernities" has appeared.[34] Emphasizing the role of religion in Muslim modernities, these mostly ethnographic studies often place their focus on the construction of contemporary pietistic Muslim identities as part of an ongoing Islamic revival.[35] In this way they provide a welcome critique of the relative absence of religion in research on modern subjectivities. Moreover, this strand of research on Islam underpins more generally the ongoing revision of classical secularization theories with their simplistic expectation of the gradual disappearance of the societal relevance of religion. This new enquiry into specifically religious Muslim modernities is part of a more general trend in research on Islam that is critical of classical modernization theories and their application to Muslim history. The authors of these studies reject the "secularist bias" of those theories and their conflation of modernization with Westernization. In short, these theoretically informed ethnographic studies declare their observations of strictly religious Muslim modernities as an alternative to what they consider to be a secularist Western modernity.

In Mahmood's book, the reader encounters a specific kind of religious urban women who, with their female mosque movement, represent a particular branch of the "larger Islamic revival in Cairo."[36] The interlocutors of Mahmood's study identify the emergence of their group with a response to the marginalization of religion in everyday life. This marginalization is supposedly caused by the "modern structures of secular governance."[37] In their pious practices, these women strongly emphasize "outward markers of religiosity," this is to say, the role of dress codes, ritual practices, and styles of comporting oneself.[38] The bodily behavior of the movement's members is at the core of the proper realization of religious norms.[39] In their acquisition of different kinds of knowledge and skills, Islamic ethics takes center stage with respect to the "various spheres of contemporary life."[40] Consequently, these female activists pursue the strategy of a conscious Islamization of modern life practices. In taking her inspiration from poststructuralist authors such as Judith Butler and Michel Foucault, Mahmood aims explicitly at challenging conventional Western theories of feminism and key features of secular-liberal thought. Through her ethnographic data she wants to show the ways in which Islamic ethics turns into a challenge of "secular-liberal understandings of agency, body, and authority" in the construction of the modern urban everyday lives of Muslim women.[41]

Then, in 2006, Lara Deeb published *An Enchanted Modern* in which she also stressed the role of Islamic imaginations of modern everyday life as counter-models to the secular liberalism of Western modernity.[42] Her ethnographic study took place among Shiite women in Al-Dahiyya, a southern suburb of Beirut that is under the political control of Hizbullah. Following the theme of Mahmood's book, Deeb aimed at the exploration of the "multiple intersections between ideas and practices of modernity and of piety" with the help of which she wanted to "underscore the inseparability of religion and politics in the lives of pious Muslims."[43] In the publicly visible piety of the women in her study, Islamic morals were intimately linked to issues such as teaching correct religious practices, doing good for others, and resisting the Israeli occupation of Arab lands.[44] Religious commitments were thus translated into political, social, and religious activities, implying individual strategies of continuous self-betterment.[45] Deeb's religious activists relied on the coexistence of scientific rationalism with faith, and they promote a combination of correct religious behavior with societal awareness.[46] In applying the well-known dichotomy of tradition versus modernity in their language, this

Shiite women's movement advocates a religiously-inspired modernization theory according to which its members constructed the modern female subject as a "pious modern" who does not "separate between issues of religion, politics and social responsibility."[47]

Jeanette Jouili, to take another example, moved the study of pious Muslim women from the Middle East to Europe.[48] In this way, her work added questions about migration and diasporic Islam to the field. In Jouili's book, female pietistic Muslim activists also represent a kind of alternative modernity to the "secularities of France and Germany," the two countries in which her fieldwork took place. Her study places its focus on the ways in which these religious activists rearticulate Islamic traditions in their "endeavor to live Islam authentically."[49] In applying concepts of the everyday, Jouili observes the enactment of this "authentic Islam" through daily practices such as prayer and bodily forms of self-cultivation. Her ethnographic study is thereby also guided by a rather strict binary distinction between the religious and the secular. She seeks to explore how these pious women "inhabit on a day-to-day basis the often hostile secular spaces of French—and German—societies."[50] In their enactment of Islamic virtues, however, they translate attributes of their social environment such as being "civil," "professional," and "refined" into "authentic Islamic qualities." In Jouili's eyes, these representatives of a diasporic Islam are engaged in specific recognition projects through which they aim to provide the compatibility of their way of life with "European modernity."[51]

This brief review of three examples of current ethnographic research on Islam—groups of Sunni, Shiite, and diasporic Muslim women—reflects only a very small but nevertheless important segment of the field.[52] Despite their preoccupation with contemporary pietistic movements, the three studies all display general features which can be discerned in the transformation of Islamic studies. While openly critical toward so-called Western theories of modernity, they remain nevertheless within the metatheoretical frame of inquiries about the relationship between Islam and modernity. In their focus on religious ethics and practices versus secularist ideologies, they articulate the topic of Islam and the West in a specific fashion with a normative attitude. In particular, they challenge the conventional wisdom of the secular nature of modernity as such. Moreover, these works refer to a number of the central new topics of Islamic studies such as gender issues, migration, the everyday, and bodily practices, as well as to the nexus between power and knowledge. In terms of sources and methods, they exemplify the move from philology to ethnology and therefore from the critical reading of religious texts to the observation of religious everyday practices.[53] Contemporary research privileges the study of Muslims over the study of Islam. Finally, in their ethnographical writings, these authors interpret anthropological data through the lenses of poststructuralist theory. In short, while at first glance limited in scope, these books are perfect examples for the fundamental changes Islamic studies has undergone since the publication of Edward Said's *Orientalism*. Yet the major theoretical and normative patterns of this kind of research should not be traced back to Edward Said alone. The assumptions, concepts, and guiding research questions of these anthropologists have their origin largely in the work of the anthropologist Talal Asad and his scholarly engagement with Islam and secularism.[54]

Talal Asad turned his attention to Islam in a seminal article from 1986.[55] In this article, based on a lecture he delivered at Georgetown University, Asad posed the question as to what kind of object Islam presents for anthropological research. In the anthropological tradition, according to Asad, Islam was basically reconstructed in terms of two opposing concepts: either as a historical totality and as such a blueprint for social order, or as an utterly heterogeneous collection of phenomena without unity. Against this conceptual opposition, Asad's article attempted to present a mediating position from which we can observe diversity in light of an organizing unity.[56] Apparently, Asad wanted to make a conceptual step toward Islam's plurality without surrendering its foundational unity. For this reconciliation of unity and diversity, he suggested a turn toward understanding Islam as a "discursive tradition." Islam is then not a systematic unity, but a body of foundational texts, authoritative narratives, and interpretative techniques to which generations of Muslims have related in their search to live authentically Islamic lives.[57] The mentioned studies on pious female Muslim activist are predicated precisely on this approach to an anthropology of Islam. Moreover, they seemingly share the intertwined concerns which characterize Asad's work. In the introduction to *Formations of the Secular*, he addresses these concerns. In his attempt to sketch out an "anthropology of secularism," Asad combines his critique of the pretension of liberal governance with that of Western expertise on Islam.[58]

Educated as part of Great Britain's anthropological establishment, Asad aimed to challenge the conceptual assumptions upon which its research relied.[59] In particular, he questioned the adequacy of a conception of religion that in his understanding could not serve cross-cultural purposes.[60] The anthropologists of the nineteenth century, according to Asad, wrongly made religion out to be "a distinctive space of human practice and belief which cannot be reduced to any other."[61] In the *Formations of the Secular*, Asad expressed his continuing "dissatisfaction with this universal category of religion" and argued that the categories of the religious and the secular are by no means clear-cut.[62] In his later work, the critique of "secular liberalism" and the barrier it provides to the integration of Muslim immigrants in Europe took center stage.[63] In this thematic move towards Muslim minorities in Europe, Asad combined his criticism of secular liberalism with that of the modern state. With its European origin and total structure, Asad perceived the modern state as a social institution that tries to exert a form of control over its citizens which has no roots in Islamic traditions at all.[64] It is this combined critique which finds its continuation and ethnographic substantiation in contemporary anthropological studies on pious Islamic movements. In a later book on religious minorities in Egypt, Saba Mahmood, for instance, reiterated Asad's critical position to argue that "modern secular governance has contributed to the exacerbation of religious tensions in postcolonial Egypt."[65]

In following Talal Asad in his normative desire to unmask the false, universalist pretensions of secular liberalism, contemporary anthropologists of Islam have a tendency to emphasize the alterity of Islamic discursive traditions vis-à-vis the so-called secular West.[66] They do so, however, by turning Islamic activists into the "paradigmatic, normal standard of religiosity."[67] They declare present piety movements as role models of an alternative Islamic modernity, an alternative to a kind of Western modernity that they identify with the secularist branch of Enlightenment thought. In their review of the state of the art concerning the study of Islam and politics in anthropology, Benjamin Soares and Filippo Osella therefore came to the conclusion that those scholars who discern in today's Islamic activism alternative forms of modernity still consider modernity to be a merely Western intellectual tradition spread by colonialism.[68] Consequently, they portray Muslims as engaging with modernity as an external force. With reference to Talal Asad, these scholars still consider Muslims to be "conscripts of Western modernity."[69] In sum, in a kind of Eurocentrism in reverse, they maintain the assumption of "Western exceptionalism."[70]

With their focus on Islam/religion, these ethnographic studies deliver a welcome critique of the often secularist and Eurocentric bias in the academic study of modernity.[71] Exploring specifically Islamic forms of modernity, they help to bring religion back in and underpin arguments against the allegation of the inherently non-religious nature of modern times. At the same time, however, these studies are very limited in scope due to their focus on both strictly religiously observant Muslims and the present. Moreover, in juxtaposing cases of pietistic Muslims with the alleged secularism of Western modernity, they have at least an implicit tendency to confirm the idea of a fundamental alterity between "Islam and the West." In applying Asad's conceptual tool of Islam as a discursive tradition, they rather uncritically follow his preoccupation with orthodoxy, that is to say, with his understanding of tradition in terms of the "authoritative prescription of the correct" in Islam.[72] In contradistinction to this focus on pietistic Muslims, Nadia Jeltoft, for instance, put the focus of her research on the variety of religious practices of Muslims who do not claim following orthodox lines of belief.[73]

In this book, I seek to overcome the limitations of this stream of ethnographic studies in three ways. First of all, instead of employing anthropological methods and theory, I observe the construction of Islamic modernities from the theoretical vantage point of a historical sociology of modernity. Adopting Talal Asad's definition of Islam as a discursive tradition, I critically revise Eisenstadt's concept of multiple modernities and apply a new theoretical perspective to the modern history of Islam. Drawing selectively from Niklas Luhmann's Modern Systems Theory, my investigation is guided by a non-normative concept of an emerging modern world society. This novel theoretical framework I present in the following chapter on theory. Second, I go beyond the present and consequently historicize this research into Islamic modernities. The empirical chapters of my book trace the idea of specifically Islamic modernities to the second half of the nineteenth century. I argue that here we find the origin of this meanwhile almost hegemonic idea in the modernization of the Ottoman Empire and Egypt, as well as in the concomitant rise of the modernist movement of Islamic reform. Third, I extend the analytical gaze on Muslim modernities beyond groups of strictly observant Muslims and the purely religious field. I do not adopt Asad's focus on orthodoxy in the discursive history of Islamic traditions. The case studies in this book integrate a variety of non-religious social sites and thematic discourses that have played a significant role in the construction of Islamic modernities. In short, my study presents a genealogy of institutions, ideas, and social practices that have led to the contemporary discursive hegemony of forms of Islamic modernities in world society.

With this approach I make a contribution to the transformation of Islamic studies that is the topic of the present chapter on the state of the art of the discipline. I later explore the pluralistic nature of modern Islam in six case studies, picking up thematic issues similar to those which I presented in the four introductory accounts of contemporary research on Islam at the beginning of this chapter. I do so from a pronounced sociological perspective.[74] However, my theoretical perspective should not be confused with what has been called the "sociology of Islam" by authors such as Bryan Turner, Georg Stauth, and Armando Salvatore. Of course, there are linkages and parallels in my book to the writings of these scholars. Especially in regards to their acknowledgment of the independent, self-reflexive, and critical contributions of Muslim intellectuals to the discourse of modernity. Yet this does not mean that I am taking part in their endeavor toward a specific sociology of Islam.

While my approach to the sociological study of Islam does not rest in Bryan Turner's studies, I have learned a great deal in my reading of parts of the comprehensive work of this sociological giant.[75] During my PhD studies, I also engaged with the work of Georg Stauth. In particular his *Islam und westlicher Rationalismus* (Islam and Western Rationalism) raised my interest in the entanglement of early sociology with Islamic studies.[76] Yet, apart from this first encounter with Stauth's writings, I have not really been further attracted by his work. In recent years, then, it has been Armando Salvatore who became the most vocal representative of the idea of a sociology of Islam. While I fully agree with him that "inserting Islam's diversity into sociological questions and paradigms becomes a potential instrument for renewing sociology's ever unfulfilled universal ambitions," my own theoretical perspective differs significantly from his.[77] Frankly speaking, beginning with my reading of his dissertation *Islam and the Political Discourse of Modernity*, I have constantly faced difficulties in following his argumentation.[78] Furthermore, I do not share his interest in the ways in which "Islamic traditions produce and modulate patterns of civility."[79] I am not pursuing a similar research agenda of investigating "the distinctive Islamic approach to building patterns of life conduct and sociability that can be subsumed under the rubric of 'civility.'"[80] Even more important, I have serious doubts that such a "distinctive Islamic approach" to social life as such really exists. Consequently, this book does not discuss in more detail the ideas of this approach to a "sociology of Islam," although my own endeavor may coincidentally look as if it was related to it.

Instead, my exploration of the contemporary hegemony of Islamic imaginations of modernity is guided by a number of more general questions that have been raised in the current research on Islam. First of all, while the new paradigm of a multiplicity of modernities has entered the field, most scholars remain silent when it comes to a generic concept of modernity. Yet, in what way can we talk about a plurality of modernities without having an explicit modernity in the singular in mind? Second, studies on contemporary Islam often re-introduce religion as a crucial factor in shaping these multiple modernities. Consequently, we must be led to re-think the role of religion in the modern world. How do religious and non-religious social realms relate to each other? Does the distinction between religion and the secular still make sense? Finally, despite Edward Said forcefully refuting the dichotomy between East and West, the idea of an in principle fundamental alterity between Islam and the West continues to inform many scholars' research on Islam. How do we escape from this historically entrenched trap? Is there a way of putting together unity and diversity in the conceptualization of modernity? The following chapter on concepts and theory takes up these three principal questions that arise from my discussion of the state of the art in contemporary Islamic studies. It presents a brief but so far as possible encompassing sociological framework within which we can find answers to these pertinent theoretical questions from the perspective of social theory.

Notes

1. Volpi, Frédéric. 2010. *Political Islam Observed*. London: Hurst, 43.
2. Hourani, Albert. 1972. Review of the Cambridge History of Islam. *The English Historical Review* 87: 348–357.

3. Jeltoft, Nadia. 2011. Lived Islam: Religious Identity with Non-organized Muslim Minorities. *Ethnic and Racial Studies* 34 (7): 1134–1151.
4. Lohlker, Rüdiger. 2008. *Islam: Eine Ideengeschichte*. Vienna: Facultas.
5. Ibid. 2.
6. Ibid. 46.
7. Ibid. 66.
8. Bamyeh, Mohammed A. 2019. *Lifeworlds of Islam: The Pragmatics of a Religion*. New York: Oxford University Press.
9. Afsaruddin, Asma. 2015. *Contemporary Issues in Islam*. Edinburgh: Edinburgh University Press.
10. Ibid. 4.
11. Ibid. 16.
12. Ibid. 206.
13. Geaves, Ron. 2010. *Islam Today*. London and New York: Continuum.
14. Ibid. 147.
15. Ahmed, Shahab. 2016. *What is Islam? The Importance of Being Islamic*. Princeton: Princeton University Press, 72.
16. McGuire, Meredith B. 2008. *Lived Religion: Faith and Practice in Everyday Life*. Oxford: Oxford University Press.
17. For a discussion of this shift in approaching Islamic studies methodologically, see also: Buskens, Léon and Annemarie van Sandwijk (eds.). 2016. *Islamic Studies in the Twenty-First Century: Transformations and Continuities*. Amsterdam: Amsterdam University Press.
18. Lawrence, Bruce B. 2010. Afterword: Competing Genealogies of Muslim Cosmopolitism. In *Rethinking Islamic Studies: From Orientalism to Cosmopolitanism*. Edited by Carl W. Ernst and Richard C. Martin. Columbia: The University of South Carolina Press, 302–323, 302.
19. Kuhn, Thomas S. 1970. *The Structure of Scientific Revolutions*. Second Edition, Enlarged. Chicago: University of Chicago Press.
20. Said, Edward W. 1978. *Orientalism*. New York: Vintage.
21. The theme of Islam and the West and European representations of Islam were already central to the following works: Daniel, Norman. 1960. *Islam and the West: The Making of an Image*. Edinburgh: Edinburgh University Press; Frye, R. N. (ed.). 1956. *Islam and the West*. S-Gravenhage: Mouton; Hitti, Philip K. (ed.). 1962. *Islam and the West: A Historical Cultural Survey*. Princeton: Princeton University Press; Rodinson, Maxime. 1974. The Western Image and Western Studies of Islam. In *The Legacy of Islam*. Edited by Joseph Schacht

and C. E. Bosworth. Oxford: Carendon Press: 9–72; Schwab, Raymond. 1950. *La renaissance orientale*. Paris: Payot; Southern. R. W. 1962. *Western Views of Islam in the Middle Ages*. Cambridge, MA: Harvard University Press; Tibawi, A. L. 1963. English-Speaking Orientalists: A Critique of Their Approach to Islam and Arab Nationalism. *The Muslim World* 53 (4): 298–313; Watt, Montgomery. 1972. *The Influence of Islam on Medieval Europe*. Edinburgh: Edinburgh University Press.

22. A number of historical events roughly coincided with the publication of *Orientalism* in 1978. Amongst those were the aftermath of the Vietnam War, the Soviet occupation of Afghanistan, the Islamic Revolution in Iran, the Lebanese Civil War, and the Camp David accords between Israel and Egypt.
23. Said 1978, 27.
24. Ibid. 339.
25. Lockman, Zachary. 2004. *Contending Visions of the Middle East: The History and Politics of Orientalism*. Cambridge: Cambridge University Press, 202–211.
26. Cf. Mongia, Padmini. 1996. *Contemporary Postcolonial Theory: A Reader*. London: Arnold; Spivak, G. C. 1985. Subaltern Studies: Deconstructing Historiography. In *Subaltern Studies IV: Writings on South Asian History and Society*. Edited by R. Guha and G. C. Spivak. Oxford: Oxford University Press: 330–363; Young, R. J. C. 2003. *Postcolonialism: A Very Short Introduction*. Oxford: Oxford University Press.
27. Kerr, Malcom. 1980. Orientalism – Book Review. *International Journal of Middle East Studies* 12: 544–547, 544.
28. Al-Azm, Sadik J. 1981. Orientalism and Orientalism in Reverse. *Khamsin* 8: 5–26.
29. I have dealt with them more intensively in: Jung, Dietrich. 2010.The Origin of Difference: Edward Said, Michel Foucault and the Modern Image of Islam. In *Islam in the Eyes of the West*. Edited by Tareq Y. Ismael and Andrew Rippin. London: Routledge: 15–31. Chapter Two in my: *Orientalists, Islamists and the Global Public Sphere: A Genealogy of the Modern Essentialist Image of Islam*. Sheffield: Equinox (2011); as well as Chapter Two in: *Der Islam in der Globalen Moderne: Soziologische Theorie und die Vielfalt islamischer Modernitäten*. Wiesbaden: Springer VS (2021).
30. Poya, Abbas and Maurus Reinkowski (eds.). 2015. *Das Unbehagen in der Islamwissenschaft: Ein klassisches Fach im Scheinwerferlicht der Politik und der Medien*. Bielefeld: Transscript, 10–11.
31. Kuhn 1970, 177.

32. Ibid. 176.
33. Maussen, Marcel, Veit Bader and Annelies Moors (eds.). 2011. *Colonial and Post-Colonial Governance of Islam: Continuities and Ruptures.* Amsterdam: Amsterdam University Press.
34. Soares, Benjamin and Filippo Osella. 2009. Islam, Politics, Anthropology. *The Journal of the Royal Anthropological Institute* 15: 1–23, 4.
35. In Chapter Seven of this book, I refer to a different strand of literature which identifies the so-called Islamic revival with new Islamic movements of an individualistic and consumerist fashion quite different from this literature on piety movements.
36. Mahmood, Saba. 2005. *Politics of Piety: The Islamic Revival and the Feminist Subject.* Princeton: Princeton University Press, 2.
37. Ibid. 4.
38. Ibid. 31.
39. Ibid. 24.
40. Ibid. 47.
41. Ibid. 191.
42. Deeb, Lara. 2006. *An Enchanted Modern: Gender and Public Piety in Shi'i Lebanon.* Princeton: Princeton University Press.
43. Ibid. 6.
44. Ibid. 8.
45. Ibid. 34, 118.
46. Ibid. 28, 116.
47. Ibid. 231.
48. Jouili, Jeanette S. 2015. *Pious Practice and Secular Constraints: Women in the Islamic Revival in Europe.* Stanford: Stanford University Press.
49. Ibid. 17.
50. Ibid. 154.
51. Ibid. 174.
52. For a different take on the same subject, see: Hafez, Sherine. 2011. *An Islam of Her Own: Reconsidering Religion and Secularism in Women's Islamic Movements.* New York and London: New York University Press. Hafez argues "that the desires of women activists in Islamic movements in Egypt today cannot be fully grasped through a focus on unitary ethical subjects based only on religious practice." Ibid. 5.
53. The everyday and ordinary religion became central sites of anthropological research in particular with reference to conceptual dichotomies such as power/

agency and unity/diversity. See: Fadil, Nadia and Myanthi Fernando. 2015. Rediscovering the 'Everyday' Muslim. Notes on an Anthropological Divide. *HAU: Journal of Ethnographic Theory* 5 (2): 59–88, 61.

54. This does not mean that they do not partly share the ambition of theorizing the intrinsic epistemological and ideological predispositions of Western thought, which is a core concern of postcolonial studies and can be traced back to the work of Edward Said. In this sense, the "Asad School" in Islamic studies shares elements of thought related to "redemptive" approaches in postcolonial theories, especially with the self-understanding of those postcolonial thinkers who take their normative starting point in a pronounced critique of Western enlightenment thinking. Cf. Nash Geoffrey, Kathleen Kerr-Koch, and Sarah Hackett. 2013. Introduction. In *Postcolonialism and Islam: Theory, Literature, Culture, Society and Film.* Edited by Geoffrey Nash, Kathleen Kerr-Koch, and Sarah Hackett. London and New York: Routledge, 1–14. In my eyes, however, in these redemptive theories the normative agenda of their authors has meanwhile increasingly superseded the analytical quality of their concepts. Borrowing from the thought of Michel Foucault, I state that the Orientalist "regime of truth" has been replaced by the attempt to establish a new regime of truth. In preaching resistance and redemption, this strand of postcolonial thought tries to achieve a hegemonic position in the humanities and to impose its own normative worldview on research on the Global South. For a more detailed critique of postcolonial theories by my pen, see: Jung 2011.
55. Asad, Talal. 1986. *The Idea of an Anthropology of Islam.* Washington, DC: Center for Contemporary Arab Studies, Georgetown University.
56. Ibid. 5.
57. Cf. Anjum, Ovamir. 2007. Islam as a Discursive Tradition: Talal Asad and His Interlocutors. *Comparative Studies of South Asia, Africa and the Middle East* 27 (3): 656–672.
58. Asad, Talal. 2003. *Formations of the Secular: Christianity, Islam, Modernity.* Stanford: Stanford University Press.
59. Scott, David and Charles Hirschkind (eds.). 2006. *Powers of the Secular Modern: Talal Asad and His Interlocutors.* Stanford: Stanford University Press, 1.
60. Asad 1986, 11.
61. Asad, Talal. 1993. *Genealogies of Religion: Discipline and Reasons of Power in Christianity and Islam.* Baltimore, MD: Johns Hopkins University Press, 27.
62. Scott, David. 2006. The Trouble of Thinking: An Interview with Talal Asad. In *Powers of the Secular Modern: Talal Asad and His Interlocutors.* Edited by David

Scott and Charles Hirschkind. Stanford: Stanford University Press: 243–303, 284.
63. Scott and Hirschkind 2006, 10.
64. Scott 2006, 291.
65. Mahmood, Saba. 2016. *Religious Difference in a Secular Age: A Minority Report*. Princeton and Oxford: Princeton University Press, 1. In a roundtable conversation with Lisa Wedeen and Schirin Amir-Moazami on the occasion of Saba Mahmood's death, this preoccupation of the "Asad school" with criticizing "secular liberalism" through ethnographic studies of Muslims was utterly explicit. See: On the Study of Islam and the Middle East after Saba Mahmood. *Sociology of Islam* 7: 345–360.
66. Bangstad, Sindre. 2009. Contesting Secularism/s. Secularism and Islam in the Work of Talal Asad. *Anthropological Theory* 9 (2): 188–208, 197.
67. Schielke, Samuli. 2010. *Second Thoughts about the Anthropology of Islam, or How to Make Sense of Grand Schemes in Everyday Life*. Working Papers, No. 2, Zentrum Moderner Orient, Berlin, 12.
68. Soares and Osella 2009, 4.
69. Ibid. 5.
70. The historian Christopher Bayly understands his work on world history as an argument against the idea of "Western exceptionalism," see: Bayly, Christopher. 2004. *The Birth of the Modern World 1780–1914*. London: Blackwell Publishing, 469.
71. However, Carool Kersten showed that a remedy to this bias can be the study of liberal Muslim intellectuals too. Kersten, Carool. 2011. *Cosmopolitans and Heretics: New Muslim Intellectuals and the Study of Islam*. London: Hurst.
72. Cf. Ahmed 2016, 273.
73. Jeltoft 2011.
74. This sociological approach puts its focus on the ways in which Muslims as individuals and collectives relate to Islamic traditions. Thus, I do not ask the question, "What is Islam" (cf. Ahmed 2016), but I am interested in the way in which social actors enact what we observe as Islamic due to the relational link of these social actions to religious traditions.
75. Cf. Turner, Bryan S. and Mohamed Nasir Kamaludeen (eds.). 2013. *The Sociology of Islam: Collected Essays of Bryan S. Turner*. Farnham and Burlington: Ashgate.
76. Stauth, Georg. 1993. *Islam und westlicher Rationalismus. Der Beitrag des Orientalismus zur Entstehung der Soziologie*. Frankfurt am Main and New York: Campus.

77. Salvatore, Armando. 2016. *The Sociology of Islam. Knowledge, Power and Civility*. Oxford: Wiley Blackwell, 6.
78. Salvatore, Armando. 1997. *Islam and the Political Discourse of Modernity*. Reading: Ithaca Press.
79. Salvatore 2016, 25.
80. Ibid. 272.

2

THE EMERGENCE OF WORLD SOCIETY: PROJECTS OF MODERNITY IN GLOBAL SOCIAL CONTEXTS

In the fall semester of 1987, I attended a course in political theory in which we discussed the works of Jürgen Habermas and Niklas Luhmann. The seminar took up a German academic controversy that had been underway since the beginning of the 1970s. The publication of *Theorie der Gesellschaft oder Sozialtechnologie* (Theory of Society or Social Technology) had launched a protracted argument between these two scholars in the field of German social theory.[1] In our seminar, we read Luhmann's *Ökologische Kommunikation* (Ecological Communication) and parts of Habermas' *Theorie des kommunikativen Handelns* (Theory of Communicative Action). In this dispute, Habermas represented the Enlightenment tradition with its reliance on rational human agency. Niklas Luhmann, by contrast, considered his Modern Systems Theory as a "final break" with the Enlightenment. In sharp distinction to Habermas, Luhmann excluded human agency from the realm of society.[2] From this point of view, Luhmann answered the central question of *Ökologische Kommunikation*—whether or not modern society would be able to meet the challenges of environmental problems—in a rather pessimistic way. Defining modern society in terms of a self-referential system of communication, Luhmann concluded that there is the possibility of a system impacting on its environment in such a way that it would later lose the ability to exist in this environment.[3] The Enlightenment optimism concerning the problem-solving capacities of human agency has, indeed, disappeared in Luhmann's theoretical world. How then does this debate between Habermas and Luhmann relate to the theoretical concerns of my book?

Almost thirty years later, an article by the German sociologist Hartmut Rosa reminded me of this dispute. Rosa proposes conceptualizing modernity in a dichotomic way. On the one hand, he suggests that modernity is a project offering the genuine promise of social progress through human action. On the other hand, he identifies modernity with a self-referential and meaningless structural process characterized by an "empty social progression." Regarding the first concept, of modernity as a project, Rosa was referring to a speech which Jürgen Habermas delivered when receiving the "Adorno Award" in the year 1980. In this speech, Habermas described modernity as an "unfinished project." He defended the promises of the Enlightenment against its postmodern and neo-conservatist critics. The project of modernity, according to Habermas, was once elaborated by the philosophers of the Enlightenment and oriented toward an all-encompassing concept of reason, including the arts, morality, law, and science. In Habermas's eyes, this project had not failed but was not yet finished.[4] Modernity considered as an empty structural progression, in Rosa's understanding, undermines this Enlightenment project of rational human progress. Referring to Luhmann's Modern Systems Theory, he describes this structural progression of modernity as a "universalistic constant" expressing modernization as a kind of ongoing and meaningless transformation. With respect to its political implications, Rosa considers this process to be easily compatible with projects other than the Enlightenment, such as those put forward by illiberal and totalitarian regimes.[5]

In the analytical framework for this book, I will use Rosa's dichotomy with respect to two different levels of social reality. Luhmann's Modern Systems Theory serves me in conceptualizing modernity in an abstract way at the macro level. The emergence of social spheres of functional differentiation is modernization as an empty social progression. By contrast, I will meanwhile employ Habermas's actor-oriented concept of modernity as an unfinished project to understand modernity at the level of "social actorhood." Projects of modernity assign meaning and purpose to modernization. I thereby understand social actorhood, in terms offered by the Stanford School on Sociological Institutionalism, as a modern cultural construction according to which individual and collective actors possess the "capacity for responsible agency."⁶ It is on this level that we can historically observe a variety of ways in which social actors imagine modernity in different forms. Among them, I perceive the project of the European Enlightenment not as a universal but as a historically specific project of modernity. There is not merely one project of modernity, but instead the global history of modernity manifests itself as a multiplicity of different modernizing projects. At the level of social actorhood, therefore, we can observe a historical diversity of projects through which social actors construct what the late Israeli sociologist Shmuel Eisenstadt once called "multiple modernities."⁷ This multiplicity of modern projects, to which the variety of specifically Islamic projects of modernity belongs, responds to the universal challenges caused by the empty structural progression of modernity which I try to grasp with the help of elements from Niklas Luhmann's theory. Modernization is both a singular process of structural change and a multiplicity of projects by social actors deeply involved in handling this change. As an empty progression, modernity is a meaningless process of a universal form of sociocultural evolution. Modern history as a multiplicity of social projects, however, is only generated by the ideas, motivations, and semantic elaborations of social actors. Thus, we must combine macro-structural theories with concepts of social actorhood.

I perceive this distinction between modernity as a structural progression and modernity as the projects of social actors as a kind of sociological complement to the writing of global and national or local histories. In his seminal book *The Birth of the Modern World* Cristopher Bayly stresses the ambivalent relationship between the global and the local, between uniformity and difference. In this book, the Cambridge historian describes a series of globally relevant developments in the nineteenth-century world. These developments not only comprised politics, science, and the economy, but also related to bodily practices, linguistic expressions, timekeeping, and sports. Significantly, Bayly pointed to the global emergence of indigenous forms of nationalism before the impact of Europe. Crucial to all these developments was how uniformity simultaneously created difference. Bayly underlined that "convergence, uniformity, and similarity did not mean . . . that all these people were likely to think or act the same way."⁸ On the contrary, in movements of nationalism and religious revivalism, social actors gave a multiplicity of answers to the fundamental changes occurring in the nineteenth century. In my own take, this simultaneity of unity and difference can be understood through the dichotomy between modern world society and modernity as multiple projects. While world society represents both a structural social reality and a means of horizontal comparison, historically different projects of modernity become constructed and enacted on national and local levels.[9] This chapter will give a brief account of my theoretical and conceptual means to make sense of what Bayly called "the multi-centric nature of change in world history."[10]

I organize this chapter with respect to four theoretical questions that are most relevant for the subsequent case studies. I do not answer them from a comparative perspective, that is to say by discussing my position in the light of other theories and possible alternative answers. As already mentioned in the Introduction, there is no room here to engage in longish theoretical debates. Instead, in this chapter, I want to familiarize my readers with the heuristic perspective and analytical concepts that will guide my case studies; and I do so by pointing to their sources and the ways in which I interpret them. This should be sufficient here. In the following section, I first pose the question about modernity as a unity and present a generic concept of global modernity that draws on Luhmann's work. At this macro level, modern society represents world society, the unity of global modernity that is internally characterized by functional differentiation. Within this theoretical context, I also define a specifically modern concept of "religion." It is at this level that modernization manifests itself as an empty progression. The next step introduces social agency as a level of social reality that is complementary to Luhmann's macro level of social systems. Here, the pertinent question concerns how social actors respond to modern structural change and concomitant perceptions of social risks and contingencies. This is the stage on which social actors launch their specific projects of modernity. I then connect this level of social agency with the historical construction of multiple projects of modernity. Eisenstadt's work on multiple modernities serves me in reconciling the macro (unity) with the micro level (diversity) and answering the question about the role of religious traditions in modernity. Finally, I put this conceptual apparatus into the metatheoretical framework of theories of social emergence. Theories of emergence help me to address two questions. First, they offer answers to questions about the linkage between the macro and the micro levels of the social. In which ways are structures, organizations, and individuals related to each other? Second, they indicate a theoretical way to overcome the deeply entrenched historical narrative about the allegedly antagonistic relationship between the "East" and the "West." What if modernization is actually a social process, one that emerges gradually and independently at different places? In the conclusions, I sum up this framework and explain the selection of my case studies and their argumentation.

The Macro Level: Luhmann and Modernity as a Meaningless Progression

In looking for a generic concept of modernity, the Modern Systems Theory propounded by Niklas Luhmann (1927–98) is a good source. In his theory, modern society represents a global and all-encompassing system of communication. Modern society is synonymous with the unity of world society.[11] Luhmann defines communication as the—in evolutionary terms—rather unlikely emergence of a unity of message, information, and understanding.[12] World society integrates all possibly articulable horizons into one communicative system. Consequently, modern society does not have any cultural, natural, political, or social boundaries. Moreover, there is no central authority that could claim any exclusive representation of society. Luhmann thus distances himself from the methodological nationalism that has characterized the conceptual ideas of the classical sociological tradition. While we may speak of American, Chinese, or Danish societies in everyday language, this equation of society with the territorial confines of modern national states no longer has any justification in Modern Systems Theory.[13]

The dominant internal structure of modern society is characterized by functionally differentiated social subsystems such as arts, economy, law, media, politics, religion, and science. To summarize Luhmann's point: Modern society is a functionally differentiated society and with this characteristic of functional differentiation it is historically unique.[14] In defining modernity by the social supremacy and spread of functional differentiation, Luhmann stands firmly in the tradition of the sociology of differentiation. From Émile Durkheim (1858–1917) to Talcott Parsons (1902–79), this tradition has interpreted modernization as an evolutionary increase of social complexity through the progressive differentiation of social life.[15] Against this background, Luhmann's definition of modern society in terms of functional differentiation is today a "commonplace of sociology."[16] However, Modern Systems Theory deviates from this tradition in three significant ways and should therefore not be confused with Talcott Parsons' structural functionalism.

First of all, Luhmann did not follow the assumption of classical differentiation theories which considered differentiation as the functional decomposition of a social whole. Classical theories of social functionalism postulated that the internal differentiation of a social system comes into existence because it is developing and maintaining a social whole or society at large.[17] Luhmann rejects this postulate and concomitant ideas that function systems would "support and reinforce each other."[18] Instead, he claims that there are always functional equivalents to existing social institutions. When talking about social functions, according to Luhmann, we always apply the "constructions of an observer."[19] Consequently, we cannot explain the existence of a social system via its function. Instead, Luhmann attributes the evolution of social systems to the problem of "double contingency," or to the idea that alter and ego mutually consider their selections as contingent.[20] In Luhmann's words: "individuals relate to themselves and to the social relationships in which they stand, they see themselves as subject and object of interaction."[21] Thus, the evolution of social systems is both a means of coping with *and* of further enhancing social contingency. But we must observe this at different levels of social reality. Borrowing this concept of social contingency from Talcott Parsons, Luhmann assigns it new meanings in the evolutionary formation of social systems.[22] Functional analysis in Luhmann's theoretical design, therefore, is mainly a heuristic instrument with the help of which we achieve knowledge through comparison with other possibilities.[23]

Second, and intimately linked to his rejection of the paradigm of functionalist decomposition, Luhmann also refutes the classical expectation that morals, norms, or forms of solidarity could serve to coordinate increasing social differentiation and therefore offer means of social integration.[24] Modern society breaks away from any claim to moral integration and, in Luhmann's words, is neither good nor evil.[25] Finally, from his evolutionary perspective, Luhmann considers modernization not as the gradual increase of functionally defined social differentiation, but as the evolutionary shift of the dominance of different forms of social differentiation. In modernity as world society, the modus of functional differentiation is globally dominant. Modernization subsequently replaces the dominance of previous forms of differentiation such as segmentation, stratification, and center–periphery relations. Yet world society does not exclude these forms of differentiation as such. The supremacy of global functional differentiation goes along with, for instance, segmentary differentiation in the internal structure of the political system as a "society of states" in which states mutually acknowledge one another as "like-units."[26]

In the theoretical design of Modern Systems Theory, Luhmann combined the tradition of social differentiation with theoretical elements of the philosophical anthropology of Arnold Gehlen (1904–76) and the German hermeneutical tradition, in particular the Phenomenology of Edmund Husserl (1859–1938). Even more important, in his drafting of social systems, he was inspired by biological theories of the self-organization of living systems. Analogous with biological systems, Luhmann defined functionally differentiated social systems in terms of their self-reliance and operational closure. The global subsystems of modern world society produce and reproduce themselves autonomously according to their own specific communicative codes. The political system, for instance, has differentiated itself through the use of the medium of power by covering collective decisions,[27] whereas the establishment of science relied on the binary code of truth/untruth and operates internally through theories and methods.[28] Borrowing from the biologist Humberto Maturana (1928–2021), Luhmann defined social systems according to these self-reliant modes of operation as "autopoietic" entities.[29] Autopoietic social systems consist, then, of communicative elements which they produce themselves. While they depend on the input of their environments, they transform these inputs according to their own specific functional semantics. In this way, social systems draw sharp boundaries to their environments, becoming autonomous and dependent at the same time. It was due to this autopoietic nature of social systems that Luhmann came to his pessimistic conclusion in *Ökologische Kommunikation*—that society cannot communicate with nature—as quoted at the beginning of this chapter.

In the context of Modern Systems Theory, religion also represents a clearly identifiable functional subsystem of modern society. According to Luhmann, religious communication is based on the binary code between transcendence and immanence.[30] In line with his theory of the autopoietic nature of social systems, Luhmann clearly rejects previous functionalist ideas according to which religion played a crucial role for the integration of society at large. In his conceptual world, modern religion is not characterized by a loss of function. On the contrary, it gains its specific religious language and therewith relative autonomy as a social system in the evolutionary course of increasing functional differentiation.[31] In this sense, Luhmann suggests understanding religion as a specifically modern concept with a temporarily limited yet nevertheless global applicability. In the sociology of religion, Peter Beyer took up Niklas Luhmann's approach. In *Religions in Global Society*, the Canadian sociologist defined religious communication in line with this approach. He based the concept of religion on binary codes such as transcendent/immanent, sacred/profane, or blessed/cursed.[32] Through these self-referential binary codes, modern religious communication has been identified with faith, with the individually experienced belief in and the communicative contact with supranatural forces. In a process of global entanglement, the nineteenth century witnessed the establishment of, in Beyer's terminology, specific "religious programs" such as Buddhism, Christianity, Hinduism, Islam, and Judaism. In the words of the German historian Jürgen Osterhammel, a new interactive organization of the religious landscape began on a global scale in the nineteenth century.[33]

As a meaningful concept "foreign to ancient cultures," religion appeared in the nineteenth century as a generic conceptual innovation. Both colonial interactions and intellectuals of different cultural backgrounds were part of this process of shaping the modern global landscape of religions.[34] It is this reconstruction of traditions with reference to the communicative code of the global system of modern religion that distinguishes religious communication from other systems of communication. Consequently, religion acquires its very specific modern form through functional differentiation. As mutually acknowledged "religions"—Beyer's religious programs—these so-called world religions represent relatively stable patterns of religious communication based on specific sets of textual, symbolic, and ritual traditions.[35] While Buddhist, Christian, Hindu, Islamic or Jewish traditions certainly existed in premodern times, Beyer argues, the way in which we understand them as religions today are specifically modern constructs.[36] In Chapter Four, I will discuss the role of Islamic modernists, in particular of the Egyptian Muhammad Abduh, in the construction of such a modern religion, this is to say of Islam as a modern religion. Thereby, Islamic modernists developed their modern understanding of Islamic tradition in continuous social interaction and discursive exchanges with other religious programs and their representatives.

With his application of conceptual tools from Modern Systems Theory, Beyer addressed two well-established forms of conceptual criticism in the academic field of religious studies.[37] On the one hand, his book is directed against the claim that we cannot study religion in its "own right." Russel McCutcheon, for instance, described "religion" as a mere conceptual invention without any ontological quality.[38] Timothy Fitzgerald, to mention a second example, also fundamentally challenged the distinction between the religious and the secular, declaring the category of religion as a distinct domain of human action to be a myth.[39] On the other hand, Beyer defended the concept of religion against scholars such as Talal Asad, who rejected its usefulness because of its origin in Christianity and the modern West.[40] However, even Talal Asad cannot deny that religion today is a concept widely applied in non-Christian and non-Western contexts. This is the main issue in Beyer's book. It is not the origin of a concept but its application that counts. The genealogical reconstruction of the meaning and usage of religion, therefore, should not start with any alleged or real European origin, but with its contemporary global use.[41]

In applying the category of religion, I do not consider religion to be a social phenomenon "that in principle exists in all cultures and languages in all historical times."[42] Religion is not a universally applicable concept in a transhistorical sense. In this sense I agree with the critique of the "Asad school" which I discussed in the previous chapter. From the perspective of Modern Systems Theory, however, we can define religion as a social subsystem of modern society inseparably linked to the larger process of functional differentiation. Religion, therefore, should not be thrown in the dustbin of conceptual history. Instead, we may use it as a historically contingent, but nevertheless, for a certain period of time, globally relevant concept. Religion is a concept that takes part in the construction and negotiation of contemporary social reality; it is an acknowledged category of both public and scholarly debate.[43] Therefore, the distinction between the religious and the secular also still makes sense, although the secular does not represent more than a residual category for non-religious realms. In Luhmann's macro-sociological approach, secularization is synonymous with the emergence of functional differentiation and describes the social environment of religion.[44] Based on its own operational code, religion observes its environment as becoming secular. Religion looks at worldly affairs in drawing boundaries between transcendence and immanence.[45] Thus, religion as a modern category of the social realm is itself a result of secularization understood in terms of the rise of specific forms of functional differentiation.[46] The secular, however, remains the environment of religion.

The Micro Level: Weber and Modernity as Ethical Polytheism

Taking my inspiration from the work of Niklas Luhmann does not necessarily mean endorsing all his theoretical assumptions. His theory supplies conceptual tools for a generic concept of modernity in which religion plays an inherent part. Yet, in my reading, Luhmann exaggerated the apartness and distinctiveness of the macro realm. In his theory of the autopoiesis of function systems, social systems remain completely indifferent to other systems and the motivation of social actors. Through the mechanism of social contingency, social order reproduces itself entirely independently from the intentions of individual and collective actors. Society in Luhmann's thought is predicated on an utterly intrinsic logic and appears to be completely detached from the lifeworld of the individual.[47] Due to differentiation processes at the macro level, the modern subject is excluded from society as a social system. The individual thereby becomes a part of the environment of social systems. Luhmann took the idea of the autonomy of society as far as possible, turning individuals as psychic systems into the environment of the social realm. While social systems operate via communication, psychic systems reproduce themselves through consciousness and thoughts. Although social and psychic systems result from a process of co-evolution and are linked via language, in Luhmann's theoretical design they represent two entirely separate realms of reality.[48] He tries to grasp the interaction of individual and social systems with the mechanism of "structural coupling." However, this mechanism can only trigger disorders or irritations in the respective other system; real communication between systems is impossible in Luhmann's thought.[49]

I do not share Luhmann's dictum that we should no longer consider human beings to be a part of the social, but to treat them as a part of society's environment.[50] More specifically, the relationship between society and individual depends on the perspective of the observer. Conceptualizing world society in terms of self-referential discursive macrostructures provides me with heuristic instruments to organize my observations of concrete social processes. Yet these social processes, as the case studies in this book will confirm, include the purposeful actions of social actors. However, how are we to grasp the linkage between social systems and social actors? What is the connection between the macro and the micro levels of social life?

In order to answer these questions, the sociology of Max Weber (1864–1920) is a good point of departure. One of the sociological master narratives tends to present the two founding fathers of the discipline, Max Weber and Émile Durkheim, as complete methodological antagonists. In *De la division du travail social* (The Division of Labor) Durkheim defines society as a *fait social*. Through this definition of society as a social fact, he describes modern "organic" society as an abstract and relatively autonomous social entity—a form of a non-palpable and coercive macro-structure.[51] Indeed, in Luhmann's Modern Systems Theory, we can easily recognize Durkheim's postulate of considering society to be a *fait social*, that is to say an autonomous social structure *sui generis*. Contrary to Durkheim, Max Weber's sociology of modernity does not start with the structural analysis of society. If we follow the interpretation of Weber's work pursued by Wilhelm Hennis (1923–2012), it was in fact the condition and "nature" of the modern human individual that was at the center of the former's lifelong enquiries. This central interest in knowledge about the modern human condition was to pave the way for Weber's specific choice of methods.[52] For Weber, according to Hennis, the modern individual is confronted with the task of representing a holistic unity in a fragmented social world of relatively autonomous social value spheres.[53] In Weber's own words, the modern individual has to decide in all the orders of life "which is God for him and which is the devil."[54] This relationship between individual and society, the tension between social order and the individual, which Weber describes in his lecture *Wissenschaft als Beruf* (Science as Vocation) in rather metaphorical words, is well worth being quoted directly:

> Today the routines of everyday life challenge religion. Many old gods ascend from their graves; they are disenchanted and hence take the form of impersonal forces. They strive to gain power over our lives and again they resume their eternal struggle with one another.[55]

In this quote, Weber repeats his comparison of modernity with a form of worldly polytheism on which he already elaborated in his essay *Zwischenbetrachtungen* (Intermediate Reflections).[56] There, Weber describes the "clash" between the ethics of the world of "brotherliness" of salvation religions with the rationalized and sublimated ethical laws of other social realms or "value spheres." By contrasting the religious with the economic, political, aesthetic, erotic, and intellectual spheres, Weber addresses—in Luhmann's language—the modern boundary demarcations between religion and the rising subsystems of economics, politics, the arts, intimacy, and science. However, he does so—as the above quote shows—from the perspective of the modern individual juggling with these competing autonomous ethics. While on the macro level these ethics may be understood as autopoietic systems of communication, social actors refer to them as "situation-specific fictions."[57] Modern function systems provide the general cognitive horizon that belongs to the "universe of significance" of modern everyday life. They offer a "texture of meaning" that makes "reciprocal perspectives" among individuals and groups possible.[58] Max Weber saw the modern individual confronted with the demands of an increasing number of rationalized and therewith impersonal spheres of social life. This is precisely what defines modern contingency at the micro level. We can understand the impersonal gods which ascended from their graves as a metaphorical expression for the empty progression of the macrostructures of modernity. Luhmann's mechanism of the autopoietic reproduction of social subsystems has a family resemblance with Max Weber's concept of formal rationalization that in modernity permeates all spheres of life.[59]

The crucial interlacement of the macro and the micro levels of the social was also part of the works of Nobert Elias (1897–1990) and Michel Foucault (1926–84).[60] In his classic *Der Prozess der Zivilisation* (The Civilizing Process), Elias put his focus on the mutual dependence in the evolution of the modern state and the modern individual, especially on the molding of the human drive economy in the context of modern state formation. According to Elias, in the "civilizing process" the coercive structures of the modern state are reflected at the micro level of the individual in the transformation of outer constraints into self-restraints. The more differentiated and stabilized self-control of modern individuals was, in Elias' eyes, intimately linked to the formation of modern states.[61] In a similar way, this connection of macro and micro levels reappears in Foucault's writings about modern subjectivation, especially in his concept of modern "governmentality." Through this concept, Foucault "translated" Elias' transformation from outer constraints to self-restraint into a move from technologies of domination into technologies of the self.[62] While the modern subject is partly the product of its own creation, it is at the same time the result of structures which determine socially acceptable forms of subjectivity. The individual and the subsystems of modern society thus meet in modern subject formation. The modern subject is constantly involved in a process of identity building, a process of self-hermeneutics, in which technologies of the self play a crucial role.[63]

There are ongoing controversies in the reception of Weber's work as to whether we should read the *Zwischenbetrachtungen* as a foundational text for theories of functional differentiation or not. The question also remains whether Weber saw the six value spheres he discussed in his essay as comprehensive or whether new ones could be added in the course of the modernization process. Important here, however, is the question of the ways in which these "cognitive fictions" exist as relevant ideas in the mind of individuals.[64] For social actors, Luhmann's different realms of communication represent discursive worlds of rules and regulations to which they consciously and unconsciously relate in their social actions.[65] This rather idiosyncratic reference to different function systems or value spheres by social actors is an important part of the construction of historically concrete projects of modernity. It is in these projects that the macro-sociological syntax of modernity, these rules and regulations of the cognitive horizon of modernity, meet with the interpretative semantics of modern social actors. It is through social agency that the construction of a multiplicity of semantics of modernity appears. This linguistic distinction between syntax and semantics of modernity I borrow from an essay by Alex Viskovatoff. He suggested perceiving the self-referential logic of Luhmann's function systems as the syntax of modernity.[66] In my theoretical language, this syntax represents the unity of modernity. It provides social actors with a set of formal rules for the construction of meaningful and therefore historically different semantics of modernity. In my framework, then, I describe these semantics as multiple projects of modernity based on the interpretative properties of social actors. According to Viskovatoff, only social actors can attach concrete meanings to the otherwise "formally rationalized" macrostructures of the syntax of modernity. How do structure and agency interlace in projects of modernity? What is the role of religion in the construction of modern social projects?

Unity and Difference: Eisenstadt and the Concept of Multiple Modernities

Since the late Israeli sociologist Shmuel Eisenstadt (1923–2010) coined the term at the turn of the millennium, "multiple modernities" has become a household word in the humanities and social sciences.[67] The meanwhile almost-random application of Eisenstadt's term, however, has reduced it into an academic buzzword that increasingly lacks conceptual substance.[68] Due to Eisenstadt's emphasis on "plurality, creativity and reflexivity,"[69] the usage of the term very often only expresses a kind of modern cultural diversity. From a more normative angle, multiple modernities are also seen in terms of alternative forms to so-called Western modernity. In sharp contrast to these loose applications of multiple modernities, Eisenstadt's approach was originally a reflective critique of some fundamental assumptions of classical modernization theories. Most important here is the fact that Eisenstadt brought religion back into the sociology of modernity. According to his revision, long-lasting religious and imperial traditions made a strong impact on the multiple trajectories which historically different modernization processes have taken. In this way, Eisenstadt made a theoretical offer to reconnect contemporary sociologies of modernity to the intellectual tradition of comparative historical sociology. More importantly, he allowed for religion to become a crucial factor in our understanding of the great variety of observable modern projects.

Modernity, in Eisenstadt's approach, represents a plurality of culturally different interpretations of an otherwise globally relevant and distinctively modern social program. This "program of modernity" Eisenstadt characterized by features such as individual autonomy, human agency, social reflexivity, the mastery of nature, social participation, and the delegitimization of previously unquestionably valid social orders.[70] At the same time, he considered modernity to be "beset by internal antinomies and contradictions." In political terms, the program of modernity can lead to visions of both totalizing and pluralistic social orders in which democracy remains an important option but is constantly challenged by Jacobin political movements propagating the total reconstruction of individuals and social orders.⁷¹ Consequently, democratic politics features prominently in contemporary projects of modernity without being a necessary marker of modern politics.

In my own approach, I translate Eisenstadt's dichotomy between the program of modernity and the multiple realizations of the modern program into Rosa's distinction between modernity as empty progression and as social projects. Furthermore, I replace Eisenstadt's rather vague definition of the unity of modernity as a program with Luhmann's concept of world society. I adopt his term of "multiple modernities," however, in regard to what I defined in the introduction to this chapter as modern projects. Historically, modernity has not developed according to a universal model or in a linear way. Modernization is not a historical process of convergence but a process of social change with a multiplicity of different faces. Eisenstadt refuted the central claim of societal convergence made by classical modernization theories that rose to prominence in the 1950s. His concept of multiple modernities stressed the plurality of modernity without affecting its unity. In Eisenstadt's view, social conditions as given by religious and other traditions play a role in shaping historically concrete modernization processes in the sense of a certain path dependency along which projects of modernity evolve.⁷² I suggest here that it is in this process of shifting modern projects among which the idea of specifically Islamic forms of modernity plays a key role. The Islamic discourse of modernity is the result of the common quest for authenticity of Muslim projects of modernity under specific historical conditions.

Taking his inspiration from the Axial Age Theory of the German philosopher Karl Jaspers (1883–1969), Eisenstadt argued that various "civilizational complexes"—Buddhism, Christianity, Confucianism, Hinduism, Islam, and Judaism—reacted to the program of modernity in different and path-dependent ways. In *Vom Ursprung und Ziel der Geschichte* (The Origin and Goal of History), Jaspers reflected upon the origin and structure of global history (*Weltgeschichte*). This origin he found in the "axial age," a period of synchronic intellectual developments among different world cultures starting around 500 BCE. Jaspers claimed to have observed in Europe, India, and China the rise of a reflexive awareness about distinct transcendent and immanent worlds. These "intuitions of the axial age," according to Jaspers' speculative philosophy, emerged simultaneously without any interaction among these different civilizations.⁷³ In Johan Arnason's interpretation of Jaspers' theory, three central ideas characterized the axial age: first, the already mentioned rise of a dichotomy between transcendent and immanent worlds; second, the belief in the superiority of the transcendent order of which the immanent world only represents a subordinated derivative; and third, the continuous comparison between the orders of the transcendent and immanent realms resulting in an "axial tension," this is to say, in a means of comparison through which intellectuals hold rulers accountable in light of the normative frameworks of transcendental orders.⁷⁴

Eisenstadt appropriated Jasper's civilizational perspective in relating the rise of multiple modernities to the religious and imperial traditions of different civilizational complexes. In this way, he was able to make them a part of modernity again. The role of traditions becomes explicitly relevant in the strategies of political and intellectual elites to claim authenticity for their modernizing projects. Axel Honneth declared authenticity a key concept for the intellectual self-understanding of modernity.⁷⁵ In the Muslim historical context, this is my hypothesis: Islamic traditions increasingly served this purpose of the justification of modern norms and institutions. Synonymous with terms such as "sincere, essential, natural, original, and real,"⁷⁶ authenticity deals with the question of essence versus mere appearance. Modernizing intellectuals oriented themselves in their search for authenticity "toward the recovery of an essence identifying the genuinely real with the help of imaginations of the past."⁷⁷ Aziz al-Azmeh claimed that the predominant literary discourses in the Middle East were local adaptations of Enlightenment and post-Enlightenment discourses linked to the modern idea of authenticity. With reference to the Arabic term *'aṣāla* (authenticity), he stressed the romantic notion of Arab history in the nineteenth-century intellectual movement of the *nahḍa* (Renaissance).⁷⁸ Christian, Jewish, and Muslim intellectuals invoked authenticity in their projects of a revival of pristine Arab culture in light of the "degraded conditions" of their contemporary situation.⁷⁹ The "trans-confessional" *nahḍa* was "closely intertwined" with the Islamic reform movement,⁸⁰ in which this quest for authenticity turned toward the purity of a "Golden Age of Islam," playing an essential role in the justification of its modernizing project. In referring to the period of early Islam, the reformers distinguished their projects of modernity from the "inauthentic" nature of the present. The Islamic discourse of modernity raised the "expectation of a truthful representation" of the past in the present.[81]

Eisenstadt's approach explains how the "program of modernity" becomes re-interpreted within the abovementioned cultural complexes by claiming authenticity in different historical forms of modernity. However, in his theory, Eisenstadt tended to deal with civilizations and religions in terms of "cultural containers."[82] In his work, civilizational complexes almost appear like hermetically demarcated cultural units, and his focus, therefore, is on the differences between those cultural macrostructures. Yet the various cases of Islamic modernities I present in this book clearly show that the religious traditions of Islam have contributed to a broad variety of different modernities within Islam. Multiple modernities originate in the social imaginaries of concrete actors, in specific projects of modernity, rather than in the cultural differences of holistic civilizational complexes. Farzin Vahdat, for instance, demonstrated the ways in which nine Muslim thinkers from various parts of the world related Islamic traditions to their different imaginations of modernity.[83] There is not merely one kind of Islamic modernity, but a multiplicity of projects that relate to—in Talal Asad's term—Islam as a discursive tradition.

Muslim intellectuals have understood Islamic modernity in quite different ways. Eisenstadt's theory of multiple modernities does not really account for these different modernizing projects within civilizations. More importantly, he did not really take into account power relations among social actors, without which the successes or failures of concrete projects of modernity remain obscure. The Tanzimat (1839–78), the major reform project of the Ottoman state elite, for instance, suffered heavily from power asymmetries between the center–periphery structures of the international system. In playing on the international level, the Ottoman bureaucrats had to translate their project of modernity into the language of their powerful European adversaries—a historical necessity often understood as the mere copy of "Western concepts" by the Ottoman state elite. From the very beginning, the Ottoman reform process was therefore subject to a language game in which international power relations to a large extent decided on the success or failure of the Ottoman project of modernity.[84] I therefore take the role of social power in its different forms seriously in my case studies.[85] Furthermore, I supplement Eisenstadt's theory of multiple modernities with some elements of other pluralistic theories of modernity such as entangled or successive modernities when necessary.

While Eisenstadt closely followed Jasper's idea of rather hermetically demarcated civilizational complex, he lost sight of the German philosopher's metatheoretical argument of social emergence. The central thought in Jaspers' book was precisely the simultaneity of the sociocultural developments of the axial age. The bifurcation between the realms of transcendence and immanence had no singular origin in time and space. In Jasper's understanding, the axial age was the backdrop to a world-historical development and therefore the very reason he was able to narrate history in form of a global history of humanity. For Eisenstadt, however, modernity did not develop simultaneously in these different civilizational complexes, but had its historical and spatial origins in Europe. The program of modernity, according to Eisenstadt, departed from Europe and spread from this place of origin over the globe.[86] Arrested in thinking in historical origins, Eisenstadt, in this respect, did not apply Jaspers' perspective of emergence. Ultimately, therefore, Eisenstadt did not go beyond the Eurocentric thought of classical modernization theory. To a certain extent, he remained within a Weberian world of modernity: though different in its forms, the modern world was initially a product of the Occident.[87] In the following section, I will introduce some elements of theories of social emergence which challenge this deeply entrenched supposition of conventional social theory. What does such a challenge by theories of emergence look like?

Modern Emergence: The Evolution of Modernity

In his theory of the axial age, Karl Jaspers described the emergence of two genuine spheres of reality—transcendent and immanent worlds—with their own distinct properties in different cultural settings at the same time. Turning from psychology to philosophy in the 1920s, Jaspers embarked on a new scholarly direction at a time when theories of emergence were moving into the center of scientific and philosophical debate. Apparently, these new theoretical discussions left their traces in Jaspers' work on the axial age. Theories of emergence first appeared in Great Britain in the nineteenth century and spontaneously addressed developing, complex adaptive systems. The concept of emergence refers to the occurrence of novel structures and properties at the macro level through processes of self-organization.[88] The core question here is the relationship between the whole and its parts. Theories of emergence deal with the mutual influence among different levels of reality. Through such means, the debate about emergence took up more general questions of the philosophy of science, revolving about the relationship among more fundamental levels of existence such as the material world, life, and mind.[89] Today, theories of emergence help in the description of a broad variety of biological, cultural, neuronal, psychical, and social systems. In the context of my discussion here, I interpret the differentiation processes of Jasper's axial age and Luhmann's rise of modern communicative social subsystems as unpredictable occurrences of novel patterns of social reality such as these. Both can be seen as the evolution of new dynamic cultural and social systems, each with their distinct properties.

Generally speaking, the paradigm of emergence offers a multilevel description of the world in which higher levels emerge from the activities of lower levels.[90] In terms of the social sciences, we can at least speak of three levels of analysis: individuals, collective actors and organizations, and social macrostructures. However, the emergence of higher from lower levels of social reality does not imply that we can reduce the properties of macrostructures to those of collective actors or individuals.[91] Even if we assign a kind of ontological priority to the individual level, as is the case with methodological individualism, we cannot reduce the properties of society at large to the social action of individuals.[92] From this theoretical position, modernity as a process of empty structural progression is the result of sociocultural evolution. Thereby, evolution is not defined in teleological terms but through complex combinations of random variations, selections, and forms of self-organization.[93] The occurrence of modern world society could not have been predicted based on those properties we can find at the individual level.[94] The specific communicative codes of function systems are the historically contingent outcomes of an evolutionary process of self-organization in a global dimension. Consequently, understanding modernity in the metatheoretical framework of emergence renders questions about the compatibility or incompatibility of Islam and modernity meaningless. The question rather is about the ways in which Islam is interpreted and practiced as a modern religion.

In my own use of theories of emergence, I am inspired by concepts of "strong emergence." While "weak emergence" builds on physical monism, strong emergence is founded on the thesis of irreducibility. In theories of strong emergence, the properties of a system are neither predictable nor are they reducible to the behavior of their parts.[95] In theories of dynamic systems, conventional concepts such as causality, continuity, linearity, irreversibility, and predictability are no longer applicable.[96] From this perspective, world society as an all-encompassing system of communication disposes over specific properties clearly distinct from those of human individuals. Social systems and individuals are autonomous but interdependent levels of social reality.[97] Even if we assume that social systems evolve from the complex web of individual action, the properties of these systems such as binary communicative codes cannot be reduced to those of individuals as such. In addition to irreducibility, "downward causation" is one of the most distinctive features of strong emergence.[98] Downward causation implies, on the one hand, that the realization of higher-level entities may have its starting point in processes on a lower level. On the other hand, once emerged, these higher-level entities provide options and constraints to lower-level processes. While the social whole emerges from lower levels, once established as a "social fact," this higher-level structure impacts on the form and properties of lower-level entities at the same time.[99] In this way, downward causation assumes the existence of "whole–part influence" within a "multinested system of constraints."[100]

Regarding my understanding of strong emergence, I roughly follow the argumentation of Keith Sawyer, who suggested we perceive the "causal force" of social structures, that is to say downward causation, on individuals as a "methodological and not necessarily an ontological claim."[101] The linkage of different social levels, then, appears as a process of "constitutive interdependence."[102] This idea of a constitutive interdependence between the macro and micro levels of social life also animated the work of Norbert Elias. Though not directly referring to theories of emergence, in his hitherto mentioned classical book Elias relied—in my eyes—on framing the civilizational process in mechanisms of emergence. In his "socio- and psychogenetical" studies, he described the abstract rationale of an unplanned, long-term process in which societal structures are shaped and sustained by the unintended outcomes of the intended acts of social actors. More precisely, in the growth of social complexity and dependency, he discerned the evolution of a more differentiated and stabilized self-control of the individual.[103] Modernization in Norbert Elias' terms is therefore a process of the mutual constitutive interdependence of social structures and modes of individual behavior. Apparently, his figurative sociology is at least implicitly committed to theoretical propositions of irreducibility and downward causation.[104]

In Luhmann's theoretical argumentation, this mechanism of downward causation is even more visible. In Modern Systems Theory, modern individualization is characterized by the differentiation between social and psychical systems. The evolution of the modern autonomous subject, therefore, is, in the end, the result of the operational closure of society and social subsystems via communication. This self-reliance on the property of communication excludes modern individuals from the social realm. Sociologists have interpreted this process of exclusion in terms of individualization. In a process of constitutive interdependence, two distinctively modern realms of social reality with their respective properties—communication and consciousness—become established. In the narrative of the observer, modernization manifests itself then as individualization or the autonomization of the individual. In his essay *Beantwortung der Frage: Was ist Aufklärung?* (Answer to the Question: What is Enlightenment?), Immanuel Kant described the autonomization of the individual as a process of emancipation. He declared "the courage to use your own intelligence without being guided by another" to be the central motto of the Enlightenment.[105] From Kant's philosophy, this interpretation of the differentiation between subject and system made its way into liberal theories of modernization, becoming a central vision in the Enlightenment project of modernity.

To sum up, according to my fusion of Modern Systems Theory with theories of emergence, modern society is a concept of world society characterized by the dominance of functional differentiation. As a "social fact," world society is the unexpected outcome of a contingent process of sociocultural evolution without any precise origin in time and space. In this context, evolution first and foremost represents the genesis of new social entities in a highly differentiated social reality. I understand Luhmann's social systems as forms of self-organization, i.e., as the spontaneous formation of social orders with a higher complexity than that of their original starting point. Function systems such as the arts, economics, law, politics, religion, and science result from communicative variations stabilized through operational closure in forms of self-organization. Luhmann's concept of functional differentiation allows me to define modernity by its historically specific but unitary form of social differentiation. While this systemic level of modernity is of a global and generic nature, social actors shape the historical realities of modernity through idiosyncratic cultural and institutional projects. In this sense, they produce multiple forms of modernity. Based on the properties of social actorhood, individual and collective actors attach meaning to the otherwise empty progression of functional differentiation in constant boundary negotiations. Social actors transform the syntactic structures of modernity into the semantics of culturally specific multiple modernities. Because of that, these analytically distinct levels of social reality are inseparably connected through historical processes of constitutive interdependence.

Conclusions: A Framework for Case Studies

In the theoretical framework presented in this chapter, the question about the compatibility or incompatibility of Islam and modernity becomes obsolete. Contemporary Islam and the great varieties of Muslim life are inherent parts of modern world society. When understanding modernity on the macro level as progressing social differentiation in terms of function systems, there is no sense in "culture" or "religion" outside the communicative structures of world society. Even more important, the contemporary category of "religion" itself is a result of this structural process. Islam as a modern religion has been shaped and is continuously being reshaped by social actors who are involved in historically relevant social boundary demarcations. World society represents the overarching horizon against which these social actions take place. The common question in the following case studies, therefore, is about the historical role social actors assign to Islamic traditions in their modernizing projects. Why have Islamic traditions assumed such a crucial role in bestowing Muslim projects of modernity with cultural authenticity? The case studies are all examples for modern boundary demarcations among emerging social realms. They all deal with social actors confronted with and acting upon the rising macrostructures of global modernity. The case studies try to give answers to the above question about the rise of a specifically Islamic discourse of modernity.

In this chapter, I have elaborated on a generic concept of modernity in an attempt to reconcile unity and diversity in the sociology of modernity.

Modern Systems Theory provides a syntax of modernity against the background of which we can decipher the multiple semantics of historically concrete projects of modernity. On the level of social actorhood, religious traditions may or may not play a significant role in the semantic construction of multiple modernities. It is on this level that we can observe social actors negotiating empirically relevant boundaries between functionally differentiated realms such as religion, politics, science, and the economy. I interpret the Islamic reform movement as a plurality of actors having engaged over time in negotiating these boundaries. In this way, the movement launched a specific discourse of Islamic modernity in the nineteenth century to which the subsequently articulated different semantics of Islamic modernities relate. The historically concrete establishment of modern function systems has happened through such boundary negotiations and therewith through the non-intended outcomes of purposeful social actions. The contemporary normative and institutional features of Islam are therefore a kind of "congealed action," objectified forms of modern interpretations of Islamic traditions, which we try to retranslate into social action in our historical analysis.[106] Luhmann's theoretical perspective offers us the heuristic means to observe these processes of the dissemination and establishment of the social patterns of modernity in different historical and cultural contexts. Luhmann constructed world society as a global system that in horizontal terms is divided by autopoietic subsystems. In his theoretical design, none of these subsystems can represent the whole of society or claim primacy over other function systems. Historically, however, we can observe that in certain periods of time, the communicative codes of specific function systems seemingly achieve hegemony over others. The negotiations of social actors refer to Luhmann's macrostructures as a cognitive horizon which does not exclude the establishment of temporary hegemonies of specific communicational codes. Richard Münch, for instance, argued convincingly that there is a visible primacy of economic communication in contemporary world society.[107] In principle, these selective preferences of social actors do not exclude any form of communication. Thus, the visible role of religious communication in contemporary projects of Islamic modernity should not be read as evidence against secularization, the latter defined in terms of the rise of a cognitive horizon of functional differentiation. Rather, we should perceive the socially acknowledged boundaries between religion and non-religious domains of the social under constant negotiation in the context of historically shifting power relations.

The Islamic reform movement, originated by Islamic modernists in the nineteenth century, has been characterized by a series of different Islamic projects of modernity. In all these projects, Muslims have tried to make sense of the meaningless structural progression of modernity at the social macro level.[108] Like Max Weber's discussion of the relationship between religion and other non-religious value spheres of modern life, the Islamic reform movement has been engaged in boundary negotiations between Islam and the emerging communicative realms of other social subsystems. In the establishment of a specifically Islamic discourse of modernity, some representatives of this diverse movement have claimed the ultimate supremacy of religion over all other systems of communication. The Egyptian Muslim Brother Sayyid Qutb (1906–66), for instance, compared the functional differentiation of modernity with the polytheist world (*jāhiliyya*) that preceded the revelation of the Qur'an. According to this "mastermind" of radical Islamist groups, "Muslims departed from the straight path of worshipping the one and only God in adhering to the many gods of a materialist world with its artistic, economic, legal and political spheres." In the name of the absolute primacy of religious communication, Qutb therefore demanded "the reintegration of functionally separated social spheres into a holistically interpreted Islamic order."[109] The quest for an Islamic state, for Islamic economics, or for Islamic science, is thus an expression of the claim of social actors that religious norms should ultimately rule over other functionally demarcated social domains.

Finally, when applying core elements of theories of emergence to the sociology of modernity, the empty progression of modernity does not have a precise origin in time or space. Together with the inclusive claims of Modern Systems Theory, this makes questions about the relationship between Islam and the West obsolete at the fundamental theoretical level. In fact, we can also expect to discern evolutionary developments toward the supremacy of functional differentiation in premodern Islamic history.[110] In Luhmann's terms, in observing Muslim history we should look for "preadaptive advances" for the rise of modernity defined in functionally differentiated realms of communication.[111] Discerning such preadaptive advances is another task of the case studies in this book. Modern Systems Theory equips us with analytical instruments to explore the autochthonous institutional and normative forms of differentiation between religion and non-religious social spheres in Islamic history.[112] This emergent structure of modernity, however, does not exclude raising the question of the impact European colonialism has registered on the modernization of the Muslim parts of the world. On the contrary, the Islamic reform movement has been molded by the changing political power configurations of the nineteenth and twentieth centuries. At the level of concrete projects of modernity, this entanglement with European colonialism and its asymmetric power relations is a main factor for the understanding of the historical path which the discourse of Islamic modernity has taken.

In this book's six case studies, I am therefore guided by both the search for preadaptive advances and the observation of modern boundary negotiations in the context of colonial entanglements shaping the discourse of Islamic modernity. In terms of social boundary negotiations, the focus of these case studies is on the role of religion in these projects without losing sight of non-religious alternatives that have also taken part in Muslim discourses on modernity. In all of the chapters, I will briefly introduce additional analytical concepts if necessary. This applies in particular to the communicative codes of the specific function systems at issue in the respective cases. In addition, these conceptual supplements will comprise modern forms of organizations, social orders, power, and actorhood. I group the six case studies in this book into two parts, one with a focus on historical political developments and one addressing three different themes. The first three cases address historical processes of state formation and their intellectual underpinnings. In this historical part, from the perspective of Modern Systems Theory, negotiations among the realms of law, politics, and religion relating to historical projects of Muslim state formation are placed center stage. Starting with the Ottoman Empire, these three chapters follow a chronological sequence from the nineteenth into the twentieth century. The second part, then, presents three thematic studies in which I examine the fields of science, economy, and modern social actorhood. In all these social realms, Muslim projects of modernity combine Islamic traditions with modern non-religious norms and institutions in their attempts to shape "authentic" projects of modernity. Together, these case studies aim to underpin my argument that there is factual fragmentation in the interpretation of Islamic traditions that has accompanied the rise of the discourse of Islamic modernity to occupying a relative hegemony.

Notes

1. Habermas, Jürgen and Niklas Luhmann. 1971. *Theorie der Gesellschaft oder Sozialtechnologie – was leistet die Systemforschung?* Frankfurt am Main: Suhrkamp.
2. Kjaer Poul. 2006. Systems in Context. On the Outcome of the Habermas/Luhmann Debate. *Ancilla Iuris* 66: 66–77.
3. Luhmann, Niklas. 1986. *Ökologische Kommunikation. Kann die moderne Gesellschaft sich auf ökologische Gefährdungen einstellen?* Wiesbaden: Westdeutscher Verlag, 38. Habermas, Jürgen. 1981. *Theorie des kommunikativen Handelns.* Zwei Bände. Frankfurt am Main: Suhrkamp.
4. Habermas, Jürgen. 1980. Die Moderne – ein unvollendetes Projekt. In *Die Moderne – ein unvollendetes Projekt. Philosophisch-politische Aufsätze 1977–1990.* Leipzig: Reclam: 32–55.
5. Rosa, Hartmut. 2014. Historischer Fortschritt oder leere Progression? Das Fortschreiten der Moderne als kulturelles Versprechen und als struktureller Zwang. In *Moderne und Religion. Kontroversen um Modernität und Säkularisierung.* Edited by Ulrich Willems, Detlev Pollack, H. Basu, Thomas Gutmann und U. Spohn. Bielefeld: Transcript: 117–141.
6. Meyer, John M. and Jepperson, Ronald L. 2000. The Cultural Construction of Social Agency. *Sociological Theory* 18 (1): 100–120, 106. I will deal more intensively with the world cultural theory of the Stanford School in Chapters Six and Eight of this book.
7. Eisenstadt, Shmuel N. 2000. Multiple Modernities. *Daedalus* 129 (1): 1–29.
8. Bayly, Christopher. 2004. *The Birth of the Modern World 1780–1914.* London: Blackwell Publishing, 21.
9. For the concept of "world society" as a means for global comparisons, see: Heintz, Bettina and Tobias Werron. 2011. Wie ist Globalisierung möglich? Zur Entstehung globaler Vergleichshorizonte am Beispiel von Wissenschaft und Sport. *Kölner Zeitschrift für Soziologie und Sozialpsychologie* 63: 359–394.
10. Bayly 2004, 451.
11. Luhmann, Niklas. 1990. The World Society as a Social System. In: *Essays on Self-Reference.* New York: Columbia University Press, 178.

12. Luhmann, Niklas. 2017. *Einführung in die Systemtheorie*. Heidelberg: Carl Ayer Verlag, 281.
13. Luhmann, Niklas. 1998. *Die Gesellschaft der Gesellschaft*. Zwei Bände. Frankfurt am Main: Suhrkamp, 618.
14. Luhmann, Niklas 1999. *Die Kunst der Gesellschaft*. Frankfurt am Main: Suhrkamp, 216–217.
15. Tyrell, Hartmann. 1978. Anfragen an die Theorie der gesellschaftlichen Differenzierung. *Zeitschrift für Soziologie* 7 (2): 175–193, 175.
16. Münch, Richard. 1992. *Die Struktur der Moderne. Grundmuster und differenzielle Gestaltung des institutionellen Aufbaus der modernen Gesellschaften*. Frankfurt am Main: Suhrkamp, 11.
17. Mahner, Martin and Mario Bunge. 2001. *Scientific Realism: Selected Essays of Mario Bunge*. Amherst: Prometheus Books, 89.
18. Cf. Kaviraj, Sudipta. 2005. An Outline of a Revisionist Theory of Modernity. *European Journal of Sociology* 46 (3): 497–526, 514.
19. Luhmann, Niklas. 2002. *Die Religion der Gesellschaft*. Frankfurt am Main: Suhrkamp, 118.
20. Luhmann adopted the concept of "double contingency" from Talcott Parsons' work. However, he rejected Parsons' assumption that social systems need values and norms in order to regulate the problem of double contingency. In Luhmann's theory, double contingency relates to the question of social order. Through its circular nature, double contingency generates social order without any metaphorical references to its origin. In an evolutionary process, double contingency leads to the emergence of social order. Luhmann 2017, 306–310.
21. Luhmann, Niklas. 1981. Handlungstheorie und Systemtheorie. In *Soziologische Aufklärung 3. Soziales System, Gesellschaft, Organisation*. Opladen: Westdeutscher Verlag: 50–66, 51. My translation.
22. Vanderstraeten Raf. 2002. Parsons, Luhmann and the Theme of Double Contingency. *Journal of Classical Sociology* 2 (1): 77–92.
23. Luhmann, Niklas 1970: Funktion und Kausalität. In *Soziologische Aufklärung. Aufsätze zur Theorie sozialer Systeme*. Band 1. Opladen: Westdeutscher Verlag: 9–30, 25.
24. To be sure, this does not exclude that social actors strive to do so. In the case studies in this book, we will see different attempts at employing religion as a means of social integration and mediating functional differentiation.
25. Luhmann, Niklas. 2008. *Die Moral der Gesellschaft*. Frankfurt am Main: Suhrkamp, 265.

26. The terms of "society of states" and "like units" are used in the field of international relations theory. See, for instance: Buzan, Barry. 2014. *An Introduction to the English School of International Relations: The Societal Approach.* Cambridge: Polity.
27. Luhmann 1986, 169.
28. Luhmann, Niklas. 1992. *Die Wissenschaft der Gesellschaft.* Frankfurt am Main: Suhrkamp, 428.
29. Maturana Humberto R. and Francisco J. Varela. 1980. *Autopoiesis and Cognition: The Realization of the Living.* Dordrecht. D. Reidel.
30. Luhmann 2002, 77
31. Ibid. 125
32. Beyer, Peter. 2006. *Religions in Global Society.* London and New York: Routledge.
33. Osterhammel, Jürgen. 2009. *Die Verwandlung der Welt: Eine Geschichte des 19. Jahrhunderts.* Munich: C. H. Beck, 1243.
34. Nongbri, Brent. 2013. *Before Religion. A History of a Modern Concept.* New Haven and London: Yale University Press, 11–13 and 107–113.
35. Ibid. 89.
36. In the empirical chapters of his book, Beyer looks more closely at different cases regarding this construction of modern religious progams.
37. Ibid. 63 and 117.
38. McCutcheon, Russel T. 1997. *Manufacturing Religion: The Discourse on Sui Generis Religion and the Politics of Nostalgia.* Oxford and New York: Oxford University Press.
39. Fitzgerald, Timothy. 2007. Introduction. In *Religion and the Secular: Historical and Colonial Formations.* London: Acumen, 1–24, 5.
40. Asad, Talal. 1993. *Genealogies of Religion: Discipline and Reasons of Power in Christianity and Islam.* Baltimore, MD: Johns Hopkins University Press, 30.
41. Bergunder, Michael. 2020. Umkämpfte Historisierung. Die Zwillingsgeburt von "Religion" und "Esoterik" in der zweiten Hälfte des 19. Jahrhunderts und das Programm einer globalen Religionsgeschichte. In *Wissen um Religion: Erkenntnis – Interesse. Epistemologie und Episteme in Religionswissenschaft und interkultureller Theologie.* Leipzig: Evangelische Verlagsanstalt: 47–132, 61–67.
42. See: Fitzgerald, Timothy. 2007. *Discourse on Civility and Barbarity. A Critical History of Religion and Related Categories.* Oxford: Oxford University Press: 9.
43. Stausberg, Michael. 2010. Distinctions, Differentiations, Ontology, and

Non-humans in Theories of Religion. *Method and Theory in the Study of Religion* 22: 354–374, 364.
44. Luhmann 2002, 126.
45. Ibid. 77.
46. Adopting Luhmann's definition of secularization, I fully agree with José Casanova, who defended the concept against Talal Asad's critique. Casanova stressed that the core of secularization theory is the assumption of an ongoing "differentiation of the secular spheres from each other and from religious institutions and norms." Casanova, José. 2006. Secularization Revisited: A Reply to Talal Asad. In *Powers of the Secular Modern: Talal Asad and His Interlocutors*. Edited by David Scott and Charles Hirschkind. Stanford: Stanford University Press: 12–30, 20.
47. Luhmann 2017, 149.
48. Ibid. 265–267.
49. It should be mentioned that not all scholars who build on Luhmann follow him in this rigid distinction. See, for instance, the discussion about inclusion/exclusion in the anthology: Stichweh, Rudolf and Paul Windolf (eds.) *Inklusion und Exklusion: Analysen zur Sozialstruktur und sozialen Ungleichheit*. Wiesbaden: VS Verlag für Sozialwissenschaften.
50. Luhmann, Niklas. 1987. *Soziale Systeme: Grundriss einer allgemeinen Theorie*. Frankfurt am Main: Suhrkamp, 288.
51. Durkheim, Emile. 1964. *The Division of Labor*. New York: The Free Press.
52. Hennis, Wilhelm. 1987. *Max Webers Fragestellung. Studien zur Biographie des Werks*. Tübingen: Mohr/Siebeck, 32.
53. Hennis 1987, 70–73.
54. Weber, Max. 1917. Science as a Vocation. In: *From Max Weber: Essays in Sociology*. London and New York: Routledge, 148.
55. Ibid. 149.
56. This text appears in English translations as "Intermediate Reflections" or "Religious Rejections of the World and their Directions".
57. Schimank Uwe. 2005. *Differenzierung und Integration der modernen Gesellschaft. Beiträge zur akteurzentrierten Differenzierungstheorie*. Wiesbaden: VS Verlag, 48.
58. Schuetz, Alfred. 1953. Common-Sense and Scientific Interpretation of Human Action. Philosophy and Phenomenological Research. 14 (1): 1–38, 7 and 9.
59. In Weber's language this empty progression appears in terms such as "formal

rationalization" and "disenchantment of the world." This is to say in the modern belief in one—in principle—can master all things by calculation. Weber, Max. 1922 [1988]. *Gesammelte Aufsätze zur Wissenschaftslehre*. Tübingen: UTB, 594.

60. It goes without saying that the works of Elias and Foucault are very different. Moreover, in his writings about governmentality, Foucault—according to my knowledge—does not refer to Elias' book. We elaborated more on similarities and differences in the perspectives of these two authors in an article on the Islamic organization Hizb ut-Tahrir: Jung, Dietrich and Kirstine Sinclair. 2020. Religious Governmentality: The Case of Hizb ut-Tahrir. *TEMENOS. Nordic Journal of Comparative Religion* 56 (1): 95–117.

61. Elias, Norbert. 1994. *The Civilizing Process: The History of Manners and State Formation and Civilization*. Oxford: Basil Blackwell.

62. Foucault, Michel. 1980. About the Beginning of the Hermeneutics of the Self. In *Religion and Culture by Michel Foucault*. Edited by Jeremy R. Carrette. Manchester: Manchester University Press, 162.

63. Foucault, Michel. 1984. What is Enlightenment?. In *The Foucault Reader*. Edited by Paul Rabinow. Pantheon Books: New York: 32–51, 41.

64. Terpe, Sylvia. 2020. Working with Max Weber's "Spheres of Life": An Actor-centred Approach. *Journal of Classical Sociology* 20 (1): 22–42, 27.

65. Ibid. 38 (my understanding of her interpretation).

66. Viskovatoff, Alex. 1999. Foundations of Niklas Luhmann's Theory of Social Systems. *Philosophy of the Social Sciences* 29 (4): 481–516.

67. Eisenstadt, Shmuel N. 2000. The Reconstruction of Religious Arenas in the Framework of "Multiple Modernities." *Millenium: Journal of International Studies* 29 (3): 591–611; Eisenstadt, Shmuel N. 2000. *Multiple Modernities*. Daedalus 129 (1): 1–29.

68. Thomassen, Bjørn. 2010. Anthropology, Multiple Modernities and the Axial Age Debate. *Anthropological Theory* 10 (4): 321–342.

69. Mota, Aurea and Gerard Delanty. 2015. Eisenstadt, Brazil and the Multiple Modernities Framework: Revisions and Reconsiderations. *Journal of Classical Sociology* 15 (1): 39–57, 41.

70. Eisenstadt 2000, 5.

71. Ibid. 19.

72. Cf. Kavira 2005, 516.

73. Jaspers, Carl. 1956. *Vom Ursprung und Ziel der Geschichte*. Frankfurt am Main und Hamburg: Fischer.

74. Arnason, Johan P. 2003. *Civilizations in Dispute: Historical Questions and Theoretical Traditions*. Leiden: Brill, 160–167.
75. Honneth, Axel. 2004. Considerations on Alessandro Ferrara's Reflective Authenticity, *Philosophy & Social Criticism* 30 (1): 11–15.
76. Lindholm, Charles. 2008. *Culture and Authenticity*. Oxford: Blackwell Publishing, 1.
77. Bendix, Regina. 1997. *In Search of Authenticity: The Formation of Folklore Studies*. Madison: University of Wisconsin Press, 8.
78. The "Arab Renaissance" or "Arab Enlightenment" was a multi-religious Arab cultural movement beginning in the mid-nineteenth century, propagating ideas of historicism, progress, rationalism, scientific knowledge, and civilizational legacies. See: Di-Capua, Yoav. 2015. Nahda: The Arab Project of Enlightenment. In *The Companion to Modern Arab Culture*. Edited by Dwight F. Reynolds. Cambridge: Cambridge University Press: 54–74.
79. Al-Azmeh, Aziz. 1996. *Islams and Modernities*. Second Edition. London and New York: Verso, 41–43.
80. Büssow, Johann. 2017. Muhammad Abduh: The Theology of Unity (Egypt, 1898). In *Religious Dynamics under the Impact of Imperialism and Globalization: A Sourcebook*. Edited by Björn Bentlage et al. Leiden: Brill, 141–159, 144.
81. Cf. Theodossopoulos, Dimitrios. 2013. Laying Claim to Authenticity: Five Anthropological Dilemmas. *Anthropological Quarterly* 86 (2): 337–360, 339.
82. For this critique, see: Wagner, Peter. 2008. *Modernity as Experience and Interpretation: A New Sociology of Modernity*. Cambridge: Cambridge University Press.
83. Vahdat, Farzin. 2013. *Islamic Ethos and the Specter of Modernity*. London and New York: Anthem Press.
84. Cf. Wigen, Einar. 2018. *State of Translation: Turkey in Interlingual Relations*. Ann Arbor: University of Michigan Press.
85. There exist different and often competing theories of power. The concept is ubiquitous in use, but its definition, conception, and manner of study are highly contested at the same time. While Max Weber defined power in terms of a social relationship and distinguished it from domination (*Herrschaft*) by the category of legitimacy, Michel Foucault considered power in terms of a rather amorphous force, a social web that penetrates social and discursive structures as a whole. In Niklas Luhmann's theory, meanwhile, power appears as a communicative media facilitating the operation of the political system. Finally, in the theory of

international relations, realist scholars define the power of states by linking it to economic, demographic, and military resources. I will further refer to these different forms of power in the case studies when needed. Cf. Anders, Andreas. 2012. *Theorien der Macht zur Einführung*. Hamburg: Junius; Baldwin, David A. 2016. *Power and International Relations: A Conceptual Approach*. Princeton: Princeton University Press; and Lukes, Steven. 2004. *Power: A Radical View*. London: Red Globe Press.

86. Eisenstadt, Shmuel N. 2001. The Civilizational Dimension of Modernity: Modernity as a Distinct Civilization. *International Sociology* 16 (3): 320–340.
87. In the *Vorbemerkungen* (Preliminary Remarks) to his essays on the Protestant Ethic, Weber explicitly formulated his question as to what the reason was for the fact that only in Europe did cultural phenomena appear and from there achieve global relevance. Weber, Max. 1920 [1984]. Vorbemerkungen zu den Gesammelten Aufsätzen der Religionssoziologie. In *Die Protestantische Ethik I. Eine Aufsatzsammlung*. Edited by J. Winckelmann. Gütersloh: Mohn, 9–26, 9.
88. Goldstein, Jeffrey. 1999. Emergence as a Construct: History and Issues. *Emergence* 1 (1): 49–72, 49.
89. Philstrom, Sami. 2002. The Re-Emergence of the Emergence Debate. *Principa* 6 (1): 133–181, 137.
90. Walby, Sylvia. 2007. Complexity Theory, System Theory, and Multiple Intersecting Social Inequalities. *Philosophy of the Social Sciences* 37 (4): 449–470, 461.
91. Stephan, Achim: Eine kurze Einführung in die Vielfalt und Geschichte emergentistischen Denkens. In: *Blinde Emergenz? Interdisziplinäre Beiträge zu Fragen kultureller Evolution* Edited by Thomas Wägenbaur. Heidelberg: Synchron Wissenschaftsverlag der Autoren, 33–47, 34.
92. Cf. Clayton, Philip. 2006. Conceptual Foundations of Emergence Theory. In *The Re-Emergence of Emergence: The Emergentist Hypothesis from Science to Religion*. Edited by Philip Clayton and Paul Davies. Oxford: Oxford University Press, 1–31.
93. Cf. Kaufmann, Stuart A. 1993. *The Origins of Order: Self-Organization and Selection in Evolution*. Oxford: Oxford University Press, 3.
94. Emmeche, Claus, Simon Køppe and Frederik Stjernfelt. 1997. Explaining Emergence: Towards an Ontology of Levels. *Journal for General Philosophy of Science* 28: 83–119, 83.
95. Stephan 1999: 49–53.
96. Wägenbaur, Thomas. 2000. Emergenz der Kommunikation. In *Blinde*

Emergenz? Interdisziplinäre Beiträge zu Fragen kultureller Evolution. Edited by Thomas Wägebaur. Heidelberg: Synchron Wissenschaftsverlag der Autoren: 121–141.
97. Schimank 2005, 73.
98. Clayton 2006, 4.
99. El-Hani, Charbel N. 2002. On the Reality of Emergents. *Principa* 6 (1): 51–87.
100. Clayton 2006, 21.
101. Sawyer, Keith. 2001. Emergence in Sociology: Contemporary Philosophy of Mind and Some Implications for Sociological Theory. *American Journal of Sociology* 107 (3): 551–585, 558.
102. Zahavi 2015.
103. Elias 1994, 443.
104. Albert, Gert. 2013. Figuration und Emergenz. Zur Ontologie und Methodologie des Ansatzes von Norbert Elias. *Kölner Zeitschrift für Soziologie und Sozialpsychologie* 65 (1): 193–222.
105. Kant, Immanuel. 1783. Beantwortung der Frage: Was ist Aufklärung. In: *Gesammelte Werke, Band 9: Schriften zur Anthropologie, Geschichtsphilosophie, Politik und Pädagogik, Erster Teil.* Darmstadt: Wissenschaftliche Buchgesellschaft: 53–61.
106. Cf. Adorno, Theodor W. 2000. *Introduction to Sociology.* Edited by Christoph Gödde and translated by Edmund Jephcott. Cambridge: Polity Press, 105.
107. Münch, Richard. 2009. Die Weltgesellschaft im Spannungsfeld von funktionaler, stratifikatorischer und segmentärer Differenzierung. In *Inklusion und Exklusion: Analysen zur Sozialstruktur und sozialen Ungleichheit.* Edited by Rudolf Stichweh and Paul Windolf. Wiesbaden: VS Verlag für Sozialwissenschaften, 283–298, 295.
108. To be sure, this is the theoretical line of interpretation to which we must add the necessary historical contextualization in order to reach the full picture.
109. I discuss this interpretation of the discourse of Islamic modernity by Sayyid Qutb in the introduction to my 2019 article: Modern Subjectivity and the Emergence of Global Modernity. Syntax and Semantics of Modern Times. In *Modern Subjectivities in World Society. Global Structures and Local Practices.* Edited by Dietrich Jung and Stephan Stetter. London: Palgrave Macmillan, 45–64. In Chapter Eight, I will again briefly discuss Qutb's thought.
110. In an almost classical study, Maxim Rodinson, for instance, identified patterns of capitalist economics in premodern Islamic settings. George Saliba, to mention another example, argued convincingly that premodern scientific findings played

a crucial role in the formation of modern science. See: Rodinson, Maxime. 1966. *Islam et capitalism*. Paris: Seuil; Saliba, George. 2007. *Islamic Science and the Making of Europe*. Cambridge: Cambridge University Press. I will refer again to Saliba's and Rodinson's work in Chapters Six and Seven respectively.
111. Luhmann 1992, 709.
112. Cf. Wohlrab-Sahr, Monika and Marian Burchardt. 2012. Multiple Secularities: Toward a Cultural Sociology of Secular Modernities. *Comparative Sociology* 11: 875–909.

PART II

MODERN STATE FORMATION AND THE ISLAMIC DISCOURSE OF MODERNITY

3

FROM EMPIRE TO NATIONAL STATES: MODERNIZATION IN THE OTTOMAN EMPIRE

In the year 2000, I published *Turkey at the Crossroads* in collaboration with Wolfango Piccoli.[1] The book was the direct outcome of my guest professorship at the International Relations Department of Bilkent University, where I had spent the 1997–98 academic year. More precisely, the study was stimulated by the everyday observations I had made on campus in Ankara and in Turkey at large throughout my stay. I arrived in Ankara on a hot summer day in late August 1997. Before I took on this guest professorship, I had never worked on Turkish affairs. The focus of my studies had been on social theory, conflict studies, and the Arab Middle East. Consequently, prior to my arrival, I could not have ever imagined writing a book on Turkey. However, this situation soon changed. While living and working in Ankara, I unwittingly engaged in a project of making participant observations; and these observations were interesting, puzzling, and thought-stirring at the same time. Within a short period of time, the fascinating social history of Turkey and the country's troubled political realities attracted my scholarly interest. Without planning it beforehand, I was subsequently sliding into the field of Turkish studies.

While teaching my courses in the International Relations of the Middle East, I began reading some of the classics on Turkish history, in particular on the modernization of Turkey in the nineteenth and early twentieth centuries. In addition, I used vacations and weekends for trips around the country that enabled me to augment my reading on Turkey with the necessary personal impressions and illustrations. These trips not only brought me to the western provinces and their cities of Bursa, Edirne, Istanbul, and Izmir, but also led me into Turkey's "far East," visiting places such as Diyarbakır, Doğubeyazıt, Gaziantep, Kars, Trabzon, and Van. The major argument of *Turkey at the Crossroads*—the thesis of a strong continuity between the Ottoman Empire and the Turkish Republic—was born out of insights from this combination of the study of scholarly literature with rather randomly gathered observations during my one-year stay in the country.

This thesis of continuity may not come as a surprise to the academic Turkey expert today, yet it was a new discovery for me. At that point of time, my historical knowledge of Turkey had been limited to the official narrative, which associated a fundamental rupture with the revolutionary establishment of the secularist republic by Mustafa Kemal Atatürk. Woven together with the paradigm of Ottoman decline, this narrative was also the core framework of some of the meanwhile contested classics on Turkish modernization with which I had begun to engage at Bilkent. Good examples for this literature are Feroz Ahmad's *The Making of Modern Turkey*, Niyazi Berkes's *The Development of Secularism in Turkey*, or Bernard Lewis's *The Emergence of Modern Turkey*.[2] In his study on late Ottoman and early Turkish history, Lewis, for instance, applied the central axioms of classical modernization theory. It is this kind of modernization theory that one could describe as paradigmatic in narrating Turkish history. Often implicitly applied, it proposes the idea of a process of linear institutional change, whose appropriateness for our understanding of the late Ottoman Empire has rightly been put into question.[3] In addition, Lewis's description of the foundation of republican Turkey closely mirrors the official historical narrative of the political elite around Mustafa Kemal Atatürk. After the Young Turk Revolution (1908), the new republican political elite "demonized" the Ottoman reform process as a kind of "distorted modernization" in comparison to the enlightened and genuine modern reforms of the Kemalist regime.[4]

When it comes to the continuity thesis of *Turkey at the Crossroads*, however, the inspiration directly resulted from my reading of Şerif Mardin's *The Genesis of Young Ottoman Thought*. In the social setting of Bilkent University, this book became the decisive eye-opener for me.[5] In his study, Mardin gives a historical account of the development of the Young Ottoman movement, whose members represented a heterogeneous group of young bureaucrats, intellectuals, and journalists and some modern-oriented *ulema* who belonged to the lower stratum of the newly educated middle class. Founded in 1865, this movement began to spread its ideas about a synthesis of the Enlightenment with Islamic traditions among the literate public.[6] The Young Ottomans formed a kind of political opposition that was nationalistic in mindset and constitutionalist in institutional approach, an opposition that reverted to the legitimizing power of Islamic traditions.[7] In short, they belonged to the core representatives in the emergence of one of the specifically Ottoman discourses of Islamic modernity. At the same time, Mardin described the state elite of the Ottoman Empire as a stratum of bureaucrats who themselves engaged in the modernization of the empire, partly taking over the established authoritative patterns of sultanic rule. Even more important, the new modernizing bureaucrats of the Tanzimat era (1839–78) assimilated the aristocratic values and elitist attitudes of the classical Ottoman state elite. To some extent, the modernizing elites were themselves acting in the style of potentates.[8] Initially the Young Ottomans, and later the Young Turk Movement, promoted their projects of Ottoman–Turkish modernity in opposition to the bureaucratic class of the empire, but they also gradually adopted the elitist attitudes of these representatives of the Tanzimat and transferred them to the new political elite of the Turkish Republic.[9]

The striking impression I gained while reading Mardin's book was the observation that this social habitus of the late Ottoman Empire was still visible in republican Turkey in the 1990s. Taking Mardin's description as an ideal type, I was able to identify the bureaucrats of the Tanzimat in the behavior of the social environment around me. Some of Mardin's descriptions of the Ottoman bureaucratic habitus could have almost been part of a non-existing ethnographic notebook written over my stay. The major theme in *Turkey at the Crossroads*, therefore, became Ottoman–Turkish continuities in terms of the political and social culture of the country. However, I must confess that I was still analyzing these continuities under the impact of the narrative of decline. In this chapter, I will not only remedy this mistake of my previous book but also extend the lines of Ottoman–Turkish continuities back into the premodern and early modern periods of the Ottoman Empire. With respect to the theoretical perspective presented in Chapter Two, I will draw this new line of continuities from preadaptive advances to modernity in the early modern empire until the Islamization of the state-driven Ottoman modernization project under Sultan Abdülhamit's reign (1876–1909). In this way, this chapter combines theses about the emergence of a discourse of Islamic modernity with those about the indigenous modernization of the empire. I unfold this argumentation by taking the chronology of Ottoman state formation as my guiding path.

In the next section, I introduce the analytical tools which I use for marching along this argumentative path. My analytical framework combines Luhmann's macrosociological understanding of the modern political system with conceptual elements of the historical political sociology of Norbert Elias, Charles Tilly, and Max Weber. Then I put the focus on the detection of the already mentioned preadaptive advances regarding first traces of functional differentiation in premodern Ottoman state formation. In this endeavor, I predominantly rely on secondary literature that belongs to the corpus of scholarly works criticizing the decline thesis. While the main emphasis in this section is on the political realm, I will occasionally refer to other social realms too. The topic of the fourth section, then, is the Tanzimat and the state-centered project of modernity of the Ottoman bureaucratic elite in the context of the European power struggle, eventually leading to the gradual Islamization of this project by Sultan Abdülhamit II. Under his rule (1876–1909), not only did the Ottoman project of modernity attain a much more Islamic look, but in this period of time we can also notice the increasing fragmentation of the ideological concept of Ottomanism into various forms of ethno-nationalisms. It was during Abdülhamit's reign that the later Kemalist Turkish-nationalist project of modernity first took shape. The chapter concludes with summing up Ottoman state formation with respect to the Islamization of its concomitant discourses on modernity.

Modern State Formation and the Political Subsystem of Modern Society

What is modern politics? There are without any doubt many answers to this question. Yet for the purpose of this chapter, two of them are most important. First of all, there is the macrosociological definition of politics as a global system of communication, and second, there is politics as the internal structure of the global political system institutionalized in the modern nation state. In this section, I will look more closely at these two levels of modern politics. In my analysis, politics as a functionally differentiated subsystem of modern world society represents the macro level, whereas the modern state as an institution and global politics as a form of interaction in a global state system constitutes the meso level. Together, they represent the realm of modern politics. In this chapter, in taking the case of the Ottoman Empire I am looking for emerging signs of modern politics in the historical development of the empire.

In Niklas Luhmann's theoretical design, modern politics evolved out of an evolutionary process of social differentiation and functional specification. In his conceptual world, politics represents one specific function system of modern society that cannot claim any kind of supremacy over other subsystems of world society. The specific code through which he defined modern politics is the production of collectively binding decisions. This code evolved around the centralization of political power by the state. In Modern Systems Theory, political power is the essential generalized medium of political communication. Political power facilitates the making of decisions and the definition of public functions, the latter implemented in state offices. Modern politics draws its boundaries to its social environment by a focus on collectively binding processes of decision-making in state offices.[10] In addition, Luhmann characterized modern politics by the differentiation between its code and its program. While the code is based on collective decision-making, the program regulates the manner in which political offices are filled. Consequently, in the modern state, the occupation of political offices is in principle contingent on legally formalized appointment processes. In Luhmann's historical analysis, the absolutist state in Europe did not yet know a clear separation between political authority and the state, which results from this differentiation between code and program. Therefore, in the concept of the state in early modernity, a legitimate distinction between government and opposition was absent. The absolutist state, was thus characterized by a form of political stratification in which the function of political programs—the regulation of the occupation of public offices—was yet unknown.[11]

From this macro perspective, the establishment of political communication is inseparably linked to the formation of the modern nation state. The evolution of politics as a function system and the state as its essential organizational agent are concomitant social processes, however on two different levels of social reality. Therefore, also in Luhmann's theory, we easily find implicit references to core features of the conceptual world of classical historical sociology. In the work of Charles Tilly, for instance, the rise of the modern nation state and of a global system of states governed by international law were the late and non-intended outcomes of intensive bargaining processes between social actors making both wars and states. Tracing this process over ten centuries of European history, Tilly abstracted from it a specific mechanism of the circularity of the state competencies of territorial control and taxation. According to this mechanism, state-makers accumulated the means of coercion, whereas entrepreneurs accumulated economic wealth. Military and civilian elites developed a new form of reciprocal relationship based on civilian demands for protection and the state-builders' need for economic extraction. In his retrospective analysis of the historical formation of European statehood, Tilly identified the central paradox of the emergence of the modern state in the observation "that the pursuit of war and military capacity, after having created national states as a sort of by-product, led to a civilianization of government and domestic politics."[12]

Even as early as the 1930s, Norbert Elias reconstructed the history of modern state formation—i.e., Tilly's circularity of territorial control and economic extraction—in terms of a double monopoly mechanism. In the *Civilizing Process*, Elias traced the origin of both internal state security and the idea of the autonomy of the modern subject back to a violent elimination contest. Essentially abstracting this from French history, he defined the centralization of political power and the concomitant extraction of economic means by taxation through two distinct phases of state monopoly formation. In the first phase, Elias described the factual emergence of monopolies of physical force and taxation in the hands of a few social actors. In the second phase, then, these monopolies shift from being a property of state-makers and become an arrangement of political and legal institutions under public control. According to Elias, the first phase of the monopoly process historically developed into absolutist forms of the state. The second phase, then, he associated with the gradual transformation of absolutist rule into forms of popular sovereignty expressed in representative democratic institutions.[13] Apparently Elias was addressing Tilly's paradox of the modern state in distinguishing between two phases of modern state formation. In this aspect, Luhmann's concept of the centralization of political power by the state and its further differentiation into political code and programs resembles the sociological reasoning of both Charles Tilly and Norbert Elias.

In my own understanding, however, the work of each of these three scholars builds on the central concepts of the political sociology that Max Weber developed at the beginning of the twentieth century. It was the German sociologist who defined modern statehood in terms of "the monopoly of the legitimate use of physical force within a given territory."[14] Weber referred to European state formation as a process of "political expropriation" in which the modern institution of the state eventually succeeded in depriving all other social actors of the means of coercion.[15] Crucial in Weber's definition, however, is his concept of legitimacy, which does not figure prominent in the works of the three scholars discussed above. The consolidation of the factual monopoly of physical force relies on an ideational factor. To some extent, according to Weber, the institutionalization of the state needed the consent of both ruler and ruled. The use of political power in terms of state authority requires a specific cultural foundation. Through the category of legitimacy, Weber distinguished between mere power relations and political authority. The establishment and maintenance of state power, that is to say, the perpetuation of historically specific forms of political authority, ultimately rests on a mutually accepted symbolic order. Moreover, in the emergence of modern statehood, we can also discern a specific change in the dominant forms of legitimacy. While the modern state is based on legal or rational authority, on the belief "in the legality of enacted rules and the right of those elevated to authority under such rule to issue commands,"[16] Weber defined premodern or traditional authority through personal ties as "the established belief in the sanctity of immemorial traditions and the legitimacy of those exercising authority under them."[17] In order to maintain its legitimacy, the modern state, therefore, may need a third monopoly, a monopoly of symbolic reproduction. Historically, we can observe the emergence of this third monopoly in the institutionalization of a modern state education system.

In this chapter, and in some of the coming chapters too, I will analyze issues of politics with the help of the conceptual tool kit provided by the above social theorists.[18] I use elements of Luhmann's theory to observe discursive processes of social boundary demarcation to investigate the ways in which the communicative establishment of function systems has accompanied modern state formation. Elias, Tilly, and Weber serve me at the meso level in the analysis of state-building processes by social actors. On this level, I explore the evolution of the institutional means of political authority such as the monopoly of physical force, forms of taxation, and military and administrative reforms. In methodological terms, I consider the concepts of this tool kit of historical sociology to be ideal types. They are instrumental means of research, however, referring in their conceptual quality to empirical observations. Ideal types are sociological constructs and, thus, they do not directly correspond to history as such. While derived from concrete empirical data, they do not copy historical reality in a descriptive way.[19] In the following sections, these ideal types provide me with the heuristic instruments to underpin my thesis that we can discern similar and indigenous processes of state formation in Ottoman history as in Europe. To be sure, in this context "similar" does not mean "the same"! It is precisely the application of ideal types that gives us the instruments for discerning historical differences. Consequently, similar processes relate to the conceptual apparatus, and they can take historically very different forms and outcomes. In short, with the help of conceptual tools of classical historical sociology, I will corroborate my thesis of a continuation of indigenous lines of state formation from early Ottoman modernity through the Tanzimat period until the establishment of the Turkish Republic.

Preadaptive Advances and the Indigenous Roots of Ottoman State Formation

In *Empire of Difference*, Karen Barkey examined the Ottoman road from empire to nation state with the help of similar concepts of historical sociology as described in the previous section. She was looking at the particular ways in which war, trade, and taxation "impinged on the networks of state-society relations."[20] In her book, Barkey turned against the decline thesis, emphasizing instead the adaptability, longevity, and resilience of the institutions of the Ottoman Empire.[21] In the classical understanding of orientalist scholarship, the empire built on traditional "Muslim principles" was embodied in the "sacred law" of Islam.[22] Modernity, consequently, appeared in the Ottoman setting of the nineteenth century as a kind of historical rupture "under Western influences" and was conducted in forms of a "systematic imitation of European techniques."[23] In this classical view, defined by the concepts of stagnation and imitation, the so-called "Napoleonic moment" marked the beginnings of the Ottoman road to modernity, eventually leading to the Tanzimat reform process.[24] According to this narrative, the French intervention initiated social and political change in the Middle East "under European influence and colonization."[25]

As early as the 1950s, Albert Hourani had criticized this position. He posed the question of whether the Ottoman Empire was indeed "decaying and lifeless" before the impact of the West. Instead, he suggested the West had entered as a new factor into the modernization of a Middle East in which indigenous developments toward modernity were already underway.[26] Today, the theses of social stagnation and institutional decline are no longer tenable, at least not in what we consider to be serious scholarship of the Middle East. This applies not only to the fields of economy and politics but also to the cultural and intellectual life in the Ottoman Empire. In particular the so-called "Tulip Age" (1718–30) and the eighteenth century at large are meanwhile considered as a period of time in which "vivacity and elegance" characterized the Ottoman arts.[27] Contemporary studies explicitly point to the neglect and misunderstanding of the eighteenth century by prior historians.[28] Since the 1990s, studies of provincial history have undermined previously held academic truisms of an Ottoman stasis and emphasized the role of center–province dynamics "as a model for understanding the origins of the Tanzimat."[29] Moreover, these studies are remarkable correctives to the traditional view on change in the Ottoman Empire, perceiving it as being almost exclusively triggered and disseminated by the imperial center in Istanbul.[30] Nevertheless, there is still not yet a firmly established body of scholarship on these provincial dynamics and the ways in which Ottoman legacies have impacted on state formation in the Middle East and the Balkans.[31] In detecting various local and not necessarily interconnected instances of indigenous modernization, however, this growing literature supports my own suggestion of perceiving global modernity as an emerging structure without specific roots in time or space. In his analysis of Ottoman state formation between the sixteenth and eighteenth centuries, Rifaat Abou el-Haj concluded therefore that the nineteenth-century Ottoman reforms did not mark a rupture but represented "the culmination of a process of change having its roots in the seventeenth century."[32]

This shift of paradigm in studies on Ottoman history makes this empire an ideal case for the search for indigenous roots of modernity in the Muslim parts of the world.[33] In the sixteenth and seventeenth centuries, it was the Ottoman Empire pushing into Europe rather than European powers impacting on the empire's domestic institutions. The empire was both a veritable threat to Europe and a significant player in its diplomatic and commercial affairs.[34] The Ottomans conquered Rhodes and Crete, attacked European trade fleets and enslaved "thousands of men and women, many of whom converted to Islam."[35] In 1627, for instance, Ottoman pirates abducted men and women as far north as Iceland and brought them to the slave markets in Morocco and Algiers.[36] From my own theoretical perspective, therefore, the growing number of studies on the early modern Ottoman Empire and its different provinces provide me with numerous indications of preadaptive advances regarding the emergence of functional differentiation in a Muslim setting.

We can find these homegrown traces of modernity in various social fields. With regard to literature, for instance, the elite culture of the Ottoman Empire in the seventeenth and eighteenth centuries featured new forms of chronicles, biographies, and moral discussions, including a "rich literature of love."[37] Harun Küçük observed in Istanbul the spread of philosophical discussions that suggest a "family resemblance to the European Enlightenment" after the establishment of the printing press in 1729.[38] More recent studies on the Islamic history of ideas have seemingly proven wrong the thesis that an intellectual stagnation occurred in the Ottoman Empire from the sixteenth century onward.[39] When it comes to economic developments in Muslim regions, these too show initial traces of capitalism long before the impact of colonialism. In an almost classical study, Maxime Rodinson claimed to have discovered elements of an emerging capitalist economy in the premodern Middle East. His book deals with boundary demarcations between religion and economics *avant la lettre*.[40]

In a more recent example, Peter Gran approached Islamic history in terms of the means of political economy and argued that the Muslim parts of the world played a critical role in the development of the modern capitalist economy "before, during and after the colonial period."[41] Focusing, like Gran, on the example of Egypt, Nelly Hanna also convincingly rejected the narrative of economic stagnation in the region. She discerned capitalist practices among Egyptian artisans in a period of the commercialization of the Egyptian economy between 1600 and 1800.[42] Although only a "minority practice," artisan entrepreneurship produced goods for the market and exchanged them in return for money. In this sense, her examination of early modern Egyptian economy led her to the conclusion that "modernity did not start through contact with the West."[43] Her examination of early modern Egyptian economy revealed pockets of modernity before the country's integration into the capitalist world market.[44] Finally, the early modern Ottoman Empire knew a specific form of legal dualism in which a combination of state legislation and customary law (*kanun*) was conceptually distinguished from the shari'a. This body of state and customary laws comprised various juridical fields such as crime, property, warfare, and the status of minorities.[45] The distinction between shari'a and *kanun* is reminiscent of a premodern differentiation between religion and law.

Most prominent, however, have been studies on politics with respect to forms of modern state formation in the Ottoman Empire. Rifaat Abou el-Haj analyzed the disintegration of the empire's "old order" in the two centuries before the Tanzimat. His data underpins the claim that in this period the Ottomans were confronted with similar problems to those of European statebuilders. In his analysis, he identified several trends of change. Among those were a breakdown in the relative consensus among the empire's ruling elite, new patterns of social mobility, a change in the system of surplus extraction, and a weakening of the symbolic power resources of the sultan.[46] In the words of Karen Barkey, the robust, flexible, and adaptive political entity of the empire, with its patrimonial center, strong army, and dependent and assimilated state elite, vanished due to structural change.[47] Through the conceptual lenses of Tilly's mechanism of territorial control and economic extraction, Ottoman rulers struggled with an increasing decentralization of power. In this situation, the establishment of state monopolies of physical force and taxation moved to the center of attention of the ruling elite. We can easily make sense of this period of Ottoman history when applying Norbert Elias' first phase of the monopoly mechanism. Consequently, early modern attempts at establishing the crucial modern state monopolies of physical force and taxation also paved the way for the coming centralization policies of the Tanzimat.[48]

Ariel Salzmann's insightful study clearly suggests that the institutional predicaments the Ottoman Empire faced were far from unique.[49] Similar to the "old regime" in France,[50] the Ottomans struggled with a decisive lack of resources for maintaining the empire's military forces and keeping the "vernacular governments of the provinces" at bay.[51] In the Ottoman's case, the patrimonial old regime was, on the one hand, characterized by a horizontal bifurcation between the privileged administrative elite of the empire (*askeri*)—officers, bureaucrats, and higher representatives of the religiously learned—on the one hand, and the rest of the Muslim and non-Muslim population (*reaya*) who had to pay taxes and duties to the state on the other. This hierarchical differentiation was accompanied by the segmentary order of the millet system, according to which the monotheistic religious minorities were allowed to autonomously administer their internal affairs.[52] A complex web of domestic and external changes—such as the rise of provincial centers with local aristocracies (*ayan*), the transformation of tax leases into private properties, and the recruitment of local militias, as well as the mounting costs of war, technological and logistical innovation, and changes in international trade routes—undermined the political economy and social fabric of the empire during the seventeenth and eighteenth centuries. In sum, these political, economic, and social transformations "tended toward a decentralization of Ottoman authority."[53]

Complimentary to this struggle of the Ottoman ruling elite to adjust to these forces of change was the "Sunnitization" of the empire.[54] In the first centuries of Ottoman rulers, "this privileged class had no basis in ethnicity, race, or religion."[55] Applying the Weberian notion of legitimate authority, however, we can observe a gradual shift toward a form of traditional legitimacy "that combined the sultan's dynasty and the Sunni orthodoxy."[56] A number of recent studies in Ottoman history have tried to analyze this development through the lenses of the more general paradigm of a Eurasian trend of "confessionalization." In the historiography of early modern Europe, this term has been applied to the formation of the absolutist state. In the language of Modern Systems Theory, it refers to the historical social boundary delimitations between the emerging realms of religion and politics. The monopolization of physical force by the state took place, at least partially, in the "guise" of religious conflicts. The priority of territorial unity and internal peace contained in the concept of the "reason of state" reflects in a certain way the historical experience of Europe's so-called religious wars.[57] In the course of this process of confessionalization, the European state of the early modern period attempted to gain a third "key monopoly," the sovereignty of the territorial princely state over the church and religious life. It is above all this claim of the early modern state to a monopoly over the means of symbolic reproduction that was sealed with the Peace of Westphalia (1648).[58]

With respect to the Ottoman Empire, this more recent literature on Ottoman historiography detects a similar trend in the emergence of an imperial religious hierarchy and the concomitant reconstruction of the "Hanafi genealogy" in a state-sanctioned orthodox way.[59] Between the sixteenth and the eighteenth centuries, processes of maintenance and re-establishment of the state monopolies of physical force and taxation were accompanied by the ulema's efforts "to define and enforce what they considered to be genuine and authentic religious practice."[60] Not surprisingly, it is also throughout these centuries that we can see the rise of Muslim heterodoxies and recurring waves of sectarian dissent.[61] As in European history, we can interpret these developments as intensive negotiations over the boundaries of religion and politics, as well as the establishment of authoritative communicational patterns within each of these social subsystems. Regarding Ottoman state formation, however, this negotiation process appears historically as a first kind of "Islamization" of the Ottoman state. Thereby, for the ruling elite the Sunnitization of the empire was less a matter of taking a "narrowly-defined" religious position than referring to Islam as a symbolic resource in the preservation of social order.[62] At the meso level of analysis, I interpret the Sunnitization of the empire as an Ottoman attempt to establish the aforementioned third monopoly of the state, the monopoly of symbolic reproduction. At the end of the nineteenth century, the symbolic resources of Islam with respect to this third monopoly again took center stage. Through the modernizing policies of Sultan Abdülhamit II, a new coalition between a dynastic ruler and orthodox Sunni *ulema* played a significant role.

From the Tanzimat to the Islamization of Ottoman Modernity: The Modernizing Project of a "Defensive" State Elite

In official historiography, the Hatt-i Sherif of Gülhane set the starting point for the Tanzimat in November 1839. Sultan Abdülmecit (1839–61) promulgated this reform edict less than five months after the death of his father and predecessor Sultan Mahmud II (1808–39). Yet it was Mahmud II who actually opened the way for the Ottoman reform project with the destruction of the Janissaries in June 1826. Two weeks after his announcement of the establishment of a new army, the Janissary Corps rose against him in open rebellion. The Janissaries, once the military backbone of the empire, had developed into a kind of state within the state. During the struggle for central power between the sixteenth and the eighteenth centuries, as described in the previous section, the Janissaries acquired substantial means of power and a certain control over the institutions of the state. With the support of the *ulema*, for the first time in Ottoman history a former commander of the Janissaries was appointed to the powerful position of the *grand vizier* in 1628.[63] From that time, tentative coalitions among the Janissaries, local notables, and lower-ranking *ulema* frequently turned against the centralization efforts of the Ottoman sultans. Consequently, the military reforms of Mahmud II posed a threat against the privileges of the Janissaries and their allies.[64]

In the night from June 15–16, 1826, five battalions of the Janissaries, followed by a violent mob, assembled in the Hippodrome of Istanbul. Mahmud II, however, was well prepared and expected the mutiny. In addition, in sharp contrast to their resistance against previous reform attempts by Sultan Selim III (1789–1807), this time the Janissaries failed to rally full support of both the religious establishment and parts of their own rank and file.[65] Mahmud II, therefore, was able to crush the rebellion with his new troops and announced the abolition of the regiment on June 17, 1826. The reform efforts of Selim III and Mahmoud II were to some extent triggered by internal and external security questions challenging the monopoly of physical force of the Ottoman state. The nineteenth-century modernization of the Ottoman Empire was not the project of a self-conscious and economically active bourgeoisie aspiring to political participation. The Ottoman project of modernity which was epitomized in the Tanzimat period was the project of an authoritarian military-bureaucratic state elite. This elite put the focus of the reform process on securing the political sovereignty and territorial integrity of the Ottoman state.[66] In short, it was a project of "defensive modernization" with which the ruling elite attempted to secure its own power position in order to forestall revolutionary upheavals from below.[67]

Irrespective of the complex motivational structures behind the Tanzimat, the reform measures clearly resemble the trajectory of a move—in Weberian terms—from traditional to legal forms of authority. The Hatt-i Sherif guaranteed in principle the property and civil rights of all citizens. It introduced a monetized and rationalized system of taxation, directly administered by the state. This abolishment of the patrimonial system of tax-farming was accompanied by the reorganization of the provincial administration. The provinces became directly administered by salaried officials from Istanbul and clearly separated private from public property. Later, the Ottoman authorities introduced secular courts of justice that were based on special codes of criminal and commercial law. In the second phase of the Tanzimat, after the promulgation of the Hatt-i Hümayun on February 18, 1856, the reform decrees emphasized principles of juridical equality, in particular with respect to the non-Muslim parts of the population. In addition, the reform measures opened up the Ottoman Empire for international trade and capital. Moreover, the Ottoman rulers built up a new secular and state-controlled education system that first and foremost had the purpose of providing well-educated military personal and administrative staff. The promulgation of the Hatt-i Hümayun took place in the context of the negotiations of the Paris Peace Congress held in February and March 1856 and the empires aspirations to become an equal part in the "Concert of Europe." The Congress ended the Crimean War (1853–56) in which the Ottoman Empire, later joined by Britain, France, and the Kingdom of Sardinia, had fought against Russia.[68]

Given the social background of the modernizing elite of the empire and its particular interests, the Tanzimat were occupied with the establishment of modern statehood in its administrative, educational, legal, and military dimensions. The reform measures mainly addressed the interests of the ruling elite, with participatory rules and representative institutions only hesitantly being implemented under internal and external pressure. With respect to the domestic opposition, it was especially the already mentioned Young Ottomans who advocated the introduction of representative elements into Ottoman rule. They were the core of an Ottoman constitutional movement, additionally supported by a group of bureaucrats and officers under the leadership of the high-ranking reformer Midhat Pasha (1822–84). In December 1876, the constitutional movement succeeded in implementing an Ottoman constitution and establishing the first Ottoman representative assembly. However, this first constitutional period ended already in 1878, when Sultan Abdülhamit II suspended the constitution and dissolved parliament.[69] Many features of the early Ottoman project of modernity are therefore reminiscent of the first monopoly process in Norbert Elias's conceptual framework, the attempt at securing the firm establishment of modern monopolies of physical force and taxation. The second phase of Elias's monopoly mechanism, in comparison, the institutional erection of public control over the state monopolies, was still in its infancy. Nevertheless, this transition from absolutist rule toward forms of legal authority and representative government increasingly became a core feature of the internal struggles in the late Ottoman Empire.[70]

In his more than 30-years reign, Sultan Abdülhamit II continued the reform process under his authoritarian rule. Avner Wishnitzer characterized the dominant trend in the Hamidian era as one of "conscious efforts to seek a synthesis between foreign and indigenous, between old and new, in an attempt to pave a distinctly Ottoman path to modernity."[71] In a way, we can see in Abdülhamit II's regency the culmination of the defensive modernization of the Ottoman Empire. In Stephen Duguid's words, Abdülhamit II continued the reforms with the purpose of achieving "unity and survival."[72] He followed the Tanzimat reformers in centralizing the state administration and enforcing state control over the provinces. Moreover, he considerably extended the reform of educational institutions and accelerated the build-up of the empire's communication infrastructure: "Railways, telegraphs, and paved all-weather roads were beginning to unite the empire, improving communications with provincial authorities while giving a solid spur to internal trade."[73] Through the "massive expansion" of educational institutions, the Hamidian period "laid the groundwork for a new elite" for which modern education became a crucial "vehicle for social advancement."[74] In this new educational system, textbooks played an important role. Closely monitoring their content, the state authorities "intended to instill positive utilitarian knowledge alongside authoritarian values."[75] In warding off external and internal threats to his power, Abdülhamit II massively built up the state security apparatus, infiltrated the broader public with a network of information services, and muzzled the emerging group of critical intellectuals and the press. Furthermore, he re-established the supremacy of the palace over the higher echelons of the Ottoman bureaucracy.[76]

However, with respect to the role of Islam in the Ottoman reform project, the regency of Abdülhamit II marked a decisive break with the Tanzimat tradition. Throughout the Tanzimat period, we can observe a gradual decline of the official role of religious dignitaries within the state elite. While reform attempts in the late eighteenth and early nineteenth centuries clearly referred to classical Islamic concepts such as *tajdīd* (renewal) and *'iṣlāḥ* (reform),[77] references to Islamic traditions became less prominent in legitimizing the state-centered reform efforts during the Tanzimat. The symbolic reproduction of state authority relied less on Islamic symbols and language than on sources which combined the religious and ethnic plurality of the empire in a complex ideology of Ottomanism. This situation visibly changed again under the reign of Abdülhamit II. The sultan began to reintegrate Islamic religious dignitaries into the state elite and surrounded himself with *ulema* and sheiks.[78] Moreover, he again laid claim to the title of Islamic Caliph, thus underpinning his pan-Islamic aspirations of rallying the global Muslim community behind the defense of the Ottoman state by strengthening ties with Ottoman Muslims and Muslim constituencies around the world.[79]

In Selim Deringil's analysis, this was Abdülhamit II's response to a double legitimacy crisis that had developed throughout the Tanzimat period. On the one hand, Deringil points to the external dimension of this crisis, the uphill struggle of defending the political integrity of the Ottoman state within the coordinates of the European power game. On the other hand, he emphasized the critical role of Weber's category of legitimacy with respect to the transformation of the empire from traditional to modern rational forms of authority. The increasing physical and ideological penetration of society by the state, according to Deringil, caused a huge deficit with respect to the cultural dimension of political authority, that is to say, the relative consent about authority structures among rulers and ruled.[80] In my own theoretical language, Abdülhamit II tried to gain again control over the symbolic reproduction of society, to which his educational efforts are a clear testimony. In short, Islamic traditions again became a core resource of political legitimacy in a territorially shrinking empire that was gradually losing the predominantly non-Muslim parts of its population.

In the thirty years under Abdülhamit II, the Ottoman Empire experienced two ideological developments that came to be crucial for the regional discourse of modernity in the twentieth century. We can clearly observe an Islamization of the Ottoman state's project of modernity. The sultan utilized the symbolic power of Islam both for the justification of his modern state-building efforts under authoritarian auspices and for the struggle of the empire against European powers. In this sense, in political terms the Ottoman sultan pushed his state-building efforts into the direction of the formation of what could be considered an "Islamic state." At the same time, however, the opposition to his regime increasingly adopted the ideas of ethnic nationalism, for which the rise of Turkish nationalism is a paradigmatic example. The territorial concept of political loyalty to the motherland (*vatan*), once introduced by the Young Ottomans, took on a more Muslim and Turkish character. In the context of the massive loss of territory and non-Muslim population, this concept gradually became geographically linked to Anatolia. In light of the simultaneously rising nationalist aspirations of the Arab, Armenian, Greek, and Slavic peoples, younger representatives of intellectual, bureaucratic, and military circles began to construct an idealized historical narrative of the Turkish nation.[81] Under the rule of Abdülhamit II, we can detect the bifurcation of Ottoman modernism into Islamic and ethno-nationalist discourses of modernity.[82]

Conclusions: End of Empires Instead of Ottoman Decline

With the abolishment of the sultanate in 1922, the Ottoman state finally disappeared from the political landscape of Europe and the Middle East. After more than 600 years, the demise of its empire was also significantly related to joining and losing the First World War on the side of the German and Habsburg empires. The end of the Ottoman Empire seemingly underpinned the orientalist narrative of decline. Furthermore, it strengthened the hegemonic understanding of the Ottoman reforms as a failed attempt to copy Western modernity. Thus, the disappearance of the Ottoman state enhanced the perception of the Tanzimat in terms of an unsuccessful Ottoman "imitation of

Europe" in the historical course of the empire from stagnation to decline.[83] Yet, instead of perceiving nineteenth-century Ottoman history as a linear process of decline, I agree with Barkey's suggestion that "the contradictory duality of saving the empire by becoming a modern nation" was behind its demise.[84] In this contradictory historical processes, the emergence of an Ottoman public sphere with its representatives such as the Young Ottomans played a significant role.[85] In addition to the internal contradiction in its state-building process, in the Ottoman case the European great powers were actively involved in the dismemberment of the imperial state.[86] Rather than being a very specific case of state failure, the Ottoman Empire was just one among many other imperial polities to disappear in a more general historical phase of the end of empires and the decolonization of the world.[87]

Charles Tilly's work clearly emphasized the factual contingency behind modern state formation. In fact, in the centuries under Tilly's inspection, more state-like entities and early modern states disappeared than eventually joined the global system of nation states. The fate of powerful European states such as the Republic of Genoa, the Kingdom of Prussia, or the Habsburg Monarchy are cases in point. However, the "failure" of these states has not been articulated in terms of pointing to alleged deficiencies on their road toward modernity. On the contrary, Prussia and its military and state bureaucracy often served as a model of early modern statehood. To be sure, the reasons for the end of the Ottoman Empire are complex and combine internal and external constraints in the transformation from empire to modern nation states. However, it was not the purpose of this chapter to engage in a highly controversial debate on the end of the empire. My aim here was much more modest. I placed my focus on aspects of the indigenous modernization of the Ottoman Empire and the ways in which the Ottoman reforms ran parallel to the emergence of a specifically Islamic discourse of modernity.

With respect to the indigenous dimension of Ottoman modernity, I have here drawn a line of continuity from premodern state-building efforts to the Tanzimat. In this way, I have tried to corroborate more recent studies on Ottoman history from my own theoretical point of view. Already long before European powers impacted strongly on the political, economic, and social fabric of the empire, we can discern local processes of modern state formation, at least when we apply the conceptual apparatus of historical sociology.

Oscillating between phases of centralization and decentralization, the early modern Ottoman state-builders tried to establish monopolies of physical force and taxation without only copying institutional blueprints from Europe. Moreover, the strengthening of the Sunni character of the empire is reminiscent of the formation of a third state monopoly over the means of symbolic reproduction and Max Weber's concomitant concept of legitimate authority. The Ottoman state elite attempted to fit modern institutional innovations to their peculiar circumstances and in so doing produced the idiosyncratic outcomes of Ottoman modernity.[88]

These state-building efforts in the Ottoman Empire characterized both the social activities of core actors in the imperial center and those of a rising provincial aristocracy. Consequently, we can observe a multiplicity of nascent processes of regional state formation. Moreover, in the history of the sixteenth to the nineteenth centuries, we can also notice ongoing boundary negotiations, indicating the emergence of artistic, economic, legal, political, and religious realms. In Luhmann's theoretical parlance, we can identify preadaptive advances to a variety of systems of functional differentiation. These findings clearly support Einar Wigen's suggestion of perceiving the Ottoman Empire of the fifteenth and sixteenth centuries as a kind of "Renaissance state that patronized some of the same artists and used many of the same military and governing techniques as its European contemporaries."[89] Similar to European absolutism, the autocratic Ottoman Empire of those times did not yet know the modern differentiation between code and program in its political communication. In addition, comparable developments in literature, music, and science accompanied these parallels in the political structures of the Ottoman and premodern European states.[90]

With respect to the fields of political and religious communication, contemporary scholarship has discussed the manners in which state-makers and the religious learned were mutually engaged in shaping the contours of Sunni Islam. In more traditional Ottoman historiography, this Sunnitization of the empire was predominantly associated with two historical developments. On the one hand, it was linked to the Ottoman conquest that incorporated Arab lands and assumed guardianship over the holy cities of Mecca and Medina in 1517. With this territorial expansion the empire became much more Muslim in its religious make-up than it had been previously. On the other hand, scholars point to the rise of the Safavid Empire, with Shiism as its "state religion," as a catalyst for the Sunnitization of the Ottoman realm.⁹¹ A new stream of historiographic literature instead put its focus on the rise of a state-endorsed Sunni orthodoxy in the broader theoretical context of processes of confessionalization that captured different regions of Europa and Asia in early modern times. Thus, they stress the aforementioned formation of a third state monopoly of symbolic representation.

In my eyes, these three explicative strategies are complementary rather than mutually exclusive, combining external aspects of a visible "Islamization" of the symbolic order of the Ottoman Empire with internal ones. In a comparable way to the processes of the early Sunnitization of the empire, the nineteenth-century project of Ottoman modernity also became more Islamic in its ideational features under the rule of Abdülhamit II (1876–1909). In his continuation of the Ottoman modernizing project, Islamic traditions increasingly became a means of unity in a situation in which the sultan was confronted with the fundamental loss of non-Muslim peoples and territories while struggling with a domestic legitimacy crisis of Ottoman state institutions at the same time. While the early modern Sunnitization of the empire was due to territorial gains, this time the shrinking of its territory went hand in hand with the Islamization of the Ottoman state. In addition, the reform of educational institutions and the emergence of a literate public generated new intellectual debate in which modernist ideas shaped projects of modernity alternative to those initiated by the state elite.⁹² Some of these projects, such as the Young Ottoman movement, we can associate with the broader stream of the nineteenth-century Islamic reform movement. The worldview of this transregional movement of Muslim intellectuals combined typical elements of nineteenth-century modernism with a conscious re-interpretation of Islamic traditions. In this way, it assumed a prominent role in launching the Islamic discourse of modernity. It is this reform movement that will be the focus of the next chapter.

Notes

1. Jung, Dietrich and Wolfango Piccoli. 2001. *Turkey at the Crossroads: Ottoman Legacies and a Greater Middle East*. London: zed books.
2. Ahmad, Feroz. 1993. *The Making of Modern Turkey*. London: Routledge;

Berkes, Niyazi. 1964. *The Development of Secularism in Turkey*. Montreal: McGill University Press; Lewis, Bernard. 1961. *The Emergence of Modern Turkey*. Oxford: Oxford University Press.
3. See: Bouquet, Olivier. 2015. Is it Time to Stop Speaking about Ottoman Modernisation? In *Order and Compromise: Government Practices in Turkey from the Late Ottoman Empire to the Early 21st Century*. Edited by Aymes, Marc, Benjamin Gourisse and Élise Massicard. Leiden: Brill, 45–67. I gave a brief description and critique of these axioms of classical modernization theory in Chapter Two when presenting my own theoretical frame of reference.
4. Gürpinar, Doğan. 2013. *Ottoman/Turkish Visions of the Nation, 1860–1950*. New York: Palgrave Macmillan, 164–165.
5. Mardin, Şerif. 1962. *The Genesis of Young Ottoman Thought. A Study in the Modernization of Turkish Political Ideas*. Princeton: Princeton University Press.
6. Ibid. 31.
7. For some primary sources of Young Ottoman thinkers in English translation, see: Seyhun, Ahmet. 2021. (ed.). *Competing Ideologies in the Late Ottoman Empire and Early Turkish Republic: Selected Writings of Islamist, Turkist, and Western Intellectuals*. London: I. B. Tauris, Part One.
8. Ibid. 108–112.
9. Mardin, Şerif. 1969. Power, Civil Society and Culture in the Ottoman Empire. *Comparative Studies in Society and History* 11 (1): 258–281.
10. Luhmann, Niklas. 1986. *Ökologische Kommunikation. Kann die moderne Gesellschaft sich auf ökologische Gefährdungen einstellen?* Opladen: Westdeutscher Verlag, 168–170.
11. Ibid. 173.
12. Tilly, Charles. 1990. *Coercion, Capital, and European States, AD 990–1990*. Oxford: Blackwell, 206.
13. Elias, Norbert. 1994. *The Civilizing Process. The History of Manners and State Formation and Civilization*. Oxford: Blackwell, 345–355.
14. Weber, Max. 1991. *From Max Weber. Essays in Sociology*. Edited by H. H. Gerth and C. W. Mills. London and New York: Routledge, 78.
15. Ibid. 83.
16. Ibid.
17. Weber, Max. 1968. *Economy and Society: An Outline of Interpretive Sociology*. Edited by Guenther Roth and Claus Wittich. Volume I. New York: Bedminister Press, 215.
18. In a chapter I contributed to a book on the continuing relevance of Tilly's work in the Social Sciences, I applied the thoughts of these sociologists to state formation

in the Middle East in a more general way. See: Jung, Dietrich. 2017. War and State in the Middle East: Reassessing Charles Tilly in a Regional Context. In *Does War Make States? Critical Investigations of Charles Tilly's Historical Sociology*. Edited by Lars Bo Kaspersen and Jeppe Strandberg. Cambridge: Cambridge University Press: 221–242.

19. Weber, Max. 1904. 'Objectivity' in Social Science and Social Polity. In *Max Weber: The Methodology of the Social Sciences*. Edited by Edward A. Shils and Henry A. Finch. New York: The Free Press [1949], 85–95.
20. Barkey, Karen. 2008. *Empire of Difference: The Ottomans in Comparative Perspective*. Cambridge: Cambridge University Press, 265.
21. Ibid. 3.
22. Gibb, Sir Hamilton and Harold Bowen. 1950. *Islamic Society and the West. A Study of the Impact of Western Civilization on Moslem Culture in the Near East*. London, New York and Toronto: Oxford University Press, 20.
23. Ibid. 19.
24. Sajdi, Dana (ed.). 2007. *Ottoman Tulips, Ottoman Coffee. Leisure and Lifestyle in the Eighteenth Century*. London and New York: I. B. Tauris, 27.
25. Hopwood, Derek. 1998. Introduction: The Culture of Modernity in Islam and the Middle East. In *Islam and Modernity. Muslim Intellectuals Respond*. Edited by John Cooper, Ronald Nettler and Mohamed Mahmoud. London: I. B. Tauris: 1–9, 2.
26. Hourani, Albert. 1957. The Changing Face of the Fertile Crescent in the XVIIIth Century. *Studia Islamica* 8: 89–122, 91.
27. Faroqhi, Suraiya. 2010. *Subjects of the Sultan. Culture and Daily Life in the Ottoman Empire*. London: I. B. Tauris, 19.
28. Barkey 2008, 97.
29. Singer, Amy. 1999. Review of State and Provincial Society in the Ottoman Empire: Mosul, 1540–1834 by Dina Rizk Khoury. *International Journal of Middle East Studies* 31 (2): 300–303, 302.
30. Wishnitzer, Avner. 2015. *Reading Clock, Alla Turca. Time and Society in the Late Ottoman Empire*. Chicago: University of Chicago Press, 9.
31. Cf. Wigen, Einar. 2018. Post-Ottoman Studies. An Area Studies that Never Was. In *Building Bridges to Turkish: Essays in Honour of Bernt Brendemoen*. Wiesbaden: Harrassowitz, 313–321.
32. Abou el-Haj, Rifaat Ali. 1991. *Formation of the Modern State: The Ottoman Empire Sixteenth to Eighteenth Centuries*. Albany: SUNY Press, 64.
33. Of course, there may be other insightful examples of indigenous processes of state formation from Asia and Africa. However, not only does the Ottoman Empire fit

my purpose very well, but it is also the case about which I would claim to have the best knowledge.
34. Goffmann, Daniel. 2002. *The Ottoman Empire and Early Modern Europe*. Cambridge: Cambridge University Press. In Chapter Seven of this book, I will take a closer look at the influence of the economic activities in premodern Islamic empires on the development of trade in medieval Europe.
35. Matar, Nabil. 1998. *Islam in Britain 1558–1685*. Cambridge: Cambridge University Press, 12.
36. Kristijánsdóttir, Dagný and Gudrídur Símonardottír. 2014. The Suspected Victim of the Turkish Abductions in the 17th Century. In *The Post-Colonial North Atlantic. Iceland, Greenland and the Faroe Islands*. Edited by Lill-Ann Körber and Ebbe Volquardsen. Berlin: Nordeuropa-Institut, 142–162.
37. Andrews, Walter G. and Mehmet Kalpaklı. 2004. *The Age of Beloveds: Love and the Beloved in Early-Modern Ottoman and European Culture and Society*. Durham, NC and London: Duke University Press, 18. See also: Sajdi, Dana. 2013. *The Barber of Damascus: Nouveau Literacy in the Eighteenth-Century Ottoman Levant*. Stanford: Stanford University Press.
38. Küçük, Harun B. 2012. *Early Enlightenment in Istanbul*. PhD Dissertation. San Diego: University of California, 2 and xiii.
39. El-Rouayheb, Khaled. 2015. *Islamic Intellectual History in the Seventeenth Century: Scholarly Currents in the Ottoman Empire and the Maghreb*. Cambridge: Cambridge University Press.
40. Rodinson, Maxime. 1966. *Islam et capitalisme*. Paris: Seuil.
41. Gran, Peter. 1979. *Islamic Roots of Capitalism. Egypt, 1760–1840*. Austin and London: University of Texas Press, at 188. For a critique of the flaws in Gran's book, cf. Sajdi 2007, 12.
42. Hanna, Nelly. 2011. *Artisan Entrepreneurs in Cairo and Early-Modern Capitalism (1600–1800)*. Syracuse, NY: Syracuse University Press, 12 and 21.
43. Ibid. 192.
44. I will take up this discussion in more detail in Chapter Seven of this book, in which I deal with boundary negotiations between Islam and economics.
45. Reinkowski, Maurus. 2005. Gewohnheitsrecht im multinationalen Staat: Die Osmanen und der albanische Kanun. In *Rechtspluralismus in der islamischen Welt. Gewohnheitsrecht zwischen Staat und Gesellschaft*. Edited by Michael Kemper and Maurus Reinkowski. Berlin: Walter de Gruyter, 121–142, 130.
46. Abou el-Haj 1991, 36–40.
47. Barkey 2008, 67.

48. Abou el-Haj 1991, 64.
49. Salzmann, Ariel. 2004. *Tocqueville in the Ottoman Empire. Rival Paths to the Modern State*. Leiden: Brill, 181.
50. Ibid. 16.
51. Ibid. 185.
52. İnalcık, Halil. 1964. Turkey. The Nature of Traditional Society. In *Political Modernization in Japan and Turkey*. Edited by Robert E. Ward and Dankwart A. Rustow. Princeton: Princeton University Press, 42–63.
53. Goffman 2002, 115.
54. Krstić, Tijana 2021. Historicizing Sunni Islam in the Ottoman Empire, c. 1450– c. 1750. In *Historicizing Sunni Islam in the Ottoman Empire, c. 1450–c. 1750*. Edited by Tijana Krstić and Derin Terzioğlu. 2021. Leiden: Brill, 1–30.
55. Goffman 2002, 51.
56. Barkey 2008, 163.
57. Scheuner, Ulrich. 1975. Staatsräson und religiöse Einheit des Staates. Zur Religionspolitik in Deutschland im Zeitalter der Glaubensspaltung. In *Staatsräson. Studien zur Geschichte eines politischen Begriffes*. Edited by Roman Schnur. Berlin: Duncker and Humboldt, 363–405, 367.
58. Schilling, Hans. 1992. *Religion, Political Culture and the Emergence of Early Modern Society. Essays in German and Dutch History*. Leiden: Brill, 216 and 230.
59. Krstić 2021, 12.
60. Erginbaş, Vefa. 2019. Introduction. In *Ottoman Sunnism. New Perspectives*. Edited by Vefa Erginbaş. Edinburgh: Edinburgh University Press, 1–11, 7.
61. Barkey 2008, 155.
62. Yılmaz, Yasir. 2019. Confessionalization or a Quest for Order? A Comparative Look at Religion and State in the Seventeenth-century Ottoman, Russian and Habsburg Empires. In *Ottoman Sunnism. New Perspectives*. Edited by Vefa Erginbaş. Edinburgh: Edinburgh University Press, 90–120, 108.
63. The *grand vizier* was a kind of acting head of the Ottoman government who executed the will of the sultan. Cf. Inalcık 1964.
64. These shifting historical power coalitions clearly show that there is no linear direction in modern state formation but a complex interaction of social actors representing different social realms. Only in retrospect can we actually construct the course of historical events in terms of a visible process of state formation.
65. In 1808, the last major revolt of the Janissary corps was able to interrupt the reform efforts of Selim III (1761–1808), who was imprisoned and subsequently

assassinated; Topal, Alp Eren. 2021. Political Reforms as Religious Revival: Conceptual Foundations of *Tanzimat*. *Oriente Moderno* 101: 153–180, 157.
66. Jorga, Nicolae. 1990. *Geschichte des Osmanischen Reiches*. Fünfter Band. Darmstadt: Wissenschaftliche Buchgesellschaft, 313–316; Matuz, Josef. 1985. *Das Osmanische Reich. Grundlinien seiner Geschichte*. Darmstadt: Wissenschaftliche Buchgesellschaft, 218; Zürcher, Jan Erik. 1993. *Turkey: A Modern History*. London I. B. Tauris, 32–37.
67. The German historian Hans-Ulrich Wehler coined this term of "defensive modernization" with respect to traditional political elites who try to safeguard the existing social order by imposing limited reforms from above against revolutionary pressures from below. In the theoretical language of Nobert Elias, processes of defensive modernization thus characterize historical struggles in the transition from the first to the second phase of the state monopoly mechanism. Wehler, Hans-Ulrich. 1989. *Deutsche Gesellschaftsgeschichte. Band 1: Vom Feudalismus des Alten Reiches bis zur defensiven Modernisierung der Reformära 1700–1815*. Munich: C. H. Beck, 532–533.
68. Data from: Hurewitz, Jacob C. 1956. *Diplomacy in the Near and Middle East. A Documentary Record: 1535–1914*. Princeton: D. van Nostrand Company.
69. In a good overview of the development of constitutionalist thought in the Ottoman Empire, Thomas Philipp shows both parallels and specific characteristics of the historical trajectories "from rule of law to constitutionalism" in the Middle East and in Europe. Philipp, Thomas. 2016. From Rule of Law to Constitutionalism: The Ottoman Context of Arab Political Thought. In *Arabic Thought Beyond the Liberal Age: Towards and Intellectual History of the Nahda*. Edited by Jens Hanssen and Max Weiss. Cambridge: Cambridge University Press, 142–166.
70. Jung and Piccoli 2001, 45.
71. Ibid. 188.
72. Duguid, Stephen. 1973. The Politics of Unity: Hamidian Policy in Eastern Anatolia. *Middle East Studies* 9 (2): 139–155, 139.
73. McMeekin, Sean. 2015. *The Ottoman Endgame: War Revolution and the Making of the Modern Middle East*. London: Penguin books, 31.
74. Wigen, Einar. 2018. *State of Translation: Turkey in Interlingual Relations*. Ann Arbor: University of Michigan Press, 2.
75. Wishnitzer 2015, 115.
76. Jung and Piccoli 2002, 47.
77. Cf. Topal 2021.

78. Züricher 1993, 83.
79. Wigen 2018, 22.
80. Deringil, Selim. 1998. *The Well-Protected Domains: Ideology and the Legitimation of Power in the Ottoman Empire 1876–1909*. London: I. B. Tauris, 166.
81. Kushner, David. 1977. *The Rise of Turkish Nationalism*. London: Frank Cass.
82. In Chapter Five, I will discuss this bifurcation with respect to the political ideologies of Kemalism and those of the Egyptian Muslim Brotherhood.
83. Einar Wigen showed the flaws of this narrative in convincingly arguing that a "wide-ranging project of 'imitating Europe'" was simply impossible to articulate in nineteenth-century Ottoman state discourse. Wigen 2018, 4.
84. Barkey 2008, 3. See also: Jung and Piccoli 2001, 54–56.
85. Şiviloğlu, Murat R. 2018. *The Emergence of Public Opinion: State and Society in the Late Ottoman Empire*. Cambridge: Cambridge University Press.
86. Fortna, Benjamin C. 2012. The Ottoman Empire and After. From a State of "Nations" to "Nation-states." In *State-Nationalisms in the Ottoman 'Empire. Greece and Turkey: Orthodox and Muslims, 1830–1845*. Edited by Benjamin C. Fortna, Stefanos Katsikas, Dimitris Kamouzis and Paraskevas Konortas. London and New York: Routledge, 1–12, 1.
87. Cf. Thorn, Gary. 2000. *End of Empires: European Decolonisation 1919–80*. London: Hodder & Stoughton.
88. For a theoretical elaboration of such processes, see: Kaviraj Sudipta. 2005. An Outline of a Revisionist Theory of Modernity. *European Journal of Sociology* 46 (3): 497–526, 522.
89. Wigen 2018, 6.
90. Faroqhi 2010, 281.
91. Krstić 2021, 6–7.
92. Cf. Şiviloğlu 2018.

4

MAKING MODERNITY ISLAMIC: THE QUEST FOR RELIGIOUS, POLITICAL, AND SOCIAL REFORM

Joseph Schacht's *Introduction into Islamic Law* was a standard reference book during my undergraduate studies at Hamburg University. Several reviewers of the book raised doubts about the success of the author's intention to provide a readable book for the not-yet specialized reader on Islamic law. The reputation and erudition of Schacht as a scholar of Islamic law, however, was not in question.[1] The book most likely introduced many young students into the subject. Already on the first page, Schacht met them with the orientalist commonplace of considering Islamic law as the embodiment of Islam as a unity. He started his book with the assertion that the shari'a is an "all-embracing body of religious duties, the totality of Allah's commands that regulates the life of every Muslim in all its aspects."[2] Sixty years before the publication of Schacht's book, Duncan Black MacDonald (1863–1943), then professor at Hartford Theological Seminary in the United States, concluded his lecture on "Muhammedanism" at the St. Louis World Fair (1904) with the words that "Islam is an essential unity and that it is practically impossible to separate the history of its religion from any other element."[3] Schacht apparently continued in this traditional tendency of classical Islamic studies. He described Islam as an all-encompassing unity, in which the sacred law—in principle—represents the central normative guideline in the lives of Muslims across the globe.

It did not take me very long to learn that this assertion was hardly tenable, at least according to my own empirical observations.[4] Teaching in Kyrgyzstan's capital of Bishkek, for instance, I noticed how difficult it was to find a mosque. Instead, I gained the impression that Vodka played a more important role in daily life for many of its citizens than the normative stipulations of the Qur'an. In the Iranian capital of Tehran, meanwhile, the ostentatious presentation of the "Islamic nature" of the country is omnipresent in public life. Yet this public image of the Islamic Republic does not necessarily find corresponding social practices in the privacy of everyday life. Living in the "laicist" Turkish Republic in the 1990s, by contrast, I observed that the mosques were packed with people, and not only at Friday prayers. Despite decades of Kemalist laicism, for many Turks Islamic traditions still played an important role in their daily lives. In my encounters with Islamic practices in Yemen, to take a last example, I entered what was for me a previously unknown cultural terrain. Evidently, this applied also to those young Muslim teachers from Egypt, who were posted to Yemen by their government in Cairo. In their eyes, the social and religious practices in the country were simply strange and "uncivilized" (*bidūn ḥaḍāra*).[5] In short, I have been unable to empirically verify Joseph Schacht's opening claim that the general way of Muslim life is universally guided by the shariʿa.

Following Edward Said's devastating critique of Western scholarship on Islam, this mismatch between scholarly representation and empirical observation should not come as a surprise. In *Orientalism*, Said rightly pointed to the fact that, for many European Orientalists, religion was indeed the core variable in explaining and determining the "otherness" of the East.[6] According to Said, European scholars constructed an understanding of Islam as a holistic, transhistorical, normative social system that has shaped the cultural, political, and social developments in the Middle East until today.[7] This is precisely what the above quotes from Joseph Schacht and Duncan Black MacDonald do. Yet in the course of my studies, while reading texts by Islamist ideologues such as Hasan al-Banna (1906–49), Ala al-Mawdudi (1903–79), and Sayyid Qutb (1906–66), I ran into the very same holistic image of an essentialist Islam in their writings. In an article from 1981, the Syrian philosopher Sadik al-Azm (1934–2016) criticized Edward Said for being blind to this phenomenon of "Orientalism in reverse."[8] Indeed, the application of the dichotomy between the East and the West by Islamists and Arab nationalists is almost absent in Said's book. Moreover, *Orientalism* remains silent regarding the holistic image that Islamist thinkers have assigned to Islam that is often predicated on the very same concept of an all-encompassing Islamic law. Apparently, Edward Said did not see the "self-application" of orientalist stereotypes. Where do these reinforcing assumptions of cultural difference come from? Why do Orientalists and Islamist share similar images of Islam?

I attempted to give a tentative answer to these questions in my book *Orientalists, Islamists and the Global Public Sphere*.[9] In this study, I traced back the origin of the essentialist image of Islam to the historical entanglements in the development of both orientalist European scholarship on Islam and Islamic modernism. A good case in point for these entanglements is the Young Ottoman Namık Kemal (1840–88), who critically engaged with the negative depiction of the Ottomans in the work of Joseph von Hammer-Purgstall (1774–1856). Not only did the Austrian historian translate the Divan of the Persian poet Hafez (1320–90) for the first time, but he is also particularly known for his then authoritative ten-volume history of the Ottoman Empire.[10] It is in the second part of the nineteenth century that we can find the intellectual environment shaping the modern image of the Islamic religion; and it is from this environment that the discourse of a specifically *Islamic* modernity grew. Moreover, this entanglement of intellectuals from the "East and the West" generated new religious movements deviating from the orthodox understandings of both Sunni and Shia Islam. Geoffrey Nash, for instance, analyzed three mahdi movements—the Ahmadiyya, Babism, and its offshoot Bahaism—and the ways in which they developed in close connection to the intellectual environment of nineteenth-century orientalist thought and to colonial power structures. The discourse of Islamic modernity and the religious programs of these new religious movements emerged within the same context of an asymmetric cultural exchange.[11]

In this chapter, I want to demonstrate the ways in which the movement of Islamic reform served as the midwife of the Islamic discourse of modernity on which later so many Muslim projects of modernity have thrived.[12] I interpret the emergence of Islamic modernism as an exemplary case for the continuously disputed efforts to demarcate the social boundaries of modern function systems. In the intellectual deliberations of nineteenth-century reform thinkers we can observe intense negotiations about the understanding of economy, law, religion, science, and politics. The following pages, therefore, are a selective investigation into the nineteenth-century Islamic history of ideas. I undertake a brief examination of Islamic modernism as the foundational step toward the global discourse of a specifically Islamic modernity.[13] Furthermore, I largely limit this analysis to boundary negotiations between religion and science, or the attempt to reconcile religion with reason as a major theme of Islamic modernism.[14] In the next section, I present some conceptual tools which I consider necessary for observing these negotiations. In addition, I will have a brief look at the state of the art and make a historical contextualization of Islamic modernism. Then, I briefly describe the life and work of the most important representatives of the modernist Islamic reform movement. In the final section, I will zoom in on Muhammad Abduh's construction of Islam as a modern religion, which has been paradigmatic for this stream of thought.

Intellectual Entanglements and the Global Public Sphere: Terms and Concepts

In 1962, the historian Albert Hourani published his *Arabic Thought in the Liberal Age*.[15] This book, which is still considered a path-breaking work on modern Arab intellectual thought, set the agenda for generations of scholars to come.[16] Hourani looked at about fifteen intellectuals, representing successive generations of Islamic modernists and both Muslim and Christian Arab secularists.[17] Treating these diverse thinkers all under the label of "liberalism," however, provoked a certain amount of criticism. Indeed, in the words of one of his critics, none of Hourani's cases "was a liberal in the strict sense."[18] In his preface to a revised edition of the book in 1983, Hourani again explained the purpose of the study and his understanding of the term "liberal." In putting the notion of liberalism so prominently in his title, Hourani's intention was to refer loosely to ideas such as democratic institutions, individual rights, governmental power, and national unity.[19] In retrospect, the self-assessment of Hourani was that *Arabic Thought* probably gave too much emphasis to breaks and ruptures at the expense of continuities. Particularly with respect to the earlier generations of nineteenth-century reformists, the focus was on the influence of European thought rather than on the rootedness of those thinkers in their own traditions.[20] For my study here, most important is the period of which Hourani considered Muhammad Abduh to be the most representative figure.[21] It was in this phase that Islamic modernists were "to reinterpret Islam so as to make it compatible with living in the modern world."[22] It was in the decades between 1870 and 1900 when Muslim intellectuals generated the specifically Islamic discourse of modernity.[23]

This period closely coincides with the "temporal center of gravity" of the nineteenth century that the German historian Jürgen Osterhammel circumscribed as the two decades from 1860 onwards.[24] During this period, Osterhammel noticed a number of crucial asymmetrical increases in efficiency in various regions of the world. This process concerned different social phenomena such as human productivity, governmental control, military power, and social mobility. In addition, he pointed to a general acceleration of daily life and an intensification of mutual cultural referencing on a global scale.[25] Both the Ottoman reforms and the intellectual production of Islamic modernists show the importance of these global references in the nineteenth century. They confirm the emergence of world society in terms of a "horizon of comparison" for social actors in different world regions.[26] To a growing extent, global developments and cultural models became horizons against which local actors have articulated their ideas of social change.[27] The Tanzimat reforms aimed at increasing the efficiency of the Ottoman state and its military forces against the backdrop of European inventions, whereas Islamic modernists reflected upon the role of Islamic traditions in meeting the challenges of both modern social change and European imperialism.

Islamic modernists developed their ideas in what some scholars, particularly in postcolonial studies, have designated as "global entanglements." The concept of entangled modernities is another critique of linear modernization theories and the assumption of a global spread and diffusion of modernity from its "European center" which still represents a central part of Eisenstadt's theory of multiple modernities. Theories of entangled modernities, however, stress relational processes of mutual construction, cooperation, and contestation behind the rise of the observable plurality of modernities.[28] Consequently, modernization is interpreted as the evolution of a multiplicity of modern projects combining colonial centers and peripheries in a circular way. Global history is therefore seen as the rise of entangled and uneven modernities in which also religious traditions can, but do not have to, play a constitutive role.[29] Even more important, in drawing our attention to the colonial periphery, these theories emphasize the historical involvement of "subaltern actors" in the construction of "modern universals based on a reflection of their own problems."[30]

This process of intellectual entanglement becomes apparent in the example of the protagonists in Hourani's book. These Arab intellectuals engaged in a global discourse about norms and institutions that Hourani labeled as liberal. However, similar to nineteenth-century thought and practice in Europe, this was a rather limited kind of liberalism with regard to its reference group. In his theory of successive modernities, Peter Wagner described it as the exclusive application of liberal norms to an elitist bourgeois minority.[31] He defined this type of "restricted liberal modernity" as a worldview that excluded the majority of the population. Instead of enjoying the promises of a bourgeois liberal order, the excluded masses of the nineteenth century were confronted with massive social inequalities and impoverishment. Their deplorable living conditions led to consecutive social and political crises and eventually to the demise of classical bourgeois modernity.[32] From this perspective, Hourani made no mistake when putting Islamic modernism under this label of a fundamentally restricted kind of liberalism. The intellectuals of his book represented the same kind of "Victorian liberalism" that served Wagner for the conceptual construction of his ideal type of restricted liberalism. As Samira Haj showed, Muhammad Abduh and his associates did not advocate the utilitarian ideals of an autonomous and self-reliant individual, at least not for the masses. Rather, the Islamic modernists of the nineteenth century combined bourgeois working ethics and constitutional thought with the prescriptive role of religious norms in the construction of moral selves.[33] Though they supported constitutionalism in principle, Abduh considered Egypt not yet ready for representative political institutions.[34]

How should we understand these nineteenth-century processes of intellectual entanglements? In my *Orientalists, Islamists and the Global Public Sphere*, I designed an analytical device for answering this question.[35] I termed this device the "global public sphere" in borrowing from Jürgen Habermas the category of the public sphere as a space of communicative, political, social, cultural, and intellectual engagement.[36] However, my notion of the global public sphere has neither a normative dimension nor any territorial limitations. In sharp contrast to Habermas, I do not assign to it a specific and intrinsic role in providing a relatively free communicative arena for fostering liberal democracy within a national state. In my conceptualization, the public sphere is a "social site," a constantly changing and evolving mesh of structural orders.[37] The global public sphere represents a culturally defined social space of discursive formations and networks of actors, permeated by power relations. The construction and diffusion of knowledge is historically always subject to modification through social power. My concept, therefore, refers to a global site of cooperation, contestation, and conflict that in operational terms is grounded in the cognitive deep structures of world society. In the following sketch of this concept of the global public sphere, I refer, on the one hand, to an emerging global reality, the communicative foundations of world society. On the other hand, I employ it as an abstract conceptual tool that analytically guides my empirical observations.

I subdivide the global public sphere into four levels. These levels serve me as different hermeneutical perspectives in the reconstruction of what appears as an empirical whole. The first level I define as the cognitive deep structure of world society. This syntax of modernity is in Foucault's sense the "archaeological fundament," the *épistémè*, of global bodies of knowledge.[38] The Canadian philosopher Charles Taylor coined the term "background knowledge," for this unconsciously applied knowledge.[39] In my own theoretical design, this background knowledge reflects the primacy of functional differentiation in the social differentiation of modern world society. It makes possible the communicative environment of cultural exchange in which Islamic modernists or the aforementioned mahdi movements could emerge. Inseparably connected to this *épistémè* of modernity is my second level on which we can observe the crucial boundary negotiations regarding the reach and relevance of modern function systems. These boundary negotiations appear in a variety of specifically modern themes such as questions about the relationships between state and religion, science and revealed knowledge, arts and economics, or the rights of individuals versus those of collectives.[40] My third hermeneutical perspective, then, deals with the different semantics of modernity in which the above questions have been discussed. It is on this level that we observe social actors articulating their historically specific projects of modernity of which Islamic modernism is only one example. These projects put the boundary negotiations of modernity in different linguistic, symbolic, narrative, and moral contexts, in this way shaping the colloquial languages, the semantics of multiple modernities. Finally, the fourth level refers to direct social interactions in the life and work of representative individuals such as the intellectuals in Hourani's *Arabic Thought*. With this analytical device in mind, I analyze in the coming sections the foundational role of Islamic modernism for the evolution of the Islamic discourse of modernity.

Islamic Modernism: The Emergence of an "Authentic" Project of Islamic Modernity

In his seminal book, Hourani limited his analysis to Arabic thought, in particular to thinkers from Egypt and Lebanon. I will concentrate on the Egyptian scene too, in particular on the life and work of Muhammad Abduh. This, however, does not suggest perceiving Islamic modernism as an Egyptian affair, with its origin in the Middle East and spreading from there to the rest of the world. Rather, we should conceive it as both an emerging intellectual movement and a discursive and social network with a number of nodal points. Islamic modernism emerged in the Middle East, South Asia, South-East Asia, and Africa in various local forms.[41] Most prominent among its representatives in the Arab context is the classical "Salafi triad" of Jamal al-Din al-Afghani, Muhammad Abduh, and Rashid Rida.[42] In South Asia, it was the Aligarh movement launched by Sayyid Ahmad Khan. In the Ottoman heartlands, as already mentioned, the Young Ottomans around Namık Kemal appeared as a modernist movement rather independent from the state. In sub-Saharan Africa we can observe reform movements that have been linked to both local Sufi networks and the protagonists of classical Arab Salafi thought.[43] In Indonesia, a merger between Islamic modernist and nationalist ideas developed under Dutch colonial rule.[44] Generally speaking, in their different forms, these intellectual movements shared reform agendas with three core elements: aiming at the revival of Islam by going back to the holy scripture of the Qur'an and the prophetic traditions (sunna), translating modern concepts into a specifically Islamic language, and addressing the problem of Western colonial hegemony through the ideological means of nationalism. I argue that these reform agendas rested in the cognitive deep structure of modernity. Consequently, Muslim intellectual debates revolved around the above-mentioned general themes and questions associated with modern social boundary demarcations among emerging communicative subsystems. Moreover, I consider "Western" and "Muslim" public spheres not as separate but as interlacing dimensions of a simultaneously emerging global public sphere.

Born in Delhi in 1817, Sayyid Ahmad Khan came from a noble Muslim family that for generations had played a part in the administration of the Moghul court. His educational background comprised knowledge in Islamic sciences, philosophy, and modern science, which he acquired in a specifically Indian intellectual context, shaped by "'Hindu thought', Western secularism and English common law."[45] Before founding the Muhammadan Anglo-Oriental College in Aligarh in 1875, Uttar Pradesh, Ahmad Khan held a position in the administration of the British East India Company and worked as a judge in the Islamic legal system of colonial India.[46] After the so-called "Indian mutiny" of 1857/58, he "tried to counteract the British belief of the specifically Islamic nature of the revolt."[47] In collaboration with the British authorities, Ahmad Khan advocated the reform of Muslim culture in India through modern education. For him, education was the means to reconcile modern science with religion against the resistance of traditionalist Islamic forces. He articulated a naturalist Islamic theology based on the idea of the consistency of the Islamic revelation with nineteenth-century rationalism.[48] The modern triad of the social subsystems of religion, science, and education was the core issue of his project of Islamic reformation, institutionalized with the foundation of the college in Aligarh.[49]

In a similar vein, the Young Ottomans pushed along their reformist agenda at the political center of the Ottoman Empire. As already mentioned in the previous chapter, the movement turned against both the higher Ottoman state bureaucracy and the traditional religious elite. Moreover, this movement propagated a kind of Ottoman nationalism, perceiving it to be above the various religious, ethnic, and regional divisions of the empire.[50] While Ahmed Khan developed his thought in combining the intellectual milieus of Muslim India with that of Great Britain, the intellectual gravity centers of the social and discursive connection of the Young Ottomans were Istanbul and Paris. Together with the bureaucratic elite of the Ottoman state, they shared an affinity with French positivism and perceived traditionalist Islam as "a major obstacle to social progress."[51] Namık Kemal, an "epic intellectual" and the leading figure among the Young Ottomans, was known for his translation of eighteenth-century French authors such as Condillac, Montesquieu,

Rousseau, and Volney.⁵² Born in 1848, he left Istanbul in 1867. During his exile in Paris, London, and Vienna, he engaged in translation, journalism, and literary work. Taking his inspiration from both Islamic thought and European philosophical and literary sources, Namık Kemal pursued a model of social reform that combined the reinterpretation of Islamic traditions with European ideas. However, he only advocated a selective borrowing from Europe after a critical evaluation of European institutions and ideas.⁵³

In Egypt, a massive state reform program was launched by Muhammad Ali (1769–1849) in 1811. In his competition with the Ottoman state elite in Istanbul and regional forces, the Egyptian ruler wanted to transform the economic, military, and political structures of the country in light of the advancements in Europe. Formally still subordinated to the Ottoman Sultan, Muhammad Ali followed an independent path of reform. He commissioned the translation of French sources on law, military affairs, and science into Arabic and sent several explorative study groups to Paris, in one of which Rifaat Tahtawi (1801–73) participated between 1826 and 1831 as its Imam.⁵⁴ Attracted by ideas such as social progress, freedom of thought, and representative institutions, he suggested learning from French models as long as they were compatible with Egypt's own traditions.⁵⁵ However, in this approach, similar to Namık Kemal's reform ideas some decades later, Tahtawi's thought on his observations in Paris was not yet deeply molded by European imperialism as a threat. In general, the diverse revivalist streams of early modern Islamic thought were instead united by the "absence of the West" as a severe challenge to their own worldviews.⁵⁶ This situation dramatically changed with respect to the life and work of the "modernist Salafiyya" associated with the names of Jamal al-Din al-Afghani and Muhammad Abduh.⁵⁷ They provided the ideological breeding ground from which the religio-political stream of modern Salafism subsequently emerged, trying to strike a balance between Islamic authenticity and modernity.⁵⁸

For these three prominent foundational figures of Islamic modernism, the imperial power structure was the given international context of their lives. Therefore, their approaches to social and religious reforms were deeply knitted into the struggle for the independence of Muslim states. This applies in particular to Jamal al-Din al-Afghani and his "paramount concern with Imperialism."⁵⁹ For Afghani, Islam became the central means of political distinction in his lifelong anticolonial fight against European and in particular British imperialism. He arrived in Cairo in March 1871, coming from Istanbul, where the Ottoman Sheikh al-Islam had declared a public lecture by Afghani to be heretical and derogatory to the dignity of Islam.[60] While in Cairo, he assembled a study group of mainly young Azhar students, discussing works of Sufism, Islamic and European philosophy, logics, and theology.[61] Besides famous Egyptian politicians and intellectuals such as Muhammad Abduh or Saad Zaghlul (1859–1927), the Hungarian orientalist Ignaz Goldziher (1850–1921) joined this circle during his "Middle Eastern Studies tour" in 1873–74. In his diary, Goldziher described Afghani's thought as "free-thinking and heretical" in its nature.[62]

Al-Afghani's life was emblematic of the construction of an Islamic discourse of modernity in an emerging global public sphere, with respect to the fourth level of my analytical device: direct social interaction. Afghani spent a number of years in Afghanistan, Mecca, and Cairo before coming to Istanbul in late 1869. He was expelled from Cairo, in September 1879, moving via India to his European exiles, first in London, then in Paris. In Paris Muhammad Abduh joined him for a short period in 1884. In 1885, Afghani moved from Paris to Iran only to be urged to leave again two years later. Until Sultan Abdülhamit II invited him to Istanbul in summer 1892, Afghani stayed in Russia, Germany, and again in London and Iran. In Istanbul, then, he was increasingly at odds with the sultan and died in March 1897 after having lived almost a year under house arrest.[63] In his restless life, Afghani was close to the political and intellectual circles of Europe, South Asia, and the Middle East. He merged his knowledge of Islamic sciences with European thought, engaging with other Islamic modernists outside the Arab realm in India, Iran, and Istanbul. Border negotiations between religion, science, and politics characterized his intellectual work. Striving for Muslim unity, Afghani became a discursive but also interactive nodal point in the construction of the modernist Islamic world of thought.

In a similar vein, Rashid Rida combined matters of religious reform with the struggle for political independence. However, in the course of his life he moved from supporting pan-Islamist ideas and the Ottoman Caliphate to pursuing Arab nationalist agendas, ultimately advocating the establishment of an Arab Caliphate.[64] Being the youngest of the three Salafi modernists, Rida was born in 1865 near Tripoli in today's Lebanon. In 1897, he left Greater Syria in order to join the Islamic reform movement in Cairo. Rida was fascinated by reading Afghani and Abduh's articles in *al-'urwa al-wuthqā* (The Firmest Bond), the fiercely anticolonial journal they published in Paris, which he found among the readings in his father's library.[65] The journal appeared only in limited editions and for a short period during 1884, but it was distributed among Muslim religious scholars, journalists, government officials, and intellectuals around the world.[66]

In the tradition of this new Islamic journalism, Rida began to publish *al-manār* (The Lighthouse) in 1898, which quickly became the global "mouthpiece" of Islamic modernism.[67] It was through *al-manār*, for instance, that Indonesian Muslims became acquainted with Muhammad Abduh's and Rashid Rida's thought. With the help of the journal, the two Arab intellectuals became central in the development of Islamic reform ideas and the reinterpretation of classical Islamic thought in Southeast Asia.[68] Both Abduh and Rida were convinced that their Muslim contemporaries could face the challenges of their time by recourse to religious traditions. Islamic principles, according to them, were the means for an authentic appropriation of features of modernity.[69] In their struggle with the cultural, economic, and political hegemony of Europe, Islamic modernists invoked a reinterpreted Islamic past as a means of achieving modern authenticity.[70] And it was through this reinterpretation of religious traditions that they constructed a specific discourse of Islamic modernity. They based this discourse on a background knowledge reflecting both the cognitive deep structures of modernity and their own philosophical and religious traditions.

In his earlier life, Rida had also followed the approach of selective borrowing from European institutions and ideas. He promoted a combination of constitutionalism, rationalism, science, and technology to initiate a renaissance of Islam. Yet, in his historical context, that is to say the subsequent frustration of his aspirations for Arab independence, Rida increasingly deviated from this path of selective borrowing. At least when our reading follows the mainstream literature on him, Rida was engaged in merging Islamic modernist ideas with the purist Sunni legal school of Hanbalism.[71] In addition, he broke with Abduh's collaborative approach toward Great Britain and returned to Afghani's radical and confrontational anti-imperialist posture. In this way,

Rashid Rida also contributed to the rising idea of a principal antagonism between "Islam and the West."[72] From Rida onward, we can observe a tendency among Islamic reformers to adopt what John Voll once described as a more "shariʿa-minded" line of thinking.[73] In this interpretation of Islam, perhaps better defined as a legalist approach, the previous "total intellectual discourse" of the shariʿa was gradually transformed into the vision of a holistic system of Islamic law.[74] The understanding of the shariʿa as a comprehensive set of rules and regulations inevitably reminds us of the concept of positive law that developed with the emergence of law as a modern function system.[75] This holistic concept of Islamic jurisprudence has played a significant role in many of the modern projects of Islamist thinkers in the twentieth century. Furthermore, it clearly resonates in the rather one-sided representation of Islam as a predominantly "legal religion" by orientalist scholars, such as Joseph Schacht in his *Introduction*.

Muhammad Abduh: Launching the Islamic Discourse of Modernity

The personal link that connected Afghani and Rida, however, was Muhammad Abduh. In his younger years, Abduh had been closely associated with Afghani, with the two of them together publishing the already mentioned fiercely anti-colonial journal *al-ʿurwa al-wuthqā* from their exile in Paris. Yet with his return to Beirut in 1885, Abduh's gradual departure from Afghani began. Even more important, he also tempered his anti-imperialist zeal and began to look more positively at the British presence in Egypt. In Lord Cromer (1841–1917), the British Consul General in Egypt (1883–1907), he found a staunch supporter of his reform activities and his struggle against conservative political and religious opponents. With the help of Cromer, Abduh returned to Egypt in 1888, where he first became a judge and was subsequently responsible for the reform of the curriculum at the Azhar. In 1899, then, Abduh took over the position of the Grand Mufti of Egypt, the country's highest religious scholar, with the support of the British authorities.[76]

Muhammad Abduh was born in a small village in the Nile Delta. His initial education he received from a traditional Qur'an teacher, before moving to the great mosque of the nearby provincial town of Tanta for further education. In 1866, he left Tanta to take up studies at the Azhar in Cairo. There he joined Afghani's study circle in 1872, adding various new bodies of European and Islamic knowledge to his previous classical religious education. The encounter with Afghani also reinforced existing traits of Abduh's thought regarding "religio-political dissidence," Islamic mysticism, and religious millenarianism.[77] Abduh further expanded this broader intellectual worldview through his contact with "cosmopolitan circles," which comprised, at different stages of his life, political émigrés, anticolonial activists, and colonial officials, as well as journalists, educators, scholars, and "religious enthusiasts." These social interactions took place in cities such as Algiers, Beirut, Brighton, Cairo, Damascus, Geneva, Istanbul, London, Oxford, and Paris.[78] Firmly anchored in traditional Islamic sciences and familiar with both Sunni orthodox and Islamic heterodox traditions, Abduh combined these sources with his study of European thought. He learned French at the age of 44 and read, among others, the works of Comte, Descartes, Guizot, Spencer, Taine, Tolstoy, and Max Nordau.[79] It was this kaleidoscopic reservoir of knowledge that Ammeke Kateman frequently stressed in her study on Abduh and his intellectual universe.[80] This plurality of knowledge makes him another nodal point in the foundational construction of the Islamic discourse of modernity. His life and thought are paradigmatic for the global entanglements out of which Islamic modernism emerged.

I will now describe this entanglement by more closely examining Abduh's *risālat al-tawḥīd* (The Theology of Unity). The book represents "a modern classic and programmatic text of reformist theology," addressing both students of Islam and a wider audience.[81] In its textbook style it represents "an accessible catechism of basic Muslim beliefs."[82] In 1898, the book was officially included in the teaching program at the Azhar.[83] Yet, it is not a catechism in the classical sense. The *risāla* is an innovative text in which Abduh reinterprets the classical schools of Asharite and Maturidite theology by drawing simultaneously on concepts and arguments from the emerging disciplines of the historical and social sciences.[84] In constructing Islam as a modern religion, Abduh combines the Islamic tradition with conceptual elements of the cognitive deep structures of world society. In doing so, however, he was not a mere puppet of the "cultural and imperial invasion" of the West. Abdulkader Tayob rightly criticized this derogatory view of Islamic modernism that is evident in some areas of contemporary scholarship. With his criticism, the South African scholar turned against the so-called Asad School, according to which Islamic modernism was not a Muslim discourse but rather the product of "Western intellectual hegemony."⁸⁵ I largely agree with Tayob's critique that this biased judgment disregards both the historical entanglements of intellectual thought and the global structural transformations that characterized the nineteenth century. Even worse, considering Islamic modernism as a mere result of the intellectual hegemony of Europe deprives Islamic modernists of their own agency.

Abduh based his book on the lectures he gave at the Sultaniyya in Beirut (1885–88). This school was opened in 1883 and emphasized the modern sciences as well as religion. Admitting both Muslim and Christian students, the foundation of the Sultaniyya was a reaction against the spread of Christian missionary schools in the region, and it predominantly catered to the local Syrian elite.⁸⁶ Abduh describes the origins of the book in the preface. At the Sultaniyya, among the subjects he taught was the "theology of unity" (*'ilm al-tawḥīd*). Yet, these theological lectures, according to Abduh, only survived in the notes of his students.⁸⁷ He himself did not have the scripts of the lectures when later writing his book. Therefore, he relied on these notes, in particular on those that his brother took from his introductory class.⁸⁸ The revision of these lectures appears as a treatise in which Abduh constructs Islam as an "empirically existing 'world religion'."⁸⁹ The *risāla* are first of all a document of what I described in Chapter Two with reference to Peter Beyer's theory on the global system of religion as the intellectual construction of modern religious programs. Abduh actively took part in transforming Islamic tradition into a modern religion distinct from other religions. Secondly, the book contributes to an "Islamic" discussion of the boundary demarcation between religion and science. This boundary was expressed by Abduh in his text through the differentiation between religion (*dīn*) and reason (*'aql*). However, the *risāla* is also an "apologetic" text. Abduh clearly argues for the primacy of both religion over reason⁹⁰ and Islam over other religions.⁹¹ For him, the autonomy of reason is subordinated to its origin in God. While Abduh clearly applies concepts of functional differentiation between religion and reason ("science") throughout the text, he does so by putting these two realms of modern communication in an unquestionable hierarchy. The Islamic revelation set free the powers of reason,⁹² but Islam retains supremacy over reason at the same time.⁹³

Taking a look at Abduh's concept of religion, his lectures strongly resemble more general nineteenth-century discussions in the emerging field of comparative religion. In conceptual terms, Islam appears in the *risāla* as a religion (*dīn*) among many other religions (*'adyān*). These religions deal with transcendence, and they are characterized by variations and differentiations in their types of worship and practices.[94] Within this plurality of religions—and this characterizes Abduh's apologetic argumentation—Islam was the first one to combine religion and reason in its holy book, making it therefore superior to all other religions.[95] Abduh conducts his comparison of religions against the background of religion as a concept in a generic sense. In other words, he considers religion to be an anthropological constant in human life and history. He describes this generic concept of religion as a natural and instinctive motivation of human beings, as the most powerful driving force among other human powers. Religion, according to him, is a general faculty of humanity.[96] Consequently, the prophetic mission appears as a necessity for humanity in establishing a perfect social order (*niẓām al-ijtimaʿī*).[97] In this way, the *risāla* clearly underpins Abdulkader Tayob's and Ammeke Kateman's general argument that the modern concept of religion was also a clear feature in the intellectual reflections of Muslim thinkers in the nineteenth century and should therefore not be treated as a mere European invention.[98] Abduh's text is a perfect example of the way in which the global system of religion and its segmentary internal structure was constructed by social agents with different cultural and intellectual backgrounds.

When it comes to the term of "unity" (*tawḥīd*) Abduh derived it from the traditionally strict monotheism of Islam.[99] God in his attributes, deeds, and fundamental existence is one.[100] Yet both Abduh and Afghani extended the meaning of *tawḥīd* beyond its religious meanings. On the one hand, they fused the concept with the notion of civilization as a cultural totality, similar to François Guizot's thought. When it comes to European authors, the literature on Abduh emphasizes the importance of his reading of Guizot's *History of Civilization in Europe*.[101] In his reconstruction of Islam as a religion, Abduh was influenced by Guizot, teaching the French thinker's philosophy of European history even as a lecturer at the Azhar.[102] Guizot reconstructed the cultural diversity of Europe as an essential unity, grounding it in an alleged intrinsic civilizational message of Christianity.[103] In his description of European history as an evolutionary process evolving from a divine plan and leading to a specific European civilization as a total way of life, the modern concepts of religion, evolution, and culture as a holistic system meet.

In making Islam the guiding power of his own evolutionary historical narrative, Abduh adopted a similar philosophy of history. He not only turned Islam into a modern religious program, but also reconstructed Islamic traditions in correspondence to an all-encompassing cultural whole. Muslim intellectuals have constructed the modern idea of Islam as a comprehensive way of life through this holistic concept.[104] On the other hand, Islamic modernists applied the concept of *tawḥīd* with respect to the unity of Muslims and therefore in describing a social collective that is defined by its adherence to Islam as a belief system. In particular for Afghani, the religious term of *tawḥīd* turned into a political doctrine of unity supporting his anti-imperialist struggle.[105] In the discourse of Islamic modernity, these two "secularized" meanings of Islam as a cultural and a political unity have been a core feature in the construction of Islamic modernities ever since.

Conclusions: The Birth of the Islamic Discourse of Modernity

Dealing with Islamic modernism in terms of the history of ideas, this chapter has argued that the nineteenth-century movement of Islamic reform was an integral part of both global negotiations about the boundaries of religion and science and the historical establishment of a global system of religion.[106] Moreover, it has considered Islamic modernism as the founding stage of a specifically Islamic discourse of modernity in which Islamic traditions are an essential means of granting authenticity to modernizing projects. This does not mean that they did not share in Enlightenment thoughts about an all-encompassing concept of reason.[107] On the contrary, they adopted this concept of reason, and many of them located it in Islam. In the thought of Islamic modernists, Islamic traditions serve in the "truthful representation" of authentic projects of modernity in light of the "inauthentic" nature of contemporary life. To illustrate this process, I employed the Egyptian scene around Abduh as a paradigmatic example for a larger reform movement that simultaneously emerged among Muslims in different parts of the world who were interpreting and negotiating modernity in localized forms.[108] In these negotiations, Islamic reformers made a significant contribution by affirming the role of Islamic traditions in the modernization of Muslim countries in contradistinction to the "secular character" of modernity in the so-called Western world.[109] In Eisenstadt's sense, Muslim reformers constructed their multiple projects of modernity with close reference to Islamic religious traditions. They turned Islam into the central signifier for their projects of modernity with respect to both domestic identification and external differentiation. In doing so, they acted within the context of European imperialism and two general historical trends: the growing importance of the modern state and the emergence of a reading public.[110] These two trends were not restricted to Egypt, but they were characteristic features of the fundamental social transformations that took place in Jürgen Osterhammel's temporal gravity center of the nineteenth century.

In zooming in on the life and work of Muhammad Abduh, I aimed to make visible the connection between the micro and macro levels of these transformative processes. On the micro level, Abduh's case demonstrates the role of discursive and social interactions in the global public sphere. At the same time, the analysis of his work—here restricted to my theoretically inspired re-reading of his *risalāt al-tawḥīd*—highlights the structural levels of this global public sphere in terms of both its *épistémè* and the demanding questions resulting from the emergence of functional subsystems as the predominant form of modern social differentiation. In Abduh's text we can discern the work of an intellectual who developed a specific modern semantics in combining the global syntax of modernity with local intellectual and religious traditions.[111] In his research on Abduh's background in mystical and millenarian streams of Islamic thought, for instance, Oliver Scharbrodt indicated that ideas of modern evolutionary thinking could be fused easily with indigenous intellectual traditions.[112] Consequently, it is wrong to understand Abduh as a mere copyist of European ideas. Rather, he was a creative producer of modern ideas in combining Islamic thought with the conceptual syntax of modernity.[113] From this perspective, I read *risalāt al-tawḥīd* as both a treatise on and a foundational document of the Islamic discourse of modernity and a testament to the intellectual entanglement that historically brought about the macrostructures of world society.

This and the previous chapter on Ottoman reform analyzed the historical foundations for the emergence of the Islamic discourse of modernity. Together, they argue for its concomitant evolution with modern state formation, educational reform aspirations, and an intellectual transformation that came about with the rise of a modern literate public. These processes not only established a new discursive platform, but also fundamentally weakened the authority of traditionally established elites. With respect to the topic of this book, most significant is the erosion of the monopoly of knowledge previously held by the religious learned. The holy scriptures of Islam and Islamic religious traditions in general became subject to the individual interpretation of Muslims who may or may not have had a form of religious education. This claim to independent reasoning (*ijtihād*) regarding religious texts is indirectly documented in *risalāt al-tawḥīd*. In this book, Abduh does not inscribe himself in the traditions of Islamic jurisprudence or Qur'an interpretations. He frequently refers directly to the Qur'an and underpins his arguments with his personal understanding of the verses of the holy book. In order to propose modern rational decisions based on religious morals, Abduh strongly rejected the tradition of *taqlīd* or "blind imitations" in religious law and practice.[114] Instead, he advocated the reflexive interpretation of the religious traditions not only for religious scholars but also for intellectuals who did not belong to the class of the religious learned.

Abduh's thought was decisive in the popularization of Islamic religious discourses and therewith indirectly for the subsequent appropriation of the means of religious interpretation by ordinary Muslims too. His work is strongly characterized by modern reflexivity in the sense of social actors assessing their own institutions, practices, and forms of conduct "from an exterior point of view."[115] From this perspective, his rejection of *taqlīd* went against two directions, the non-reflexive application of the Islamic tradition and the blind following of European innovations without critical discrimination. In the following chapter, I will discuss the popularization of the nineteenth century's elitist religious discourse of reform with respect to the Muslim Brotherhood movement. At the same time, I will juxtapose this prototype of an Islamist ideological movement with the Kemalist project of Turkish modernity, which despite its secularist nature had its origins in the same streams of institutional modernization and modernist Islamic thought of the nineteenth century. The Kemalists and the Muslim Brothers serve as exemplary cases for the bifurcation that Islamic modernism has taken since the beginning of the twentieth century.

Notes

1. For example: Coulson, N. J. 1965. Reviewed Work(s): An Introduction to Islamic Law by Joseph Schacht. *The International and Comparative Law Quarterly* 14 (1): 336–338 and Holland, W. J. D. 1965. Review: An Introduction to Islamic Law by Joseph Schacht. *Journal of African Law* 9 (3): 187–188.
2. Schacht, Joseph. 1964. *An Introduction to Islamic Law*. Oxford: Oxford University Press, 1.
3. MacDonald, Duncan B. 1906. The Problems of Muhammadanism. In *Arts and Science: Universal Exposition, St. Louis, 1904, Vol. 2: History of Politics and Economics, History of Law, History of Religion*. Edited by H.J. Rogers. Boston: Houghton, Mifflin & Company, 518–536, 536. Duncan Black MacDonald gave his lecture together with the Hungarian Orientalist Ignaz Goldziher in the section on "Muhammedan history" at the Congress of Arts and Science in St. Louis. In addition to these two Orientalists, scholars such as the sociologist Max Weber and the theologians Ernst Troeltsch and Adolf von Harnack participated in the academic gatherings at this World Fair. Georg Stauth even alluded to the idea that Weber might have been a silent listener at the lectures on Islam given by Goldziher and probably also MacDonald. Stauth, Georg. 2000. *Islamische Kultur und moderne Gesellschaft*. Bielefeld: Transcript, 211.
4. My critique of MacDonald and Schacht is a scholarly critique due to my own observations that does not imply branding them as Orientalists conspiring with colonial interests. In this respect, I pretty much agree with Najib G. Awad, who convincingly rejected deeming Duncan Black MacDonald as being, in Saidian terms, "a colonially driven orientalist." Awad, Najib G. 2016. "Understanding the Other From-Within": The Muslim Near East in the Eyes of Duncan Black Macdonald. *The Muslim World* 106: 523–538, 529.
5. Touring the country in the 1980s, I met with several young Egyptian teachers who were posted to Yemen as their first teaching placement. They often combined their critique of this practice with comments on the behavior of the students and their relatives with whom they had to engage.
6. But not for all of them, as the example of Carl-Heinrich Becker shows. In his programmatic article *Islam as a Problem*, Becker argued that it is wrong to understand the "Islamic civilization" from their presumed religious origins alone. Becker, Carl-Heinrich. 1910. Islam as a Problem. *Der Islam* 1 (1): 1–21.
7. Said, Edward W. 1978. *Orientalism*. New York: Vintage, 301.

8. Al-Azm, Sadik J. 1981. Orientalism and Orientalism in Reverse. *Khamsin* 8: 5–26.
9. Jung, Dietrich. 2011. *Orientalists, Islamists and the Global Public Sphere: A Genealogy of the Modern Essentialist Image of Islam*. Sheffield: Equinox.
10. For a discussion of Namık Kemal's reception of Hammer-Purgstaller, see: Gürpinar, Doğan. 2013. *Ottoman/Turkish Visions of the Nation, 1860–1950*. New York: Palgrave Macmillan, 24–25.
11. Nash, Geoffrey. 2022. *Religion, Orientalism and Modernity: Mahdi Movements of Iran and South Asia*. Edinburgh: Edinburgh University Press. See also the earlier book by Scharbrodt: Scharbrodt, Oliver. 2008. *Islam and the Baha'i Faith: A Comparative study of Muhammad 'Abduh and 'Abdul-Baha 'Abbas*. London and New York: Routledge.
12. The variety of these Islamic projects of modernity is broad, and it goes without saying that many Islamic intellectuals of the twentieth century no longer endorsed the thought of earlier Islamic modernists. Yet also important here is the role of Islamic modernists as being modern switchmen in putting an Islamic discourse of modernity on track. The argument here is that the modernists launched an intellectual process of finding modern authenticity in Islamic traditions.
13. It is important to note that not only Islamic modernists took part in this shaping of the Islamic discourse of modernity. The responses to modern challenges in the nineteenth century took various forms, from secular to traditionalist movements. In particular, neo-traditionalist movements took an antimodernist stance. However, they should nevertheless be seen as "modern" responses to social and religious change. I will come back to this issue of multiple contributions to the Islamic discourse of modernity in the conclusions of the book. Cf. Ghazzal, Amal. 2016. "Illiberal" Thought in the Liberal Age. Yusuf al-Nabhani (1849–1932), Dream Stories and Sufi Polemics against the Modern Era. In *Arabic Thought Beyond the Liberal Age: Towards an Intellectual History of the Nahda*. Edited by Jens Hansen and Max Weiss. Cambridge: Cambridge University Press, 214–233 and Metcalf, Barbara. 2002. *"Traditionalist" Islamic Activism: Deoband, Tablighis, and Talibs*. Leiden: ISIM Papers.
14. See: Sallah, Asmahan. 2015. Islamic Modernism and Discourse on Reason as a Reconciliatory Argument between Islam and Western Enlightenment. *International Journal of Islamic Thought* 7: 11–24.
15. Hourani, Albert. 1983. *Arabic Thought in the Liberal Age, 1798–1939*. Revised edition. Cambridge: Cambridge University Press.

16. Hansen, Jens and Max Weiss. 2016. Introduction. Language, Mind, Freedom and Time: The Modern Arab Intellectual Tradition in Four Words. In *Arabic Thought Beyond the Liberal Age: Towards an Intellectual History of the Nahda*. Edited by Jens Hansen and Max Weiss. Cambridge: Cambridge University Press, 1–37.
17. Reid, Donald M. 1982. Arabic Thought in the Liberal Age Twenty Years after. *International Journal of Middle East Studies* 14: 541–557, 547.
18. Goodman. L.E. 1986. Review of Arabic Thought in the Liberal Age, 1798–1939. *The International History Review* 8 (1): 107–111, 108.
19. Hourani 1983, iv.
20. Ibid. ix.
21. In contradistinction to Hourani, Samira Haj almost overemphasized the continuities in Abduh's and other reformers thought; Haj, Samira. 2009. *Reconfiguring Islamic Tradition: Reform, Rationality, and Modernity*. Stanford: Stanford University Press.
22. Hourani 1983, vi.
23. However, in my eyes, it is an utter mistake to consider Islamic modernists as modern only based on a periodization of time—because "they lived in the modern world"—a simplistic understanding of modernity against which I profoundly argue with this book. Cf. Wood, Simon. 2019. Reforming Muslim Politics. Rashid Rida's Visions of Caliphate and Muslim Independence. *Journal of Religion & Society* (Supplement 18): 63–78, 64.
24. Osterhammel, Jürgen. 2009. *Die Verwandlung der Welt: Eine Geschichte des 19. Jahrhunderts*. Munich: C. H. Beck, 17.
25. Ibid. 1290–1293.
26. Cf. Heintz, Bettina and Tobias Werron. 2011. Wie ist Globalisierung Möglich? Zur Entstehung globaler Vergleichshorizonte am Beispiel von Wissenschaft und Sport. *Kölner Zeitschrift für Soziologie und Sozialpsychologie* 63: 359–394.
27. This is also one of the core arguments in the world cultural theory of the so-called Stanford School on Sociological Institutionalism around the sociologist John Meyer. In Chapter Eight, I will refer to this sociological school with respect to their concept of modern social actorhood. See also the paradigmatic essay of the school: Meyer, J. W., Boli, J. Thomas, G. M. and Ramirez F. O. 1997. World Society and the Nation-State. *American Journal of Sociology* 103 (1): 144–181. I discussed the school's approach to world society critically in chapter seven of my: Jung, Dietrich. 2021. *Der Islam in der globalen Moderne: Soziologische Theorie und die Vielfalt islamischer Modernitäten*. Wiesbaden: Springer VS.

28. Therborn, Göran. 2003. Entangled Modernities. *European Journal of Social Theory* 6: 293–305.
29. Randeria, Shalini. 2002. Entangled Histories of Uneven Modernities: Civil Society, Caste Solidarities and Legal Pluralism in Post-Colonial India. In *Unravelling Ties—From Social Cohesion to New Practices of Connectedness*. Edited by Yehuda Elkana, Ivan Kratev, Eísio Macamo, and Shalini Randeria. Frankfurt am Main and New York: Campus, 284–311.
30. Getachew, Adom. 2016. Universalism After the Post-Colonial Turn: Interpreting the Haitian Revolution. *Political Theory* 44 (6): 1–25, 1–2; Jung, Dietrich. 2017. *Muslim History and Social Theory: A Global Sociology of Modernity*. Cham: Palgrave Macmillan, 22.
31. I will also discuss Wagner's theory of successive modernities in Chapter Seven.
32. Wagner, Peter. 1994. *A Sociology of Modernity: Liberty and Discipline*. London: Routledge; Wagner, Peter. 2010. Successive Modernities and the Idea of Progress: A First Attempt. *Distinktion* 11 (2): 9–24.
33. Haj 2009, 98 and 109.
34. Scharbrodt 2008, 69.
35. Jung 2011, 81–93. For a shorter version with the historical example of Muhammad Abduh, see: Jung, Dietrich. 2012. Islamic Reform and the Global Public Sphere: Muhammad Abduh and Islamic Modernity. In *The Middle East and Globalization: Encounters and Horizons*. Edited by Stephan Stetter. London and New York: Palgrave Macmillan: 153–170.
36. Cf. Habermas, Jürgen. 1962. *Strukturwandel der Öffentlichkeit*. Neuauflage 1990. Frankfurt am Main: Suhrkamp.
37. Schatzki, Theodore R. 2002. *The Site of the Social: A Philosophical Account of the Constitution of Social Life and Change*. University Park: Pennsylvania State University Press.
38. The concept of *épistémè* (episteme) refers to the works of the "young Foucault," see: Foucault, Michel. 1989. *Archaeology of Knowledge*. London and New York: Routledge; Foucault, Michel. 1994. *The Order of Things*. London and New York: Routledge.
39. Taylor, Charles. 1991. *The Ethics of Authenticity*. Cambridge, MA: Harvard University Press, 37.
40. It is at this level that in a cross-cultural context the mutually asked questions appear which Ammeke Kateman emphasized in her book on Muhammad Abduh. Kateman, Ammeke. 2019. *Muhammad 'Abduh and His Interlocutors: Conceptualizing Religion in a Globalizing World*. Leiden: Brill.

41. I consider Islamic modernism to be a part of the global evolution of modernist thought, taking off in the second part of the nineteenth century. This global intellectual movement was driven by "a self-reflexive concern with formal innovation in the face of perceived historical and moral crises." Boehmer, Elleke and Steven Matthews. 2011. Modernism and Colonialism. In *The Cambridge Companion to Modernism*. Edited by Michael Levenson. Cambridge: Cambridge University Press, 284–300, 285.

42. There is an ongoing debate about the right application of the terms Salaf, Salafi, Salafiyya in studies on Islam for which here is not the place to discuss it further. My own application follows the suggestions of Frank Griffel and Itzchak Weismann, who state that we can trace back a historical continuity to these three reformers in the nineteenth century. They represent an elitist modernist movement in search of Islamic authenticity, with Abduh as its key figure; see: Griffel, Frank. 2015. What do We Mean by "Salafi"? Connecting Muḥammad 'Abduh with Egypt's Nūr Party in Islam's Contemporary Intellectual History. *Die Welt des Islams* 55: 186–220 and Weismann, Itzchak. 2017. A Perverted Balance: Modern Salafism between Reform and Jihad. *Die Welt des Islams* 57: 33–66. Jakob Skovgaard-Petersen summed it up perfectly when he described Abduh as somebody who completely ignored classical discussions of Islamic jurisprudence in his juridical opinions and went directly back to the Qur'an. Skovgaard-Petersen, Jakob. 1997. *Defining Islam for the Egyptian State: Muftis and Fatwas of the Dār al-Iftā*. Leiden: Brill, 125. See also: Coruh, Hakan. 2019. The Qur'an and Interpretation in the Classical Modernism: Tafsircentric Approach of Muhammad 'Abduh. *Australian Journal of Islamic Studies* 4 (2): 1–21. For this direct emphasis on the Qur'an, see also: Scharbrodt 2008, 133.

43. It is necessary to mention that this classical Salafi stream of thought was not restricted to Egypt and the figures of Afghani, Abduh, and Rida. Other important nineteenth-century Salafist thinkers with different stands were, for instance, Tahir al-Jazairi (1852–1920) and Jamal al-Din al-Qasimi (1866–1914) in Damascus and Khayr al-Din al-Alusi (1836–99) in Baghdad.

44. For the history of Islam in Indonesia, see: Kersten, Carool. 2017. *A History of Islam in Indonesia: Unity in Diversity*. Edinburgh: Edinburgh University Press; Laffan, Michael. 2002. *Islamic Nationhood and Colonial Indonesia: The Umma Below the Winds*. London and New York: Routledge; Laffan, Michael. 2011. *The Making of Indonesian Islam: Orientalism and the Narration of a Sufi Past*. Princeton: Princeton University Press. Reform movements in Africa are discussed in Loimeier, Roman. 2003. Patterns and Peculiarities of Islamic

Reform in Africa. *Journal of Religion in Africa* 33 (August): 237–262. See also Chapter Three in: Østebø, Terje. 2022. *Routledge Handbook of Islam in Africa*. London and New York: Routledge. See also Moaddel, Mansoor. 2001. Conditions for Ideological Production: The Origins of Islamic Modernism in India, Egypt, and Iran. *Theory and Society* 30 (5): 669–731.

45. Bayly, C. A. 2016. Indian and Arabic Thought in the Liberal Age. In *Arabic Thought Beyond the Liberal Age: Towards an Intellectual History of the Nahda*. Cambridge: Cambridge University Press, 325–350, 327.
46. Peters, Rudolph. 1989. Erneuerungsbewegungen im Islam vom 18. bis zum 20. Jahrhundert und die Rolle des Islam in der neueren Geschichte: Antikolonialismus und Nationalismus. In *Der Islam in der Gegenwart*. Edited by Werner Ende and Udo Steinbach. Munich: C. H. Beck, 90–127, 112.
47. Lelyveld, David. 1996. *Aligarh's First Generation: Muslim Solidarity in British India*. New Delhi: Oxford University Press, 4.
48. Ibid. 110.
49. Ibid. 146. For a good overview on the life and work of Sayyid Ahmad Khan, see: Saikia, Yasmin and M. Raisur Rahman (eds.). 2019. *The Cambridge Companion to Sayyid Ahmad Khan*. Cambridge: Cambridge University Press. A classical read on Ahmad Khan is: Troll, Christian W. 1978. *Sayyid Ahmad Khan: A Reinterpretation of Muslim Theology*. New Delhi et al.: Vikas Publishing House. I will come back to Ahmad Khan in the introduction to Chapter Six. On Islamic reform in India more generally, see: Metcalf, Barbara. 2014. *Islamic Revival in British India: Deoband, 1860–1900*. Princeton: Princeton University Press; Robinson, Francis. 2000. *Islam and Muslim History in South Asia*. New Delhi: Oxford University Press; Robinson, Francis. 2008. Islamic Reform and Modernities in South Asia. *Modern Asian Studies* 42 (2–3): 259–281. A recent overview on nineteenth-century Islamic reform in India is provided by: Mazher, Hussain et al. 2022. Rise of Muslim Modernist Discourse in the Nineteenth Century India: A Thematic. *Multicultural Education* 8 (1): 211–217.
50. Karpat, Kemal H. 1972. The Transformation of the Ottoman State, 1779–1908. *International Journal of Middle East Studies* 3: 243–281, 262–265.
51. Hanioğlu, Şükrü. 2005. Blueprints for a Future Society: Late Ottoman Materialists on Science, Religion, and Art. In *Late Ottoman Society: The Intellectual Legacy*. Edited by Elisabeth Özdalga. London and New York: Routledge, 28–116, 28.
52. Gürpinar 2013, 15; Al-Azmeh. Aziz. 1996. *Islams and Modernities*. Second Edition. London and New York: Verso, 107.

53. Menemencioğlu, Nermin. 1967. Namık Kemal Abroad: A Centenary. *Middle Eastern Studies* 4 (1): 29–49, 32.
54. 'Arafāt, 'Alā' al-Dīn. 2001. *Al-alaqāt al-maṣriyya al-faransiyya min al-ta'āwun ila al-tawāṭū 1906–1923*. (Egyptian–French Relations from Cooperation to Agreement 1906–1923). Cairo: Al-Arabi, 382.
55. Livingston, John W. 1995. Muhammad Abduh on Science. *The Muslim World* 85 (3–4): 215–234, 219.
56. Dallal, Ahmad. 1993. The Origins and Objectives of Islamic Revivalist Thought, 1750–1850. *Journal of the American Oriental Society* 113 (3): 341–359, 359.
57. Barber Johannsen pointed to the extremely ambivalent relationship this generation of Islamic modernists had toward Europe. Due to the colonial conditions, they could neither fully embrace European advances in science, politics, and intellectual liberties nor reject them outright: Johansen, Barber. 1967. *Muhammad Husain Haikal: Europa und der Orient im Weltbild eines ägyptischen Liberalen*. Beirut: Orientinstitut der Deutschen Morgenländischen Gesellschaft, 12. In the twentieth century, then, the devastating consequences of the First World War, as well as the rise of Fascism and Stalinism, seemingly confirmed Muslim narratives about the moral decay of European culture and the failure of secular liberalism; cf. Gershoni, Israel. 1999. Egyptian Liberalism in an Age of "Crisis of Orientation": Al-Risala's Reaction to Fascism and Nazism, 1933–39. *International Journal of Middle East Studies* 31: 551–576; and Johansen 1967, 125–158.
58. Weismann 2017, 64.
59. Euben, Roxanne L. 1999. *Enemy in the Mirror: Islamic Fundamentalism and the Limits of Modern Rationalism*. Princeton: Princeton University Press, 99.
60. Adams. Charles. C. 1933. *Islam and Modernism in Egypt: A Study of the Modern Reform Movement Inaugurated by Muhammad Abduh*. London: Oxford University Press, 6.
61. Hildebrandt, Thomas 2002. Waren Jamal Ad-Din Al-Afghani und Muhammad Abduh Neo-Muataziliten? *Die Welt des Islams* 42 (2): 207–262, 215.
62. This according to Goldziher's diary. Goldziher, Ignaz. 1978. *Tagebuch*. Edited by Alexander Schreiber. Leiden: Brill, 68. For a portrait of Goldziher against the background of my thesis of the connectiveness between Islamic modernists and European Orientalists, see: Jung, Dietrich. 2013. Islamic Studies and Religious Reform. Ignaz Goldziher—A Crossroads of Judaism. Christianity and Islam. *Islam—Journal of the History and Culture of the Middle East* 90 (1): 106–126.

63. For Afghani's biography, see: Keddi, Nikki R. 1972. *Sayyid Jamal ad-Din al-Afghani: A Political Biography*. Berkely: University of California Press; Keddi, Nikki. 2005. Sayyid Jamal al-Din al-Afghani. In *Pioneers of Islamic Revival*. New edition. Edited by Ali Rahnema. London: zed books, 11–29.
64. Haddad, Yvonne. 2005. Muhammad Abduh: Pioneer of Islamic Reform. In *Pioneers of Islamic Revival*. New edition. Edited by Ali Rahnema. London: zed books, 30–63, 254.
65. Ryad, Umar. 2009. *Islamic Reformism and Christianity: A Critical Reading of the Works of Muhammad Rashid Rida and His Associates (1898-1935)*. Leiden: Brill, 3.
66. Scharbrodt 2008, 71.
67. Zemmin, Florian. 2021. The Modern Prophet. Radhid Rida's Construction of Muhammad as Religious and Social Reformer. In *The Presence of the Prophet in Early Modern and Contemporary Islam Series: Volume 2: Heirs of the Prophet: Authority and Power in Early Modern and Contemporary Islam*. Edited by Rachida Chih, David Jordan and Stefan Reichmuth. Leiden: Brill, 349–369, 349.
68. See: Burhanudin, Jajat. 2005. Aspiring for Islamic Reform: Southeast Asian Requests for Fatwas in *al-Manar*. *Islamic Law and Society* 12 (1): 9–26, 26; and Kersten, Carool. 2016. *Islam in Indonesia: The Contest for Society, Ideas and Values*. Oxford: Oxford Scholarship, 211.
69. Brown, Carl. 2000. *Religion and State: The Muslim Approach to Politics*. New York: Columbia University Press, 139.
70. Dallal, Ahmad. 2000. Appropriating the Past: Twentieth-Century Reconstruction of Pre-Modern Islamic Thought. *Islamic Law and Society* 7 (1): 325–358.
71. Based on Rida's "Hanafi fatwas" concerning the business activities of Muslims in China, Leor Halevi argued against this "reductive narrative." Halevi does not reject Rida's increasing closeness to Hanbali thought and Ibn Saud, but he gives proof of a more ambiguous pluralism in Rida's thought. Halevi, Leor. 2019. *Modern Things on Trial: Islam's Global and Material Reformation in the Age of Rida, 1865-1935*. New York: Columbia University Press, 234–237.
72. Tauber, Eliezer. 1989. Rashid Rida as Pan-Arabist before World War I. *The Muslim World* 85 (2): 102–112.
73. Voll, John. 1979. The Sudanese Mahdi: Frontier Fundamentalist. *International Journal of Middle East Studies* 20: 145–166.

74. In the introduction to his book, Messick described the shariʿa as a total intellectual discourse that represented a vast field of religious, scholarly, and social deliberations and reflection in premodern Islamic history. Messick, Brinkley. 1993. *The Calligraphic State: Textual Domination and History in a Muslim Society*. Berkeley: University of California Press.
75. Cf. Scharbrodt 2008, 159.
76. Regarding the details of Abduh's biography, I rely on: Sedgwick, Mark. 2010. *Muhammad Abduh*. London: Oneworld.
77. Scharbrodt 2008, 19–29.
78. Büssow, Johann. 2015. Re-Imagining Islam in the Period of the First Modern Globalization: Muhammad Abduh and His Theology of Unity. In *A Global Middle East: Modernity, Materiality and Culture in the Modern Age, 1880–1940*. Edited by Liat Kozma et al. London and New York: I. B. Tauris, 273–320, 280.
79. ʿArafāt 2001, 377.
80. Kateman, 2019.
81. Büssow, Johann. 2017. Muhammad Abduh: The Theology of Unity (Egypt, 1898). In *Religious Dynamics under the Impact of Imperialism and Globalisation: A Source Book*. Edited by Björn Bentlage et al. Leiden: Brill, 141–159, 141–143.
82. Scharbrodt 2008, 134.
83. Kateman 2019, 71.
84. Büssow 2017, 147.
85. Tayob, Abdulkader. 2018. Decolonizing the Study of Religions: Muslim Intellectuals and the Enlightenment Project of Religious Studies. *Journal of the Study of Religion* 31 (2): 7–35, 16. In his article, Tayob particularly refers to the works of Charles Hirschkind and Saba Mahmood. I discussed the "Asad school" in chapter one of this book.
86. Sedgwick 2010, 60.
87. Abduh, Muhammad. 2006. *Al-ʾaʿmāl al-kāmila lī al-imām al-shaykh Muhammad ʿAbduh, ṭabʿa al-thaniyya, al-juz al-thālitha*. Cairo: dār al-shurūq, 379.
88. Ibid. 380.
89. Büssow 2015, 302.
90. Abduh 2006, 449. Here, for example, Abduh makes this very explicit in referring to the superiority of the "authority of religion" (*sulṭān al-dīn*) over the "authority of reason" (*sulṭān al-ʿaql*).

91. Ibid. 471
92. Ibid. 469.
93. While I agree with Elie Kedourie that Abduh was a "free thinker" combining heterodox ideas in his thought, I nevertheless perceive him to be a modern Islamic apologist, rather than an agnostic. Cf. Kedourie. Elie. 1966. *Afghani and Abduh: An Essay on Religious Unbelief and Political Activism in Modern Islam*. London: Frank Cass, 12–14.
94. Abduh 2006, 472. In terms of different religious communities, Abduh also applies the term (*milla*), ibid. 411.
95. Ibid. 382.
96. Ibid. 451–452.
97. Ibid. 448.
98. Tayob 2018. Kateman 2019.
99. The core of Islam is the teaching of the unity of God (*tawḥīd allah*); Abduh 2006, 465.
100. Abduh 2006, 401.
101. Guizot, François. 1828. *Cours d'histoire modern—Histoire général de la civilisation en Europe*. Paris: Pichon et Didier, chapters 11 and 12. The role of Guizot in Abduh's thought is examined, for instance, in 'Arafāt 2001, Livingstone 1995, and Sedgwick 2010.
102. Sedgwick 2010, 16.
103. Guizot 1828.
104. Jung 2011, 242–244.
105. Cf. Euben 1999.
106. An excellent study on the history of modern ideas in Arab thought is delivered by Florian Zemmin in his book on the concept of society as it appeared in *al-manār*. Zemmin, Florian. 2020. *Modernity in Islamic Tradition: The Concept of "Society" in the Journal al-Manar (Cairo 1898–1940)*. Berlin and Boston: Walter de Gruyter.
107. See my references to Jürgen Habermas's "modernity as an unfinished project" in the introduction to Chapter Two.
108. Cf. Aydin, Cemil. 2007. *The Politics of Anti-Westernism in Asia: Visions of World Order in Pan-Islamic and Pan-Asian Thought*. New York: Columbia University Press, 193.
109. Cf. Nafi, Basheer M. 2004. The Rise of Islamic Reformist Thought and its Challenge to Traditional Islam. In *Islamic Thought in the Twentieth Century*. Edited by Suha Taji-Farouki and Basheer M. Nafi. London: I. B. Tauris, 28–60.

110. Skovgaard-Petersen 1997, 77.
111. For a similar example of these modern boundary negotiations, see Florian Zemmin's analysis of the thought of Rafiq al-ʿAzm (1865–1925), who was a "core contributor" to *al-manār*; Zemmin, Florian. 2019. Validating Secularity in Islam: The Sociological Perspective of the Muslim Intellectual Rafiq al-ʿAzm (1865–1925). *Historical Social Research/Historische Sozialforschung* 44 (3): 74–100, 76.
112. Scharbrodt, Oliver. 2007. The Salafiyya and Sufism: *Muḥammad ʿAbduh* and His *Risālat al-Wāridāt* (Treatise on Mystical Inspirations). *Bulletin of SOAS* 70 (1): 89–115.
113. On this, see again the study by Kateman 2019.
114. Here Abduh was following a general trend in Islamic modernism which, for instance, is also clearly expressed in the thought of Sayyid Ahmad Khan in India; cf. Troll 1978.
115. Kaviraj, Sudipta. 2005. An Outline of a Revisionist Theory of Modernity. *European Journal of Sociology* 46 (3): 497–526, 523.

5

DIVERGING DIRECTIONS: "ISLAMIST" AND "SECULARIST" PROJECTS OF MUSLIM MODERNITIES

I will never forget my first Sunday walking tour, taking me through the center of Turkey's capital, Ankara, late in the summer of 1997. This walk began at the *hisar*, the old citadel on a hill north of the city center that then was populated by rural migrants mainly from Eastern Anatolia. From there I passed through the *gecekondu* Altındağ, taking the direction via Ulus along Atatürk Boulevard toward the fancier residential area of Çankaya.[1] There is no doubt that this walk does not rank prominently among Turkey's numerous tourist attractions. On the contrary, the modern functional architecture that forms the backdrop for most of this walking tour seemingly corroborates the negative image which most travel guides usually paint of the Turkish capital. Yet Ankara is not as bad in terms of interesting places as this image may purport at first glance. In fact, taking this path through central Ankara offers a multiplicity of insights into both the history of the Turkish Republic and the various different lifestyles which actually characterize Muslim life in Turkey. These lifestyles correlate with differences in economic status, educational background, ethnic origin, political orientation, religious affiliation, and social class.

The view from my starting point, the old *hisar*, offers a petrified image of the two essential forces that in various ways have characterized modern Ottoman-Turkish history. Looking over Ankara from there, you will see on the left-hand side the huge Kocatepe Mosque. The mosque is a neo-classicist building completed in 1987. In terms of architecture, it is a clear replication of those Ottoman imperial mosques which were once designed by the famous architect Mimar Sinan (1490–1588). Sinan worked for over 40 years as the "chief architect" of the Ottoman Empire, in a period in which the "Sunnitization" of the Ottoman state took place.[2] When turning your gaze to the right, you will see the Anıtkabir, the mausoleum of Mustafa Kemal Atatürk. This building reminds us of an antique temple. Built in a neo-classicist style, the mausoleum was completed in 1953 and gives home to the sarcophaguses of both Atatürk and his successor İsmet İnönü.[3] Moreover, it includes a museum with various paraphernalia from Atatürk's life and work. With its reference to antiquity the mausoleum is also an expression of Turkish republican nationalism tracing its origin back into ancient pre-Islamic times.

For the careful observer, my walking tour through Ankara, as already mentioned, provides an encounter not only with Turkey's petrified history but also with the country's lively and multifaceted social life. In particular, you can spot the very peculiar cultural merger of Kemalist secularism and Islam. The tour takes you through quarters populated by different socioeconomic classes, and the streetscape changes in character with this. These changing streetscapes are accompanied by people who, in clothing and physical appearance, also represent the different cultural forces of secularist Kemalism and Islam. With respect to this book, however, the view over Ankara with its two landmarks, the Kocatepe Mosque and the Anıtkabir, as well as these visible different cultural forces, illustrate more than simply two pillars of modern Turkish-Ottoman history. In my own perception, they represent the more generally "secularist" and "Islamist" poles of the eventual bifurcation that Islamic modernism took in the twentieth century at which I hinted at the end of the previous chapter.

In his discussion of the thought of Muhammad Abduh's Egyptian disciples, Albert Hourani firstly wrote some pages on the deep tension he discovered in Abduh's work. Each side of this tension, according to Hourani, came with its own "inescapable" demands. On the one hand, there was Abduh's strict adherence to Islam as a sincere Muslim believer. In all his efforts, religious reform had priority, and Islamic traditions provided his social and moral compass. On the other hand, Abduh was convinced of the "irreversible movement of modern civilization." In order to remedy the ills of the country and achieve independence, Egypt had to modernize. Abduh tried to reconcile this tension, in Hourani's eyes, through his search for a kind of "true Islam" that could accommodate modernity within the moral cosmos of Islamic teachings. Yet Hourani also stressed the apologetic nature of Abduh's efforts. He emphasized that in the case of conflict between the two sides, the Islamic reformer always took the religious side. For Abduh, Hourani concluded, Islam exposed "certain moral and doctrinal imperatives" on which he never compromised.[4] This uncompromising attitude, however, was not the case for all his disciples.

In the generation following Abduh, the tension that Hourani identified in the work of the Egyptian reformer diverged into two different streams of thought. To put it in simple terms: we can notice the increasing "Islamization" and the gradual "secularization" of Islamic modernism. As described in the previous chapter, Rashid Rida (1865–1935) played a crucial role in the Islamization of modernist thought, becoming a kind of intellectual father of the Islamist ideologies of the twentieth century. Mustafa Abd al-Raziq (1885–1947), rector of the Azhar from 1945 until his death in 1947, and his brother Ali Abd al-Raziq (1888–1966) meanwhile represent the second stream. Both considered themselves close disciples of Abduh, and their father was a friend of the Imam.[5] Mustafa studied at the Sorbonne, and in his rationalization of Islamic thought he applied concepts from the German-born British philologist Max Müller (1823–1900) and the French sociologist Émile Durkheim (1858–1917).[6] After having received his degree from the Azhar, Mustafa's brother Ali went to study at Oxford until the First World War. In 1925, he then published his famous book on the fundaments of governance in Islam (*al-islām wa uṣūl al-ḥukm*). In this book, Ali Abd al-Raziq came to the conclusion that a specifically Islamic system of government does not exist. The Islamic Caliphate, according to him, was a mere religious institution that did not represent anything like a Muslim state. Advocating a separation between Islam and the institutions of the state, the book raised a fundamental controversy in Egypt. In the course of this debate, Rashid Rida declared Ali Abd al-Raziq's book "an attempt of the enemies of Islam to weaken and divide it from within."[7] Looking at this controversy, Rida and the al-Raziq brothers, all three close followers of Abduh, perfectly personify the conflicting tendencies of his thought. Yet this bifurcation applies not only to Abduh's reformist ideas but also to the intellectual stream of Islamic modernism more generally.

Ali Abd al-Raziq's book was published in the year after the abolition of the Islamic Caliphate in March 1924 by the republican government of Turkey under Mustafa Kemal Atatürk. This move by Atatürk triggered a storm of indignation throughout the Islamic world, yet without leading to the establishment of an alternative caliphate. On the contrary, in the fierce discussion about the establishment of a successor to the Ottoman Caliphate, no alternative could gain legitimacy among a majority of Muslims.[8] While certainly not a disciple of Abduh, Atatürk was nevertheless socialized in the world of thought which characterized the broad stream of Islamic modernism of the late Ottoman Empire. His educational background and military career made him a perfect child of the state-driven Ottoman modernization process. In his political thought, he was to a significant extent an heir of Ottoman constitutionalism, which began with the Islamic modernism of the Young Ottoman movement. However, Atatürk belonged to the generation of Turkish nationalists who replaced the Ottomanism and Islamic reformism of the Young Ottoman Namık Kemal (1840–88) with a new kind of staunch ethnic Turkish nationalism.

In this chapter, I will compare the two—at first glance—very different projects of modernity that are associated with the life and work of Hasan al-Banna, the founder of the Egyptian Muslim Brotherhood, and Mustafa Kemal Atatürk. This comparison sets two extreme poles against each other which nevertheless have their roots in the intellectual environment of nineteenth-century Islamic modernism. In comparing the Islamist ideology of the Muslim Brotherhood with Turkey's republican secularism, I want to shed light on the contextual conditions under which the Islamic discourse of modernity and its various facets evolved. In this way, these two cases serve to underline the historicity of the rise of a specifically Islamic discourse of modernity. The paths that modernist Islamic thought has taken are historically contingent. Consequently, the current hegemony of Islamic discourses of modernity is not the result of any specific essence of Islam and is therefore also subject to historical change. In the following section, I will first introduce some analytical tools for the comparison of these two streams of thought, drawing from the sociological concepts of Peter Wagner and Andreas Reckwitz.[9] This theoretical discussion will also show that Banna's Islamism and Atatürk's secularism are not so different after all. They share important institutional and organizational features which had a global relevance in the first part of the twentieth century. Following this, I will move on to the two case studies. I first look at the life and thought of Hasan al-Banna and then move on to Mustafa Kemal Atatürk and his cultural revolution.

Organized Modernity: Egyptian Efendis and Turkish Kemalists in Search of Social Order

In her *The Age of Efendiyya*, Lucie Ryzova described a specific kind of Egyptian man who became the social bearer of Egyptian nationalism in the first part of the twentieth century.[10] These "efendi subjects" she defined as belonging to an emerging middle class of bureaucrats, journalists, teachers, white-collar workers, and writers from an urban or recently urbanized background.[11] Many of them grew up in provincial areas of Egypt before moving to Cairo for further education. Claiming agency on behalf of the nation, the efendis pursued a project of modernity for which they claimed authenticity with respect to both their "correct interpretations" of Egyptian and Islamic traditions as well as their rejection of a kind of Western modernity that was "conflated with colonialism."[12] Efendi culture was nationalist in nature and directed against both the ruling political and religious establishment and the colonial administration of Great Britain.[13] The efendis constructed a modernizing project based on their secular education and articulated themselves through new media such as the emerging film industry, the printing press, and publishing houses.[14] Some figures of this new efendi class achieved national and international prominence by founding schools, hospitals, scientific associations, cultural clubs, and grass-roots social movements.[15] Most significantly, these successful efendis felt like vanguards on a mission to change Egyptian society.[16] One of them was undoubtedly Hasan al-Banna, who founded the Egyptian Muslim Brotherhood in 1928. At first a rather insignificant religious association, the Muslim Brotherhood gradually developed into the largest politico-religious organization in the Middle East.

Before looking more closely at the evolution of the Brotherhood movement, however, we have to qualify Ryzova's observations. The cultural type of an Egyptian efendi that she discovered through her analysis of autobiographical works, movies, and novels was probably less peculiar for Egypt than her book would have us assume. In a voluminous study, the German sociologist Andreas

Reckwitz identified three different cultural types that have characterized three successive steps of modernity since the nineteenth century. The first of these historically hegemonic types, the classical bourgeois, epitomized the period which Peter Wagner labeled "restricted liberalism." The classical bourgeois, according to Reckwitz, represented a kind of rationalistic and introverted self who gained moral formation through daily practices of disciplined work related to literacy. Writing and reading were central practices in this process of bourgeois' self-formation. To a certain extent, the intellectuals in Albert Hourani's *Arabic Thought* resemble this cultural type of the classical bourgeois. The rise of the Egyptian efendi, however, marks the emergence of a new cultural type of the modern subject that, according to Reckwitz, became hegemonic after the decline of restricted liberalism toward the end of the nineteenth century.[17]

In Peter Wagner's conceptual design, a form of organized modernity gradually replaced the social order of the classical bourgeoisie. The restricted liberalism of nineteenth-century society gave way to various historical forms of an "organized mass society." These forms of organized mass society comprise very different social orders: of a Fordist, nationalist, socialist, or fascist nature. The culturally different projects of organized modernity in the first part of the twentieth century shared, more or less, a number of general features such as a belief in progress, an instrumental rationality, the employment of developmental schemes, the control of the population by bureaucratic means, and the in-principle possible top-down management of society. Revolving around the central institution of the modern national state, for these projects of modernity top-down governance and attempts at social engineering became essential tools for the political integration and the social containment of the masses. In this chapter, I propose perceiving both Hasan al-Banna's concept of Islamic governance and the republican regime of Atatürk as variations on this global theme of organized modernity. The ideology of the Muslim Brotherhood and Kemalism share essential features of a social order that refers to this ideal type of organized mass society.[18]

Against this conceptual background, it should not come as a surprise that many of the characteristics of the Egyptian efendi mirror the social patterns of Kemalism. These parallels are clearly visible in the veneration of Atatürk. The founding father of the Turkish Republic is portrayed in innumerable images representing social types such as the elder statesman, the orderly bureaucrat, the disciplined officer, the enlightened teacher, or the urban bohemian presiding over the cultural reproduction of the Turkish nation.[19] In these "multiple faces of Mustafa Kemal Atatürk" we can detect the social strata of the early Turkish Republic. They closely match the social profiles in Ryzova's definition of Egyptian efendi subjectivity. Even more important, as in the case of the efendiyya, the modern state in Turkey was also "the largest producer and consumer" of Kemalist subjects.[20] Coming back to Reckwitz' study, again, both the efendi subject and the Kemalist subject built on more general patterns of a cultural type which was seemingly prevalent in the subjectivity formation of early twentieth-century modernity.

According to Reckwitz, the rather introverted literacy of the classical bourgeoisie was superseded by new social practices. Firstly, the transformation of material culture and the invention of new technological means led to a reorganization of time and space. Together with the dissemination of new scientific bodies of knowledge, this technological transformation enabled, secondly, the construction of new forms of collectivity based on strong ideas concerning the social engineering of the population. Thirdly, new social movements discovered the human body as an object for social technologies that positioned their ideal of a "peer-group-oriented" subject of mass society visibly against the cultural representations of the classical bourgeois elite.[21] In the subjectivity formation of organized modernity, new print and audiovisual media facilitated previously unknown modes of consumption including practices of the body and collective public performances. However, these new features of organized modernity were still nested within a system of the coordination of social action. The cultural type of organized society claimed to be all-inclusive and advocated social adaptation, but it did so in the form of a peer-group-oriented culture of the masses. Adopting some of the ideas of top-down regulation and control from the previous bourgeois order, the vanguards of organized modernity tried to steer the subjectivity formation of the population according to their own cultural ideals. In this respect, the life and action of Hasan al-Banna and Mustafa Kemal Atatürk were also paradigmatic. The political ideals of both the Muslim Brotherhood movement and the Turkish nationalists closely resemble this shift toward the collective and individual features of organized modernity. Let us first have a look at Hasan al-Banna's project of an Islamic organized modernity.

Hasan al-Banna: Constructing the Modern Muslim Subject

In 1927, Hasan al-Banna finished his studies at the Dar al-Ulum in Cairo and moved to Ismailia taking up his first position as a schoolteacher. The Dar al-Ulum was founded as a college for the education of teachers. The historical literature on Egypt considers it as a predecessor of the modern Egyptian university system. Providing both education in religion and modern sciences, the college represented an alternative to the traditionalist clerical milieu at the Azhar. It was one of the typical new educational institutions in which the effendiyya was formed. Banna joined the Dar al-Ulum in 1923 in order to complement his previous traditional Islamic education and his initial training as a teacher in the provincial town of Damanhur. In Ismailia, then, the young Banna started his religious mission by preaching ideas about "true Islam" in the coffeehouses of the town. In the eyes of the young primary school teacher, a high level of religious ignorance characterized his fellow Egyptians. While studying in Cairo, he was appalled by the features of the city's social life and what he perceived as the disregard of the educated youth for an Islamic way of life.[22] Together with a small group of like-minded men, Hasan al-Banna organized what he called a "School of Moral Education" (*madrasa al-tahdhīb*). There young religious activists met to discuss correct forms of worship and Islamic behavior. Moreover, they aimed to spread their religious reform ideas for the improvement of the moral status of Egyptian society at large. Understanding themselves as "brothers in serving Islam," the group adopted the name Muslim Brothers (*al-ikhwān al-muslimūn*).[23] Founded as a predominantly religious movement, the Muslim Brotherhood developed into one of the most influential organizations of Islamist thought in the twentieth century. The Ikhwan popularized a specific version of the Islamic discourse of modernity and disseminated it far beyond the borders of Egypt.

Born in 1906, Hasan al-Banna grew up in a small provincial town less than 100 miles from Cairo. His father was a watchmaker and became the local Imam in 1913. With his literary leanings, Banna's father made his children familiar with Islamic texts such as Qur'an exegesis (*tafsīr*), Islamic jurisprudence (*fiqh*), and the traditions of the Prophet (*hadith*). In addition, he introduced his children to non-religious and fictional literature.[24] While receiving a rather traditional form of Islamic education in his childhood, Hasan al-Banna soon sought to acquire a modern secular education, first by attending a modern primary school, and then at the teacher training school in Damanhur, and finally in the Dar al-Ulum. The biography of Hasan al-Banna clearly reflects the becoming of an "efendi subject." This applies to the trope of departure, the move from the countryside to Cairo, the personal metamorphosis in the course of his education, and the social activism that increasingly accompanied his personal career.[25] Even in his hometown, Mahmudiyya, he already joined a religious association for the moral education of Egyptian youth. Later he continued this engagement in Islamic benevolent societies until he founded the Brotherhood. In this way, Banna combined modern forms of social activism with the Islamic call to religious missionhood (*daʿwa*).[26] As in the biography of Isam al-Din Galal, an Egyptian pharmacologist and public health official who is described in Ryzova's book, Hasan al-Banna followed the "formulaic course" of becoming an efendi in his "development of a passion for reading, peer friendships and political activism."[27] Moreover, in founding the Muslim Brotherhood, he combined his missionary religious zeal with his role as a vanguard in the project of engineering a specific kind of modern Islamic social order. The Brotherhood and its leader are an example of a modern movement aiming at the establishment of an Islamic social order that builds on the historical ideal type of organized modernity.

In the Muslim Brotherhood ideology, Banna constructed a project of modernity that bears the imprint of Rashid Rida's thought. According to Gudrun Krämer's biography, Banna was a "diligent reader" of Rida's journal *al-manār*.[28] In Cairo, he frequented reformist circles, meeting among others Rashid Rida and Muhib al-Din al-Khatib (1886–1969). The latter was the co-founder of the Salafiyya Press and Bookshop whom Banna described as a "hard-working scholar and journalist."[29] The ideas of classical Islamic modernism, therefore, entered Banna's thought in the form of the Salafist interpretation for which Rashid Rida stood for in his later years. This applies in particular to Rida's modernist understanding of the shariʿa as being close to the modern concept of positive law. In the discussion about the Islamic Caliphate, Rida envisaged it as an independent Arab state in Greater Syria (*bilād al-shām*) enforcing Islamic law.[30] Hasan al-Banna appropriated this concept of the shariʿa as the blueprint for an authentic Islamic order. Consequently, he utilized Islamic law as the primary source for claiming moral integrity and cultural authenticity for the politics of the Muslim Brotherhood.[31] In this way, Banna radicalized some elements of the intellectual fundaments of nineteenth-century Islamic reform. In the conscious recollection of the early Islamic community represented by the Prophet Muhammad and the four "rightly guided Caliphs" he saw the main resource for the religious and social transformation of Egypt.[32] The fourth leader of the Brotherhood, Muhammad Hamed Abul Nasr (1913–96), described this position when he recalled a situation in which Hasan al-Banna compared the lamentable contemporary condition of the Islamic community with the glorious past under the guidance of the Salaf.[33] Moreover, Banna shared Rida's appreciation for the Saudi King, Ibn Saud (1876–1953), and tried to enlist his financial support for the funding of the Muslim Brotherhood.[34] In July 1939, he even continued the publication of *al-manār*, which was interrupted after the death of Rashid Rida in August 1935.[35]

With the foundation of the Muslim Brotherhood, the thought of the classical Islamic modernists—Afghani, Abduh, and Rida—eventually left the narrow world of intellectual circles. Hasan al-Banna took the "defense of Islam" directly to the Egyptian people.[36] The success of the Brotherhood was due to the lasting colonial situation and the failure of Egyptian liberal nationalism to achieve the political independence of the country after the First World War. In wartime, Saad Zaghlul (1857–1927) formed a nationalist group among the representatives of the Egyptian parliament. This nationalist movement tried to mobilize the population for their call for independence from British colonial administration. Demanding the right to participate at the Paris Peace Conference (1919–20), Zaghlul's group became known as the "delegation" (*wafd*).[37] The British authorities, however, rejected Zaghlul's demands and arrested him in March 1919. The subsequent deportation of Zaghlul to Malta then sparked the Egyptian Revolution of 1919, the first popular mass movement with countrywide demonstrations in Egyptian history. In 1922, Great Britain granted Egypt a kind of restricted independence, allowing it to remain the mandatory power controlling the international affairs of the country. For a short while, Saad Zaghlul served as prime minister in 1924. The Wafd Party's policies of liberal secular nationalism, however, did not achieve full independence for the Egyptian population nor an improvement in their living conditions. Even worse, the Egyptian king and the British authorities undermined the legitimacy of subsequent liberal governments and contributed further to the failure of Egypt's liberal bourgeois project of modernity.[38]

Against this historical background, Hasan al-Banna experienced modern social contingency in the context of British Imperialism and founded a revivalist movement with the aim of shaping new social practices for Muslim individuals and the Egyptian nation in general. The conceptual fundament of his modernizing project, however, rested in what I defined as the *épistémè* of an emerging global public sphere.[39] Hasan al-Banna built his Islamist world of thought on the syntax of modernity. The Islamist semantics of the Brotherhood relied on conceptual tools given by the confrontation with the social logic of functional differentiations. Thereby, Hasan al-Banna constructed an idiosyncratic modern vernacular combining Islamic traditions with modern concepts in constructions such as Islamic culture and civilization, organicist theories of an Islamic system, and an evolutionary teleology that rested in an imagined Islamic past. In one of his "epistles" (*rasā'il*), for instance, he explained his concept of Islamic governance (*niẓām al-ḥukm al-islāmī*). In this he built on the idea of the social contract (*al-ʿaqd al-ijtimāʿī*) between ruler and ruled, as well as on the modern institution of the public good (*al-maṣlaḥa al-ʿāma*). Hasan al-Banna gained the specific Islamic justification for these two core concepts of modern governance through tracing them back to the practices of rule by the first Caliph Abu Bakr (573–634 CE).[40] Even more important, he used the organizational patterns of his times in transforming the benevolent religious missionary group of the Ikhwan into a highly bureaucratized political and religious organization with administrative offices throughout the country. These offices connected the organization's local membership and their welfare and student associations with an effective line of communication to the center in Cairo.[41] On the occasion of the fifth conference of the Muslim Brotherhood in 1939, Hasan al-Banna declared that "Islam is creed and worship, nation and nationality, religion and state, spirituality and work, Holy book and sword."[42] The political role of the Brotherhood was further enhanced by the foundation of the organization's "Special Apparatus" in 1939–40 and the establishment of paramilitary units actively involved in the militant resistance against British troops in Egypt and in the armed struggle in Palestine.[43]

The Muslim Brotherhood became the organizational tool for Hasan al-Banna's project of establishing a truly authentic Islamic modernity. The ideology of the Brotherhood represented an Islamic version of the peer-group-oriented selfhood of modernity framed according to the then globally predominant type of organized society. Center stage in this project of organized modernity was Islamic law, which Banna transformed from an independently used reference for the formation of moral subjects to a collectively binding set of norms and laws. In his ideological thought, Islamic traditions were expected to play the role of a technology of domination in dealing with Egypt's contingent historical reality by coercive legal means. In addressing the pressing political, economic, and social questions of the country, the Brotherhood employed the templates of then contemporary mass organizations. The ideal type behind the organization's paradigmatic member closely resembles Reckwitz' cultural type of the peer-group-oriented modern subject of organized modernity. The Brothers adopted extroverted modes of performance such as the use of badges, dress codes, and public marches and ceremonies. In its boy scout- and paramilitary-style units the organization emphasized the new role of the human body. Hasan al-Banna constructed an ideal of the modern Muslim who was mainly a male, clean, industrious, modest, physically active, punctual, and temperate subject morally anchored in religious practices and Muslim community life. In short, leaving specifically Egyptian and Islamic attributes aside, the ideal Muslim Brother mirrored the templates of the subject of organized modernity whose historical emergence Christopher Bayly described in his *Birth of the Modern World*. Hasan al-Banna and the Egyptian Muslim Brotherhood are an integral part of what Bayly described as the "multi-centric nature" of global change.[44]

Mustafa Kemal Atatürk: Constructing the Modern Turkish Subject

In 1928, the same year in which Hasan al-Banna founded the Muslim Brotherhood, the words "The religion of the Turkish state is Islam" were deleted from the republican constitution of Turkey. In April 1924, only one month after the abolition of the caliphate, the Grand National Assembly in Ankara promulgated the first republican constitution. While the regime in Ankara dissolved religious courts and abolished the function of the chief mufti (*sheikh ül-Islam*) as well as the ministries of religious affairs and pious foundations, the republican government first retained the constitutional status of Islam as the Turkish state religion. It was not until February 1937 that secularism entered the Turkish constitution as one of the core ideological pillars of the Kemalist republic.[45] Declaring secularism a Turkish state doctrine one year before the death of then President Atatürk in 1938 marked the final point of a cultural revolution with a very strong iconoclast posture.[46]

This revolution started with the abolition of the Ottoman Sultanate in 1922.[47] Atatürk launched an institutional and symbolic transformation process through which the new political elite demonstrated its claim over the Turkish national state. These fundamental institutional, ideological, and symbolic measures of the Kemalist revolution comprised among others: the declaration of the Turkish Republic in October 1923; the abolition of the caliphate and the introduction of co-education for boys and girls in 1924; the so-called hat-law (prohibiting the Fez, the symbolic headgear of the Ottoman bureaucracy) and the subsequent closure of religious brotherhoods, convents, sacred tombs, and other places of worship in 1925; the establishment of secular law codes together with the introduction of the Gregorian Calendar and the Latin alphabet in 1926; and the prohibition of the pilgrimage to Mecca and the shift from Friday to Sunday as the official Islamic day of rest in 1935. Atatürk and his associates transformed the Turkish polity from an empire based on religious and dynastic legitimacy—in Max Weber's terms, from a system of traditional authority—to a republican regime resting on both a type of legal authority and on the sovereignty of the Turkish nation. This revolutionary process was as much a reform of the political institutions of the country as it was a bold cultural justification for the complete replacement of the previously ruling Ottoman royal elite.[48] In order to underpin this fundamental cultural change with "scientific evidence," in 1931 Atatürk founded the Turkish Historical Society and in 1932 the Turkish Linguistic Society under his own leadership. With the "Turkish Historical Thesis" and the "Sun Language Theory," these two associations provided the essential arguments for anchoring Turkish nationalism historically before the advent of Islam and geographically in Central Asia. They both represent core institutions for the way in which the Kemalist state elite "invented traditions" in the construction of their nationalist modern project.[49]

In responding to the admiration for Atatürk and his reforms expressed by Mustafa al-Nahhas (1879–1965), who served on five occasions as Prime Minister of Egypt between 1928 and 1952, Hasan al-Banna criticized the

Egyptian politician for his suggestion that Egypt should follow the Turkish leader on this path and liberate herself from all forms of Islamic manifestations. Nahhas expressed his appreciation for the Kemalist reforms to the Turkish news agency Anadolu in June 1935. According to Banna, in his veneration for Atatürk the Egyptian prime minister completely forgot that the Turkish leader would not have been in power without the help of Islam. In Banna's eyes, Atatürk achieved his military victories and therewith power in Turkey as a Muslim, "carrying his *misbaḥa*, reading the Qur'an and kneeling through his prayers in the desert among the Arabs and Muslims of Anatolia."[50] Therefore, it would be utterly wrong, Banna continued, to attribute the successes of republican Turkey to the empty and atheist manifestations of the Kemalist revolution that actually set Turkish people back rather than moving them forward.[51]

Hasan al-Banna's opinion of Mustafa Kemal Atatürk is relevant with regard to two points. First of all, it shows the principal admiration of Muslims for Atatürk in using military means to salvage a part of the Ottoman state and territory in the form of the Turkish Republic. Arabs and Muslims beyond the Middle East reacted rather ambiguously to the political development in Turkey, but at the point of the end of the "Turkish War of Independence" (1919–22) most of them considered Atatürk as a Muslim war hero.[52] Second, and even more important for the foundation of the Turkish Republic, it was only gradually that the Kemalists pushed away the Islamic legacy of Turkey's Ottoman modernist origins. During the War of Independence against Greek troops, references to Islam served the nationalist movement as a crucial means of social cohesion and military mobilization.[53] The majority of the loose alliance of army officers, state bureaucrats, professionals, merchants, and Anatolian landlords behind the national resistance were fighting for the restoration of the Ottoman state.[54] The ordinary population of Anatolia apparently shared Hasan al-Banna's opinion in considering the victory in the War of Independence as a "triumph of Islam over the infidels."[55] With the Treaty of Lausanne and the establishment of the Turkish Republic in 1923, the national movement abandoned this Ottoman legacy of the unifying power of Islam.[56] The following Kemalist revolution,[57] then, orchestrated the gradual replacement of religious traditions in the symbolic reproduction of the Turkish state. Consequently, the new political elite heavily drew on the specific resources on which their social power rested. The officers, bureaucrats, and white-collar workers of the Kemalist state employed the means of organizational and cognitive knowledge afforded by their modern-style education.[58] The iconoclast reform measures aimed at providing the specific symbolic means on which the legitimacy of the new ruling elite rested.[59]

Mustafa Kemal, the son of a customs officer, was born in Salonika in 1881. After graduating from the Staff College in Istanbul, Kemal was a founding member of the nationalist Committee of Union and Progress (CUP) and joined the so-called Young Turk Revolution in 1908.[60] The members of the CUP, and Mustafa Kemal in particular, were typical representatives of the new Ottoman military bureaucracy who found in the modernized Ottoman education system the core institutions of their personal social advancement. In deposing Sultan Abdülhamit II less than a year after the Young Turk Revolution in 1909, some members of this new educated Turkish middle class assumed power over the governing institutions of the Ottoman state. The decision of the new rulers to enter the First World War on the side of Germany and Austria-Hungary, however, ended in a complete disaster. Since the late eighteenth century, the Ottomans were increasingly drawn into the European power struggle and eventually into the First World War. Lacking the economic, military, and communicative means to fight a major war, this involvement on the side of the Axis powers led to the collapse of the Ottoman state.[61] The only remarkable military success was the defense of the Dardanelles at Gallipoli, in which the 34-year-old Mustafa Kemal played an important role on the side of the Prussian officer Liman von Sanders. On October 31, 1918, Sultan Mehmet VI (1918–22) signed the empire's unconditional capitulation in the Truce of Mudros, and the CUP leadership fled Istanbul aboard a German submarine the day after.[62] In the immediate post-war situation, formal power again went to the sultan. Yet Mehmed VI was completely at the mercy of the victorious war allies. Signing the treaty of Sèvres in 1920, he further discredited the dynastic legitimacy of the empire. The military successes at Gallipoli and in the War of Independence, as well as the abolition of the never-implemented clauses of Sèvres in the peace negotiations at Lausanne in 1923, then opened the way for the nationalist movement to seize power under the charismatic figure of Mustafa Kemal Atatürk.[63]

In the consolidation of republican rule, Atatürk combined his iconoclast measures with the willful construction of the Kemalist Turkish subject. In this process of social engineering, the Kemalists closely followed the then-powerful ideas of an organized modernity. In the course of the Kemalist revolution, the regime prescribed new cultural types for the individual identity construction of the Turkish population at large. Measures such as the compulsory adoption of surnames, the introduction of dress laws, the opening of public beaches for women, and the staging of the first Miss Turkey contest in 1929 symbolize this top-down construction of a new Turkish subject that was expected to sever its ties from the Ottoman past. This distancing from the past essentially reflected the change in the claim to legitimacy undertaken by the new political elite. Atatürk further bolstered this process of state-controlled identity construction with his performances in public. This applies to his own "Western-style" appearance, his self-representation as the teacher of the nation, the visible socializing of the president with women, and his public consumption of alcoholic beverages. From 1926 onwards, the regime further underline this role of Atatürk as the "model of modern Turkishness" by erecting statues of the president first in Istanbul and then in Ankara, Kayseri, Samsun, and many other provincial towns.[64] Together, the cultural revolution, the "scientific" construction of a national narrative by the Turkish Historical and Linguistic Societies, and the omnipresent veneration of the Atatürk model contributed to the manufacturing of a standardized national culture from above. In the early Turkish Republic, the domestic policies of the Kemalist regime aimed at the formation of an organized modern society with a peer-group-oriented modern nationalist Turkish subject. Atatürk and his associates, thereby, represented the vanguards in this project, combining educational with coercive means.[65]

In the establishment and consolidation of the Turkish Republic, the doctrine of secularism as a political ideology played a central disciplinary role. This became apparent with the death of Atatürk and the institutionalization of his charismatic authority first in the Republican Peoples Party (RRP) and after the Second World War in the hegemonic political role of the Turkish armed forces. Turkey's secularism worked as a Foucauldian technology of domination. The republican state represented a form of a "Kemalist panopticon." In abstracting from the model of a prison, Michel Foucault defined the panopticon as a "political technology" that induces a state of conscious and permanent visibility to assure the automatic functioning of power. Political power is exercised in forms of open and implicit surveillance. The move from a visible to a hidden disciplinary mechanism thereby characterizes the transition from state technologies of domination to technologies of the self.[66] In the Kemalist project of modernity, secularism became the central instrument for controlling and managing the masses, the embodiment of the specific Turkish way of constructing a form of organized modernity. The secularist doctrine represented a disciplinary mechanism with the help of which the RPP and the military tried to maintain their respective positions of power. In the omnipresence of Atatürk in public and private spaces we can detect Foucault's fictious mechanism in which factual forms of surveillance become combined with self-imposed means of social control.

With the introduction of multiparty politics in 1946, the RPP lost its role as a vanguard and as the ultimately ruling institution in Turkey. Under the government of Prime Minister Adnan Menderes (1950–60) and his Democratic Party (DP), therefore, we can observe the first reappearance of Islamic legacies which the RPP forcefully suppressed during President İnönü's autocratic rule (1938–50).[67] The Menderes government abandoned Atatürk's prohibition of the Arabic call to prayer, permitted once more the activities of religious brotherhoods (*tarikat*) and communities (*cemaat*), and re-opened previously closed public places of worship. With these measures, Menderes appealed in particular to the voters of the Anatolian provinces. Thus, breaking with the ideological heritage of Atatürk, the Menderes government crossed a red line. In May 1960, the Turkish armed forces intervened in Turkish politics through a military coup. Putting themselves into the vanguard position of Turkish modernization, the officer corps controlled Turkish politics for more than 40 years. Drawing heavily on the heritage of Atatürk's charismatic authority, the armed forces developed into a state within the state, building the state's relative autonomy on political institutions such as the National Security Council, on a broad range of its own economic enterprises and joint ventures with private businesses, and on its own educational system. These educational institutions provided both academic knowledge and military ethics based on Kemalist values. In its high schools and military academies, the army educated young officers in a spirit that set them apart from the rest of the population. According to the tenet of this spirit, the Turkish armed forces traced a direct line from the charismatic authority of Atatürk to their own role as the guardians and trustees of the republican revolution. Again, Atatürk served here as the role model and secularism as the core ideological feature in the justification of the moral and political superiority of the military over civil society.[68]

Conclusions: Empirical Observations and Theoretical Implications

In June 2012, the Muslim Brother Muhammad Mursi (1951–2019) became President of Egypt. For the first time in Egyptian history, a member of the Muslim Brotherhood held the presidency of the country. The development from a tiny religious association to a powerful political party seemed at its successful end. Yet Mursi's time in office only lasted for a year. On July 3, 2013, the Egyptian military ended the political advancement of the Brotherhood by a coup. Since the presidential elections of 2014, the country has been ruled by Abdel Fattah al-Sisi, the officer behind the coup against Mursi. The Brotherhood is once again experiencing massive state repression. While the Egyptian military re-established its political role by force, the Turkish armed forces today have apparently lost their vanguard role in a long historical process rich in conflicts between secularist and Islamist social forces. In the political framework of Turkey's post-Second World War multiparty system, a rising "counter elite" challenged Kemalist modernity in the form of an alternative project with references to Islam.[69] In 2002, the political wing of this social movement, the Justice and Development Party (AKP), eventually assumed power. The AKP combines the authoritarian-minded and state-centered Turkish nationalist heritage of the Kemalist movement with the discourse of Islamic modernity. From the 1970s until the AKP came to power, Necmettin Erbakan (1926–2011) and his political parties represented the Islamic political discourse in Turkey. First as prime minister and then as president, Recep Tayyip Erdoğan, representing the AKP, took over this political legacy from Erbakan, who was only able to assume premiership for a short period in 1996–97.[70] Once in power, Erdoğan and the AKP succeeded in subsequently undermining the social and political power of the military, which finally lost its dominant role in Turkish politics after the abortive military coup against Erdoğan in July 2016. Since then, an explicitly Turkish version of the Islamic discourse of modernity has achieved relative supremacy—though heavily contested—in the political life of the Turkish Republic.[71]

This chapter's two case studies underpin my argument about the rise of a specific Islamic discourse of modernity during the twentieth century. Both the successful coup in Egypt and the abortive military intervention in Turkey perfectly illustrate this claim. In Egypt, the armed forces could only counter the claim to political leadership of the Muslim Brotherhood by military force. In Turkey, military control over the state was eventually replaced by a civilian government willing to compromise some of the secularist features of the republic. To be sure, the contemporary hegemony of Islamic imaginations of modernity in these two cases is not without public contestation. The two case studies, therefore, also represent the factual but conflictual co-existence of Islamic and secular-nationalist projects of modernity among Muslims at the same time. Even more important, the histories of Kemalism and of the Muslim Brotherhood movement perfectly show that the successes and failures of such projects heavily depend on their specific historical and social contexts. Nevertheless, at this point of time, Islamic projects of modernity can apparently muster a majority of support among both the Egyptian and the Turkish population. Even the Egyptian regime under Sisi, like those of Presidents Anwar El Sadat (1970–81) and Hosni Mubarak (1981–2011) before him, has partly submitted to the discursive pressure of the Islamic discourse of modernity with respect to its rhetoric and public appearances.

Finally, these two case studies also have some theoretical implications. First of all, they show the framing of Muslim modernities by more globally relevant patterns of modernity. With their origins in the interwar period of the twentieth century, both Turkey's secular-nationalist movement and the Egyptian Muslim Brotherhood built on the then-prevalent ideas of an organized type of society. Hasan al-Banna's Islamic system and Atatürk's republicanism were firmly anchored in the organizational and institutional templates of their time. In this sense, they represent particular forms of the historical articulation of global modernity. The conceptual ideals of Wagner and Reckwitz serve as instruments for detecting this differentiation between the universal and the particular very well. Second, the Egyptian Brotherhood and the Turkish National Movement are modern organizations mediating between the systemic and the individual levels of modernity.

According to Luhmann, modern organizations generalize motivation and action through membership. In this way, they guarantee specific modes of behavior for the partial inclusion of social actors in the functional realms of world society, yet without reflecting these social functions adequately. Social functions cannot be delegated to organizations in general.[72] The shift of the Muslim Brotherhood from a benevolent religious association to a religio-political organization illustrates this theoretical assumption. We can interpret the internal tension of the movement, its oscillation between religion and politics, as an expression of this only partial inclusion of their members in one or the other communicative system. Lastly, at least on the meso level of social organizations, we can therefore observe the relative dominance of specific forms of functional communication. The autopoiesis of function systems does not apply to other social systems such as institutions, movements, or organizations. In the modern social boundary negotiations on the meso level, we can discern a continuing struggle for supremacy of different forms of communication. The two case studies are thereby paradigmatic for the shifting boundary demarcations between religion and politics. In both cases we can observe that the closer the association with the institution of the modern state, the more it is political communication that dominates religion. In the following two chapters, I will take up boundary negotiations between Islam and science, as well as Islam and economics. If we put on Luhmann's conceptual glasses, in both cases we will observe similar struggles of communicative supremacy in which religion—in vain—wants to assume dominance over the two other modern function systems.

Notes

1. A *gecekondu* is a squatter settlement, and the name indicates that its houses have been erected "overnight," thereby enabling the authorities to move its squatters out by force. Since 1945, Turkish cities have faced a dramatic growth in population, with many new residents finding their homes in a *gecekondu*, see: Wedel, Heidi. 1996. Binnenmigration und ethnische Identität—Kurdinnen in türkischen Metropolen. *Orient* 37 (3): 437-452.
2. See my discussion of this process of Sunnitization in Chapter Three.
3. Mustafa Kemal adopted the surname Atatürk ("father of the Turks") after the name law of 1924. I use the names Mustafa Kemal and Atatürk throughout this text interchangeably and not in following the historically correct chronology. İsmet Pasha adopted the surname İnönü too. The surname alludes to the battles of İnönü under the War of Independence.

4. Hourani, Albert. 1962. *Arabic Thought in the Liberal Age 1798-1939*. Cambridge: Cambridge University Press, 161.
5. Adams, Charles C. 1933. *Islam and Modernism in Egypt: A Study of the Modern Reform Movement Inaugurated by Muhammad Abduh*. London: Oxford University Press, 252.
6. 'Arafāt, 'Alā' al-Dīn. 2001. *Al-alaqāt al-maṣriyya al-faransiyya min al-taʿāwun ilā al-tawāṭū 1906–1923* (The Egyptian-French Relations from Cooperation to Agreement 1906–1923). Cairo: Al-Arabi, 413.
7. Hourani 1962, 189.
8. For an informative overview on the history and understanding of the Islamic Caliphate, see the anthology: Al-Rasheed, Madawi, Carool Kersten, and Marat Shterin (eds.). 2015. *Demystifying the Caliphate: Historical Memory and Contemporary Contexts*. Oxford: Oxford University Press.
9. These two sociologists will appear again in chapter seven of this book when discussing boundary negotiations between Islam and economics.
10. Ryzova, Lucie. 2014. *The Age of Efendiyya: Passages to Modernity in National-Colonial Egypt*. Oxford: Oxford University Press.
11. Ibid. 4–11.
12. Ibid. 9.
13. Ibid. 176.
14. Ibid. 21.
15. Ibid. 242.
16. Ibid. 23.
17. Reckwitz derives his cultural types from empirical data that was collected with regard to historical developments in Europe and North America. Yet he does not claim that the applicability of his conceptualization of modern subject formation would not be possible outside the "West."
18. Therefore, it comes as no surprise to read in a footnote of Ryzova's book that "there was a substantial overlap between the Muslim Brotherhood and the Communists in terms of their analysis of the ills of the Egyptian society, as well as their social appeal and following" (Ryzova 2014, 77, fn. 67).
19. I discussed these images of Atatürk in more detail in a book chapter: Jung, Dietrich. 2018. The Multiple Faces of Mustafa Kemal Atatürk: Authority, Iconography, and Subjectivity in Modern Turkey. In *Reframing Authority: The Role of Media and Materiality*. Edited by Laura Feldt and Christian Høgel. Sheffield: Equinox 207–228.
20. Ryzova 2014, 19, argues that the Egyptian state played this role in the evolution of the efendi class.

21. Cf. Jung, Dietrich and Kirstine Sinclair. 2015. Multiple Modernities, Modern Subjectivities and Social Order: Unity and Difference in the Rise of Islamic Modernities. *Thesis Eleven* 130 (1): 22–42, 29.
22. Mitchell, Richard P. 1969. *The Society of the Muslim Brothers*. London: Oxford University Press, at 5.
23. Al-Banna, Hasan. 2013. *Mudhakirāt al-daʿwa wal-dāʿiyya*. Cairo: Dār al-kalimah, 91–97.
24. Ibid. 40–42.
25. Cf. Ryzova 2014, 174.
26. Itzshak Weismann argued that it was this idea of Islamic mission (*daʿwa*) that was at the heart of the ideological make-up of the Muslim Brotherhood and not the concept of jihad as so prominently contended in the current debate about Islamist movements. Weismann, Itzshak. 2015. Framing a Modern Umma. The Muslim Brothers' Evolving Project of Da'wa. *Sociology of Islam* 3: 146–169.
27. Ibid. 148
28. Krämer, Gudrun. 2010. *Hasan al-Banna*. Oxford: One World, 16.
29. Banna 2013, 67.
30. Haddad, Mahmoud. 1997. Arab Religious Nationalism in the Colonial Era: Rereading Rashid Rida's Ideas on the Caliphate. *Journal of the American Oriental Society* 117 (2): 253–266, 256.
31. Krämer 2010, 114.
32. Mitchell 1969, 201.
33. Jung, Dietrich and Ahmed Abu El Zalaf. 2022. Islamic Politics of Imagination: The Case of the Muslim Brotherhood. In *Debating Imaginal Politics: Dialogues with Chiara Bottici*. Edited by Suzi Adams and Jeremy C. A. Smith. London: Rowman & Littlefield, 121–142, 133.
34. Weismann, Itzshak. 2017. A Perverted Balance: Modern Salafism between Reform and Jihad. *Die Welt des Islams* 57: 33–66, 48.
35. Hourani 1962, 360.
36. Mitchell 1969, 211.
37. Rogan, Eugene. 2009. *The Arabs: A History*. London: Penguin books, 167.
38. Marsont, Afaf Lutfi al-Sayyid. 2007. *A History of Egypt: From the Arab Conquest to the Present*. Cambridge: Cambridge University Press, 105. For a comprehensive study on the failure of Egyptian liberalism, see: Maghraoui, Abdeslam M. 2006. *Liberalism without Democracy: Nationhood and Citizenship in Egypt 1922–1936*. Durham, NC and London: Duke University Press.
39. Jung, Dietrich. 2011. *Orientalists, Islamists and the Global Public Sphere: A Genealogy of the Modern Essentialist Image of Islam*. Sheffield: Equinox, 81–93.

40. Al-Banna, Hasan. 2011. *Mushkilatunā fī ḍaw' al-nizām al-islamī (nizām al-ḥukm)* (Our Problematic in Light of the Islamic System (The System of Governance). Cairo: Muasasat Iqraa, 5.
41. Abdel Halim, Mahmoud. 2013. *Al-ikhwān al-muslimīn, aḥdāth ṣana'at al-tārīkh, ru'yā min al-dākhil* (The Muslim Brotherhood, Events that Shaped the History, a View from Inside). (vols. I–III). Alexandria: Dār al-Da'wa, 245; Zaki, Muhammad Shawqi. 1954. *Al-ikhwān al-muslimīn fī al-mujtama' al-miṣrī* (The Muslim Brotherhood in the Egyptian Society). Cairo: Dār al-'ahd al-Jadīd, 107–108.
42. Al-Banna, Hasan. 2004. *Majmu'āt rasā'il al-imām al-shahīd Hasan al-Banna* (The Collection of Epistels of the Imam and Martyr Hasan al-Banna). Beirut: Al-Islamiyyah, 119.
43. Zalaf, Ahmed Abou El. 2019. Det specielle apparat hos det Muslimiske Broderskab. *Babylon—Nordisk Tidskrift for Midtøstenstudier* 17 (1): 8–17; Zalaf, Ahmed Abou El. 2022. The Special Apparatus (*al-Nizam al-Khass*): The Rise of Nationalist Militancy in the Ranks of the Egyptian Muslim Brotherhood. *Religions* 13 (77): 1–18. For a comprehensive study on the repression of the Brotherhood under Nasser, see: Zalaf, Ahmed Abou El. 2023. *The Muslim Brotherhood and State Repression in Egypt: A History of Secrecy and Militancy in an Islamist Organization*. London: Bloomsbury.
44. This paragraph is based on Jung and Sinclair 2015, 34. Cristopher Bayly's book I discussed briefly in Chapter Two.
45. In May 1931, the third congress of the Republican Peoples Party adopted six principles of Kemalist ideology that since then are symbolized by six arrows in the party's emblem: nationalism, populism, republicanism, revolutionism, secularism, and statism. In February 1937, these principles then were incorporated in the Turkish constitution. Jung and Piccoli 2001, 75.
46. Jung, Dietrich. 2006. "Secularism": A Key to Turkish Politics. *Intellectual Discourse* 14 (2): 129–154, 134.
47. The Ottoman Sultanate was abolished after a contentious debate and vote on November 2, 1922, and "astounded Muslims within the former Ottoman realms and outside." In his speech to the Grand National Assembly, Atatürk declared the sultan "a traitor to the nation, its people, and to Islam." Provence, Michael. 2017. *The Last Ottoman Generation and the Making of the Modern Middle East*. Cambridge: Cambridge University Press, 140.
48. Jung, Dietrich and Wolfango Piccoli. 2001. *Turkey at the Crossroads: Ottoman Legacies and a Greater Middle East*. London: zed books, 60–61.

49. According to the Turkish Historical Thesis, the original Turks were forced by natural disasters to leave Central Asia, migrating to different parts of the world. The thesis describes the Hittites and Sumerians as predecessors of the Anatolian Turks, drawing a line of historical continuity between them and the nationalism of the Turkish Republic. The Sun Language Theory underpins this historical thesis in defining "ancient pure Turkish" as the origin of many other languages and of clear distinctions to Middle Eastern and Islamic cultures. Alici, D. M. 1996. The Role of Culture, History and Language in Turkish National Identity Building: An Overemphasis on Central Asian Roots. *Central Asian Survey* 15 (2): 217–231. Both theses are perfect examples for what Hobsbawm and Ranger described as the nationalist "invention of traditions," see: Hobsbawm, Ernest and Terence O. Ranger (eds.). 1992. *The Invention of Tradition.* Cambridge: Cambridge University Press.
50. The *misbaḥa* is the Islamic string of prayer beads counted while praying.
51. Abdel Aziz, Jumʿah Amin. (ed.) 2006. *Min turāth al-imām al-Banna: Al- daʿwa wa al- ḥukūmāt wa al-hayʾāt (From the Heritage of Imam al-Banna: Missions, Governments and Institutions).* Port Said: dār al-tawzīʿ wa al-nashr al- islāmiyyah, 174–175.
52. These ambiguous and shifting responses call for a longer footnote on this subject. The Indian Khilafat movement, founded in 1919, honored Atatürk, for instance, with the title "The Sword of Islam," and the Indian reformer Muhammad Iqbal praised Mustafa Kemal and the Turkish national movement in his poems; Aydin, Cemil. 2007. *The Politics of Anti-Westernism in Asia: Visions of World Order in Pan-Islamic and Pan-Asian Thought.* New York: Columbia University Press, 137. However, the movement's decisively Islamic origin and linkage to the Ottoman Caliphate as a renewed symbol of identity and pan-Islamic solidarity made it factually incompatible with Atatürk's nationalist movement in the long run. A more ambiguous picture of the relationship between the Turkish nationalist movement and the Khilafat, therefore, is presented by: Trivedi, Raj Kumar. 1981. Mustafa Kemal and the Indian Khilafat Movement (to 1924). *Proceedings of the Indian History Congress* 42: 458–467. See also: Malik, Jamal. 2020. *Islam in South Asia: Revised, Enlarged and Updated Second Edition.* Leiden: Brill, 438–445. The ambivalence of Muslim activists regarding the establishment of the Turkish Republic is further documented in the contradictory standpoint of Rashid Rida, who politically supported the new Turkish government, and the deposition of the Ottoman dynasty yet completely rejected the secularist way of governance that the new regime in Ankara adopted, see: Wood, Simon. 2019.

Reforming Muslim Politics: Rashid Rida's Visions of Caliphate and Muslim Independence. *Journal of Religion & Society* (Supplement 18): 63–78. In his study on Sati al-Husri (1880–1968), William Cleveland reported on the high praise and admiration the Arab nationalist had for Atatürk's conduct of the war and that he even approved of the abolition of the Islamic caliphate, Cleveland, William L. 1971. *The Making of an Arab Nationalist: Ottomanism and Arabism in the Life and Thought of Sati al-Husri*. Princeton: Princeton University Press, 116. In his book on Shakib Arslan, however, Cleveland described this Arab nationalist as an ardent opponent of Atatürk and the Turkish Nationalist Movement that undermined Arslan's own kind of pan-Islamic nationalist ideology; Cleveland, William L. 1985. *Islam against the West: Shakib Arslan and the Campaign for Islamic Nationalism*. London: Al Saqi Books. Generally speaking, the initial Muslim and Arab appreciation of Mustafa Kemal Atatürk's role at the end of the First World War only gradually shifted toward a pejorative image of the Turkish leader after the abolition of the caliphate. In Egyptian newspapers, temporal political power was only associated with the sultanate, and there was no consensus of opinion about the right place for the Caliphate within the global Muslim community. Yet increasingly the Egyptian press discussed the Kemalist revolution more critically, see: Hattemer, Richard. 1997. *Atatürk und die türkische Reformpolitik im Spiegel der ägyptischen Presse*. Berlin: Klaus Schwarz Verlag; and Hattemer, Richard. 1999. Atatürk and the Reforms in Turkey as Reflected in the Egyptian Press. *Journal of Islamic Studies* 11 (1): 21–42.
53. Heper, Metin. 1981. Islam, Polity and Society in Turkey: A Middle Eastern Perspective. *Middle East Journal* 35 (3): 346–363, 350.
54. Ahmad, Feroz. 1993. *The Making of Modern Turkey*. London: Routledge, 52.
55. Stirling, Paul. 1958. Religious Change in Republican Turkey. *Middle East Journal* 12 (4): 395–408, 400.
56. At Lausanne, İsmet İnönü was the chief negotiator of the Turkish Nationalist Movement. In the War of Independence, he was a leading officer and deputy to Atatürk. In abandoning claims to speak in the name of the Arab population of the empire, he emphasized the right of the Kurdish- and Turkish-speaking people of Anatolia to political self-determination. Provence 2017, 149–150.
57. Although I use here the term "revolution," we should not understand Kemalism as a "radical rupture with the Ottoman past." Hanioğlu, Şükrü M. 2011. *Atatürk: An Intellectual Biography*. Princeton: Princeton University Press, 227.
58. Mardin, Şerif. 1971. Ideology and Religion in the Turkish Revolution. *International Journal of Middle East Studies* 2: 197–211, 201.

59. Atatürk was profoundly influenced by the thought of Ziya Gökalp. However, he did not follow the Islamic modernism of Gökalp, who promoted a form of Turkified Islam as a means of social cohesion and authentic reforms. See: Hanioğlu 2011, 62–67. There is not enough room here to look more closely at the relationship between the thinking of Atatürk and Gökalp. I dealt more with it in Jung and Piccoli 2001, 61 and 178.
60. Macfie, A. L. 1994. *Atatürk*. London and New York: Longman, 34.
61. Regarding the end of the Ottoman Empire, see also my references to the Ottoman–German jihad in Chapter Eight.
62. Zürcher, Jan Erik. 1993. *Turkey: A Modern History*. Reprint 1998. London: I. B. Tauris, 139.
63. Jung and Piccoli 2001, 59–65.
64. Zürcher, Jan Erik. 2012. In the name of the Father, the Teacher, and the Hero: The Atatürk Personality Cult in Turkey. In *Political Leadership, Nation and Charisma*. Edited by Vivian Ibrahim and Margret Wunsch. London and New York: Routledge, 129–142.
65. Cf. Jung, 2018.
66. Foucault, Michel. 1977. *Discipline and Punish: The Birth of the Prison*. London: Penguin.
67. The planning and building of the Kocatepe Mosque that I mentioned in the introduction to this chapter can be seen as a step in this process.
68. Cf. Birand, Mehmet A. 1991. *Shirts of Steel: An Anatomy of the Turkish Armed Forces*. London: I. B. Tauris. For İsmet İnönü, see: Heper, Metin. 1998. *İsmet İnönü: The Making of a Turkish Statesman*. Leiden: Brill. A brief analysis on the economic role of the Turkish Armed Forces is provided by: Parla, Taha. 1998. Mercantile Militarism in Turkey: 1960–1998. *New Perspectives on Turkey* 19: 29–52.
69. Göle, Nilüfer. 1997. Secularism and Islamism in Turkey: The Making of Elites and Counter-Elites. *Middle East Journal* 51 (1): 46–58.
70. In 1996, Erbakan became Turkish prime minister in a coalition government of his Welfare Party with the True Path Party under Tansu Çiller. In the so-called 28 February Process, the Turkish military gradually put pressure on Erbakan in a carefully calibrated campaign which led to his stepping down after a meeting of the National Security Council on February 28, 1997. In Turkish history, this process was labelled a "postmodern coup"; Jung and Piccoli 2001, 96–97.
71. Similar to the extraordinary presidential power of Atatürk, Erdoğan tries to control the legislative, executive, and judicial powers of the country and considers

parliamentarism a means rather than an end in itself. Cf. Hanioğlu 2011, 115–117.
72. Luhmann, Niklas. 2008. *Die Moral der Gesellschaft*. Frankfurt am Main: Suhrkamp, 214–221.

PART III

SCIENCE, ECONOMICS, AND AGENCY IN THE ISLAMIC DISCOURSE OF MODERNITY

6

BOUNDARY NEGOTIATIONS BETWEEN ISLAM AND SCIENCE: THE ISLAMIZATION OF KNOWLEDGE AND THE IDEA OF AN ISLAMIC UNIVERSITY

On a foggy morning in December 2008, we left New Delhi en route to the city of Kol, better known as Aligarh. Our destination was the Aligarh Muslim University. The university's Centre of West Asian Studies had invited my PhD student Luke Patey and myself to give talks in its "Extra Mural Lectures" series. An Indian friend of mine organized a taxi ride for the roughly 150 km through the densely populated countryside southeast of Delhi.[1] This journey turned out to be a very long and rather tough ride, living up to all the clichés of Indian road traffic. With a little less than a million inhabitants, Aligarh is a "minor" provincial town in Uttar Pradesh. Yet for me, giving a lecture there was a kind of historically grounded event. The Aligarh Muslim University was formally established in 1920. Today an Indian national university, it is the successor of the Muhammadan Anglo-Oriental College once founded by Sayyid Ahmad Khan in 1875. The college was one of the core projects of Islamic modernity in India. The tomb of the famous Indian reformer is on campus. Lecturing at Aligarh, therefore, was in some way a journey back to the foundational scene of Islamic modernism. Walking through its red entrance gate almost felt like a time machine bringing me into contact with the boundary negotiations between Islam and science of the late nineteenth century.

Today, the Aligarh Muslim University caters for almost 40,000 students in thirteen faculties. It states its mission as being "a leading and vibrant institution of excellence in teaching, research and innovation." The purpose of the university is to contribute to the achievement of "the national goals of a self-reliant, technologically strong and modern India."[2] In contemporary Indian university life, the Islamic background of the Aligarh Muslim University is not prominently displayed. Yet for its founder, Ahmad Khan, the Muhammadan Anglo-Oriental College was the central means for the advancement of learning and knowledge among the higher class of North Indian Muslims.[3] To a certain extent, Sayyid Ahmed Khan epitomizes the theme of this chapter. He represents both an advocate of a specific kind of Islamization of knowledge and a precursor for the establishment of explicitly modern Islamic educational institutions. In the words of Zaituna Umer, Ahmad Khan was a complex personality driven by "an overriding concern with education."[4] Similar to Muhammad Abduh in Egypt, Ahmad Khan placed education at the heart of his Islamic reform agenda. However, his reconstruction of Islamic traditions along the lines of modern rationalism had already begun about twenty years earlier than Muhammad Abduh's reform activities.[5] The intellectual thought of Ahmad Khan is a genuine expression of nineteenth-century Islamic modernism deeply rooted in a specifically Muslim experience of modernity.[6]

In his search for "true Islam," Ahmad Khan put a very strong emphasis on science and education.[7] In the late 1840s, he still defended the geocentric Ptolemean worldview according to which the earth is stationary with the heavenly bodies circling around it.[8] When he eventually converted to the Copernican system and popularized it in public, he was subjected to heavy attacks from his Muslim compatriots. It was in this conflict-laden situation that Ahmad Khan "first developed his mature conception of the scientific method and its relationship to Islam."[9] In the 1870s, he elaborated in more detail on the reconciliation of the evidence of the Qur'an with the Copernican worldview. Ahmad Khan considered scientific truth as subject to change in theories and methods, whereas the Qur'anic revelation remains over time, if only interpreted in a correct and thus historically contextualized way.[10] Consequently, "the laws of nature are the material artifacts of God's creative activity."[11] However, "whenever the natural laws and the statements of the Qur'an appear to contradict each other, the Qur'anic statement must be interpreted allegorically."[12] Consequently, Ahmad Khan considered science and religion to be "totally different subjects."[13] True Islam, according to him, provides a holistic perspective on the otherwise fragmented experiences of social life and the disparate elements of knowledge. In Ahmad Khan's reformist reading, this unifying power of Islam is the sound meaning of the religious term *tawḥīd* that has often been narrowly misconceived as the mere unicity of God.[14]

Sayyid Ahmad Khan's search for the reconciliation of revealed knowledge with modern science falls within a century in which we can observe the accelerated differentiation of science as a subsystem of modern society. The nineteenth century was a period of the multiplication, deepening, and dissemination of modern bodies of knowledge.[15] This applies not only to Europe, but to the world as a whole. The prototype of the modern university as core institution of the modern scientific system was founded in Berlin in 1810.[16] This institutional blueprint of the modern university spread over the globe in the second half of the nineteenth century.[17] It was this concept of the modern university that inspired Ahmad Khan to found the Muhammadan Anglo-Oriental College in Aligarh.[18] Science and education were also major issues in the reform efforts of nineteenth-century Islamic reformers in the Middle East and their confrontation with the activities of Christian missionaries.[19] In their engagement with modern science, however, Muslim intellectuals in India and the Middle East could authoritatively relate to their indigenous roots. In the centuries between 800 and 1500 CE, scholars in Baghdad, Bukhara, Cairo, Cordova, Damascus, Nishapur, and Samarqand were the "uncontested leaders in science."[20] This "golden age" of Islamic or Arabic science was an important precursor to the modern system of science.[21]

Against this background, the purpose of this chapter is twofold. First, I will present modern science and education as social systems and as global cultural institutions. In this part, I draw theoretically from Niklas Luhmann's Modern Systems Theory and the Stanford School on Sociological Institutionalism. Then, I move on to argue that the golden age of Arabic science represents a period of preadaptive advances toward the modern system of science. In this period, we can already detect boundary negotiations between emerging systems of religion, science, and education, at least when we apply the certainly anachronistic lenses of Modern Systems Theory to this premodern age. Consequently, we can find in Islamic history indigenous roots on the path toward modern science. Therefore, in terms of modern science, we should not perceive modernity as a merely European invention. Second, I look more closely at attempts to make science Islamic. I selectively discuss different approaches to the diverse ideological streams of the Islamization of knowledge as inherent parts of the Islamic discourse of modernity. I understand these ideologies as both attempts to establish the social priority of religion over science and to make modern science Islamically authentic. First, I deal with Said Nursi's (1878–1960) project of reconciling science and religion, which the Kurdish religious thinker launched against the secularist educational policies of republican Turkey. Then, I move on to the Shiite Iranian scholar Seyyed Hossein Nasr and his anti-modernist mission of reinventing sacred Islamic science in the ideological context of Traditionalism.[22] Both thinkers pursue different but influential kinds of Islamization of knowledge. Finally, I look at the institutionalization of some of the ideas of the Islamization of knowledge movement, which was launched at the First World Conference of Muslim Education at Mecca in 1977. In so doing, my specific focus is on the example of the International Islamic University Malaysia (IIUM). I will conclude with the thesis that we can interpret the problems which these attempts at an Islamization of knowledge face by applying Luhmann's concept of the "operational closure of modern social systems."

Modern Systems of Science and Education: Luhmann and the Stanford School

For the scholars of the Stanford School on Sociological Institutionalism, science is a core cultural model of world society.[23] Since the nineteenth century, thus the thesis of the school, models for science and education have become essential meta-frames of world culture.[24] The expansion of higher education is a global pattern for achieving social progress that is visible in all developmental ideologies.[25] Indeed, the examples of Sayyid Ahmad Khan and Muhammad Abduh clearly show the ways in which the modernist ideology of Islamic reform was animated by these global cultural models. In this process, the global spread of science and education has occurred in the context of the diffusion of two other world cultural institutions: the modern national state and the modern individual based on the idea of the sovereignty of social actorhood.[26] Meyer and his colleagues argue further that modern science is "serving some of the same functions as religion and partially replacing it."[27] In Luhmann's terms, science and religion became autonomous social systems through centuries-long boundary negotiations and specific forms of operational closure.

As a "generalized cognitive cultural model," the sociological institutionalists consider modern science as being organized according to globally acknowledged categories, models, standards, and forms of communication.[28] Historically, the Stanford School argues that scientific expansion occurred first in the West as a Europewide phenomenon with "deep cultural roots in Western visions of universalism and rationalism."[29] Therefore, the scholars around John Meyer keep "Western science sharply distinct from non-Western, premodern, or indigenous knowledge systems."[30] The school holds that the institutionalization of science on a global level became organized in industrialized Western nations. According to the institutionalist approach of the Stanford School, contemporary variations of global science are defined as different "styles of science" which nevertheless all closely reflect the general organizational features of the global cultural model of science.[31]

I largely agree with this description of the globally relevant general features of modern science and education. Yet I strongly question the Eurocentric and historically myopic narrative of the emergence of these features as put forward by the Stanford School. What is labeled "Western science" in its institutionalist parlance is historically the product of long-lasting, multifaceted, and extremely complex cultural interactions. And in these interactions, Arabic science played a significant role.[32] Thus, many of the meanwhile global patterns of modern science, such is my argument, were already visible in its infancy during the golden age of Arabic science. Of course, these patterns had not yet developed into globally dominant institutional features before the nineteenth and twentieth centuries; and it was at some places in Europe that they were reinvented and institutionalized. As mentioned before, the establishment of modern universities, combining scientific research with higher education, is historically a very recent development. This becomes evident in Meyer's statistical data about university enrolments over time. While the number of students at university around the year 1900 amounted to about half a million worldwide, it had reached a hundred million in 2000.[33] Modern science and higher education were not firmly established institutions of world society before the twentieth century. Yet the evolution of scientific communication has been an older, cross-cultural, and therewith emergent global process without a single origin. The emergence and evolution of modern science is a true instance of entangled modernities.[34]

According to the Modern Systems Theory of Niklas Luhmann, the rise of scientific communication is the evolutionary result of a specific kind of second-order observation based on the binary distinction between true and untrue.[35] This code remains universal in the sense of being applicable to all experiences and observations. These also comprise human action, however, not in the sense of the appropriate selection of specific forms of action. The distinction between true and untrue is not attributed to the observers themselves. The scientific code does not serve selective processes in a normative sense, but it provides a means for the expansion of the possibilities of the dissolution and recombination of experiences. Scientific knowledge, therefore, appears as a product of analysis and synthesis. Through this specific form of operational closure, the scientific system has gradually differentiated itself from religious and moral communications.[36] Empirically, we can observe this separation as a historical process of the differentiation between revealed knowledge and scientific knowledge, an intense boundary negotiation between faith and truth. This boundary negotiation was part of the intellectual deliberations of both the golden age of Arabic science and the history of Islamic reform. The distinction between divine and human knowledge, for instance, entered the thought of Thomas Aquinas (1225–74) through the translated writings of Ibn Sina (980–1037), the Persian medic, philosopher, and Islamic theologian in Europe better known under his Latin name Avicenna.[37]

Following Modern Systems Theory, the scientific code of true/untrue creates a state of permanent uncertainty. This state of uncertainty generates the internal differentiation of science into different programs defined as theories and methods. New theories and methods cope with the persistent contingency of scientific knowledge production.[38] In this sense, the evolution of modern science feeds into the experience of modern contingency that I already discussed in chapter two. In historical terms, scholarly writing and academic publications guarantee the autopoietic reproduction of scientific communication across time and space, representing both production and depiction of scientific knowledge.[39] Moreover, scientific programs shape a structure of horizontal differentiation in terms of disciplinary subsystems of science that are oriented toward internally constructed problems.[40] In the modern university system, these disciplinary subsystems are established in scientific departments and different faculties. In higher education, they appear in form of specific curricula and educational paths. In this way, internal differentiation does not occur as a kind of decomposition of the system. Instead, it takes place in processes of the splitting off and formation of new disciplines.[41] The emergence of each new form demands prior developments, which appear in Luhmann's theory as preadaptive advances.[42] I turn now toward early appearances of modern scientific communication, this is to say to preadaptive advances in science, during the golden age of Arabic science.

Preadaptive Advances to Modernity: Scientific Communication in the Golden Age of Arabic Science

Jim al-Khalili begins chapter twelve of his *House of Wisdom* with a quotation from Abu Rayhan al-Biruni (973–1048). Coming from a Persian-Shiite background, Biruni was a typical polymath of the golden age of Arabic science. In retrospect, he is known among other things as an astronomer, encyclopedist, geographer, historian, mathematician, pharmacist, philosopher, and physician.[43] In the quote, Biruni poses a question about the benefits of these "natural" sciences solely pursued by men. He concludes that science is a peculiar human activity conducted only for its own sake.[44] In Niklas Luhmann's conceptional language, Biruni thereby considers science to be a form of "self-referential communication." With this quote as his starting point, Jim al-Khalili describes the relationship between Biruni and his contemporary Ibn Sina, who represents another famous scholar of the golden age. In his *Canon of Medicine*, Ibn Sina combined the medical knowledge of Greek, Indian, and Persian origins with his own intellectual thought. In this way, he produced an academic text "with a shelf life of almost six hundred years.".[45] Furthermore, his synthesis of Greek philosophy with Islamic theology became a "direct and indirect source" for the work of Thomas Aquinas and other Scholastic theologians.[46] In his classic *Introduction to the History of Science*, George Sarton therefore refers to Ibn Sina as "the most famous scientist of Islam and one of the most famous of all races, places, and times.".[47]

A century later, the Andalusian jurist, philosopher, physicist, and theologian Ibn Rushd (1126–98) further enhanced the impact of the Greek–Islamic philosophical synthesis on European thought. In his encyclopedic book,

George Sarton described Ibn Rushd as a giant in philosophy because of his perfect knowledge of Aristotle. In light of and against Ghazali's critique of the Islamic philosophers, Ibn Rushd returned to a purer Aristotelianism of a "positivist" and "scientific" philosophical nature.[48] For Jonathan Lyons, it was in particular this "Arab Aristotle," in Europe known as Averroes, and "not so much the pagan thinker of classical Greece, who ultimately triumphed in the West."[49]

This short historical detour into the life and work of Biruni, Ibn Sina, and Ibn Rushd clearly shows the ways in which these polymaths of Arabic science already distinguished between communicative realms of scientific enquiry and religious beliefs.[50] They were engaged in the crucial boundary demarcation between religion and science. And it was precisely in the context of these intellectual societal negotiations that Abu Hamid al-Ghazali (1058–111) strongly advocated the primacy of religion, accusing philosophy of leaving no room for faith.[51] In his autobiographical *Deliverance from Error*, Ghazali poses the question of the nature of true knowledge.[52] His answer evolves from a discussion of the validity of empirical, philosophical, and revealed knowledge. First, he repudiates knowledge based on experiments and observations and then the philosophical thought of the Muslim philosophers. In the end, it is mystical experience alone that leads him to real truth in the divine revelation.[53] In this autobiographical account, Ghazali's argumentation precisely follows Sarton's formalist definition of Scholastic thought. He first subordinates experience to reason and then reason to faith.[54] Yet in this argumentation, Ghazali also plainly distinguishes between different bodies of knowledge and therewith between scientific and religious communication. Despite the refutation of his critique of the philosophers by Ibn Rushd, the theological position of Ghazali has remained influential in Islamic theological thinking until our days. Even more important, for the conventional historical narrative, the works of Ghazali and his theological successors have been declared responsible for the decline in scientific curiosity and intellectual deliberation in the Muslim regions of the world.[55]

Ghazali's critique of the philosophers plays a crucial role with respect to the boundary negotiations between science and religion of the golden age of Arabic science. Conventionally, this flourishing of Arabic sciences is related to the Abbasid Caliphate (750–1258). It began with the reign of the second

Abbasid Caliph Abu Jafar al-Mansur (754–75 CE), whose court was "surrounded by established centers of Christian, Persian and pagan learning." Moreover, he invited an Indian delegation to Baghdad who brought with them essential texts of Hindu knowledge on astronomy and mathematics, including the Indian decimal system.[56] Baghdad thereby became a hub of scientific activities, and under the rule of Caliph al-Mamun (813–33 CE) its library grew into the "largest repository of books in the world."[57] While Arabic sciences were conducted at many places, the urban intellectual culture of the Abbasid capital Baghdad was at its center for several centuries. Baghdad disposed over a large infrastructure of academies and libraries as well as research and teaching institutions. As early as the eighth century, the population of the Abbasid capital exceeded two million inhabitants.[58] In Islamic cities such as Baghdad, "urban merchants and traders generated the surpluses of cash and leisure time," making possible the scholarly life of authors, booksellers, intellectuals, librarians, and philosophers.[59] Evidently, we can discern there a premodern, nascent infrastructure reminding us of the Stanford School's cultural model of science and higher education. Over centuries, theological, philosophical, and scientific questions were discussed controversially in the intellectual milieu of Baghdad.[60] Moreover, these scientific deliberations combined bodies of knowledge from different world regions. Muslim scholars produced astronomical, historiographical, geographical, and theological literature, as well as handbooks on administrative and political affairs.[61] In short, the Abbasid capital knew early the institutional features of the scientific system.

With a particular emphasis on the field of astronomy, George Saliba therefore suggested granting a more "revolutionary role" to Arabic science in the development of modern science.[62] The classical narrative of Islamic sciences—moving from translation via a golden age into stagnation and decline—meanwhile represents a rather narrow and Euro-centric understanding of the rise of the modern system of science.[63] It is a perfect example for those narratives of modernity that are animated by the idea of—in the words of the historian C. A. Bayly—European exceptionalism. In Saliba's view, the production of scientific knowledge did not face a straight decline with the fall of Abbasid rule. For him, Muslim scholarship did not merely represent a transitory period in the translation and transmission of Greek knowledge to Europe. With their innovative scientific achievements, Arabic-speaking scientists contributed to the development of the global system of science more generally. In fact, according to Saliba, the so-called modern scientific revolution in Europe cannot be separated from its complex entanglement with Asian, Greek, and Islamic cultures of knowledge.[64] Medicine, for instance, was one of the important areas of this entanglement. Medical sciences were considered as a common good (*mushtarak*) and therefore something that communicated "across the religious and military boundaries."[65] When writing the history of science from the perspective of pathbreaking discoveries, a telling case in point is the Arab physician Ibn al-Nafis (1213–288).

The Muslim medical doctor lived and worked in Cairo and Damascus, two cities that replaced Baghdad as the centers of Arab medicine in the tenth and eleventh centuries.[66] In his *Commentary on Anatomy in Avicenna's Canon*, Ibn al-Nafis fundamentally revised the Galen scheme with respect to the pulmonary circulation of the blood. About 300 years before European scholars came to the conclusion that "blood has to pass through the pulmonary circulation and could not move directly from the right to the left ventricle" of the heart, Ibn al-Nafis described this process in his *Commentary*.[67] While there is seemingly evidence for a gradual decline in the relatively open reception and discussion of philosophical and scientific knowledge since Ghazali, it is historically wrong to simply claim a centuries-long stagnation of scientific thought in the Islamic regions of the world. This also applies for the sciences in the Ottoman Empire. The previously entrenched narrative about the alleged "lack of a scientific history" in the Ottoman realm has been increasingly revised in recent decades.[68] Some scholars argue that the culture of science in the empire lived on into the eighteenth century.[69]

In the Arab and Ottoman contexts, however, these boundary negotiations between religion and science never became conclusive before they were sparked anew in the nineteenth century. In etymological terms, this becomes visible in the mere concept of science. Until the nineteenth century, the modern Arabic term for science (*'ilm*) remained a generic and encompassing concept for different bodies of knowledge. This unity of knowledge also appeared in the previously mentioned character of the Arab and Iranian medieval scientists as polymaths. The factual internal division of science into different disciplines and its clear separation from Islamic law and theology, the classical Islamic sciences, was only in the making. This applies also to the institutional features of modern science. The first endeavors to establish modern Ottoman universities, for example, began in 1863, and one of the most conspicuous shortcomings in late Ottoman science was its lack of research.[70] In this sense, the high level attained by Arabic science was a legacy of the past and almost "absent from the modern period."[71] The necessary conversion of Sayyid Ahmad Khan to the Copernican worldview can almost be understood as proof of this verdict.

The debate about the causes for the rise and decline of Arabic science, however, is not what I want to engage in here. I do not intend to replace one narrative by another. My focus is on the differentiation of functionally defined modes of communication and respective preadaptive advances to modern boundary demarcations between science and religion in Islamic history. For me Ghazali's critique is an important intervention in the boundary negotiations between revealed and scientific knowledge, between faith and truth. From a comparative perspective, we can observe in medieval Islamic history similar discussions about the relationship between religious belief and philosophical truth to those in European Scholasticism.[72] In this process, the factual entanglement of Scholastic Christian and Islamic thought is documented in the reception of Ibn Sina and Ibn Rushd in Europe. The philosophers, scientists, and theologians of the golden age of Arabic science and those of medieval Europe were entangled in their premodern boundary negotiations between religion and science.

In the Middle East, this entanglement continued in the nineteenth century but under reversed conditions. Now, the activities of Christian missionaries influenced societal negotiations about religion and science in a Muslim context. These negotiations took place through a kind of "Arabization" of the modern scientific discourse. In contrast to "positivist ideas" of a "universal protocol language" of science, Marwa Elshakry pointed to the "problem of translation."[73] While the modern social subsystem of science rests on an autonomous code of communication, this syntax of modern science has to be translated into the semantics of vernacular languages, which are not neutral with respect to cultural, historical, and social contexts. The eventual translation of modern science into Arabic largely took place in the second half of the nineteenth century, thereby reducing the term *'ilm* to the meaning of science in the modern sense. This process was characterized by "sharper distinctions between sensory or empirical knowledge and matters of belief."[74] It is this reduction of *'ilm* to the "narrow" concept of modern scientific knowledge against which the different protagonists of the Islamization of knowledge have directed their activities. While mostly accepting the achievements of modern science, they promote the reintegration of science and sacredness in an Islamic unity of knowledge.[75] Precisely this aim makes them significant projects in the contemporary discourse of Islamic modernity.

Attempts Toward an Islamization of Knowledge: Said Nursi, Seyyed Hossein Nasr, and the International Islamic University Malaysia (IIUM)

In 1977, the First World Conference on Muslim Education took place in Mecca. The conference stood under the sponsorship of Saudi Arabia's King Abdulaziz University. On the initiative of the former Saudi Minister of Commerce, Sheikh Ahmed Jamjoon (1923–2020), about 350 Muslim scholars participated at the conference with the purpose of addressing the rather depressing status of Muslim education against the background of the "contemporary conditions of life."[76] The Mecca conference's vision of the Islamization of knowledge was supposed to generate a dynamic process in the development of Islamic scholarship "which would lead to the reconstruction of the Islamic world view." In this reconstruction, Islamic knowledge combines both dimensions, revealed perennial knowledge and knowledge acquired through empirical methods.[77] While its origin at this conference in the 1970s testifies to "the novel and modern aspect of the discourse,"[78] the relationship between revealed and scientific knowledge has been a key feature of the discourse of Islamic modernity since its inception. The example of Sayyid Ahmad Khan at the beginning of this chapter and the analysis of the thought of Muhammad Abduh in Chapter Four are only two cases in point for this assumption. Hence, the idea of an Islamization of knowledge has been part and parcel of the attempt "to construct an Islamic version of modernity."[79] In the following two sections, I will first look briefly at two Muslim thinkers who developed their very different ideas about Islamic science independent from the Mecca conference. I begin with the life and work of the Sunni scholar Bediüzzaman Said Nursi (1876/77–1960) from Turkey[80] and then move on to the Shiite philosopher Seyyed Hossein Nasr, who moved from Tehran to the United States. The third section, then, brings up the case of the International Islamic

University Malaysia (IIUM), whose establishment in 1983 is directly linked to the Mecca conference and its educational initiatives.

Making Science Islamic: The Anti-materialist View of Said Nursi

Said Nursi was born in the mid-1870s into a Kurdish family in a small village in the eastern Anatolian province of Bitlis.[81] Conventionally, his biography is divided into the two periods of the old and the new Said. The period of the old Said coincides with the long authoritarian reign of Sultan Abdülhamit II (1876–1909), the Young Turk Revolution (1908), and the following rule of the Committee of Union and Progress (1909–18), as well as the First World War. In this period, Said Nursi studied the classical Islamic sciences at different madrasas and made himself familiar with philosophy and the empirical sciences during his stay in the city of Van. There, the Ottoman governor Tahir Pasha (1898–1906) invited him to move into his residence. It was in the library of Tahir Pasha that Said Nursi immersed himself in the study of a broad range of modern scientific disciplines such as "history, geography, mathematics, geology, physics, chemistry, astronomy, and philosophy."[82] Becoming acquainted with the reformist thoughts of the Young Ottomans and Jamal al-Din al-Afghani, the old Said also combined his search for knowledge with forms of political activism. He supported the ideas of the constitutionalist movement of the Ottoman Empire and propagated educational and constitutional reforms in an Islamic way.[83] One of his own major reform ideas was the establishment of an Islamic university in eastern Anatolia. In November 1907, he went to Istanbul in order to get support for this educational project from the Ottoman government.[84] In his proposal for an Islamic university, Said Nursi suggested combining the traditional institutions of education, the madrasa and the Sufi *takiyya*, with the new secular schools that were established during the Ottoman reform process. In this way, the university proposal reflected his general life-long mission of combining the teaching of religious with modern sciences.[85] In the end, Said Nursi's Islamic university never saw the light of the day, and the new Said continued his mission in a different way.

The new Said emerged from the First World War and the end of the Ottoman Empire. Said Nursi commanded a militia force in eastern Anatolia and went into combat against Russia at the Caucasian front in January 1916. He ended up as a prisoner of war in a Russian detention camp for more than two years, eventually returning to Istanbul through Europe in the spring of 1918.[86] In November 1922, the Grand National Assembly welcomed Said Nursi in Ankara, where he also met with Mustafa Kemal. Unsurprisingly, Nursi's ideas about an Islamic government did not resonate much among the republican nationalists in Ankara. Consequently, he withdrew from the new Turkish capital to Van in April 1923.[87] Until the establishment of the democratically elected government of Adnan Menderes in 1950, the new Said lived a life characterized by "persecution, imprisonment, and displacement to other places where he was kept in enforced residence."[88] In contradistinction to the old Said, the new Said disengaged from political activity and replaced previous tendencies toward an almost arrogant "awareness of his own talents" with personal modesty and the retreat into religious scholarship.[89] Said Nursi dedicated the second part of his life to writing his *risale-i nur*. From the 1920s, Nursi disseminated this blend of Qur'anic truths with modern science "in order to address the mentality of modern man."[90] He replaced instruction from the charismatic religious teacher with the written text, making the message of the Qur'an intelligible to a large audience through accessible language.[91] Written in the language of Turkey's social periphery, his discourse on an Islamic modernity was able to generate a large followership among Muslims in Turkey and beyond.[92] Even more important for this chapter, Said Nursi developed an Islamic sacralization of modern science in which the study of nature acquired "a sacred quality" as a "theophany of God."[93]

Following Bekim Agai's interpretation of Said Nursi's thought, the main purpose of conducting science is to achieve knowledge about the creator. There is no autonomous purpose of science; seeking empirical knowledge is a religious duty.[94] Nursi himself confirms this interpretation throughout his writings. For him, science is worth nothing in itself as it cannot help "on the road to post-eternity."[95] Anyone whose study of science is not in the name of religion is a "self-centered seeker of benefit" and not a sincere student and servant of God.[96] Ultimately, engineering, medicine, and the natural sciences at large are nothing other than worldly manifestations of God.[97] Said Nursi's often allegorical interpretations of scientific findings completely reject the self-referential claims of modern scientific communication. The above quotes combine his condemnation of modern individualism with the reduction of science and education to "footnotes" of the faith.[98] Said Nursi advocated engaging in science as a means of bringing development and progress to the Muslim people, however, only if this was done in accordance with Islamic principles.[99] Science, therefore, is only an instrument for social advancement when clearly subordinated to religion. In his study among German members of the Nurcu movement, Levent Terzan observed this subordination of science to religion. The German followers of Said Nursi consider science to be a tool of belief. They strongly bless science and technology, yet they do so in terms of them giving witness to God on earth.[100] There is no scientific truth outside the eternal truth of the Qur'an.

With this kind of the Islamization of knowledge, Said Nursi and the Nurcu movement became a major force in "the formulation and dissemination of Islamic creationism."[101] Once developed in Turkey in the 1970s, it has meanwhile assumed a broad followership among Muslims in Europe.[102] In his writings, Said Nursi did not address theories of evolution directly. However, he attacked the basic mechanism of self-organization in evolutionary thought. In this way, Nursi opposed the materialist worldview that was widespread among Turkey's Kemalist elite.[103] This is apparent when Nursi writes that philosophy and science "have confused unconscious nature, blind chance, and lifeless causes" with the wise activity of God. Modern sciences without religious motivation are "falling into the darkness of misguidance."[104] In the mind of Said Nursi, explanation of the rules of nature was only acceptable on the premise that there was an "active intelligence" at work in shaping these patterns.[105] While applying the modern cultural models of science and technology as a means of achieving social progress through higher education, Said Nursi, at the same time, rejected the autonomous claims of scientific communication. He wanted to employ the essentially constant uncertainty of modern scientific knowledge in order to confirm eternal truth.

Said Nursi inspired a number of Islamic movements to follow him on his path of the Islamization of knowledge. In arguing for the necessity of a conscious creator, the Nurcu movement, for instance, initiated an Islamic creationist debate, which also plays a role in the religious ideology propagated by Fetullah Gülen. Though not a part of the inner circle of the Nurcu movement,[106] Gülen has advocated a similar synthesis of religion and science, which his followers successfully disseminate throughout social networks and educational institutions around the world.[107] According to one of his biographers, Jon Pahl, Said

Nursi's Qur'an interpretations in the *risale-i nur* were among the central experiences of Gülen's intellectual life, leading him to the promotion of science and technology among pious Muslims.[108] Previously a functionary in the Diyanet, the Turkish State Directorate of Religious Affairs, Gülen became the leader of a globally operating reformist religious movement. In presenting the modern world as being in moral degeneration, Gülen developed a "framework for the engagement of conservative Islamic educators in secular scientific pedagogy" based on Said Nursi's worldview.[109] In 2016, Gülen's Hizmet movement was linked to a network of about 1,200 schools, colleges, and universities in 180 different countries.[110] Since 1999, Fethullah Gülen has been living in exile in the United States.[111] The Turkish President Recep Tayyip Erdoğan made him personally responsible for instigating the failed military coup on July 15, 2016, and has persecuted his followers in Turkey ever since.

The Call for "Islamic Science": The Traditionalist View of Seyyed Hossein Nasr

Said Nursi's writings confront the reader with an often-baffling synthesis of traditional and modernist modes of interpretation. Yet, while Nursi's traditionalism was nevertheless strongly impacted by Ottoman Islamic modernism, Seyyed Hossein Nasr has been following a very different path. In his approach to the Islamization of science, Nasr staunchly rejects modernist ideas. Born in Teheran in 1933, he comes from a family of scholars and physicians that also has a background in Shiite religious studies and Sufism. In his childhood, Nasr not only experienced the Persian school curriculum, but he also encountered the intellectual thought of European and Eastern civilizations. In this regard, he mentions long conversations about religion and philosophy with his father. After having received his primary education in Iran, Nasr moved via Baghdad and Cairo to the United States at the age of twelve. There, he attended high school at The Peddie School, a top-ranked, at that time Baptist, educational institution south of New York.

Nasr described the four and a half years at Peddie as a period in which he felt "full dislocation culturally as well as emotionally." He characterized these years as both "traumatic and very constructive." While at Peddie, he learned about the American way of life, "whose popular aspects" he experienced as completely repulsive.[112] In the summer of 1955, then, Nasr moved to Boston and took up studies in physics at the Massachusetts Institute of Technology (MIT). Through these studies, he aimed at "gaining knowledge about the 'nature of things.'"[113] At MIT, he met prominent scholars such as Robert Oppenheimer (1904–67), Bertrand Russell (1872–1970), and Norbert Wiener (1894–1964), gradually becoming more interested in philosophy and the history of science. Moreover, he made the encounter with the Traditionalist literature of René Guénon (1886–1951), Ananda K. Coomaraswamy (1877–1947), and Fritjhof Schuon (1907–98). The reading of these Traditionalist authors Nasr considered crucial in determining the course of his life.[114] In 1956, he received his MA degree in geology and geophysics from Harvard and now engaged fully in the field of the history of science. When working at the department founded by George Sarton at Harvard, Nasr also traveled through Europe and North Africa, deepening his intellectual contacts with the Francophone world. He finally obtained his PhD in the history of science with an emphasis on Islamic science, philosophy, and technology, eventually returning to Tehran in the fall of 1958.

From 1958 to the Islamic Revolution of 1979, Nasr was Professor of the History of Science and Philosophy in the Faculty of Letters at Tehran University. He also gave lectures at various other Iranian universities as well as on radio and television stations. In terms of research, his publications included a number of monographs in Persian and English and critical editions of the texts of Suhrawardi (1154–1191) and Sadr al-Din Shirazi (1571–1640) and on the exchange of letters between Ibn Sina and Biruni. Moreover, Nasr began to develop a complete biography of the Islamic sciences. In 1973, Seyyed Hossein Nasr was put in charge of establishing an Iranian Academy of Philosophy. Under the patronage of the Empress of Iran, he founded the Imperial Iranian Academy of Philosophy. The academy has continued to work until today, though without maintaining the international character for which it was known under Nasr. In January 1979, Nasr left Iran "for what was intended as a two-week-journey."[115] While staying with his family in London, his house was plundered by a revolutionary mob and his library confiscated, and due to his close association with the Shah and his wife, a return was not considered advisable. After a short period at the University of Utah, Nasr was appointed Professor of Islamic Studies at Temple University before moving on to a chair at George Washington University in 1984.

Seyyed Hossein Nasr has continued his endeavor of an Islamization of knowledge in the USA. His philosophical mission, however, does not aim at a reconciliation of religion and modern science as in Said Nursi's case. On the contrary, Nasr's mission is clearly directed "against the modern world."[116] In his contribution to a commemorative anthology on the South Asian Islamist thinker Ala al-Mawdudi (1903–79), Nasr made this bluntly clear. With reference to the founding father of the Traditionalist movement, René Guénon, he described "modern Western civilization" as an anomaly in human development.[117] According to Nasr, "the curve of life of modern Western civilization . . . has gone from 'renaissance' to deviation to decadence."[118] Only by remaining faithful to the eternal principles of Islam, he concludes, can the present crisis of the modern world can be solved.[119] This book chapter is a manifest of the Traditionalist worldview as so aptly described in Mark Sedgwick's book. In identifying the Orient with tradition and the West with modernity, René Guénon aimed at saving the "West from collapse by means of Oriental tradition."[120] Guénon directed his ideology of orientalism against science, rationalism, and objectivity, basically producing an inverted form of Edward Said's orientalism.[121] At the heart of his ideology is a kind of perennial philosophy according to which all religions/traditions share their origin in a common truth. It is on the negation of this supramundane truth that the modern world and modern science rest.[122]

Hossein Nasr's Islamization of science basically represents Guénon's Traditionalism put into intellectual action. He employs ideas of perennial philosophy in terms of a transhistorical body of knowledge that in principle is the inner core of all religions and traditions.[123] Islam, however, as the last "terrestrial expression of this Truth" is best equipped to remedy the plight in which modern people of both the East and the West must live.[124] Modernity brought "havoc and confusion beyond comparison," and since the Renaissance, modern Western civilization has developed into a "failed experiment."[125] It is Islam, according to Nasr, that inherited perennial knowledge from various previous traditions. Yet in its concept of *tawḥīd* (unity), Islam added to them a very strong unitarian point of view with an immutable and permanent character.[126] From this perspective, Islam and in particular the classical Islamic sciences became the heir to the intellectual heritage of all major civilizations. In Nasr's reasoning, Islam is the last expression of eternal truth. The Islamization of knowledge and science, therefore, is the intellectual campaign against all the vices of modern life to reinstate these eternal truth claims that are an inherent part of civilizational traditions.

In *Science and Civilization in Islam*, Nasr presented his account of the scholars of the Arabic golden age. This book seems to be proof for his "genealogical approach" in which historical figures, the wise men (*ḥukamā'*, sing. *ḥakīm*), appear as "prototypes" for contemporary Muslims. Abu Nasr al-Farabi, al-Biruni, Ibn Sina, Abu Hamid al-Ghazali, and Ibn Rushd are examples for these "universal figures of Islamic science," of which the Prophet Muhammad serves as the ultimate example and role model for humankind.[127] Throughout Islamic history, these wise men transmitted both perennial wisdom and the sciences. They were astronomers, mathematicians, philosophers, physicians, poets, and theologians, but above all they were "sages."[128] Clearly the polymaths of the golden age represent in Nasr's thought the ideal scholars of Islamic science. In his eyes, the unity of the divine principle is the matrix within which these Islamic scholars gave science a meaning.[129] While these Islamic sciences were already distinct from the supreme science of metaphysics, they were still necessarily linked to it in terms of "knowledge pertaining to the manifested and created order."[130] Only in the revitalization of the unity of wisdom and science, in which the Qur'an is "the counterpart to the text of nature" can the sciences be salvaged from the onslaught of Western rationalism. Therefore, the recourse to the classical representatives of Islamic science gives the direction for Nasr's call for the re-establishment of sacred sciences.

In a critical assessment of Nasr's work, Mehdi Aminrazavi characterized him as a metaphysician deeply entrenched in medieval Islamic philosophy.[131] However, it would be a grave mistake to consider Seyyed Hossein Nasr as a thinker of the past. In fact, he combines the world of premodern Islamic traditions with the anti-modernist ideology of twentieth-century Traditionalism. Nasr closely follows the recipe of the French Perennialist René Guénon, who wanted to save "the West from collapse by means of Oriental tradition."[132] He even treated Guénon and his friend the Swiss Frithjof Schuon as "sages" in one line with the figures of Islamic sciences.[133] In Sedgwick's analysis, Nasr connected Traditionalism for the first time with "non-Western" Islamic scholarship and made this anti-modernist ideology of the twentieth century consumable for segments of modern Muslim intellectual life.¹³⁴ In doing so, Nasr's thought largely builds on utterly modern narratives and concepts, clearly taking part in the modern discourse of authenticity. His language combines gnostic and hermetic concepts with the organicist vocabulary of the late nineteenth and early twentieth centuries. His holistic understanding of the world as an "organic totality" has its origins in the culture of modernity rather than in medieval Islamic philosophy. Only in this modern perspective do the Hindu Vedas and the Qur'an appear as foundational texts for the "harmony between the parts and the whole."¹³⁵ Seyyed Nasr implicitly adopts the Eurocentric narrative of the European origin of modernity. He basically confirms the position of the Stanford School, which perceives science as a purely Western invention. Moreover, in his references to premodern traditions, he closely follows the nineteenth-century civilizational discourse about framing Buddhism, Christianity, Hinduism, Islam, Judaism, and Taoism as "world religions."¹³⁶ In this sense, the Traditionalist Seyyed Hossein Nasr is clearly a representative of the Islamic discourse of modernity. His discourse rests on the syntax of modernity though with a strong anti-modernist stance.

Islamic Universities: The Example of the International Islamic University Malaysia (IIUM)

Said Nursi's project of an Islamic university eventually failed, and Seyyed Hossein Nasr has not designed his own version of an Islamic institute of higher education. The ideas of both concerning the Islamization of knowledge, however, have left their traces on contemporary Islamic education. The different branches of the Nurcu movement and in particular the educational network of Fetullah Gülen are obvious examples for the continuing importance of Said Nursi's work. Seyyed Nasr's thought has entered various educational institutions through his own teachings and those of others in "the East and the West." The latter becomes visible in the curricula of Islamic universities with a Traditionalist orientation such as the Cambridge Muslim College in the United Kingdom and the Zaytuna College in the United States.¹³⁷ In this sense, they both take part in and impact on the Islamic discourse of modernity. It was the First World Conference on Muslim Education in Mecca, however, that put a strong emphasis on the foundation of Islamic universities. Unlike either Nursi's or Nasr's visions, the aim of these universities was to combine education in the revealed knowledge of Islam with the study of contemporary acquired sciences.[138] This hybrid nature of fusing a religious institution with the modern university clearly distinguishes this new kind of institution from those forms of Islamic universities that put their focus on religious education alone.

The Islamic University of Medina (IUM), for example, represents such a university. Founded in 1961 as a "missionary venture," the IUM was a project in competition with the Egyptian al-Azhar.[139] IUM, therefore, can be perceived as an institution with the aim of expanding Saudi influence through religious educational means. The focus of its teachings is on classical Islamic sciences such as jurisprudence (*fiqh*), Qur'anic exegesis (*tafsīr*), and theology (*kalām*). Explicitly targeting Muslim students from all over the world, the university's task is to spread conservative religious interpretations in these fields of Islamic science. In the 1960s, the university played an essential part in Saudi Arabia's Islamic "counter-project" against the Arab nationalist politics of Egyptian President Gamal Abd al-Nasser.[140] Since the 1980s IUM has increasingly taught its students in a "Wahhabi"-oriented, Salfi interpretation of the Islamic sciences. Educating young Muslims in the classical Islamic sciences at IUM, therefore, is closely knitted into the geopolitical and the national power context in which the Saudi regime operates.[141]

While political contexts also play a role in the establishment and functioning of the new hybrid Islamic universities, they nevertheless are very different from IUM in their educational content. In the remaining part of this section, I will describe this by taking up the case of the International Islamic University Malaysia (IIUM), whose foundation was closely linked to the Mecca conference. In particular, the educational visions of the Palestinian-American Ismail al-Faruqi (1921–86), the Saudi Abdul Hamid Abu Sulayman (1936–2021), and the Malayan Syed Muhammad Nagib al-Attas (b. 1931) played an important role in the foundational phase of IIUM. While we can still observe the contrasting views of al-Attas and al-Faruqi at work, teaching and research at IIUM are meanwhile dominated by Faruqi's approach. The university largely follows his idea of integrating Islam and modern science instead of the proposition of an alternative form of Islamic science formulated by Attas.[142]

Arriving at Gombak campus in March 2005, I had no doubt that this was an Islamic university. The campus is about twenty kilometers drive from

Kuala Lumpur's city center, and its architecture reminded me of a form of orientalism in stone. A huge mosque with two high and slender minarets and a blue dome dominates the university's faculty buildings, student dormitories, sport complexes, and catering facilities. IIUM disposes over separate prayer rooms for men and women, and every day at noon the campus resounds with the call to prayer. Students and staff appear in modest dress, women wearing a headscarf. Graphical signs such as flyers and posters remind you of this dress code, and Islamic symbolism characterizes the announcement boards. The various food courts on campus offer a broad range of cuisines, all with halal certifications.[143] Moreover, instead of using the term "faculty," the academic units of the university are named by the Arabic word "*kulliyyah*." Teaching, however, is organized in 16 standard faculties of which only one appears to be specifically Islamic, the Kulliyyah of Islamic Revealed Knowledge & Human Sciences.[144] In 2018, IIUM catered for about 26,000 students from 117 countries and gave work to over 2,000 faculty members.[145]

The hybrid character of IIUM is explicitly expressed in the university's mission statement. The university aims at "becoming a leading international centre of educational excellence" by producing "better quality intellectuals, professionals and scholars." This goal is to be achieved by integrating "faith," "knowledge," and "good character," producing a kind of "holistic excellence which is imbued with Islamic moral-spiritual values." IIUM wants to produce young Muslim scholars and professionals "who are motivated by the Islamic world-view" and who will be able "to serve as agents of comprehensive and balanced progress as well as sustainable development in Malaysia and in the Muslim world." The catchwords of the summary of IIUM's mission are: integration, Islamization, internationalization, and comprehensive excellence.[146] According to the Research Management Centre at IIUM, established in 1991, the university aims at promoting "research that seeks to restore the dynamic and progressive role of the Muslim Ummah in all branches of knowledge."[147] The mission statements of IIUM, thus, closely follow the recommendations of the Mecca conference and its propositions for the Islamization of knowledge. At least in a rhetorical fashion, IIUM is organized and works as a modern university under a holistic Islamic umbrella. Yet how are these normative statements put into practice in the daily working routines of the university?

The working conditions at IIUM in both research and teaching are very similar to other universities in Malaysia, characterized by rather low research grants and a relatively heavy teaching load. Given the working load of the staff and the comparatively scarce funding for research, IIUM does not really figure as a research university.[148] A good part of the university's research is published in about twenty academic journals by IIUM Press, some of which are indexed in international databases. Some of these journals, such as *al-Burhan, al-Risalah, Journal of Islamic Finance*, and *Halalsphere*, address specifically Muslim audiences. The journal *Revelation and Science* is directly associated with the Islamization of knowledge project, being "dedicated to the integration of science and religion." The publishing process, however, closely adheres to the standard routines of refereed academic journals. This was at least my impression when publishing an article in the IIUM journal *Intellectual Discourse* and working as a reviewer for it. In the years between 1991 and 2013, the university produced more than 3,000 MA and PhD theses, most of them submitted in English. The majority of these theses present research from an Islamic perspective while simultaneously taking into account local and international scholarship in their literature reviews.[149] In this way, they clearly show efforts in combining Islamic revealed knowledge with international scientific knowledge production.

In terms of teaching, the IIUM wants to provide for its students a "learning ecosystem" that is "founded on the Tawhid."[150] The courses at IIUM fall into four categories: courses with conventional content, courses with a minor integration of Islamic perspectives, courses with a substantial integration of these perspectives, and those with purely Islamic content. There are only a few courses with pure Islamic content, and Psychology appears to be the subject with most substantial integration, with up to about 44 percent of the learning content having an Islamic perspective.[151] In her fieldwork at IIUM, however, Gry Hvass Pedersen came to the conclusion that the university's Islamization policies do "not follow a coherent, uniform approach." While the different study programs all emphasize the university's mission of the Islamization of knowledge, in everyday teaching it is more or less the teachers themselves who decide upon "what the Islamic perspective consists of and how it is interpreted and added to the course."[152] Also, in the seminars I taught at IIUM, I could not detect a specific and uniform kind of Islamic worldview in the discussions with my students. These students represented an extremely mixed group of young Muslims from many countries with apparently different attitudes to practicing their religion. Of course, class discussions put more focus on matters relevant to the Muslim parts of the world, but this should not come as a surprise. Generally speaking, despite very few students trying to play the "Islamic role model," the teaching experience was no different from other places at which I happened to teach. This even applies to topics such as secularization and the role of religion in the modern world.

The students at IIUM first and foremost look for professional education. The informants in Pedersen's thesis generally listed a number of pragmatic reasons for enrolling at IIUM. These comprise arguments such as its academic standard, educational reputation, English language curriculum, international flair, and the relatively easy accessibility of the university. Students take up their studies with specific career and life expectations that are not necessarily connected to their religious practices. This does not mean, however, that the Islamic character does not play a role in their enrolment at IIUM. For about half of the students in Pedersen's focus group, the Islamic character of the university played an additional role. The religious moral education at IIUM was mentioned as important either for the students themselves or with respect to their parents' decision to endorse their choice of studies. For a minority of the interlocutors, the Islamic perspective of IIUM was even the main reason for taking up studies there.[153] Yet the specifically normative-religious environment of IIUM does not exclude that the university also becomes a site of ordinary life beyond professional and moral advancement. Therefore, also at IIUM you will observe students sitting together in mixed gender groups, even starting intimate relationships. As one of Pedersen's female interviewees put it: "I guess the difference in dating in Islamic university [sic] compared to elsewhere is that you don't hold hands in public; . . . You just walk next to each other, . . . but once you are out of the gates, you do whatever you want."[154] Evidently, for its students, IIUM is both an Islamic place and a normal university.

The specific features of IIUM's Islamization strategies have been closely knitted into Malaysian state politics and its foundation "during the height of Mahathir-era Islamization and New Economic Policy (NEP)."[155] The NEP was launched by the government in 1971 with the aim of breaking the dominance of the Chinese population in economy and finance. These economic policies were accompanied by a gradual Islamization of the country during the more than twenty years under the premiership of Mahathir Mohammad (1981–2003).[156] The central reason of the NEP "was to produce a generation of entrepreneurial Malay-Muslim capitalists." The aim was for the mostly rural and rather poor segments of the Malayan Muslim population to gain access to higher education, thus shaping a new specifically Malayan middle class. Classifying Malay Muslims as *bumiputera*, the original representatives of the Malay nation, the NEP combined national politics with an Islamization of sorts.[157] The graduates of IIUM were to become employed in Islamic finance and halal industries as well as serving as staff in Malaysia's educational sector and state bureaucracy.[158] In this way, the purpose of IIUM recalls Sayyid Ahmad Khan's aim with the foundation of the Anglo-Muhammedan College in Aligarh, namely the conscious construction of a class of Muslim professionals. The educational policies of subsequent Malaysian governments have clearly aimed at redressing the economic imbalances among the country's different ethnic groups.[159] However, these policies also brought a further "push towards greater Islamization" and have therefore intensified the potential for ethnic and religious conflicts in the country.[160] Furthermore, it strengthened the role of Islamist parties such as the "Parti Islam Satanah Melayu" (PAS) which call for Islamic governance and the implementation of Islamic law.[161] As a consequence, the ruling "United Malays National Organization" (UMNO) restructured Islamic education in the country.[162] The ultimate aim of this reconstruction was to install state control over the religious field and the dissemination of a particular interpretation of Islam among the Malayan population.[163] The development of IIUM must be understood in the context of these policies and explains the university's shift from an international profile to a more national one.[164]

Conclusions: The Islamization of Knowledge and its Systemic Constraints

This chapter has dealt with the boundary negotiations between religion and science in the history of Islamic thought. In the Islamic discourse of modernity, science has taken on an ambiguous role. On the one hand, Islamic reformers perceived science and technology as instrumental for social reforms and the liberation of Muslim lands from the yoke of colonialism. In this way, the Enlightenment narrative of progress through scientific knowledge also resonated strongly in Muslim reformist thought. Sayyid Ahmed Khan, Muhammad Abduh, Namık Kemal, and Rashid Rida were prominent examples for this trend in late nineteenth-century Islamic modernism. Said Nursi, Ala al-Mawdudi, and Hasan al-Banna pursued an Islamization of modern scientific knowledge in the twentieth century. The First World Conference on Muslim Education in Mecca only continued this trend in Islamic modernity. On the other hand, Muslim intellectuals identified modern science with the power of imperialist Europe. The need for science and technology therefore had to be negotiated with the perils of its assumed Western origin. The adoption of modern scientific knowledge became increasingly fused with the claim of making it "authentically" Islamic. It is this ambiguity in the Muslim approach to modern science that has driven the Islamization of knowledge until today. Only an anti-modern Traditionalist like Seyyed Hossein Nasr was willing to reject the rationalism of "Western science" completely as an inseparable part of the "onslaught of the West." Yet, while negotiations between religion and science have characterized the Islamic discourse of modernity to a large extent, Muslim intellectuals have never agreed upon where exactly to draw the line between them or what relationship should actually be maintained between Islam and science.

In reviewing Stenberg's thesis on the Islamization of science, Abdul Rashid Moten, a former professor at the political science department at IIUM, came to the conclusion that the four scholars in Stenberg's study—Maurice Bucaille, Seyyed Hossein Nasr, Ziauddin Sardar, and Ismail Raji al-Faruqi—have much in common but essentially hate each other.[165] The study, according to Moten, shows "the fractured nature of the community of Muslim scholars and their vulnerability to Western temptations."[166] The fractured nature of scholarly communities may not come as a surprise, in particular when taking seriously the systemic logic of scientific communication. Applying Modern Systems Theory, the communicative medium of the scientific system—truth—is only temporal and subject to constant criticism and revision. Consequently, scholars are in continuous conflict in establishing historically contingent claims of truth. In light of this operational logic of modern science, attempts such as by Said Nursi to utilize scientific truth for the confirmation of the perennial truth of Islamic revealed knowledge is a contradiction in terms. Faith and scientific truth, at least in their systemic nature, are incompatible.[167]

The observation of theory and practice at the IIUM can lead to more paradigmatic conclusions regarding the boundary demarcations between Islam and science in contemporary times. At IIUM we can observe two parallel logics at work. Against the backdrop of the cultural model of the modern university, closely resembling the description given by the Stanford School, IIUM becomes a laboratory for this negotiation process on institutional and individual levels. Since its inception, the university has been a stage for shifting boundaries whose temporal demarcations are drawn in the context of national and international power relations converging in differing governmental strategies. The history and development of IIUM nicely illustrate the entanglement in which the competing claims of revealed and scientific knowledge have been engaged. As such, boundaries have moved without having disappeared. Most significantly, the economic and political interests of a variety of social actors have conditioned these social boundary negotiations between religion and science. Consequently, doing science based on an Islamic worldview has been subject to divers and even competing interpretations of the Islamic traditions. The Islamization of knowledge, therefore, is a good example for Talal Asad's suggestion of treating Islam as a discursive tradition. Authentic Islamic science must relate to Islam, yet the way in which this happens is up to the discretion of different social actors.

This brings me back to the premodern historical part of this chapter. Evidently, the polymaths of the golden age such as Biruni, Ibn Rushd, Ibn Sina, and Ghazali already had a sense of these incommensurable logics of science and faith. Simultaneously dealing with science and religion, they tried to avoid confusing them. In this sense, we can observe preadaptive advances to the modern concept of science. In examining the golden age of Arabic science, however, the fragmentation of knowledge appears first of all as a feature of the individual scholar rather than of society at large. The life and work of the Muslim polymaths show the way in which the individual juggles with but is also able to combine science and faith. At least at the micro level these two spheres of social communication are seemingly not incommensurable. Individuals can live with eternal and temporal truths. This applies even to Ghazali, although he aimed at turning communicative differentiations into a hierarchical order. However, when it comes to the institutional level of modern society, then Max Weber's dictum applies that "every scientific 'fulfilment' raises new 'questions'; it *asks* to be 'surpassed' and outdated." The meaning of science—or its operational logic—is the infinite replacement of temporary truths with new knowledge.[168] From this perspective, modern science will never be able to confirm faith. Despite all competition, power differentials, and hate among social actors, these systemic constraints are clearly visible in the history of the Islamization of knowledge.

Notes

1. In particular, I would like to thank my friend and colleague Prof. Gulshan Dietl, who introduced me to the academic world of India. Without her help, I never would have lectured at the Aligarh Muslim University.
2. For the data on Aligarh University, see the university's homepage: *https://www.amu.ac.in*.
3. Lelyveld, David. 1996. *Aligarh's First Generation: Muslim Solidarity in British India*. New Delhi: Oxford University Press.
4. Umer, Zaituna Y. 1974. Introduction. In Major-General G. F. I. Graham. *The Life and Work of Sir Syed Ahmed Khan*. Karachi: Oxford University Press, v–xvii, vii.
5. Troll, Christian W. 1978. *Sayyid Ahmad Khan: A Reinterpretation of Muslim Theology*. New Delhi et al.: Vikas Publishing House, xv.
6. Hussain, Khurram. 2020. *Islam as Critique: Sayyid Ahmad Khan and the Challenge of Modernity*. London: Bloomsbury, 6.
7. Ibid. 43.
8. Troll 1978, 144.
9. Hussain 2020, 97.
10. Troll 1978, 155–157.
11. Hussain 2020, 41.
12. Dallal, Ahmed. 2010. *Islam, Science, and the Challenge of History*. Yale: Yale University Press, 168. See also: Riexinger, Martin. 2017. Die Diskussion über die Evolutionstheorie in der islamischen Welt. *Nova Acta Leopoldina* 414: 179–200.
13. Riexinger, Martin. 2016. Al-Ghazālī's "Demarcation of Science": A

Commonplace Apology in the Muslim Reception of Modern Science—and Its Limitations. *In Islam and Rationality: The Impact of al-Ghazālī: Papers Collected on His 900th Anniversary.* Vol. 2. Edited by Frank Griffel. Leiden: Brill, 283–309, 305.
14. Ibid. 13.
15. See Chapter XVI of Osterhammel, Jürgen. 2011. *Die Verwandlung der Welt: Eine Geschichte des 19. Jahrhunderts.* Munich: C. H. Beck.
16. Ibid. 1133.
17. Ibid. 1135.
18. During his stay in Great Britain (1869–70), Sayyid Ahmad Khan drew his inspiration for the college from the universities of Oxford and Cambridge. Jung, Dietrich. 2011. *Orientalists, Islamists and the Global Public Sphere: A Genealogy of the Modern Essentialist Image of Islam.* Sheffield: Equinox, 222. Moreover, as a member of the Delhi society, which advocated the establishment of universities, the translation of European scientific works, and teaching in vernacular languages as medium of instruction, he represented a broader stream of the "domestication" of modern science in nineteenth-century India. See: Habib, Irfan S. and Dhruv, Raina. 2004. *Domesticating Modern Science and Culture in Colonial India.* New Delhi: Tulika Books.
19. Christian missionaries were also strongly involved in these boundary negotiations between science and religion. I am not able to deal with this issue in this chapter. For literature on this subject, see: Baron, Beth. 2014. *The Orphan Scandal: Christian Missionaries and the Rise of The Muslim Brotherhood.* Stanford: Stanford University Press; Dogan, Mehmet Ali and Heather J. Sharkey (eds.). 2011. *American Missionaries and the Middle East: Foundational Encounters.* Salt Lake City: University of Utah Press; Elshakry, Marwa. 2013. *Reading Darwin in Arabic, 1860-1950.* Chicago: University of Chicago Press; Makdisi, Ussama. 2008. *Artillery of Heaven: American Missionaries and the Failed Conversion of the Middle East.* Ithaca: Cornell University Press; Sedra, Paul. 2011. *From Mission to Modernity: Evangelicals, Reformers and Education in Nineteenth-Century Egypt.* London: I. B. Tauris. I briefly discuss the relationship between missionary activities and science in the Middle East in a book chapter: Jung, Dietrich. 2020. "Modernization in the Name of God": Christian Missionaries, Global Modernity, and the Formation of Modern Subjectivities in the Middle East. In *Middle East Christianity: Local Practices, World Societal Entanglements.* Edited by Stephan Stetter and Mitra Moussa Nabo. Cham: Palgrave Macmillan, 69–90.

20. Livingston, John W. 2017. *The Rise of Science in Islam and the West: From Shared Heritage to the Parting of the Ways, 8th to 19th Centuries*. London: Routledge, xi.
21. I will use the term "Arabic science" in this chapter, following the conceptual suggestions of Jim Al-Khalili, who stresses two points. First of all, we are talking about scientific work written in Arabic as a language of science. Second, while many of the scholars of the golden age were Muslims, non-Muslims also played prominent roles among them. See: Al-Khalili, Jim. 2011. *The House of Wisdom: How Arabic Science Saved Ancient Knowledge and Gave Us the Renaissance*. New York: Penguin Press, xxv–xxix.
22. I use Traditionalism in its capitalized form to designate the ideological movement of Traditionalism. Otherwise, I spell the concept in its non-capitalized form as "traditionalism."
23. Drori, Gili S., John W. Meyer, Francisco Ramirez and Evan Schofer. 2003. *Science in the Modern World Polity: Institutionalization and Globalization*. Stanford: Stanford University Press.
24. Krücken, Georg and Gili S. Drori (eds.). 2009. *World Society: The Writings of John W. Meyer*. Oxford: Oxford University Press, 217.
25. Ibid. 366.
26. Ibid. 217. See also my references to the Stanford School in Chapters Two and Eight of this book.
27. Drori et al. 2003, 6.
28. Ibid. 16.
29. Ibid. 82.
30. Ibid. 6.
31. Ibid. 196–198.
32. Freely, John. 2009. *Aladdin's Lamp: How Greek Science Came to Europe Through the Islamic World*. New York: Alfred A. Knopf, 4.
33. Krücken and Drori 2009, 357.
34. The British botanist Alexander Moon (1755–1825), for instance, in his catalogue of the plants of Ceylon fused his knowledge of European botany with the local natural history which he had learned about in Kandy. See: Sivasundaram, Sujit. 2010. Sciences and the Global: On Methods, Questions, and Theory. *Isis* 101 (1): 146–158, 152.
35. Luhmann, Niklas. 1992. *Die Wissenschaft der Gesellschaft*. Frankfurt am Main: Suhrkamp, 170.
36. Luhmann, Niklas. 1986. *Ökologische Kommunikation: Kann die mod-*

erne Gesellschaft sich auf ökologische Gefährdungen einstellen? Opladen: Westdeutscher Verlag, 153–158.
37. Lyons, Johnathan. 2009. *The House of Wisdom: How the Arabs Transformed Western Civilization*. New York et al.: Bloomsbury Press, 190.
38. Luhmann 1992, 428.
39. Ibid. 432–433.
40. Ibid. 451.
41. Ibid. 448.
42. Ibid. 709.
43. Al-Khalili 2011, 175.
44. Ibid. 172.
45. Ibid. 178.
46. Colish, Marcia L. 2006. Avicenna's Theory of Efficient Causation and Its Influence on St. Thomas Aquinas. In *Studies in Scholasticism*. Aldershot and Burlington: Ashgate, Variorum, 3; Richardson, Kara. 2013. Avicenna's Conception of the Efficient Cause. *British Journal for the History of Philosophy* 21 (2): 220–239.
47. Sarton, George. 1927. *Introduction to the History of Science: Volume I: From Homer to Omar Khayyam*. Baltimore: The Williams & Wilkins Company, 709.
48. Sarton, George. 1932. *Introduction to the History of Science: Volume II: From Rabbi Ben Ezra to Roger Bacon*. Baltimore: The Willimas & Wilkins Company, 287.
49. Lyons 2009, 197.
50. Al-Khalil 2011, 184.
51. Leaman, Oliver. 1999. *A Brief Introduction to Islamic Philosophy*. Cambridge: Polity Press, 7.
52. For an English translation of Ghazali's book, see: McCarthy, Richard J. 1980. *Freedom and Fulfillment: An Annotated Translation of Al-Ghazālī's Al-Munqidh Min Al-Dalāl and Other Relevant Works of Al-Ghazālī*. Woodbridge: Twayne Publishers.
53. For a more detailed presentation of this argument, see: Jung, Dietrich. 2022. "*Abu Hamid al-Ghazali and Niklas Luhmann: Boundary Negotiations between Religion and Science in the Abbasid Empire.*" Working Paper Series of the CASHSS "Multiple Secularities—Beyond the West, Beyond Modernities" 26. Leipzig University.
54. For Sarton, Scholasticism was not only a Christian philosophy, but a

cross-cultural mode of thought characteristic for medieval philosophy more generally. Sarton 1927, 21–29.

55. This narrative has meanwhile come under massive pressure. See the collection of articles in: Griffel, Frank. (ed.). 2016. *Islam and Rationality: The Impact of al-Ghazālī: Papers Collected on His 900th Anniversary*. Vol. 2. Leiden: Brill. For a good critique with regard to astronomy in the Ottoman Empire, see: Ben-Zaken, Avner. 2004. The Heavens of the Sky and the Heavens of the Heart: The Ottoman Cultural Context for the Introduction of Post-Copernican Astronomy. *British Journal of the History of Science* 37 (1): 1–28.
56. Lyons 2009, 62.
57. Al-Khalil 2011, 71.
58. Lombard, Maurice. 1992. *Blütezeit des Islam: Eine Wirtschafts- und Kulturgeschichte des 8.—11. Jahrhunderts*. Frankfurt am Main: Fischer, 129.
59. Lyons 2009, 159–160.
60. Günther, Sebastian. 2016. Bildung und Ethik im Islam. In *Islam. Einheit und Vielfalt einer Weltreligion*. Edited by Rainer Brunner. Stuttgart: Kohlhammer, 210–236, 214.
61. Hourani, Albert. 1992. *Die Geschichte der arabischen Völker*. Frankfurt am Main: Fischer, 252–255.
62. Saliba, George. 2007. *Islamic Science and the Making of the European Renaissance*. Cambridge: Cambridge University Press.
63. Cf. Ragab, Ahmed. 2017. Making History: Identity, Progress and the Modern-Science Archive. *Journal of Early Modern History* 21: 433–444.
64. Saliba, George. 2002. Greek Astronomy and the Medieval Arabic Tradition. *American Scientist* 90 (4): 360–367. For a different opinion, see the work of Toby Huff. He takes the position that European scientific innovations are absolutely unique, although he admits to considering the very idea of a "scientific revolution" to be a retrospective twentieth-century invention. Huff, Toby. 2011. *Intellectual Curiosity and the Scientific Revolution: A Global Perspective*. Cambridge: Cambridge University Press, 12.
65. Matar, Nabil. 2009. *Europe Through Arab Eyes 1578–1727*. New York: Columbia University Press, 25.
66. Dallal, Ahmad. 1999. Science, Medicine, and Technology. In *The Oxford History of Islam*. Edited by John Esposito. Oxford: Oxford University Press, 155–214, 198.
67. West, John B. 2008. Ibn al-Nafis, the Pulmonary Circulation, and the Islamic Golden Age. *Journal of Applied Physiology* 105: 1877–1880.
68. See: Ben-Zaken 2004; Küçük, Harun B. 2012. *Early Enlightenment in Istanbul*.

PhD Dissertation. San Diego: University of California; Küçük, Harun B. 2017. Early Modern Ottoman Science: A New Materialist Framework. *Journal of Early Modern History* 21: 407–419; İhsanoğlu, Ekmeleddin, Kostas Chatzis, and Efthymios Nicolaidis (eds.). 2003. *Multicultural Science in the Ottoman Empire*. Turnhout: Brepols.

69. Dallal 2010, 154.
70. İhsanoğlu, Ekmeleddin. 2004. *Science, Technology and Learning in the Ottoman Empire*. Aldershot: Ashgate, 240.
71. Dallal 2010, 150.
72. Schneider, Werner L. 2011. Religion und funktionale Differenzierung. In *Soziale Differenzierung Handlungstheoretische Zugänge in der Diskussion*. Edited by Thomas Schwinn, Clemens Kroneberg and Jens Greve. Wiesbaden: VS Verlag, 181–210, 193.
73. Elshakry, Marwa. 2008. Knowledge in Motion. The Cultural Politics of Modern Science Translations in Arabic. *Isis* 99 (4): 701–730, 702.
74. Elshakry, Marwa. 2010. When Science Became Western: Historiographical Reflections. *Isis* 101 (1): 98–109, 103–104.
75. Dallal 2010, 175.
76. Ghulam, Nabi Saqeb. 2000. Some Reflections on Islamization of Education Since 1977 Makkah Conference: Accomplishments, Failures and Tasks Ahead. *Intellectual Discourse* 8 (1): 45–68, 47.
77. Ibid. 48.
78. Abaza, Mona. 2002. *Debates on Islam and Knowledge in Malaysia and Egypt: Shifting Worlds*. London and New York: Routledge, 9.
79. Stenberg, Leif. 1996. *The Islamization of Science: Four Muslim Positions Developing an Islamic Modernity*. Lund: Lund Studies in History of Religions, University of Lund, 336.
80. The honorary title *Bediüzzaman* (miracle of the age) was conferred on Said Nursi by his followers, see: Riexinger, Martin. 2020. Evolution, the Purpose of Life and the Order of Society. How a Nurcu Connects Worldview and Normativity in Pseudo-Biographical Narratives. *Marburg Journal of Religion* 22 (2): 1–19, 1.
81. Though his father served as a village mullah, there are no official records that would underpin later claims that the genealogy of his family could trace descendance from the Prophet and therefore justify the title of a Said. Cf. Turner, Colin and Hasan Horkuc. 2009. Said Nursi. *Makers of Islamic Civilization*. London: I. B. Tauris, 5.
82. Ibid. 10–11.

83. Vahide, Şükran. 1999.The Life and Times of Bediuzzaman Said Nursi. *The Muslim World* LXXXIX (3–4): 208–244, 217.
84. Vahide, Şükran. 2011. *Beduizzaman Said Nursi: Author of the Risale-I Nur*. Kuala Lumpur: Islamic Book Trust, 40.
85. Ibid. 51. On the history, role, and nature of the madrasa as an institution of Islamic education, see the excellent introduction in: Moosa, Ebrahim. 2015. *What is a Madrasa?* Edinburgh: Edinburgh University Press.
86. Vahide 1999, 220.
87. Ibid. 222–223.
88. Mardin, Şerif. 1989. *Religion and Social Change in Modern Turkey: The Case of Bediüzzaman Said Nursi*. Albany: SUNY Press, 36.
89. Algar, Hamid. 1979. Said Nursi and the Risala-i Nur: An Aspect of Islam in Contemporary Turkey. In *Islamic Perspectives: Studies in Honour of Mawlana Sayyid Abul Ala Mawdudi*. Edited by Khurshid Ahmad and Zafar Ishaq Ansari. London and Jeddah: The Islamic Foundation, 313–334, 318.
90. These are the words of his hagiographic biographer. Sükran 2011, ix.
91. Mardin 1989, 36–37.
92. Ibid. 7.
93. Ibid. 216.
94. Agai, Bekim. 2017. The Religious Significance of Science and Natural Science in the Writings of Bediuzzaman Said Nursi. In *Ein traditioneller Gelehrter stellt sich der Moderne: Said Nursi 1876–1960*. Edited by Martin Riexinger und Bülent Uçar. Osnabrück: V&R unipress, 121–143, 122.
95. Nursi, Said. 1996. *The Words: On the Nature and Purposes of Man, Life, and All Things*. Istanbul: Sözler, 44.
96. Ibid. 145.
97. Ibid. 270.
98. Cf. Riexinger, Martin 2017a. Freiheit und Moderne im Denken Said Nursis und seiner Schüler. In *Ein traditioneller Gelehrter stellt sich der Moderne: Said Nursi 1876–1960*. Edited by Martin Riexinger und Bülent Uçar. Osnabrück: V&R unipress, 63–73, 70.
99. Agai 2017, 131.
100. Terzan, Levent. 2005. The Problems of Religious Modernity. *AJSS* 33 (3): 506–528, 513–515.
101. Riexinger, Martin. 2010. Islamic Opposition to the Darwinian Theory of Evolution. In *Handbook of Religion and the Authority of Science*. Leiden: Brill, 483–510, 502

102. Riexinger, Martin. 2017. Die Diskussion über die Evolutionstheorie in der islamischen Welt. *Nova Acta Leopoldina* 414: 179–200, 181.
103. Ibid. 186–187. Riexinger further emphasizes that in Kemalist materialism the work of Darwin did not play a central role. Rather the Young Turk and Kemalist intellectuals adopted the materialist and atheist thought of German authors such as Karl Vogt (1817–95), Ludwig Büchner (1824–1899), and Ernst Häckel. Ibid, 185. For an analysis of the intellectual sources of Kemalism, see: Hanioğlu, Şükrü. 2005. Blueprints for a Future Society: Late Ottoman Materialists on Science, Religion, and Art. In *Late Ottoman Society: The Intellectual Legacy*. Edited by Elisabeth Özdalga. London and New York: Routledge, 28–116.
104. Nursi, Said. 1997. *Letters 1928–1932*. Istanbul: Sözler, 111.
105. Mardin 1989, 213.
106. Riexinger 2017, 192.
107. For an account of the activities of the Gülen movement in Europe, see: Celik, Gürkan, Johan Leman and Karel Steenbrink (eds.). 2015. *Gülen-Inspired Hizmet in Europe: The Western Journey of a Turkish Muslim Movement*. Brussels: P.I.E. Peter Lang.
108. Pahl, Jon. 2019. *Fethullah Gülen: A Life of Hizmet: Why a Muslim Scholar in Pennsylvania Matters to the World*. Clifton, NJ: Blue Dome Press, 16.
109. Tee, Caroline and David Shankland. 2013. Said Nursi's Notion of "Sacred Science": Its Function and Application in Hizmet High School Education. *Sociology of Islam* 1: 209–32, 226.
110. Ibid. 17.
111. Yavuz, Hakan M. 2013. *Toward an Islamic Enlightenment: The Gülen Movement*. Oxford: Oxford University Press, 43.
112. For the following bibliographical notes, my source is Nasr's own brief autobiography: Nasr, Seyyed Hossein. 2001. Intellectual Autobiography of Seyyed Hossein Nasr. In *The Philosophy of Seyyed Hossein Nasr*. Edited by Lewis Edwin Hahn et al. Peru, Illinois: Open Court Publishers, 1–86, 13.
113. Ibid. 15.
114. Ibid. 19.
115. Ibid. 71.
116. Sedgwick, Mark. 2004. *Against the Modern World: Traditionalism and the Secret Intellectual History of the Twentieth Century*. Oxford: Oxford University Press.
117. Nasr, Seyyed Hossein. 1979. *Islamic Perspectives: Studies in Honour of Mawlana*

Sayyid Abul Ala Mawdudi. Edited by Kurshid Ahmad and Zarfar Ishaq Ansari. London: The Islamic Foundation, 35–42, 37.
118. Ibid. 40
119. Ibid. 41.
120. Sedgwick 2004, 25.
121. Ibid. 264–266.
122. Ibid. 24–28.
123. Steenberg 1996, 102.
124. Nasr, Seyyed Hossein. 1975. *Islam and the Plight of Modern Man*. London and New York: Longman, xi.
125. Ibid. 3 and 12.
126. Nasr, Seyyed Hossein. 1987. *Science and Civilization in Islam*. Second Edition. Cambridge: The Islamic Text Society, 21–25.
127. Cf. Stenberg 1996, 149. Nasr 1987, Chapter One.
128. Nasr 1987, 41.
129. Ibid. 22.
130. Nasr, Seyyed Hossein. 1993. *The Need for a Sacred Science*. Richmond: Curzon Press, 95.
131. Aminrazavi, Mehdi. 2001. Philosophia Perennis and Sciencia Sacra in a Postmodern World. In *The Philosophy of Seyyed Hossein Nasr*. Edited by Lewis Edwin Hahn et al. Peru, Illinois: Open Court Publishers, 551–562, 551.
132. Sedgwick 2004, 25.
133. Stenberg 1996, 136.
134. Sedgwick 2004, 267.
135. Nasr 1993, 81.
136. Masuzawa, Tomoko. 2005. *The Invention of World Religions*. Chicago and London: University of Chicago Press. For Nasr, see: Nasr 1981, 67 and Nasr 1976, 10.
137. On these two universities: Sinclair, Kirstine. 2016. "Liberal Arts are an Islamic Idea": Subjectivity Formation at Islamic Universities in the West. *Review of Middle East Studies* 50 (1): 38–47; Sinclair, Kirstine. 2017. Er klinisk psykologi brugbart, sheikh? En undersøgelse af subjektivitetsformation på islamiske universiteter i vesten. *Tidsskrift for islamforskning* 11 (1): 83–98. For a brief overview on Islamic learning in Europe, see: Bano, Masooda. 2022. Islamic Authority and Centres of Knowledge Production in Europe. *Journal of Muslims in Europe* 11: 1–16.
138. Ghulam 2000, 50.

139. Farquhar, Michael. 2017. *Circuits of Faith: Migration, Education, and the Wahhabi Mission.* Stanford: Stanford University Press, 3.
140. Ibid. 77.
141. Ibid. 84.
142. For more about these two scholars and their approaches, see: Hanafi, Sari. 2021. From Streaming to Mainstreaming "Islamization of Knowledge": The Case of the International Islamic University of Malaysia. *American Journal of Islam and Society* 38 (1–2): 101–135; Keim, Wiebeke. 2016. Islamization of Knowledge—Symptom of the Failed Internationalization of the Social Sciences? *Méthod(e)s: African Review of Social Sciences Methodology* 2 (1–2): 127–154; Stenberg 1996, Chapter Four.
143. In Chapter Seven, I will go into the issue of halal products in the context of Islamic economics in more detail.
144. The other faculties are put together in these seven units: Medicine & Healthcare; Science; Law; Economics and Management Sciences; Engineering; Architecture & Environmental Design; Information & Communication Technology.
145. Hanafi 2021, 103.
146. https://www.iium.edu.my/office/odrail/vision-and-mission-10; accessed March 22, 2022.
147. https://www.iium.edu.my/centre/rmc; accessed March 24, 2022.
148. Hanafi 2021, 107.
149. Ibid. 121.
150. https://www.iium.edu.my/page/educational-goals-1; accessed March 24, 2022.
151. Hanafi 2021, 111.
152. Pedersen, Gry Hvass. 2020. *Modernity, Islamic Tradition and Higher Education: Visions of Modern Muslim Selfhoods among Contemporary Students at Islamic Universities in Asia.* PhD Thesis. Odense: University of Southern Denmark, 136. Pedersen's observations about varieties in the very understanding of an Islamic worldview confirm the excellent analysis of the Islamization of knowledge movement by Wiebeke Keim. In her article, Keim discerned three general approaches in the "Islamization of the social sciences" with respect to the claim that international social sciences possess a universal character: Keim 2016.
153. Ibid. 218–222.
154. Ibid. 223.
155. Sloane-White, Patricia. 2017. *Corporate Islam: Sharia and the Modern Workplace.* Cambridge: Cambridge University Press, 38. Regarding

state-building and economic policies in Malaysia, see also chapters seven and the conclusions in this book.
156. Anadaya, Barbara Watson and Leonard Y. Andaya. 2017. *A History of Malaysia*. Third Edition. London: Palgrave Macmillan, 307.
157. Sloane-White 2017, 6.
158. Ibid. 12–13.
159. Kraince, Richard G. 2009. Reforming Islamic Education in Malaysia: Doctrine or Dialogue? In *Making Modern Muslims: The Politics of Islamic Education in Southeast Asia*. Edited by Robert W. Hefner. Honolulu: University of Hawai'i Press, 106–140, 117. For a comprehensive study of the historical development of the educational sector in Malaysia, see Hashim, Rosnani. 2004. *Educational Dualism in Malaysia: Implications for Theory and Practice*. Second Edition. Kuala Lumpur: The Other Press.
160. Andaya and Andaya 2017, xiii.
161. Ibid. 283.
162. The UMNO was established in 1946 as a political movement that brought together various social actors such as aristocrats, civil servants, and religious leaders in anticolonial politics. See: Andaya and Andaya 2017, 271–273.
163. See: Kraince 2009.
164. I come back to these policies of the Malaysian government in Chapter Seven, when discussing the idea of an Islamic economy.
165. This opinion is confirmed by Sedgwick, who mentions a book review by Ziauddin Sardar which reviews a number of Nasr's books. Apparently, he starts this review with Nasr's praise of Frithjof Schuon by linking it to charges of child molestation and sexual battery raised against Schuon which were later dropped; Sedgwick 2004, 175.
166. Moten, Abdul Rashid. 1998. Book Review: The Islamization of Science: Four Muslim Positions Developing an Islamic Modernity. *Intellectual Discourse* 6 (1): 88–98, 98.
167. To be sure, this conclusion on the systemic level does not exclude a full fusion on the micro level. The followers of the Nurcu movement, for instance, can conduct science as religious subjects without differentiating between the two bodies of knowledge. Here it is in the individual that the diverse ethics of social systems collapse into idiosyncratic positions. Moreover, also in the Christian context there were many attempts to proof the truth of the revelation by scientific methods. A good example is the theologian and orientalist William Robertson Smith (1846–1894) on whom I elaborated in: Jung, Dietrich. 2016.

Sociology, Protestant Theology, and the Concept of Modern Religion: William Robertson Smith and the "Scientification" of Religion. *Journal of Religion in Europe* 8 (3–4): 335–364.
168. Weber, Max. 1919 [1991]. Science as a Vocation. In *From Max Weber: Essays in Sociology*. London and New York: Routledge, 129–156, 138.

7

BOUNDARY NEGOTIATIONS BETWEEN ISLAM AND ECONOMICS: ISLAMIC FINANCE, HALAL MARKETS, AND THE MUSLIM ENTREPRENEUR

My personal encounters with the economy of the Middle East have been threefold. During the 1980s and 1990s, I observed instances of outrageous exploitation, rampant corruption, and runaway inflation. In fall 1982, I arrived in the United Arab Emirates. Through the help of my father, I got a job on a building site in the Emirate of Sharja. To be sure, despite my formal high school graduation and my license to drive lorries, I did not have any professional qualifications at this point in my life. I took up the tasks of a driver, a kitchen-helper, and supervisor of a group of Indian contract workers. Without any doubt, my Indian colleagues would not have had any need of my supervision. They were skilled in their crafts and knew their work perfectly. My role as a supervisor was due to the fact that I was working as a German for a German company that had hired "local staff," who turned out to be mostly Indian as well as a few Iranian and Arab nationals. Consequently, I profited from a kind of asymmetric colonial relationship in the postcolonial era. This asymmetric relationship was profoundly borne out in our salaries: I was receiving about ten times as much as my much more skilled colleagues. Moreover, we Europeans had single rooms in our airconditioned "residential containers," while the non-European staff lived six men together in approximately the same space, some without air conditioning. Looking at it from today's perspective, this was utter exploitation of them by the German company and the UAE investor.

Three years later, I used my lorry license to transfer travel coaches from Stuttgart to Amman. Together with two friends, we drove two buses to Jordan, which a Jordanian businessman had purchased in Germany. Paying our salaries and return travel expenses, was cheaper for him than transporting the coaches by ship. For us, it was a good salary and undoubtedly an adventurous tour, leading us through Austria, former Yugoslavia, Bulgaria, Turkey, and Syria to Jordan. From Belgrade onwards, we could only make progress by continuously paying bribes to policemen and customs officers. In Syria we even had to transit the country in a military-guided convoy. Getting on this convoy entailed a day-long negotiation and heavy bribes at the Bab al Hawa border crossing between Turkey and Syria. Our Jordanian business partner had given us the money for all these extra expenses, however, in advance. They were an immanent part of the whole business transaction.

Finally, I learned what it means to work under the conditions of runaway inflation. While teaching as a guest assistant professor at Bilkent University from 1997 to1998, I was paid in Turkish Lira. At that time, the inflation rate was at about 85 percent—officially—but in reality, probably above 100 percent. The employees of the campus supermarket at Bilkent were basically busy continuously changing the price tags on their goods. Receiving my salary at the end of the month, it was necessary to withdraw the whole sum from my bank account, rush down to Ankara city center and change all my Liras into German Marks. At that time, downtown Ankara was full of *döviz büroları*, the then-mushrooming currency exchange offices. Again, I profited from my status as a privileged foreigner, getting my salary roughly adjusted every month and being able to transfer my whole salary into foreign currency. Do not ask me how this financial situation was handled by Turkey's poor.

These personal experiences in no way reflect the kind of "Islamic economics" which Umer Chapra has envisioned. The Pakistani-born former senior economic advisor to the Saudi Arabian Monetary Agency declared Islamic economics to be an alternative to conventional economics, one which calls for political accountability and socio-economic justice. Similar to the advocates of Islamic science described in the previous chapter, Chapra demanded the embedding of economic behavior in a normative Islamic worldview. According to him, this Islamic worldview gives "primacy to moral values, human brotherhood, and socio-economic justice." Muslims should conduct economics in this kind of Islamic way, instead of relying—as conventional economics does in his opinion—solely on secularist, materialist or even social-Darwinist rationalities realized through the state or the market.[1] In Chapra's eyes, "the practical wisdom of Islamic economics" has gradually developed since the Prophet's time, having made "valuable contributions over the centuries."[2] Apparently, the Saudi economic advisor considered premodern Islamic economics as a valuable model for economic action in modern times.

In his vision of Islamic economics, Umer Chapra made references to another golden age of Islam, a premodern golden age of commerce and trade. Yet, the origins of the idea of an all-encompassing system of Islamic economics should be found in the twentieth century. The essential intellectual positions took shape in late-colonial India and "gained currency" through the sermons, speeches, and publications of the Indian Islamist Ala al-Mawdudi (1903–79).[3] In the context of the anti-colonial struggle in South Asia, the founder of the Pakistani Jamaat-i Islamia promoted Islamic economics as a means of reinvigorating an authentic Muslim culture.[4] The economist Timur Kuran emphasized that the pan-Islamists of the late nineteenth and early twentieth century did not yet talk about a recognizable Islamic economic agenda. Only in the second part of the twentieth century did Islamist intellectuals suggest solving a wide range of socio-economic problems through recourse to economic institutions inspired by Islamic religious traditions.[5] In this sense, Islamic economics was a latecomer to the Islamic discourse of modernity, one actually preceded by ideas on modern Islamic politics and science.[6] Islamic finance, today's flagship of Islamic economics, had its conceptual roots in the 1950s, with the first institutional manifestations in the 1960s and 1970s.[7] While pioneered by actors from Egypt, Malaysia, and South Asia, Islamic financial institutions only gained economic significance in the 1990s due to the enormous investment sources of the countries of the Gulf Cooperation Council (GCC).[8] Since then, these countries represent the "bulk of the addressable Islamic finance market."[9]

In this chapter, I will first briefly discuss premodern Islamic economics in light of Luhmann's Modern Systems Theory and some conceptual reflections of early sociologists on the social function of money. Against this theoretical background, I then again look for preadaptive advances to modernity, in this case among medieval Muslim traders and their economic networks. Can we observe in classical Islamic economics the preliminary boundary negotiations between religion and economics? Are there even "Arab roots of capitalism"?[10] The next section takes up contemporary ideas and institutions of Islamic economics. Does Islamic economics indeed represent "the emergence of a new paradigm," an alternative to global capitalism?[11] The answer to this question is closely connected to the twentieth-century evolution of the Islamic discourse of modernity. Strongly influenced by other critiques of capitalism, Islamic economists competed with them in designing alternative economic institutions and strategies aiming at authenticity in referring them to Islamic traditions.[12] Consequently, the discourse on Islamic economics has been an inherent part of the emergence of global modernity. After this critical review of present-day proposals of Islamic economics, the final part of this chapter takes a closer look at new forms of Islamic activism. The focus in this section is on more recent social developments in the discourse of Islamic modernities. More precisely, it discusses the merger of Islam and neoliberal values of creative entrepreneurship in the identity constructions of the managers and volunteers of contemporary Egyptian youth organizations.

The "Vices of Money" and Premodern Islamic Economies

According to Niklas Luhmann's Modern Systems Theory, the modern economy is characterized by a double communicative code. Economic communication operates based on the code of possessing and not possessing. Yet the economy only achieves its complete differentiation and therewith operational closure as a specific functional subsystem of society through a second code, the binary code of *to pay or not to pay*. Consequently, only a fully monetized system of economic exchange represents the economic subsystem of modern society. It is through its "monetary centralization" that the economy established itself as a circular and self-referential modern social system.[13] In the evolution of modern society, the economic system transformed the medium of property into money.[14] In this process, it regulates its internal operations through the price mechanism.[15] The contact between the economic system and its environment takes place via the language of the price.[16] Money, market, and price are the core concepts with which we describe economic exchange. The autopoiesis of the economic system is eventually epitomized in the circularity of its communicative medium money.

This conceptualization of modern economics by Luhmann brings us directly to the Islamic prohibition of *ribā* (usury), that is to say the prohibition of charging interest in the Islamic tradition. Interpreting *ribā* in terms of "money is breeding money,"[17] it is precisely this autopoietic notion of modern economics that characterizes the institution of interest-based lending. As a core feature of modern economic life, interest became a major target of the proponents of Islamic economics and finance. However, Islamic tradition is far from unique in its pejorative attitude toward interest.[18] Aristotle had already stressed the destructive social power of money in his *Politika*. The Greek philosopher distinguished between economic actors and usurers, contrasting the use of money as a means of exchange against its tendency to generate surplus through multiplying itself.[19] Since antiquity, numerous theologians and philosophers have critically discussed this tendency of money and its economic institutionalization in the form of interest.[20] All three monotheistic religions condemn the charging of interest "as the motor of capitalism." They only authorize it—if at all—when it is pursued by strangers.[21] Even among the aristocracies of Europe, the charging of interest was a socially suspect kind of human activity.[22]

Long before Luhmann, the "autopoietic character" of money was also a central theme of classical sociology. This applies in particular to the work of Karl Marx (1818–83). For Marx the unfolding of the value relationship through three subsequently developed functions of money was the central stage in the emergence of modern society. In Marx's theory, the medium of money hides an abstract form of social relationship, relations as commodity owners, which are mediated by value relations.[23] This abstract social relationship, in Marx's reasoning, undermines all "ancient types" of social formations such as the family, clan, guild, or local communities: "Commodities as such are indifferent to all religious, political, national and linguistic barriers. Their universal language is price, and their common bond is money."[24] Religious commandments are thus directed against this socially destructive power of money. According to Marx, money develops from a measure of prices via that of a means of exchange to money in its third form as money itself. Now, money appears as an end in itself. In Luhmann's conceptual wording, economic communication has reached the status of self-reference and thus of operational closure. It is due to this development that money has often been perceived as the "source of all evil."[25] Today's Islamic economists follow Marx's three steps in their perception of money in considering it as shariʻa-compliant in its form as a measurement of value and as a medium of exchange. Yet, from the normative perspective of Islamic economy, money should not be used in its third form, whereby money is exchanged for a price.[26]

With this third form of money in mind, Max Weber (1864–1920) described money as the most abstract and impersonal thing in human life.[27] Weber concluded that money—understood as a non-ethical contract of purpose—was suitable as a means of eliminating the magical or sacramental character of legal acts and, in this way, strongly contributed to the advancement of the formal rationality of modernity.[28] For Weber, "consociation through exchange in the market" was the archetype of all rational social action.[29] Finally, Georg Simmel (1858–1918) wrote at book-length on the *Philosophy of Money*. In this seminal volume, Simmel described money as a contradictory social institution that connects people while at the same time separating them.[30] In pointing to this paradox, he emphasized the role of money in making possible the high level of individualization in modern society. In short, classical sociology assigned the institution of money a crucial role in the emergence of modern society. Can we also observe the evolutionary steps of the unfolding of Marx's value relationship in the era of premodern Islamic economics?

There are a number of scholars who have argued that we can discern some roots of capitalism in the economy of premodern Islamic empires.[31] While the dominant narrative relates the origins of capitalism exclusively to Europe, these scholars claim that a golden age of Islamic commerce was a necessary predecessor to the evolution of modern capitalist economics in Europe. Both narratives are closely linked to the role of Italian city-states in medieval trade. The city of Amalfi is a case in point. Today a provincial town relegated to touristic interest alone, Amalfi was once one of the leading commercial centers in medieval trade. For about three centuries (800–1100 CE) the Italian town vied with Venice for the position of the major intermediary trade hub between "East and West."[32] As the Geniza papers disclosed, traders from Amalfi were deeply involved in the distribution of expensive goods from Constantinople, and their representatives were continuously present in Egypt during the tenth and eleventh centuries.[33] In the course of these intense contacts with Middle Eastern economies, the merchants of the Italian city-states developed economic institutions directly borrowing some features from Muslim traders.[34]

Medieval Islamic economics "preserved, enriched, and then extended the economic precepts of antiquity," transmitting "arche-typical tools of modern capitalism" to Europe.[35] These comprise in particular financial instruments such as bank checks, bank deposits, bonds, letters of credit, and promissory notes.[36] This transfer of business knowledge is clearly visible in the large number of concepts from Arabic commercial terminology that subsequently appeared in medieval Europe.[37] Moreover, European merchants became acquainted with advanced methods of commerce based on writing and recording from their Muslim counterparts.[38] This implied the crucial introduction of double-entry bookkeeping based on Arabic numerals.[39] Initially having originated in India, these numerals were used by Muslims in their scientific work rather than in commerce. However, having learned them due to their interaction with Muslim people, European merchants began to apply them around the year 1200.[40] In Europe, deposits and therewith identifiable bank money as means of payment were otherwise not recognized before the early fifteenth century.[41]

Seemingly, the golden age of Islamic science, one of the topics of Chapter Six, was somehow accompanied by a golden age of trade. In this age we can detect the evolution of similar forms of capital as those later developed in Europe. Moreover, in medieval Arab trade, basing economic exchange on money was a standard practice.[42] Already in the ninth century, real barter exchange was increasingly replaced by economic exchanges via money, even in provincial regions.[43] The circulation of money developed rapidly and "spanned over the entire Islamic world."[44] Wealthy non-merchants accumulated surplus capital in looking for lawful avenues of "investment," reflected in specific books of Islamic law, in Arabic the *kutub al-ḥiyal* (sing. *kitāb al-ḥiyal*).[45] These books document the ways in which Islamic jurists developed means to deal with the theoretical prohibition of *ribā*.[46] The *ḥiyal* are legal devices using legal means for extra-legal ends: "They enabled persons who would otherwise have had no choice but to act against the provisions of the sacred Law, to arrive at the desired result while actually conforming to the letter of the law."[47] In particular the Meccan verses of the Qur'an are "replete with the enunciation of the economic injustice of contemporary Meccan society."[48]

There is also a vast body of literature on *ribā* in the Prophetic Traditions (*sunna*), however, with a "lot of contradiction" and "insoluble complexities." Therefore, no commonly accepted definition of *ribā* has been agreed upon in light of both the Qur'an and the Traditions.⁴⁹ In addition, in Islamic law, commerce and trade are not only economic but also social and moral relations. In the Hanafi school of law, for instance, an economic contract relies in principle on the legal model of direct face-to-face relationships, making market exchanges cumbersome if not practically impossible.⁵⁰ These normative and practical obstacles to a monetized economy were addressed in numerous medieval juridical discussions. These discussions gave expression to the historical fact that the "Islamic economics" of premodern times were already characterized by the production of commodities and an orientation toward the exchange value of these commodities expressed in money.⁵¹ Yet, it would be wrong to consider "Arab economic policies" between the seventh and the eleventh centuries as delineated by a kind of uniformly applied set of regulations and rules. While the available sources give the general impression "that the market should be competitive and that prices should be determined by the forces of supply and demand," the medieval Arab economy was primarily agricultural with a relatively high autonomy of local structures.⁵² In dealing with these circumstances, medieval Muslim law applied a double strategy. On the one hand, the juridical discussion invoked its direct filiation with the divine word. On the other hand, Islamic jurists adapted their rulings to local practices, local knowledge, and customary law.⁵³

This brief assessment of the golden age of Islamic economics shows that the rise of specifically economic patterns of communication played a part in the intellectual debates of this time. The emergence of a money economy led to ongoing discussions among Islamic legal scholars about where to draw the line between admittable economic gain and illicit enrichment. These discussions reflect the emergence of the autopoietic nature of economic communication, epitomized in Marx's third form of money, in which money breeds money. While the prohibition of usury is a central issue in the Qur'an and the sunna of the Prophet, the precise meaning of *ribā* is not fixed in the shari'a.⁵⁴ Therefore, the famous Islamic modernist thinker Fazlur Rahman (1919–88) came to the conclusion that modern interest rates are mere price-mechanisms and should not be understood as forms of usury.⁵⁵

Historically, this tacit acceptance of money in its third form has been confirmed. The charging of interest has not been unknown in the history of Muslim commercial activities. In his work on the rules of purchase on the market, the Hanafi scholar Al-Sarakhsi (1090 CE), for instance, described mercantile lending as a quintessential market imperative.[56] In the Ottoman Empire, *ribā* was often only related to specific goods and modest interest rates up to 15 percent were "in the order of the day."[57] In seventeen- and eighteenth-century Egypt, Cairine merchant families disposed over complex and geographically widespread commercial networks as they carried out their business along mercantile capitalist lines. At the same time, we can observe the growing commercialization of artisan production in Egypt and a general development toward the exchange of goods and services in return for money.[58] Given the fact that the dependency of the Ottoman economy did not start before the turn of the nineteenth century, Nelly Hanna's conclusion that the empire knew internal roots of modernity also makes sense in its economic dimension.[59] In short, the century-long juridical debates about the very meaning of *ribā* represent boundary negotiations between emerging religious and economic realms. In the Middle East, preadaptive advances to economic modernity are undeniably observable in precolonial times.

The Idea of Islamic Economics: Islamic Finance, Halal Markets, and the Muslim Critique of Capitalism

The crucial role of *ribā* in the Qur'an and in Islamic tradition has fundamentally shaped the boundary negotiations between religion and economics among Muslims. To be sure, the holy scriptures of Islam are ambiguous with respect to economic issues. Economic activities such as the pursuit of profit, trade, and production for the market are favored by both the Qur'an and the sunna.[60] At the same time, however, the religious scriptures strongly condemn usury. It is therefore not surprising that the charging of interest occupies such a central position in the Islamic critique of modern capitalism too. In the eyes of some Muslim intellectuals, the capitalist economy has transformed the vices of *ribā* into the virtues of modern economic action. Islamic economists, therefore, have propagated the restoration of a moral economy in governing economic action by Islamic norms.[61] In normative terms, this conduct of Islamic economics has been directed against social behavior such as excessive individualism, moral egotism, profit-oriented action, and wholesale commodification.[62] The intellectuals behind the Islamic discourse of economic modernity identified the West with an excessive capitalist culture of greed.[63] In this way, Islamic economics have been presented as a third way of doing economics beyond capitalism and socialism, as the establishment of an "economy with moral purpose."[64] From this perspective, for instance, the new shariʿa-compliant generation of Malayan entrepreneurs has been driven by the "powerful conviction that Islam presented a perfect conjuncture of the spiritual and corporate economy that would lead" Malaysia and its citizens into a bright future.[65]

The concept of an Islamic economy basically rests on three pillars. The first one is the already several times mentioned ban on interest. To a large extent "the prohibition of *ribā* came to summarize the moral gulf" separating Islamic ethics from global capitalism.[66] Second, there is the idea of a redistribution of wealth through the institution of zakat, the Qurʾanic requirement of giving alms. Third, proponents of Islamic economics consider the application of Islamic norms in general as a means for the moral improvement of economic behavior.[67] While Islamic financial institutions, in particular banks, were already introduced to more than 60 countries in the mid-1990s, only a few, very different state-run systems to collect zakat exist. These zakat institutions were established by the governments of Libya, Malaysia, Pakistan, Saudi Arabia, and Yemen.[68] The more complex field of normatively guided Islamic economics comprises additional fields such as construction, production, services, tourism, and trade. Here, shariʿa-compliant companies do business while following interpretations of the general principles of the shariʿa (*maqāsid al-shariʿa*).[69] In the economic realm, three of these principles are particularly relevant: the subordination of individual interests to the benefit of the community; the precedence of relieving hardship over the promotion of benefit; and a balanced risk policy on loss and harm.[70] In particular the production and certification of goods as halal, i.e. as permissible with respect to Islamic law, has developed into a prosperous industry. The shariʿa-affinity of different economic realms thereby goes hand in hand with the spread of Islamic financial institutions interacting with companies in the globally expanding halal market. In the remaining part of this section, I will therefore cast a closer look on Islamic finance and the halal market.

Islamic banking aims at circumventing the charging of interest by applying alternative instruments as they are described in *fiqh* literature, the classical field of Islamic jurisprudence. The Qurʾan contrasts *ribā* with the obligation to pay zakat. In addition, numerous traditions forbid *ribā* without defining it more closely. Those who are involved in *ribā* "are cursed, the guilty are threatened with hell."[71] This strong religious condemnation of *ribā* gave rise to juridical methods—or tricks, the aforementioned *ḥiyal*—in order to evade the religious prohibition in economic practice.[72] It is these juridical methods to which contemporary instruments of Islamic banking also refer. Most important here is the recourse to the classical Islamic concept of *muḍāraba* as an "efficient revelation device."[73]. While in conventional financial transactions the bank will act as a lender of money and gain its profit through interest, *muḍāraba* is characterized by a special form of sharing risks and profits in the economic transaction. The concept is treated as a commercial association in *fiqh* and has found the approval of all four schools of law. It describes a fiduciary relationship that played an essential role in medieval long-distance trade. Thereby an investor entrusted capital to an agent "who trades with it and shares with the investor a pre-determined proportion of the profits." While financial losses "are the responsibility of the investor," the agent would have lost time, effort, and expected profits.[74] Today, *muḍāraba* refers to a form of "cost-plus financing" in which "the bank buys a product at a price and sells it back to you at a higher price."[75] Islamic finance, in this way, avoids conventional lending by rooting surpluses in the exchange of assets and not by using money as a commodity, that is to say exchanging money at a price.[76]

In circumventing interest by *muḍāraba* transactions, however, Islamic banking can hardly be said to have established a clear alternative to capitalist finances.[77] Rather than having an antagonistic relationship to conventional banking, Islamic banking employs the vocabulary of *fiqh* to reach an accommodation to rather than a rejection of the capitalist system.[78] This is also apparent in the fact that Islamic banking services have meanwhile become an established part of major conventional financial institutions such as HSBC, Citybank, Deutsche Bank, UBS, and Standard Chartered.[79] The successful rise of Islamic banking is largely due to two reasons. On the one hand, there is the increasing financial importance of a number of superbly rich Gulf investors. Global collaboration with their investment capital, therefore, demands a certain sensitivity to their normative religious requirements. On the other hand, the growing cultural assertiveness of Muslim identity discourses has produced an ever-growing reservoir of shariʿa-minded Muslim customers. Consequently, these religious customers represent an interesting additional market to the still predominant conventional banking market in Muslim parts of the world.[80] Islamic banking has thus developed into a profitable niche in the global financial market "engaging with capitalism rather than confronting it."[81]

This engagement with the capitalist market also applies to the diverse field of companies who address the growing segment of pious Muslims in the world market with their products and services. Parallel to the Islamic banks we can observe a multiplicity of new Islamic enterprises such as retailers, publishers, construction firms, and factories for various specifically Islamic products that create shari'a-compliant markets.[82] In her book on the "commodification of piety," Faegheh Shirazi argued that in these new Islamic markets pietism plays the role of a "marketing tool."[83] One of the central conceptual tools of this industry is the Islamic legal distinction between halal and *ḥarām*. In his *The Lawful and the Prohibited in Islam* the famous *'ālim* (religiously learned) Yusuf al-Qaradawi (1926–2022) discusses the question of the permissibility of things in light of the shari'a.[84] Thereby, Qaradawi applies a quite reformist approach in the merging of juridical opinions from different schools of law (*madhāhib*; sing. *madhhab*). This practice of *talfīq*, often critically perceived but with an occurrence in all schools of law already in premodern times, was also a part of Muhammad Abduh's reform agenda in the nineteenth century.[85] Qaradawi's book attempts to comprise the full range of aspects of contemporary life such as belief, business transaction, food, leisure activities, marital relationships, and work. In this way, it provides an encompassing guidance for those who want to participate in a sharia-conscious way in this new market of halal products and services.[86]

I had bought Qaradawi's book in an English translation during one of my stays in Malaysia, which is an important country in both Islamic finance and halal markets. In her "ethnography of corporate Islam," Patricia Sloane-White conducted fieldwork among Malaysia's new corporate "shari'a elite." The business activities of these people—corporate, salaried urban professionals—make Malaysia a key site for understanding the role of Islam in modern corporate everyday life.[87] Many bureaucrats and professionals of this shari'a generation are graduates from the International Islamic University Malaysia (IIUM), which served me as a case study in the previous chapter. The director of IIUM's school of Islamic management described his students as deeply pious Muslims fluent in both English and modern business. In Malaysia, the state-controlled educational policies of "moral character-building" based on Islamic principles created a new pious Muslim middle class that has been instrumental in making the country a significant pioneer in Islamic economics.[88] In its identity formation, this Malayan middle class combines the invocation of an Islamic worldview with a broad range of consumer practices and lifestyle choices.[89] In Sloane-White's words, Malaysia's corporate Islam "combines the triumph of capitalism with the triumph of Islam."[90]

The "halalization" of the Malaysian economy constructed strong "linkages between, class, consumption, market relations and the state,"[91] in this way, turning shopping into a "national duty."[92] Meanwhile global companies such as Carrefour, Colgate-Palmolive, Nestlé, and Unilever have made significant investments in this emerging market and have expanded their product range with halal goods.[93] According to some estimations, up to 70 percent of Muslims follow halal standards, thus making halal industries a profiting economic endeavor. Since the beginning, food products have been at the center of the halal market, whose estimated growth rates are about seven percent annually.[94] Due to the elaborate dietary requirements of Islam, pious Muslims are compelled to find religiously proper food at home and abroad. With Muslims making up approximately 16.6 percent of global food expenditure, the halal market "is one of the largest food markets in the world."[95] In Malaysia, the menus of McDonald's and Kentucky Fried Chicken have acquired their halal certifications by Malaysian state institutions.[96] Increasingly also restaurants and shops of the country's Chinese population display halal certifications in order to appeal to Muslim customers.[97] The certification of halal food is an integral part of this emerging global market that influences both consumer preferences and purchase behavior.[98] Generally speaking, participating in an ever-growing market with an abundance of halal and non-halal products, religious Muslim consumers experience increasingly uncertainties regarding normatively correct consumption. Consequently, the spread of modern consumer culture among Muslims goes hand in hand with the establishment of more rigid and stringent general standards for halal products.

The total number of halal certification bodies is estimated in the order of about 500 institutions. These institutions have been "founded as a business, non-government organization, a unit within a mosque, or a government department." Given the highly dynamic nature of halal standards and the continuous growth of certification bodies, the question of the integrity of halal-certified products became a highly relevant issue.[99] Consequently, Muslims "demand a near-zero risk halal environment," calling for "halal reputation management strategies."[100] This becomes visible in the halal tourism industry. Halal tourism is distinguished from Islamic tourism through its purpose. While the latter is motivated in religious terms, for instance performing the pilgrimage to Mecca (hajj), the purposes of halal tourism are no different from ordinary tourism. Yet, Muslim tourists often look for shariʿa-compliant travel destinations that provide for religious-related needs such as halal food, considerations of religious sensitivities, halal-conscious service staff, and local prayer facilities.[101] These demands include reliable halal certifications for restaurants and hotels on a global scale. It is expected that Muslim tourists will spend about USD 300 billion in 2026, making halal tourism an important growing market.[102] Participating in this market also demands from non-Muslim countries that they apply reliable standardized halal certifications in their tourism sector. In the long run, these certification policies by private and state agencies will lead to more rigid and standardized normative behavior among Muslims. The whole complex of halalification will contribute to the eradication of individual strategies of the "benefit of doubt" that for centuries have characterized compliance with religious rules in individual consumption.[103]

This brief examination of Islamic finance and the halal market tends to confirm Charles Tripp's conclusion that Islamic economics is a part of rather than an alternative to global capitalism. Invoking the vocabulary of classical Islamic jurisprudence in contemporary economics, according to him, represents an "alphabet of appropriation" for profit-oriented Islamic businesses, which try to attract an ever-increasing number of pious Muslim customers.[104] In particular the global halal market seems to be proof for this conclusion. Having its origins in food products, this market has expanded to include all kinds of commodities from cosmetics, lingerie, and various fashion accessories to tourism.[105] Even halal sex shops have entered a market which promises extraordinary business rewards.[106] In this commercial hype, the initially normative dimension of the Islamization of modern economics has apparently withered away. At least in Patricia Sloane-White's assessment of the Islamic economy of Malaysia and its shariʿa-compliant new corporative world, economic Islamization has not let to a visible concern for "serving the everyday needs of the hardcore poor." On the contrary, corporate Islam has privileged the members of the new corporate shari'a elite themselves. Heavily relying on political connections and the support of the state, this new Malayan business elite reproduced for them the "same opportunities, class distinctions, inequalities, and elite definitions of self-worth (and moral loopholes)" which characterized their predecessors. Apparently, the shari'a-compliant business generation has been following the path of the Malayan middle class, whose origin was in the New Economic Policy era of the 1970s and 1980s.[107]

Volunteers and Muslim Entrepreneurs: "Post-Islamist" Discourses of Islamic Modernities

Islamic economics do not necessarily "transform the selfish and acquisitive homo economicus into a paragon of virtue."[108] At least this is the tentative conclusion to be drawn from the previous section. The increase in the shari'a-affinity of Islamic businesses might make capitalism more "authentic," but not automatically less materialist than conventional economics has appeared in the eyes of Islamic economists. In addition, as seen in the example of Malaysia, corporate Islam turned the working place into another space of state policies of nationalist Islamization. This state-induced Islamization promotes a financially powerful form of conservative Islam calling for stricter shari'a laws also in other walks of life.[109] The rather state-centered, paternalistic, and conservative mindset of Malaysia's shari'a generation reminds us of the ideals of the organized Islamic society propagated by the Muslim Brotherhood ideology that was the topic of Chapter Five. However, alternative projects of Islamic modernities have increasingly challenged this state-centered vision of an Islamic social order based on state-controlled, collectively binding, religiously inspired rules. In the literature, these alternative projects have been discussed under the concept of a new kind of "post-Islamist" middle-class Islamic activism. This activism is "sustained by Islamic counter-elites" and takes place "in the context of a changing economy."[110] It represents a new trend in religious movements that "tend toward a liberal state model that allows individual agency, choice, and autonomy with respect to religious, economic, political, and civic action."[111] According to Asef Bayat, we should observe in these new Islamic movements a marriage of "Islam with individual choice and freedom." In what he labeled a "post-Islamist" discourse Bayat discerns a new emphasis on "religiosity and rights."[112] In the remaining part of this chapter, I will take a closer look at these newer projects of Islamic modernities which distance themselves from both the version of Islamist modernism promoted by the Muslim Brotherhood and from Islamic projects of modernity closely associated with the power of authoritarian states.[113]

In his theory of successive modernities, Peter Wagner pointed to the rise of a new paradigmatic type of liberal modernity that gradually replaced the ideals of an organized society in Europe after the Second World War. Other sociologists described this historical shift between two different forms of modernity as the turn toward "second," "reflexive," "late," or "liquid" modernity.[114] These authors more or less share Wagner's diagnosis of the emergence of a new pluralist form of modernity with a decisive shift in social priorities from the collective to the individual.[115] Wagner builds his theory of successive modernities on—in his eyes—the specifically modern ambivalence between mastery and autonomy to which social actors can only find temporary solutions.[116] Imaginations of organized modernities emphasize mastery by autonomous collective actors, whereas pluralist modernities employ visions of the autonomous agency and liberal rights of the individual. According to liberal thought, these modern individuals are not controlled from above, that is to say by state institutions, but they are largely masters of themselves. In contrast to the patterns of organized modernity, the social orders of pluralist modernities are characterized by "multiple choices, entrepreneurial strategies and an increasing pluralization of social practices,"[117] In putting his focus on processes of subjectivation, Andreas Reckwitz complemented this pluralist form of social order with a specific cultural type of modern subjectivity. According to Reckwitz, we can observe the emergence of a "postmodern" type of subjectivity formation whose central features are individualized patterns of consumption, creative action, and self-reliance. The individual of this postmodern subjectivity formation is of a dynamic kind, exhibits an entrepreneurial mentality, and is continuously engaged in shifting projects. This type of modern subjectivity rejects the peer-group-oriented average culture of organized society with its ideals of rational calculation, bureaucratic organization, and technical coordination of social life. Instead, it appreciates an individualized working culture and a social order that has its focus on the dignity and rights of the individual.[118]

The theoretical designs of Wagner and Reckwitz describe a form of modernity in which principles of individual self-control replace the top-down control of the population by state authorities. In the conceptual language of Michel Foucault: in the neoliberal order, technologies of the self take the place of the previously disciplining technologies of domination coerced by the modern state.[119] The demand for individual development opportunities supersedes programs of state-controlled modernization. To be sure, in many states with Muslim majority populations, this concept of a pluralistic order can hardly be said to describe the contours of contemporary social and political life. In most of them, authoritarian regimes and illiberal democracies prevail, representing approximations to different forms of organized modernity. Yet the here-discussed examples of new Islamic activism share at least some features displayed by the ideal type of pluralist modernity, thus indicating possible avenues of social change. Ideas of individual autonomy, social plurality, and diversity in religious practices have characterized the societal visions of some "post-Islamist" movements.[120] In Egypt, this applies especially to the political visions that were displayed during the revolutionary weeks on Tahrir Square in 2011. In the context of the so-called "Arab Spring," elements of a much more pluralist notion of modern life animated many of the anti-governmental protests. The model of social order implemented by the demonstrators in Tahrir was vehemently directed against the patriarchal and exclusivist governmental practices of the Mubarak regime. The opposition in the square practiced a way of life that combined elements of a collectivist society with those of a pluralistic modernity. In this way, the activists tried to bring the disregarded economic needs and political rights of both the Egyptian people and the individual Egyptian citizen into agreement.[121] However, signs of these social transformations were already visible before the years of Arab upheavals of 2011–12.[122]

In Egypt, some of the first signs indicating a more pluralist direction in the nature of Islamic activism appeared in a growing number of Islamic youth organizations. These organizations combine social commitment based on religious ethics with accepted forms of consumer behavior. This combination corresponds above all to the everyday experiences of the younger generation of Egypt's urban upper middle class.[123] The members of these organizations found some of their core inspirations in the thought of a new group of religious lay preachers. These religious actors introduced new projects of modernity that clearly diverged from the rather hegemonic Islamist visions with which the Muslim Brotherhood has dominated the Islamic discourse of modernity for several decades. Instead of presenting their messages in the authoritative voice of the classical Arabic of Al-Azhar's religiously learned sheikhs, these lay preachers addressed their audiences in the vernacular of colloquial Arabic, using new kinds of media such as the internet, chat rooms, and satellite TV. As one of their major representatives, Amr Khaled, put it: "My main concern is to make young people love religion instead of fearing it."[124] Born in Cairo in 1967, Amr Khaled was one of the leading figures in this new Islamic movement. The son of an Egyptian upper middle-class family and business-school graduate, he started preaching in the early 1990s while still working as an accountant. Given this background, he perfectly combined Islamic ethics with contemporary business attitudes. In 2001, he first appeared on TV with the Ramadan show "Words from the Heart." Rapidly increasing his audience, Khaled left Egypt in 2002 and produced his programs from Great Britain until his return to Egypt in 2007.[125] Through different satellite channels such as Iqra, Dream TV, and Orbit, his messages reached millions of young Muslims around the globe. In addition, people followed him on his extensive website and by consuming his audio and videotapes.[126]

Amr Khaled and other lay preachers such as Mustafa Hosni, Khaled el-Guindy, Moez Masoud, and Mona Abdel-Ghani became diverse catalysts for a broader trend of religious reorganization among Islamic movements. In the context of the technological advancement of digital media, the traditional forms of religious organization were challenged by emerging new religious actors. Instead of adopting the disciplining voices of traditional sheikhs, some of these new religious actors addressed their audiences in a soft and compassionate style. They were young Egyptians with a middle-class background, religious autodidacts not educated in the traditional Islamic sciences. In underlining this distance from the traditional establishment of learned sheikhs, Amr Khaled declared himself an "average Muslim" who engages in missionary work and not in Islamic jurisprudential deliberations.[127] He often presented his shows in a suit and tie, adopting a similar style to American televangelists. The programs of Amr Khaled wove together Qur'anic stories and questions of contemporary everyday life. His themes usually comprised issues such as love, forgiveness, morality, and social responsibility. At the same time, he reconciled the enjoyment of life with the observance of Islamic norms. Amer Khaled declared becoming wealthy through business activities as in accordance with being a sincere practician of the Islamic faith. In this way, the young Islamic lay preachers propagated an understanding of Islam fully compatible with the personal and economic life expectations of Egypt's young urban middle classes. In their projects of modern Islamic reforms, we can detect some elements of the rising type of "postmodern" subjectivity, particularly when they described modern Muslim believers as creative, consumption-oriented, and self-reliant entrepreneurs at the same time.[128] In the terminology of Mona Atia, in the discourse of these lay preachers we can discern the construction of an ideal type of the "pious neoliberal subject," combining features such as entrepreneurship, individualism, volunteering, and faith.[129]

In the years 2006 and 2007, we conducted fieldwork among Islamic youth and welfare organizations in Egypt and Jordan.[130] The social engagement and working spirit of our interlocutors in these groups clearly showed the mobilizing power of this kind of Islamic reform discourse propagated by the new lay preachers. Among these organizations, the Egyptian "Resala Association for Charity" was the most influential. Starting as a student initiative in 1999, Resala grew into the largest Arab-Muslim youth organization, with more than 200,000 volunteers and 63 branches spread over the whole country.[131] The organization provides educational, health, and social services for the poor, mainly based on monetary and in-kind donations. On the Egyptian scene, Resala represents an Islamic organization with both civic and national visions.[132] The communication of these youth organizations with their members, potential staff, and volunteers, as well as with donors and the general public, takes place via websites, mailing lists, blogs, Facebook groups, and chat rooms. Generally speaking, they identify the major problems of Egyptian society in poverty-related phenomena such as illiteracy, illness, and unemployment. Moreover, our interlocutors emphasized the negative status of Egypt's youth characterized by the widespread underemployment of graduates of higher education, their exclusion from public institutions, and a general mood of social apathy among them.[133] In order to tackle this situation, the organizations promoted a new kind of Islamic activism, combining youth voluntarism with social entrepreneurship and Islamic morality with neoliberal business and management strategies.[134] In their vocational training courses, board members, staff, and volunteers learn about micro-financing, human capital building, and sustainable development strategies linked to religious narratives. The references to religious traditions bestow these central buzzwords of the "global developmental industry" with a kind of Islamic authenticity. The volunteers are driven by a form of "active piety," a deep desire to influence others in their beliefs and social behavior, in order to achieve change in society.[135]

These new projects of Islamic modernities are epitomized in the model of the Muslim professional, fusing religious ethics with some essentials of neoliberal economic ideology. This ideal type of Islamic creative worker and entrepreneur represents the role model for both the leaders of the youth organizations and their volunteers. Rather than contrasting modern business strategies with Islamic values, as the protagonists of Islamic economics predominantly have done, in the Muslim professional these two become complementary attributes. "The Muslim professional dresses in the right way, works efficiently and has high moral standards."[136] In their career development courses, the young participants learn efficient technologies of the self, derived from both religious and non-religious discursive practices, aiming at their self-fashioning according to the desired role model.[137] In accordance with the messages of Amr Khaled's programs, religious commitment and economic success meet in the Muslim professional. With reference to the voluntary activities of Resala's members, the founder and chairman stated: "In all this we're only talking about the rewards in the afterlife. But is the reward only in the afterlife? The rewards are in this life as well. What is the reward that God gives in this life as well? Success! Self-Satisfaction! People's love"![138]

The, often elegantly dressed, directors and board members of these organizations serve as role models for the younger volunteers. Even more important, they are living examples of success in this life. This was clearly acknowledged in our interview with the founder of Bayan, who concluded: "We are role models. I am not preaching perfection, but I am teaching total project management."[139] The leaders of these youth organizations, thus, are the major "social carriers" of a new kind of Islamic movement articulating a specific spirit of identity-building through social activism.[140] Taking inspiration from globally acknowledged features of contemporary corporate life, they merge business philosophies and entrepreneurial spirit with Islamic norms, providing an important frame of reference for the identity construction of their volunteers and course participants. In contradistinction to Malaysia's religiously conservative shariʻa generation, however, these projects of Islamic modernity do so by keeping at a distance to Islamist concepts about a fully shariʻa-compliant state. Rather, they emphasize the crucial role of the Muslim individual and therewith traits of a kind of subjectivity of which we can make sense with reference to Reckwitz' cultural type of the "postmodern" subject.

Conclusions: The Mirage of Islamic Economics

In his interview with *Foreign Policy*, Hamza Yusuf declared the trend toward opening halal sex shops a reflection of "the adaptive qualities of capitalism." The founder and president of the Islamic Zaytuna College in Berkeley, California, concludes that in the end this "all goes back to the monetization of religion."[141] Indeed, especially the quickly growing global halal market apparently corroborates Hamza Yusuf's judgment. The global expansion of halal products underlines the commodification of religious traditions in a market that combines religious motivations with the distribution of goods for money. From this perspective, Islamic economics indeed represents a variation upon, rather than an alternative to, modern capitalism. The modern economic system has seemingly colonialized religion. This is at least the common denominator I could find among authors such as Johan Fisher, Timur Kuran, Charles Tripp, Faegheh Shirazi, and Patricia Sloane-White, all of whom point to the relative dominance of economic reasons over religious values. In his study on *Gulf Capital & Islamic Finance*, Aamir Rehman suggests we look at the "factual relevance of Islamic Financial Institutions" instead of "focusing on their Islamic character."[142] The relevance of Islamic financial products is also increasing, according to Rehman, albeit from a very low level in comparison to the size of the conventional financial market. In his eyes, "Islamic finance has proven its viability," but it still has to "strengthen its posture" in the competition with conventional products on international financial markets.[143] Consequently, in order to enhance their economic viability, Islamic enterprises have to follow the rules of competitiveness of a global market economy.

In this context, the recourse to medieval Islamic institutions such as *muḍāraba* serves the purpose, on the one hand of making economic modernity authentic. In this sense these institutions also play an important role in contemporary identity politics. Consequently, the *kitāb al-ḥiyal* literature of classical Islamic jurists provides a large reservoir for the contemporary Islamic discourse of modernity in its economic dimension. Furthermore, the ideas of Islamic economics also prove Eisenstadt's contention that projects of multiple modernities draw from the sources of religious traditions. The semantics of Islamic financial markets employ religious traditions when applying the general syntax of modernity. The Islamic economy as a "third way" is a religiously framed project of modernity.

On the other hand, the recourse to premodern deliberations in *fiqh* also supports the argument that we can observe in Muslim history preadaptive advances in the boundary demarcations between emerging religious and economic systems. In medieval Islamic economics we can observe similar processes of preservation, transformation, and extension of the conceptual and institutional devices from antiquity as in Islamic science. Thus, it should not come as a surprise that scholars of medieval economics echo those of science not only in discussing a golden age of Arab economics, but also in employing the bridge metaphor, that is to say understanding this historical period as a transition from antiquity to "European modernity." From the perspective of Modern Systems Theory, however, the *kitāb al-ḥiyal* literature indicates more than a mere transitional epoch. This genre of classical Islamic jurisprudence can be read as a series of reflections upon the gradual emergence of economic value relationships in a non-European context, which later led to the fully monetized modern economic system.

The contemporary Islamic economist resembles the medieval jurist who worked for the accommodation of Islamic precepts to the autonomous logics of specifically economic communication. To be sure, this does not justify the talk about the so-called "Arab roots of capitalism." From the theoretical perspective of this book, an emerging modern system of economic communication does not have "roots." Instead, the functionally differentiated system of the modern economy is the contingent but selective result of a process of sociocultural evolution. However, we *can* talk about non-European advances to modern capitalism, which according to the works of authors such as Peter Gran, Nelly Hanna, and Maxime Rodinson continued to appear in the centuries after the Islamic/Arab golden ages. Also in this respect, we should undertake a critical revision of the predominant narrative of Arab and Ottoman decline. Furthermore, the logics of economic communications were also not merely an export product from Europe. Consequently, the field of Islamic economics, old and new, invites further studies on the process of the conceptual provincialization of European history in the sociology of modernity.

While the monetization of religion is an apparent feature of the relationship between Islam and economics, it does not represent the whole story. Rather we should perceive this relationship in ambiguous and co-constitutive terms. The interlacement of economic and religious discourses leads to a new type of religious modern subjectivity in which piety and consumption closely intersect.[144] The case of Malaysia shows how the promotion of Islamic finance and halal markets can also go hand in hand with state policies of nationalist Islamization. In Malaysia the promotion of Islamic economics also aimed at creating nationalistic Malayan consumers.[145] Moreover, economic strategies, state policies, and religious motivations have intersected in the evolution of the country's shari'a generation. Ironically, the developmentalist modernization policies of Prime Minister Mahathir Mohamad—largely based on the precepts of classical modernization theories—simultaneously propagated a distinctively conservative kind of Islam in practice.[146] Modern economic and political communication thus contributed to the rise of more purist and conservative practices in Islamic traditions in Malaysia.[147] Our fieldwork in Egypt and Jordan, by contrast, documented a different combination of economic and religious forms of communication. Here the intersection of religion and economics becomes instrumental in the identity construction of a new generation of young Muslims, whose identity constructions resemble the more general cultural type of subjectivation which Reckwitz described as the modern creative worker and entrepreneur. In the concept of the "Muslim entrepreneur" prevalent among contemporary Islamic youth and welfare organizations we can detect a more individualistic pattern of the interlacement of religion with neoliberal market mechanisms.[148]

This leads me to my final point in this chapter. The social negotiations between Islam and economics here have implications for the theoretical framework of this book. They provide some empirical material for reflections upon the "Eurocentric conceptual tools" which I presented in Chapter Two. In contemporary Islamic economics we can observe a kind of double-bind between the economic and the religious systems. At the macro level, we can conceptually treat them as two distinct social systems with each having a self-referential code of communication. At the level of social actors, however, the boundaries between system and environment become blurred. Here we can see historical processes of the mutual appropriation of communicative elements from the respective other system by religious and economic actors. The shariʿa generation in Malaysia and the new post-Islamist Islamic movements show ways in which religion can take specific shapes and religious adherence grow stronger among individuals and collectives in modern life. In this sense, secularization defined by functional differentiation may lead precisely to the opposite of religious decline, as once propagated by classical modernization cum secularization theories. However, one might say this does not come without a price. The relative success of Islamic economics has been predicated on the tacit acceptance of the commodification and monetization of religious communication by the economic system. Though this may only be of a temporary nature, this brings the question of dominance among function systems into play. The empirical material of this chapter also underpins the argument that one function system—here the economic system—may have a relative but limited hegemony over others which occur in different historical periods of modernity. And it is this relative hegemony of other systems over religion that conservative religious intellectuals like Hamza Yusuf bemoan.

Notes

1. Chapra, Umer M. 2000. Is It Necessary to Have Islamic Economics? *The Journal of Socio-Economics* 29: 21–37, 29. To some extent, Chapra's suggestions sound like an Islamic variation over a meanwhile well-known normative business strategy of socially responsible entrepreneurship or Corporate Social Responsibilty (CSR): Cf. Choi, David Y. and Edmund R. Gray. 2008. Socially Responsible Entrepreneurs: What Do They Do to Create and Build Their Companies? *Business Horizons* 51: 341–352.
2. Ibid. 32.
3. Abu Ala al-Mawdudi was born in Hyderabad, where he was brought up in a religious environment and received a traditional Islamic education. After moving to Delhi, he worked as a journalist and supported the Indian Khilafat movement. His later writings on Islam and political authority became foundational for the development of radical Islamist thought. In 1938, Mawdudi moved to Punjab, today in Pakistan, and founded the Jamaat-i Islami in Lahore in 1941. While not supporting the aim of the Indian Muslim League to establish

a Muslim state in South Asia, he strongly opposed the secular nationalism of the Indian Congress. After the separation of South Asia into India and Pakistan, he made the Islamization of the Pakistani state the major project of his and the Jamaat's political activities. See: Jung, Dietrich. 2011. *Orientalists, Islamists and the Global Public Sphere: A Genealogy of the Modern Essentialist Image of Islam.* Sheffield: Equinox, 252–255.

4. Kuran, Timur. 2004. *Islam and Mamon: The Economic Predicaments of Islamism.* Princeton: Princeton University Press, 82–85.
5. Ibid. ix–x.
6. At the same time, we can also observe the rise of an Islamist discourse on positive law and the shari'a which was in a similar way triggered by cultural anxieties regarding Muslim identity and the authenticity of modern legal systems rather than by juridical practices. See: Fahmy, Khaled. 2018. *In Quest of Justice: Islamic Law and Forensic Medicine in Modern Egypt.* Oakland: University of California Press, 28–35.
7. Rehman, Aamir A. 2010. *Gulf Capital & Islamic Finance: The Rise of the New Global Players.* New York: McGraw Hill, 102.
8. In Malaysia, for instance, an Islamic finance industry was already launched with the "Islamic Banking Act" in 1983. See: Sloane-White, Patricia. 2017. *Corporate Islam: Sharia and the Modern Workplace.* Cambridge: Cambridge University Press, 36.
9. Ibid. 18.
10. Heck, Gene W. 2006. *Charlemagne, Muhammad, and the Arab Roots of Capitalism.* Berlin: Walter de Gruyter.
11. Cf. Presley, John R. and John G. Sessions. 1994. Islamic Economics: The Emergence of a New Paradigm. *The Economic Journal* 104 (424): 584–596.
12. Tripp, Charles. 2006. *Islam and the Moral Economy: The Challenge of Capitalism.* Cambridge: Cambridge University Press, 8.
13. Luhmann, Niklas. 1986. *Ökologische Kommunikation: Kann die moderne Gesellschaft sich auf ökologische Gefährdungen einstellen?* Opladen: Westdeutscher Verlag, 103.
14. Luhmann, Niklas. 1998. *Die Gesellschaft der Gesellschaft.* Vol. 1. Frankfurt am Main: Suhrkamp, 148.
15. Luhmann 1986, 104.
16. Ibid. 122.
17. Tripp 2006, 66.
18. Therefore, it is also a flawed argument to point to its purpose of regulating and

organizing not only divine but also material life when distinguishing Islam from Judaism and Christianity. All three religions have expressed these kinds of claims to regulate social action beyond the narrowly described religious realm. For such argumentation, see: Presley and Sessions 1994, 585.

19. Aristoteles. 1958. *Politik*. Übersetzt und mit erklärenden Anmerkungen und Registern versehen von Eugen Rolfes. Hamburg: Felix Meiner, 22–23.
20. Cf. Müller, Rudolf. 1977. *Geld und Geist: Zur Entstehungsgeschichte von Identitätsbewußtsein und Rationalität seit der Antike*. Frankfurt am Main: Campus.
21. Fontaine, Laurence. 2014. *Le Marché: Historie et usages d'une conquête sociale*. Paris: Gallimard, 16.
22. Ibid. 20.
23. Marx, Karl. 1974. *Grundrisse der politischen Ökonomie* (MEW 13). Berlin: Diez Verlag, 75.
24. Marx, Karl. 1976. A Contribution to the Critique of Political Economy. In *Collected Works*. Volume 29. London: Lawrence and Wishart, 257–420, 384.
25. Ibid. 129–134.
26. Rehman 2010, 95.
27. Weber, Max. 1920. *Gesammelte Aufsätze zur Religionssoziologie*. Vol. I. Tübingen: UTB [1988], 544.
28. Weber, Max. 1972. *Wirtschaft und Gesellschaft: Grundriß der verstehenden Soziologie*. Studienausgabe. Tübingen: Mohr, 403.
29. Weber, Max. 1968. *Economy and Society: An Outline of Interpretive Sociology*. Vol. II. New York: Bedminister Press, 635.
30. Simmel, Georg. 1989. *Philosophie des Geldes*. Frankfurt am Main: Suhrkamp, 667.
31. Gran, Peter. 1979. *Islamic Roots of Capitalism: Egypt, 1760–1840*. Austin and London: University of Texas Press; Hanna, Nelly. 2011. *Artisan Entrepreneurs in Cairo and Early-Modern Capitalism (1600–1800)*. Syracuse, NY: Syracuse University Press; Heck 2006; Rodinson, Maxime. 1986. *Islam und Kapitalismus*. Mit einer Einleitung von Bassam Tibi. Frankfurt am Main: Suhrkamp.
32. Citarella, Armand O. 1968. Patterns in Medieval Trade: The Commerce of Amalfi Before the Crusades. *The Journal of Economic History* 28 (4): 531–555, 531.
33. Ibid. 535 and 553. The Geniza papers comprise documents from all over the Mediterranean from the eleventh to the thirteenth century which were preserved in the so-called Cairo Geniza, see: Goitein, S. D. 1960. The Documents

of the Cairo Geniza as a Source for Mediterranean Social History. *Journal of the American Oriental Society* 80 (2): 91–100.
34. Heck 2006, 4.
35. Ibid. 6.
36. Ibid. 109.
37. Lieber, Alfred E. 1968. Eastern Business Practices and Medieval European Commerce. *The Economic History Review* 21 (2): 230–243, 230.
38. Ibid. 231.
39. Heck 2006, 219.
40. Lieber 1968, 243.
41. Usher, Abbott Payson. 1934. The Origins of Banking: The Primitive Bank of Deposit, 1200–1600. *The Economic History Review* 4 (4): 399–428.
42. Rodinson 1986, 30 and 64.
43. Lombard, Maurice. 1992. *Blütezeit des Islam: Eine Wirtschafts- und Kulturgeschichte des 8.—11. Jahrhunderts*. Frankfurt am Main: Fischer, 232.
44. Ibid. 120. Interestingly, this highly developed commerce by money made coins into a vital source for historians of early Muslim history. Due to the scarcity of primary documents prior to the fifteenth century, they largely have to rely on secondary sources such as chronicles, often written much later than when the factual events took place. Here numismatics became a valuable substitute, as coins of the classical period of Islam often bear texts of up to 150 words. This texts comprise important information about names and hierarchies of power in a time period of "the first six-and-a-half centuries of Islam." See: Heidemann, Stefan. 2010. Numismatics. In *The New Cambridge History of Islam: Volume I: The Formation of the Islamic World, Sixth to Eleventh Centuries*. Edited by Chase Robinson. Cambridge: Cambridge University Press, 648–663, 648–649.
45. Heck 2006, 93,
46. Rodinson 1986, 65.
47. Schacht, Joseph. 1979. Ḥiyal. In *The Encyclopaedia of Islam: New Edition*. Vol. III. Leiden: Brill: 510–513, 511.
48. Rahman, Fazlur. 1964. Ribā and Interest. *Islamic Studies* 3 (1): 1–43, at 3.
49. Ibid. 12–21 and 30.
50. Udovitch 1987, 12.
51. Rodinson 1986, 87.
52. Tuma, Elias H. 1965. Early Arab Economic Policies (1st/7th–4th/10th Centuries). *Islamic Studies* 4 (1): 1–23, 13.

53. Udovitch 1987, 27.
54. Rahman 1964, 26.
55. Ibid. 37
56. Heck 2006, 92.
57. Çağatay, Neşet. 1970. "Ribā and Interest Concept and Banking in the Ottoman Empire. *Studia Islamica* 32: 53–68, 65.
58. Hanna 2011, 23.
59. Ibid. 192.
60. Rodinson 1986, 41.
61. Tripp 2006, 65 and 47.
62. Ibid. 97.
63. Sloan-White, 26.
64. Tripp 2006, 112.
65. Sloane-White 2017, 23.
66. Tripp 2006, 133.
67. Kuran 2004, xiv.
68. Kuran, Timur. 1995. Islamic Economics and the Islamic Subeconomy. *Journal of Economic Perspectives* 9 (4): 155–173, 160; Sloane-White, 135 and fn. 11.
69. There is no definitive list of these principles that could be found in the Qur'an and the traditions of the Prophet (sunna). While they generally relate to the purpose of Islamic law in serving the social well-being of the Muslim community, the four schools of law have differed in their interpretations of them. For a more detailed discussion of the principles of the shari'a, see: Duderija, Adis (ed.). 2014. *Maqāṣid al-Sharī'a and Contemporary Reformist Muslim Thought and Contemporary Reformist Muslim Thought*. London: Routledge.
70. Todorof, Maria. 2018. *Shariah*-compliant FinTech in the Banking Industry. *ERA Forum* 19 (1): 1–17, 2–3.
71. Schacht, Joseph. 1995. Ribā. In *Encyclopaedia of Islam: New Edition*. Vol. VIII. Leiden, Brill: 391–393.
72. It should be mentioned that not all Islamic jurists agreed with these methods of evaluation. While the Hanafi school was most at ease with it, the Hanbali school rejected the *ḥiyal* almost completely. In particular Ibn Taymiyya (1263–1328 CE), a classical icon for contemporary Salafist thinkers, declared them as invalid in general. See: Schacht 1979.
73. Presley and Sessions 1994, 595.
74. Wakin, Jeanette. 1993. Muḍāraba. In *The Encyclopaedia of Islam: New Edition*. Vol. VII. Leiden: Brill: 284–285, 284.

75. Todorof 2018, 7.
76. Rehman 2010, 95–97.
77. Similar forms for the funding of risky start-ups can be found outside Islamic finance on the conventional capital market, in particular with regard to new lean start-up businesses: Blank, Steve. 2013. Why the Lean Start-Up Changes Everything. A Faster, Smarter Methodology for Launching Companies May Make Business Plans Obsolete. *Harvard Business Review* 91 (5): 63–72.
78. Tripp 2006, 68.
79. Rehman 2010, 90.
80. Ibid. 187.
81. Tripp 2006, 199.
82. Cf. Turan 1995, 155.
83. Shirazi, Faegheh. 2016. *Brand Islam: The Marketing and Commodification of Piety*. Austin: University of Texas Press, 7.
84. Born in Egypt in 1926, Yusuf Qaradawi was one of the leading Sunni sheiks in recent decades. Having had a background in the Egyptian Muslim Brotherhood, Qaradawi later aired his interpretations of Islam through TV programs from Doha in Qatar. For a comprehensive overview on him, see: Gräf, Bettina and Jakob Skovgaard-Petersen (eds.). 2009. *The Global Mufti: The Phenomenon of Yusuf al-Qaradawi*. London: Hurst. See also: El-Wereny, Mahmud. 2018. Reichweite und Instrumente islamrechtlicher Normfindung: Yūsuf al-Qaraḍāwīs *iğtihād*-Konzept. *Die Welt des Islams* 58 (1): 65–100.
85. Krawietz, Birgit. 2002. Cut and Paste in Legal Rules: Designing Islamic Norms with Talfiq. *Die Welt des Islams* 42 (1): 3–40.
86. Al-Qaradawi, Yusuf. 2001. *The Lawful and the Prohibited in Islam*. Translated by: Kamal El-Hebawy, M. Moinuddin Siddiqui and Syed Shukry. Reprint of the Malaysian Student's Edition. Kuala Lumpur: Islamic Book Trust.
87. Sloane-White 2017, 6.
88. Ibid. 75–78.
89. Fischer, Johan. 2008. *Proper Islamic Consumption: Shopping Among the Malays in Modern Malaysia*. Copenhagen NIAS Press, 8.
90. Ibid. 183.
91. Fischer 2008, 17.
92. Ibid. 10.
93. Shirazi 2016, 13.
94. Yuhanis, Abdul Aziz and Nyen Vui Chok. 2013. The Role of Halal Awareness, Halal Certification, and Marketing Components in Determining Halal

Purchase Intention among Non-Muslims in Malaysia: A Structural Equation Meddling Approach. *Journal of International Food & Agribusiness Marketing* 25 (1): 1–23, 2.
95. Ab Talib, Mohamed Syazwan, Siti Salwa Md. Sawari, Abu Bakar, Abdul Hamid and Too Ai Chin. 2015. Emerging Halal Food Market: An Institutional Theory of Halal Certificate Implementation. *Management Research Review* 39 (9): 987–997, 988.
96. Fischer, Johan. 2011. *The Halal Frontier: Muslim Consumers in a Globalized Market*. New York: Palgrave Macmillan, 56.
97. Ibid. 46.
98. Ab Talib et al. 2015, 988.
99. Tieman, Marco. 2018. Measuring Corporate Halal Reputation. A Corporate Halal Reputation Index and Research Propositions. *Journal of Islamic Marketing* 11 (3): 591–601, 592.
100. Ibid. 593 and 594.
101. Xiong, Jia and Zhang Chaozhi. 2020. "Halal Tourism": Is it the same Trend in Non-Islamic Destinations with Islamic Destination? *Asia Pacific Journal of Tourism Research* 25 (2): 189–204.
102. Yoksamon Jeaheng, Amr Al-Ansi and Heesup Han. 2019. Halal-friendly Hotels: Impact of Halal-Friendly Attributes on Guest Purchase Behaviors in the Thailand Hotel Industry. *Journal of Travel & Tourism Marketing* 26 (6): 729–746, 729.
103. Fischer 2011, 164.
104. Tripp 2006, 195.
105. Cf. Shirazi 2016.
106. Fosset, Karelyn. 2013. What Makes a Sex Shop Halal? *Foreign Policy*, October 23rd.
107. Sloan-White 2017, 185–186.
108. Kuran 1995, 159.
109. Sloan-White 2017, 89.
110. Wickham, Carrie Rosefsky. 2002. *Mobilizing Islam: Religion, Activism, and Political Change in Egypt*. New York: Columbia University Press, at 8; Clark, Janine A. 2004. *Islam, Charity, and Activism: Middle-Class Networks and Social Welfare in Egypt, Jordan, and Yemen*. Bloomington and Indianapolis: Indiana University Press, 11.
111. Çevik, Neslihan. 2016. *Muslimism in Turkey and Beyond: Religion in the Modern World*. New York: Palgrave Macmillan, 6.

112. Bayat, Asef. 2007. *Making Islam Democratic: Social Movements and the Post-Islamist Turn*. Stanford: Stanford University Press, 11.
113. Another dimension of this post-Islamist turn is due to recent developments in Islamic thought. Since September 11, 2001, an increasing number of Muslim intellectuals have been drawn into public debate. These Islamic thinkers often "try to elaborate a vision of Islam in conformity with political liberalism" in order to counter the essentialist image of Islam among European and North American publics; Brahimi, Mohamed Amine and Houssem Ben Lazreg. 2021. Post-Islamism and Intellectual Production: A Bibliometric Analysis of the Evolution of Contemporary Islamic Thought. *Religions* 12 (49): 1–25, 16.
114. Baumann, Zygmunt. 2007. *Liquid Times: Living in an Age of Uncertainty*. Cambridge: Cambridge University Press; Beck, Ulrich. 1992. *Risk Society: Towards a New Modernity*. London: Sage; Giddens, Anthony. 1991. *The Consequences of Modernity*. Stanford: Stanford University Press.
115. Wagner, Peter. 2010. Successive Modernities and the Idea of Progress: A First Attempt. *Distinktion* 11 (2): 9–24.
116. Wagner, Peter. 2001. *Theorizing Modernity: Inescapability and Attainability in Social Theory*. London, Thousand Oaks and New Delhi: Sage Publications, 118.
117. Jung, Dietrich. 2017. *Muslim History and Social Theory: A Global Sociology of Modernity*. London and New York: Palgrave Macmillan, 28.
118. Reckwitz, Andreas. 2006. *Das hybride Subjekt: Eine Theorie der Subjektkulturen von der bürgerlichen Moderne zur Postmoderne*. Weilerwist: Velbrück Wissenschaft, 441–630. See my summary, in: Jung 2017, 72–73.
119. For a good overview on Foucault's concept of governmentality, see: Bröckling, Ulrich, Susanne Krasmann and Thomas Lemke (eds.). 2007. *Governmentality: Current Issues and Future Challenges*. London and New York: Routledge.
120. Bayat 2007, 13.
121. Mex-Jørgensen, Line. 2020. Imaginaries of the Good Life from the Egyptian Revolution in 2011: Pride and Agency. In *Muslim Subjectivities in Global Modernity: Islamic Traditions and the Construction of Modern Muslim Identities*. Edited by Dietrich Jung and Kirstine Sinclair. Leiden: Brill, 216–237.
122. For a brief account of Egyptian youth groups on the way to the Arab rebellions, see: Shehata, Dina. 2014. Youth Movements and the 25 January Revolution. In *Arab Spring in Egypt: Revolution and Beyond*. Edited by Bahgat Korany and Rabab El-Mahdi. Cairo and New York: American University of Cairo Press: 105–124.

123. Peterson, Mark Allen. 2011. *Connected in Cairo: Growing up Cosmopolitan in the Modern Middle East*. Bloomington and Indianapolis: Indiana University Press, 114. For a comprehensive study of the ways in which new modes of consumption have transformed the everyday life of Cairo's middle classes since the epoch of President Nasser, see: Abaza, Mona. 2006. *Changing Consumer Cultures of Modern Egypt: Cairo's Urban Reshaping*. Leiden: Brill.
124. Quoted in: Wise, Lindsay. 2006. *Amr Khaled versus Yusuf Al Qaradawi: The Danish Cartoon Controversy and the Clash of Two Islamic TV Titans*. https://www.ikhwanweb.com/article.php?id=4529. Accessed: May 4, 2022.
125. Rock, Aron. 2010. Amr Khaled: From Da'wa to Political and Religious Leadership. *British Journal of Middle Eastern Studies* 37 (1): 15–37, 16.
126. Jung, Dietrich, Marie Juul Petersen, and Sara Lei Sparre. 2014. *Politics of Modern Muslim Subjectivities: Islam, Youth, and Social Activism in the Middle East*. New York: Palgrave Macmillan, 120.
127. Wise, Lindsay. 2003. *"Words from the Heart": New Forms of Islamic Preaching in Egypt*. M.Phil. Thesis, Oxford University, 58.
128. Jung et al. 2014, 121. It is necessary to mention that many observers dismissed the image of Amr Khaled as a "liberal Muslim thinker." Asef Bayat (2007) and Aron Rock (2010) rightly pointed to his conservative perceptions regarding the role of women in society. Moreover, the new lay preachers had to face the criticism of "pacifying" Egyptian youth in supporting political quietism. Yet often this criticism disregarded the high mobilizing force of this kind of new Islamic activism as shown in our fieldwork experiences.
129. Atia, Mona. 2012. "A Way to Paradise": Pious Neoliberalism, Islam, and Faith-Based Development. *Annals of the Association of American Geographers* 102 (4): 808–827, 811.
130. This fieldwork took place in the framework of a larger research project that was funded by the Danish Royal Ministry of Foreign Affairs. I conducted the project at the Danish Institute for International Studies (DIIS) together with two research assistants. Marie Juul Petersen (Jordan) and Sara Lei Sparre (Egypt) undertook fieldwork in November and December 2006, as well as between March and June 2007. The first results of our project were published in a DIIS Report (13/2007): *Islam and Civil Society: Case Studies from Jordan and Egypt*. The data in this paragraph on Egyptian youth organization and the Muslim professional is a summary from Jung et al. 2014, chapter eight.
131. Sparre, Sara Lei. 2018. Experimenting with Alternative Futures in Cairo: Young Muslim Volunteers between God and the Nation. *Identities: Global Studies in*

Culture and Power 25 (2): 158–175, 160. For a map over the branches of Resala: Atia 2012, figure 4, 819.

132. Sparre 2018, 163.
133. The potential for conflict due to this critical status of Egyptian youth becomes clear when taking into account that in the year 2016 about 20 percent of the Egyptian population was aged between fifteen and twenty-four. Moreover, some ten million of these young Egyptians were in secondary or tertiary education, certainly shaping their expectations for a professional future. At the same time, young people figure highest when it comes to Egypt's unemployment rates. This mismatch of expectations and the real situation contributed strongly to the uprisings in 2010–12. Cf. Springborg, Robert. 2018. *Egypt*. Cambridge: Policy Press, 149. For a brief description of the grievances of Egypt's youth right before the Arab rebellion, see: Herrera, Linda. 2010. Young Egyptians' Quest for Jobs and Justice. In *Being Young and Being Muslim: New Cultural Politics in the Global South and North*. Edited by Linda Herrera and Asef Bayat. Oxford: Oxford University Press, 127–143.
134. In discussing the motivation of Resala's volunteers in the chapter "Caravan to Paradise," Amira Mittermaier describes them as some kind of "pious entrepreneurs" whose major concern is about their own road to salvation; Mittermaier, Amira. 2019. *Giving to God: Islamic Charity in Revolutionary Times*. Oakland: University of California Press.
135. Cf. Bayat 2007, 150.
136. Jung et al. 2014, 142.
137. In a similar way, the Indonesian "Krakatau Steel" tried to enhance the productivity and competitiveness of the company in combining Islamic tradition and Euro-American management knowledge in the training program for its employees: Rudnyckyj, Daromir. 2009. Spiritual Economies. Islam and Neoliberalism in Contemporary Indonesia. *Cultural Anthropology* 24 (1): 104–141. Another example for this merger of neoliberal business ideologies with Islamic traditions we find in the so-called *homo islamicus* propagated by MÜSİAD, the Islamic Independent Industrialist and Businessmen Association in Turkey: Gökarıksel, Banu and Anna J. Secor. 2009. New Transnational Geographies of Islamism, Capitalism and Subjectivity: The Veiling-fashion Industry in Turkey. *Area* 41 (1): 6–18, 12.
138. Jung et al. 2014, 168.
139. Ibid 143.
140. Wickham, Carrie Rosefsky. 2004. Interest, Ideas and Islamist Outreach in

Egypt. In *Islamic Activism: A Social Movement Approach*. Edited by Quintan Wiktorowicz. Bloomington: Indiana University Press, 231–249, 238.
141. Fosset 2013. Zaytuna College was founded in 2009 and provides its students with a liberal art education in Islamic studies. The college aims at educating "morally committed professional, intellectual, and spiritual leaders who are grounded in the Islamic scholarly tradition and conversant with the cultural currents and critical ideas shaping modern society"; https://zaytuna.edu/#mission, accessed May 18, 2022. This mission statement is reminiscent of that of the International Islamic University Malaysia (IIUM), though with a "Traditionalist touch," see Chapter Six of this book.
142. Rehman 2010, 5.
143. Ibid. 286 and 291.
144. For a well-argued article on this interlacement, see: Sandıkcı, Özlem. 2018. Religion and the Marketplace: Constructing the 'New' Muslim Consumer. *Religion* 48 (3): 453–473.
145. Cf. Duffy, Andrew and Ginnette Ng Hui Xian. 2021. Edible Communities: How Singapore Creates a Nation of Consumers for Consumption. *Journal of Consumer Culture* 21 (4): 782–799, 784.
146. Liow, Joseph Chinyong. 2016. *Religion and Nationalism in Southeast Asia*. Cambridge: Cambridge University Press, 150.
147. The promotion of more conservative attitudes through new technological and economic devices can also been observed in what has been labeled as "halal-dating," a specific form of new Muslim youth culture. Regarding this halal discourse in the social field of intimacy, smartphones and dating apps play a significant role. Bøel, Marianne. 2017. Halal-dating som ungdomskultur. Forhandlinger om ekteskaps—og samlivspraciser blant norsk ungdom med mulimsk bakgrunn. *Prismet Forskning* 68 (1–2): 9–26; Hasan, Farah. 2021. Keep it Halal! A Smartphone Ethnography of Muslim Dating. *Journal of Religion, Media and Digital Culture* 10: 135–154.
148. With respect to Islamic welfare organizations, a similar development has been observed in Turkey: Vicini, Fabio. 2020. "Worship is Not Everything:" Volunteering and Muslim Life in Modern Turkey. In *Muslim Subjectivities in Global Modernity: Islamic Traditions and the Construction of Modern Muslim Identities*. Edited by Dietrich Jung and Kirstine Sinclair. Leiden: Brill, 97–120; Zenciri, Gizem. 2020. Markets of Islam: Performative Charity and the Muslim Middle Classes in Turkey. *Journal of Cultural Economy* 13 (5): 610–625. In her book *Muslimism in Turkey and Beyond*, Neslihan Çevik coined the term

"Muslimism" for these kinds of new Islamic movements. According to her analysis, Muslimists "tend toward the liberal state model that allows individual agency, choice, and autonomy with respect to religious, economic, political and civic action." In the conceptual language of the sociologist Andreas Reckwitz, they come close to the "postmodern" type of modern subjectivity formation. In her book, Çevik describes the emergence of Muslimism in the economic context of the financial liberalization polices in Turkey since the 1980s. See: Çevik 2016, 6.

8

MULTIPLE JIHADS: MODERN SOCIAL ACTORHOOD IN THE NAME OF ISLAM

Today, there is no longer any need for a transcription of the Arabic term *jihād*. Often translated as "holy war," in recent times this classical Islamic concept has entered European everyday languages in its original Arabic form. This is with no doubt due to the events of September 11, 2001, and the rise of so-called jihadist movements in general. Calling for war against both unbelievers in the West and fellow Muslims whom they deny are following the true path of the Islamic faith, these movements are now often featured on prime-time news. Radical Islamist groups employ the concept of jihad to justify the violent means with which they pursue their political ends. And this radical understanding of jihad appears to have assumed relative hegemony in public debate. Against this public representation of jihad as a war against the infidel, many Muslims advocate a different understanding of the concept, by emphasizing its non-militant character. Muslim advocacy groups often connect their social activism with the institution of jihad. They understand their public engagement as a kind of jihad for the advancement of the individual and collective good.

Frequently in my public lectures, I have experienced audiences clashing with each other in propagating one of these two—at first glance—contradictory interpretations of jihad. In Denmark, scholars are expected to disseminate their academic knowledge to a broader non-academic audience through public lectures, newspaper contributions, and background interviews for journalists.

In the scholarly community, this is perceived as a kind of obligation to the taxpayer, who after all is funding research and teaching at Danish universities. Therefore, we are used to presenting and discussing our academic work in non-academic fora. My own encounters with the Danish public have clearly shown that talk about jihad is on everyone's lips. The very meaning of the concept, however, is thereby openly contested, and not only by Muslims alone. Behind many of these contestations—at least in my interpretation—there is not only a dispute regarding the proper meaning of jihad as such. In these contemporary debates on jihad, it is actually the "very nature" of Islam that is at stake. These debates reflect disputes about the essentially violent or peaceful character of the Islamic religion. More important still: discussions about the nature, role, and meaning of jihad are a core issue in the broader debate about Islam and modernity as such.[1]

The current global public relevance of the Islamic institution of jihad is a striking historical development, at least when we look more closely at the discussion of this religious concept in Islamic studies. A good example is the more than century-old controversy between the Dutch orientalist Christiaan Snouck Hurgronje (1857–1936) and his German colleague Carl-Heinrich Becker (1876–1933). It was the declaration of the last official jihad in Islamic history that ignited this dispute between these two scholars. In November 1914, the Ottoman Sultan and Caliph Mehmet V (1909–18) called upon every Muslim to defend Islam against its enemies. This proclamation of a jihad in defense of Islam was endorsed by the juridical opinion (*fatwa*) of the highest religious learned of the Ottoman Empire. The sultan's call to jihad was accompanied by the decision of the Ottoman ruling elite—the Committee of Union and Progress—to join the First World War on the side of Germany and the Hapsburgian Empire. Consequently, this jihad positioned the war opponents of the Axis—France, Great Britain, and Russia—as the enemies of Islam. While the text of the proclamation closely followed the instruction of traditional Islamic jurisprudence in formal ways, its actual content was a remarkable deviation from Islamic tradition: the *fatwa* united the Islamic Ottoman Empire with the Christian powers of Germany and Austria in the defense of Islam.[2] Even more puzzling, the initiative for this declaration of jihad did not come from Istanbul. Apparently, the strategic move to rally the world's Muslims behind the Axis powers was conceived in the German foreign office in Berlin.[3]

It was this origin of the Ottoman–German jihad in the foreign office in Berlin that pitted Snouck Hurgronje and Carl-Heinrich Becker against each other. Hurgronje suspected his German colleague Becker of being deeply involved in Germany's religious politics. In 1915, the Dutch scholar and former colonial advisor in Aceh (1889–1906) published an article in which he expressed his disappointment that Becker had been "swept away" by the "jihad-craze" conjured up by German politicians.[4] Yet Hurgronje's opinion was that this German appeal to pan-Islamist sentiments would not work. The idea of any kind of "world conquest by Islam," in his eyes, had "lost its hold on all sensible adherents of Islam."[5] Hurgronje reminded Becker that he himself once declared the so-called solidarity of Islam a mere phantom. Now from Hurgronje's vantage point, Becker was standing in stark contrast to his academic erudition by supporting a thoughtless war propaganda that invoked a "mixture of deceit and nonsense."[6] For Hurgronje, the Islamic jihad was an atavist medieval religious doctrine that no longer resonated among educated modern Muslims.

In his swift reply, Becker admitted that as a scholar he definitely shared the dismissive attitude of his Dutch colleague concerning the role of jihad in the modern world. For Becker too, jihad was an institution without any real relevance for modern life. However, he considered this Ottoman–German declaration of jihad not to be a matter of scholarship but of real politics. Therefore, Becker, who was at that time a professor at the University of Bonn and later became Minister of Culture in Prussia (1925–30), asked his Dutch colleague: Why not try to employ a medieval institution as a "possibly effective means in times of existential war"? According to Becker, the German government was not calling for religious hatred, as Berlin was merely supporting the empire's use of a traditional religious institution as a political weapon.[7] What is significant here is that based on their oriental scholarship both Becker and Hurgronje "perceived *jihad* as a remnant of traditional Islamic orthodoxy that will hardly be able to survive in modern times."[8]

To cut a long story short, the Ottoman–German jihad failed in every respect. The Muslims under the imperial control of France and Great Britain did not turn against their colonial masters. On the contrary, in the First World War many Muslims fought against the Ottoman army and did so under the flags of France and Great Britain. The last official jihad ended in disaster. The military defeat of the Ottoman Empire alongside Germany and Austria was its final and fatal result. In retrospect, however, the history of the twentieth century has also proven the judgment of the two leading European scholars of Islam to be equally wrong. The concept of jihad has not disappeared, but instead it has experienced a striking renaissance.

When it comes to contemporary scholarship on Islam, "Jihadology" is still "a virtual subfield" of research in Islamic studies, and this not only with regard to the classical understanding of the concept in Islamic jurisprudence (*fiqh*).[9] Even more important, the discussion of its allegedly belligerent nature is by no means a theme of public debate alone. In his book review of Asma Afsaruddin's *Striving in the Path of God*, for instance, the Oxford historian Christopher Melchert emphasizes the meaning of jihad as an "aggressive war on unbelievers in the Islamic legal tradition."[10] Afsaruddin's study on jihad[11] intended to highlight "internal contestations" among Muslim scholars by retrieving "non-legal perspectives."[12] It was not by taking Islamic law as her source that she wanted to reconstruct "a more holistic understanding of jihad in the premodern world" but by using broader scholarly perspectives.[13] In this way, Afsaruddin aimed to underpin arguments for the non-belligerent character of the concept. However, Melchert accuses her of pressing the "case too hard" in the process.[14] According to Melchert, in her attempt to emphasize classical positions beyond the martial understanding of jihad, the Professor at Indiana University had left the path of historical scholarship on Islam and presented Islam "as it ought to be like."[15]

This contemporary controversy between two scholars about the very nature of jihad in Islamic history underscores the ongoing relevance of this "medieval" concept for current scholarly and public debate on Islam as such.[16] Yet what is then the correct meaning and practice of jihad? This chapter does not aim to answer this question in the normative sense. Rather, I address it in order to illustrate further the core arguments of my book. In the course of history, Muslims—both lay and scholars—have answered this question in very different ways. Consequently, there is no single authoritative understanding of jihad in contemporary Islamic practices. Many Muslims employ the concept to justify their social and political projects, but in vastly different ways. The range of the application of jihad in this process goes from violent terrorist acts to benevolent humanitarian activities. Therefore, the conceptual history of jihad is a perfect example to underline both of my claims concerning the relative hegemony of the specifically Islamic discourse of modernity and its factual fragmentation in the interpretative realm. References to jihad provide Muslims with religious and therewith moral legitimacy for a broad variety of social and political projects. The term jihad became an integral part of the multiple semantics of modernity in Islam and thus perfectly serve as the last case study in this book.

I will underpin my argument by four steps. Firstly, I introduce the concept of "modern social actorhood" from the Stanford School on Sociological Institutionalism. In the contemporary use of jihad, I discern a fusion of this Islamic institution with the modern concept of social actorhood as defined by this school. Then, I take a look at the classical understanding of jihad and its two versions of the "lesser" and the "greater" jihad. Thirdly, I will describe the erosion of this classical understanding of jihad in the course of the nineteenth and twentieth centuries. I will argue that this erosion started with its re-interpretation by the Islamic modernists who were the theme of Chapter Four. In the conclusion I briefly demonstrate the rather random contemporary application of jihad by different social actors, thus substantiating my argument that the term has taken on an essentially modern meaning.

Islamic Modernism and World Culture: Jihad and Modern Social Actorhood

Islamic modernists understood themselves as reformative activists. They perceived dynamic social engagement as a core principle of Islam. In their worldview, not only do Islam and modern civilization share a foundation in rationalism, but both also call upon individuals to actively engage in society. Therefore, the principles of Islam and those of modernity are not in contradiction. On the contrary, in the opinion of these nineteenth-century reformers, Islamic and modern principles mutually reinforce each other. In their reconstruction of Islam as a discursive tradition, Islamic modernists aimed at addressing the cultural, economic, and political challenges of their countries; and pursuing this kind of sociopolitical engagement "is the meaning of the term *jihad* in its most general sense."[17] Taking this quote from the Lebanese reformer Shakib Arslan (1869–1946),[18] Albert Hourani pointed to the fusion of the Islamic concept of jihad with the modern notion of social activism.

The reform of social life and—often even more important—the nationalist aspirations for political independence from colonial rule demanded this activist stance of the Islamic modernists. However, not only Islamic modernists but also a number of Christian Arab nationalists employed the term jihad in calling for the liberation of their homelands and their struggle against the influence of American Protestant missionaries.[19] This clearly shows the degree to which the non-religious meaning of social activism began to take possession of this classical Islamic institution during the nineteenth century. Together with other Islamic concepts such as justice (*'adāla*), positive law (*sharī'a*), nation (*umma*), and unity (*tawḥīd*), the reform movements of the nineteenth century integrated jihad into their modern reformist vocabulary by essentially changing its classical meaning. In their specifically Islamic discourse of modernity, so my argument goes, the Islamic reformers employed jihad in the generic sense of the concept of modern social actorhood as defined by the Stanford School on Sociological Institutionalism.

In Chapter Two, I briefly introduced this concept of social actorhood with regard to my discussion of modernity as a project. I argued that the projects of modernity and therewith multiple modernities evolve through social actors who construct different semantics of modernity. The concept of social actorhood plays a pivotal role in the world cultural theory of the Stanford School. In its theoretical framework, the concept of the self-conscious social actor is one of the characteristic features of modernity. The group of sociologists around the Stanford scholar John W. Meyer has been working with a theory of world society as an alternative to Luhmann's definition, based on the global dominance of functional differentiation. The world cultural theory of the Stanford School applies at a lower level of abstraction and claims that there has been a rise in the global homology of social structures since the nineteenth century. Modern world culture, then, is characterized by a notable isomorphism with respect to both organizations and cultural models associated with the modern individual.[20] This overarching world culture shapes a singular arena of action and discourse with distinct patterns of modern culture. It is embedded in formal organizations and defines the purpose and nature of social action on a global scale.[21] The emergence of this form of a world society has been driven by the rise of the global as the most relevant social horizon, by processes of rationalization and standardization, and by an emphasis on voluntaristic authority. Furthermore, these processes have been accompanied by a specifically modern culture of social actorhood and the empowerment of collective and individual actors.[22]

These dynamic factors of an emerging world culture are clearly visible in the thought and action of Islamic modernists. Their attempts to rationalize Islamic principles, their desire for the standardization of Islamic law, and their rejection of the authoritative interpretation of the Holy Scriptures by the religious elite are all cases in point. In Chapter Four, I described the ways in which Muhammad Abduh developed his re-interpretation of Islamic traditions as a means of social reform. In this endeavor, Abduh closely followed the transformative lines described by the Stanford School. His disciple Rashid Rida even reconstructed the personality of the Prophet Muhammad in accordance with these nineteenth-century templates of rationality and voluntaristic authority. In his highly popular book *The Revelation of Muhammad* (*al-waḥī al-muḥammadī*), Rida drew a picture of the Prophet as a figure whose main character traits were his rationality and his independence of mind.[23] In this context, the Prophet appears as the model of a modern religious and social reformer. In this way, the various actors of Islamic reform have participated in the enactment of these global cultural structures identified by the Stanford School.[24] I will now take a closer look at the conceptualization of social actorhood by the sociological institutionalists and the way in which this global cultural model has entered the modern interpretation of jihad.

The Stanford School defines "social actorhood" as "a historical and ongoing cultural construction."[25] Social actorhood is not a transhistorical, natural property of humanity, but it is the historically constructed idea of an individual or an organization bestowed with the "capacity for responsible agency." Modern social actors, collectives, and individuals claim agency along three lines: for themselves, for other actors, and for normative principles.[26] As the prototype of a modern collective actor, organizations self-consciously dominate in economic, educational, political, religious, or scientific realms.[27] In these social realms, they claim social actorhood according to the three ways described above. The threefold nature of modern social actorhood is a core pattern in the ideological cosmos of contemporary Islamist movements. As a formal organization, the Muslim Brotherhood, for instance, claims to act according to its own interests, on behalf of all Muslims, and in the name of Islamic principles. In this way, the Muslim Brothers employ the "highly standardizing models for agency and scripts for activity" in their own fashion.[28] In the ideologies and practices of Islamist organizations we can discern global cultural scripts, an often unconsciously applied syntax of modernity, in reference to which Islamist activists construct their own historically specific semantics of modernity. In doing so, they claim legitimate agency and they participate directly in the shaping of world culture.[29] Non-European actors do not passively follow a given path, but they are directly involved in forming contemporary world culture.[30] The modern social world is "filled with models of actorhood." The cultural model of the self-conscious social actor is the preferred, if not even the demanded, identity that "persons and groups eagerly pursue."[31]

This global model of modern social actorhood is an essential element of the Islamic discourse of modernity once launched by Islamic modernists. In their fusion of this model with the concept of jihad, the modernists conferred authenticity on this world cultural idea of social agency. In this modern reconstruction of an Islamic institution, the semantic breadth of the Arabic root *jahada* facilitated the widespread and diverse application of the term jihad. The verb *jahada* in its basic form carries meanings such as to engage, to exert, to strain, to strive, to struggle, or to try hard. The noun *jahd* can be translated as effort, endeavor, exertion, hardship, strain, or struggle. Jihad is only one of the derivatives of the root *jahada*. Its narrower meaning of a holy struggle or holy war is largely due to its centuries-long application in Islamic jurisprudence, as the next section of this chapter will show. In addition, there are other derivatives such as *majhūd* (commitment, effort, zeal), *mujāhada* (combat, fight, struggle against), *mujāhid* (officer, policeman, warrior), and the two technical terms of *fiqh*: *ijtihād* (independent reasoning) and *mujtahid* (jurisprudent).[32] Apparently it is not only the Islamic connotation of the term but also its broad range of possible meanings that made jihad a perfect semantic carrier for the modern model of social actorhood in Islamic discourse. The resilience, spread, and diverse application of the concept in modern times is due to the multiplicity of semantic opportunities it provides. However, as I will demonstrate in the next section, in translating jihad into modern actorhood, the Islamic modernists also deviated to a large part from its traditional application in *fiqh*.

The Concept of Jihad in Premodern Islamic Legal Tradition

In the classical period of Islamic empires, jihad was primarily known as a legal institution of Islamic jurisprudence. A good example illustrating this is *bidāyat al-mujtahid*, a legal handbook by the jurist and philosopher Ibn Rushd (1126–98 CE).[33] More precisely, a book in which Ibn Rushd explains the principles behind those differences which occur in the juridical argumentations by the four Sunni schools of law (*madhāhib*; sing. *madhhab*).[34] In Europe better known under his Latin name Averroes, Ibn Rushd adhered to the Malikite school of law and lived in Andalusia. Integrating Aristotelian philosophy with Islamic theology, he was "one of the most important philosophers of all time," with a sustained impact on the development of modern European thought.[35]

In the first volume of his juridical handbook, one chapter is dedicated to the concept of jihad. This chapter represents a legal corpus on the justification, conditions, forms, and aims of warfare according to Islamic law. The book of jihad discussed what in Latin technical terms is known as *ius in bello* and *ius ad bellum*. Ibn Rushd described the different opinions of the Sunni schools of law about the legitimate use of physical force by Islamic rulers. Who has the right to wage war? How should military actors behave in warfare? These are the main questions in juridical texts about jihad. Ibn Rushd compares the often-diverse opinions from the four schools of law, pointing to differences and concords among them. In accordance with the classical schools of war, Ibn Rushd defined jihad as a collective responsibility in order to defend and/or extend the realm of Islamic rule. Political and religious authorities were allowed to proclaim jihad as long as the conduct of war was subordinated to the jurisdiction of Islamic jurists (*fuqahā'*; sing. *faqīh*). This jurisdiction concerned the adversaries in war as well as the means and forms of conduct in war. In principle, jihad was directed against non-Muslims; only those Muslims who were in open rebellion against legitimate Islamic rulers could become the target of jihad.[36] Consequently, in Islamic jurisprudence, jihad was a largely restrictively defined institution of justified war, closely knitted into the stratified authority structures of classical Islamic empires.

Through the lenses of Eisenstadt's civilizational theory, the above juridical concepts of jihad represent a historically specific combination of religious and imperial traditions. These two kinds of traditions have largely characterized Islam as a premodern civilizational complex. The juridical opinions on jihad were the result of many centuries of intellectual deliberations among the religious learned and rulers. Two points are important in this premodern conceptualization of jihad. First of all, these deliberations took account of the fact that the Qur'an does not contain a clear doctrine of jihad.[37] There is no doubt that the Qur'an has a lot to say about war, religious struggle, and military campaigns. However, this multiplicity of narratives related to violent strife is of a rather unsystematic character and leaves us with an inconsistent notion of jihad in the Qur'an.[38] These inconsistencies in the Qur'an regarding jihad are partly linked to the broad range of semantic meanings from which the concept evolved that I discussed in the previous section. The verbal root *jahada* knows many derivatives, by far not all of them with a religious connotation and only a few implying war or physical force. Secondly, the debates among religious specialists about the meaning of jihad were also an expression of the historical contexts in which they emerged. This becomes particularly visible in the sources of these deliberations, which predominantly refer to the large corpus of prophetic traditions, the so-called sunna of the Prophet, rather than to the Qur'an itself. This corpus of prophetical traditions evolved together with the expansion of the early Islamic empires during the early centuries after the death of the Prophet Muhammad. Together with the Qur'an, many of these traditions subsequently achieved the status of authoritative sources for Islamic jurisprudents. Ibn Rushd, for instance, based his elaborations on these sources and on the canon of syllogistic conclusions arrived at by previous scholars of religious law.

The discursive development of the concept of jihad was further conditioned by historical circumstances. We should understand the meanings of jihad in both historical and geographical contexts. A good example is provided by the differences between the conceptual meanings of jihad according to the geographic location of their origins. In the frontier areas of Islamic empires, fighting war in order to defend and extend territories under Muslim rule apparently impacted the prevalent meaning of jihad much more clearly than was the case in the pacified core territories of those empires. The emphasis on the military dimension of jihad in frontier areas is documented in a specific corpus of traditions according to which the Prophet declared the defense of boarders as specifically rewarding in religious terms.[39] In conclusion, the concept of jihad evolved through centuries of methodologically guided deliberations among Islamic jurists. In Islamic jurisprudence jihad predominantly represents a legal category defining the legitimate form of military campaigns in defense of and for the expansion of Islam. In short, the concept revolves around "the rules of killing at war."[40]

This premodern juridical interpretation of jihad as justified warfare in defense of Islam was essentially what the two Orientalists Snouck Hurgronje and Carl-Heinrich Becker considered to be an atavistic remnant of the imperial Islam of the Middle Ages. It was this understanding of jihad in classical *fiqh* that, according to their reasoning, would disappear in modern times. European Orientalists mainly based their knowledge on the reading of classical texts and therefore emphasized the one-sided Islamic legal interpretations of Islamic institutions such as could be found in the handbook of Ibn Rushd. These formal elaborations on the doctrine of jihad by Islamic jurists in the age of Islamic empires, however, certainly did not reflect the entire range of social and religious practices among Muslims. Albrecht Noth pointed to this difference between formal legal doctrines and religious practices regarding jihad in his use of the conceptual dichotomy of "holy war" and "holy struggle." According to Noth, in early Islamic history we already find personal forms of jihad apart from the juridical dogmas and authorized forms of warfare.[41] This personal holy struggle could comprise both the military engagement of individual believers and the moral battle of pious Muslims with respect to religious virtues such as charity, fasting, and the conduct of prayers.[42] In the legal discussion of classical Islamic jurisprudents, however, these moral and spiritual dimensions of jihad do not play a significant role.[43]

With respect to Albrecht Noth's dichotomy between struggle and war, Reuven Firestone argued against a quasi-evolutionary development of the concept of jihad from a category of spiritual struggle for Islam to one of justified warfare by Islamic rulers. Instead, he suggested that a constant competing dualism in these meanings has been at work throughout Islamic history. Firestone assumed that this dualism already had its roots in the early Muslim community.[44] Evidently, this dualism is still at work today and it often finds its expression in the heated debates about the purpose and meaning of jihad in the public contexts already mentioned.

Looking more closely at the intellectual history of Islam, we find the concept of the spiritual character of jihad in particular in Sufism, the so-called mystical branch of Islam. This form of jihad is almost completely detached from the military connotations of the concept elsewhere so prevalent in Islamic jurisprudence.[45] In Sufi reasoning, jihad is predominantly directed against human desires and plays an important role in the justification of mystical practices.[46] It is this understanding of jihad which Afsaruddin also wants to highlight in her *Striving in the Path of God*. Moreover, this classical *non-military* interpretation of jihad also connects to the application of the concept by contemporary Muslim advocacy groups in their societal engagement. Scholars identified the evolution of this spiritual concept of jihad as occurring in the ninth century, which then in the twelfth century found its doctrinal manifestation in the teachings on the greater jihad by the jurist and theologian al-Ghazali (1058–1111 CE). According to Ghazali, the greater jihad is a struggle concerning the moral self and the public good, whereas the lesser jihad refers to the military defense of Islam.[47] Yet these spiritual and moral forms of jihad did not play a significant role in the history of Islamic legal tradition until the modern Islamic reform movement reinvented them in the nineteenth century in the context of colonial domination and domestic aspirations for social and political change.

Modern Interpretations of Jihad: Fusing Islamic Tradition and Modern Agency

In Chapter Four, I described the ways in which nineteenth-century Islamic reformers proclaimed a return to the original sources of the revelation. Islamic modernists rejected the established authority of the comprehensive interpretations that are documented in the huge legal corpuses of classical Islamic jurisprudence. One of their core arguments was that only independent reasoning with reference to the pristine Islamic principles would provide an authentic platform for the building of a just and legitimate modern order. Consequently, the Islamic reform movement made the liberation of independent reasoning (*ijtihād*) from the institutional control of the religious learned (*'ulamā'*/sing. *'ālim*) a core issue of religious reform. It was not the firmly established methods of *fiqh* but a fresh and independent reading of the Holy Scriptures that they wanted to apply in addressing the social, political, and moral questions of their times.

In the coercive straitjacket of imperialist power relations, the religious language of Islam facilitated the propagation of modern ideas and institutions without giving up the explicitly modern claim to cultural authenticity. This, in the end, lies at the heart of the contemporary hegemony of the specifically Islamic discourse of modernity. The ideas of nineteenth-century Islamic reform constituted a fusion of Islamic religious concepts and narratives with the functionally differentiated conceptual language of modern economic, educational, legal, and political communication. In this way, the discourse of Islamic modernity combined the syntactic rules of modernity with the cultural program of what in Eisenstadt's language is the "Islamic civilizational complex." Islamic modernists narrated the fundamental social transformation toward an increasingly functionally differentiated social life in an Islamic idiom. They related to Islam as a discursive tradition in a new way, now within the new cultural context of a genuine syntax of modernity.

This specifically Islamic discourse of modernity generated a conceptual resource for the reflexive semantics of modernity from which subsequent Muslim thinkers have selectively drawn. The conceptualization of shari'a in terms of positive law, the re-interpretation of *shura* as a form of representative government, the definition of alms (*zakāt*) as an Islamic form of taxation, and the association of *ribā* with capitalist interest-charging are only some of the significant cases which I have also discussed throughout this book. With strong reference to the specifically modern mode of social differentiation, that is to say the distinction of societal realms of functionally differentiated forms of communication, the Islamic reform movement bestowed religious concepts with new meanings. In this way, modern Islamic reformers laid the foundations for the rise of the fragmented and polysemic nature of Islamic discourses of our times.

As an essential part of this process, the institution of jihad also attained a variety of new meanings linked to the concept of modern social actorhood. In his revolutionary efforts, Jamal al-Din al-Afghani, for instance, applied the term to the mobilization of Muslims against colonial rule and to his conception of pan-Islamic struggle. In his world of thought, jihad became a central concept of anticolonial agitation. Meanwhile the Egyptian reformer Muhammad Abduh, who underpinned his call for reform in theological terms, defined jihad as the religiously motivated effort to work hard in everyday life for the revival of Muslim society.⁴⁸ Even more importantly, in the long run Abduh put a new emphasis on jihad as an individual duty. In the classical discussion among Islamic jurisprudents, a majority of scholars considered jihad as a collective duty (*farḍ kifāyya*); not every single Muslim but the armed units of the Islamic polity shared a responsibility for the defense of Islam. Only in specific circumstances could rulers proclaim jihad in terms of an obligation for the individual Muslim (*farḍ 'ain*). In his zeal for social reform and the moral improvement of Egyptian society, Abduh promoted a reformist, spiritual jihad as individual obligation which meanwhile also entered the militant discourse of Jihadist groups.⁴⁹

For both Afghani and Abduh, Islam was synonymous with social activism, understood as a form of jihad. They employed the premodern notion of holy struggle as a new means of mobilizing the population for their modernizing projects. Taking up the distinction defined by Ghazali, late nineteenth-century reformers interpreted the spiritual form of the greater jihad as a kind of collective and individual striving for social reform. They assigned a key role in the resistance against colonialism instead to the narrower military concept of the lesser jihad. Premodern anticolonial movements in British India, North Africa, and the Sudan already perceived themselves as being engaged in a jihad against the colonial powers. However, their worldview did not yet know the nationalist impact that dominated the meaning of jihad in the fight for independence later in the nineteenth and early twentieth centuries.⁵⁰ The dualism in the meaning of jihad, together with the semantic variations of its linguistic roots, provided the Islamic reform movement of the nineteenth century with a religious template for conceptual innovations. Most significantly, this re-interpretation supplied a template for the justification of various forms of modern social actorhood. Stripping jihad of its institutional and interpretative constraints, Islamic modernists opened the door for the flourishing of new applications of the term in a multiplicity of ways.

In the year 1928, the foundation of the Muslim Brotherhood by Hasan al-Banna was a decisive turning point for this decoupling of jihad from its classical institutional and interpretative constraints. Chapter Five dealt with the ways in which Hasan al-Banna translated the Islamic discourse of modernity from an elitist language among Muslim intellectuals into the vernacular of a religio-political movement. The Muslim Brotherhood was crucial in initiating an ongoing process of the "centrifugal ideologization" of Islam. According to the sociologist Siniša Malešević, this process is "a mass phenomenon that historically spreads from the centre of social organisations (or social movements, or both) to gradually encompass an ever wider population."[51] In so doing, the ideological activities of the elite and the broader masses of the population mutually reinforce each other, tying together the ideological narrative on the macro level with individual forms of solidarity on the micro level.[52] This popularization, societal dissemination, and ultimately intellectual trivialization of the Islamic reform discourse by the Muslim Brotherhood movement contributed significantly to the evolution of the polysemic voices of contemporary Islam on the semantic level.

The ideology of the Brotherhood was predicated on the idea of an Islamization of modernity. In this process, jihad became a metaphor for social engagement fused with the organizational logic of a modern mass movement. In Hasan al-Banna's usage, the term "jihad" represented a whole range of meanings from militant resistance against British colonial domination to the striving for social reform and the struggle for the moral betterment of individual Muslims. References to jihad "pervaded his entire discourse."[53] He seemingly fused the military and spiritual notions of the concept, virtually transgressing the boundaries between the lesser and the greater jihad. Yet in contradistinction to the reformers of the late nineteenth century, Banna put a new stress on the military character of jihad. He firmly associated jihad with notions such as violent struggle, death, and martyrdom.[54]

Hasan al-Banna further radicalized the idea of authenticity in his application of Islamic concepts. In contradistinction to Abduh, he aimed at the establishment of an authentic Islamic order without any conscious borrowing from the normative and institutional achievements of Europe. At the same time, the regulative claims of the Brotherhood were gradually expanded toward the imagination of a reorganization of the functionally differentiating realms of economics, politics, law, education, arts, and religious practices under a form of Islamic governance.[55] From the theoretical perspective of this book, the idea of Islamic governance attained the role of giving an all-encompassing answer to the complexity of modern problems generated by society's increasing functional differentiation. The imposition of Islamic government on the diverging logics of different realms of society was thus translated into various forms of jihad. In a process of centrifugal ideologization, the Islamization of modern social realms such as education, economics, law, politics, and science became synonymous with an Islamic program for the societal integration of an increasingly differentiated population.

In political terms, the major Islamist ideologists of the twentieth century further radicalized the notion of jihad. In particular, the intellectual thought of Abul Ala al-Mawdudi (1903–79) and that of Sayyid Qutb (1906–66) were instrumental in making it the core concept for revolutionary Islamist groups. Mawdudi's career as a mastermind of Islamist thought began with the publication of his *Jihad in Islam* (*al-jihād fī-l-islām*). In this book, the Indian Muslim intellectual presented a systematic discussion of jihad in Islamic history. Based on his historical analyses, he presented his own theory of a comprehensive holy struggle for social justice and faith in the absolute unity of God.[56] Following on from this, he later developed his theory of an Islamic state—which remains largely an ideological state without any elaborated institutional framework. The legitimacy of this state he derives from the theological concepts of the "unity" (*tawḥīd*) and of the "sovereignty" (*ḥākimiyya*) of God. In this way, Mawdudi combined the holistic interpretation of the unity of Islamic civilization with the claim to sovereignty of the modern state. In 1939, then, he founded the Jamaat-i Islami in Lahore, which became an Islamist cadre party. After the division of the Indian subcontinent, Mawdudi and the Jamaat played an instrumental role in the Islamization of the politics of the independent state of Pakistan.[57]

For the Egyptian Sayyid Qutb, Abu Ala al-Mawdudi's theories on jihad and the Islamic state became an important source of inspiration. After serving a number of prison sentences, Qutb, a member of the Egyptian branch of the Muslim Brotherhood, was executed in 1966 in the context of President Gamal Abdel Nasser's violent suppression of the Brotherhood movement. In his ideological thought, Sayyid Qutb fundamentally revised three concepts of the Islamic tradition: justice (*'adāla*), the "authority/sovereignty" of God (*ḥākimiyya*), and the pre-Islamic period of "ignorance" (*jāhiliyya*). In this revision, the Islamic concept of *'adāla* was fused with the modern call to revolutionary social reforms in which an Islamic order represents a kind of third way between capitalism and socialism. This social dynamism was linked by Qutb to a political authority structure in which the absolute sovereignty of

God, *ḥākimiyya*, was combined with the diagnosis of living in times of ignorance, *jāhiliyya*. Qutb identified the increasing ethical differentiation of social realms, that is to say functional differentiation, with the polytheist *jāhiliyya*, a modern form of ignorance, where people have lost the one and only path of God.[58] He called for an existentialist jihad against this modern *jāhiliyya*, which he justified through the exemplary narratives about the life and struggles of the Prophet. His combination of *'adāla*, *ḥākimiyya*, *jāhiliyya*, and jihad achieved a foundational role in the justification for a call to Islamist revolution. Numerous Islamist groups employed this thoroughly revised concept of the lesser jihad in their militarization of Qutb's existentialist political philosophy. In declaring the modern world to be in a state of ignorance, Qutb's ideology justifies, in principle, a ubiquitous application of jihad against everybody, circumventing all the institutional and normative constraints that once characterized the rule-guided circumscription of jihad in the legal tradition of Islamic jurisprudence.[59] Today, it is this liberation of jihad from all institutional constraints on which the militant wave of jihadist groups thrives.

Conclusions: Contemporary Understandings of Jihad

Looking at the dispute between Snouck Hurgronje and Carl-Heinrich Becker from the perspective of the twenty-first century, these two erudite Orientalists evidently completely failed in their mutual assumption concerning the gradual disappearance of the "medieval institution of jihad" in modern times. In fact, the contrary has occurred. The invocation of jihad by both Islamist organizations and civil Islamic activists has rather become ubiquitous. This observation applies to both the lesser jihad in its narrow military sense and the greater jihad in its more amorphous sense of the justification of various kinds of social engagement and personal advancement. The Ottoman–German jihad, the source of conflict between the Dutch and the German Orientalists, was the last jihad in Islamic history that—at least in formal terms—followed the rules of Islamic jurisprudence. Today, the application of jihad has lost its previous containment within political rules and juridical regulations.

At first glance, contemporary interpretations of the lesser jihad also look as if they are based on the classical models of *fiqh*. The Palestinian Abdallah Azzam (1941–89), for instance, justified Islamist militancy in close reference to the argumentation of the "justified war" literature in traditional Islamic jurisprudence. Azzam developed the ideological foundations of contemporary jihadist groups in the context of the Soviet occupation of Afghanistan. In organizing the resistance of foreign fighters in Afghanistan, he invoked jihad in defense of Islam. According to Azzam, all Muslims were individually obliged to wage war as long as there was any Islamic territory under siege.[60] Osama bin Laden (1957–2011) and al-Qaida further radicalized this position. According to his theory of global jihad, bin Laden also stripped the obligation to wage war of its territorial confines. In the worldview of transnationally operating jihadist organizations, Muslims must constantly defend Islam against internal and external enemies across all boundaries. While the semantics of today's jihadists are closely linked to the classical terms of the Islamic legal tradition, they are combined with a completely new content. Militant Islamist organizations use the core concepts of classical Islamic theology and jurisprudence in order to mobilize Muslims for a transnationally fought armed struggle against the alleged enemies of Islam. Thereby, the concept of a global jihad plays a central role in the justification of violent means.

In present times, radical Islamists disseminate their modern jihadist discourse based on a global media infrastructure via DVDs, movies, pamphlets, social media, and the various channels and platforms of the internet.[61] In the popularized versions of this "Islamist cultural industry," the modern semantics of jihad becomes a property of the side of its consumers. Using modern media technology, every single Muslim is potentially able to proclaim jihad today. Consequently, the lesser jihad has lost its character of being the exclusive prerogative of Islamic rulers that was restrictively defined by legal, political, and religious authorities. In its modern form, the military jihad has become a globally and freely available instrument for the legitimization of the use of physical force in the name of Islam. Beginning with the revision of the Islamic traditions by the Islamic modernists of the nineteenth century, the lesser jihad has almost completely lost its embeddedness in structures of political and religious authority. The call to jihad meanwhile appears to be in some way the individual right of each Muslim.

Parallel to the unleashing of the lesser jihad from all of its institutional and normative constraints, we can observe the relatively arbitrary application of the concept of the greater jihad to individual and collective endeavors in effectively all walks of life. The Malaysian author Azly Rahman, for instance, lamented a culture of religiously charged public discourse in his country. According to him, people are "urging this or that kind of jihad at times for reasons unknown."[62] This statement is underpinned by Malaysia's new shariʿa-compliant business elite, which was one of the topics of the previous chapter. This new corporate group applies the concept of jihad to their struggle against interest-charging and immoral capitalist business habits.[63] Against that background, a Malaysian bank, for instance, described its business mission as its specific kind of "financial jihad."[64]

Rahman's observation, however, does not just fit the scene in Malaysia alone. The invocation of jihad in terms of social activism has become a fully global phenomenon. Jihad now almost appears synonymous with "religiously inspired social activism" in world society. Lara Deeb, for instance, described forms of public piety and community work among her female interlocutors in the Shiite quarter of al-Dahiyya in Beirut as a specific kind of women's jihad.[65] In fighting their jihad, these women were "engaged in defining, reinforcing, and prioritizing certain religious discourses and practices over others, constantly distancing themselves from those considered traditional."[66] In their modern vernacular, they define their aspiration for religious and social reforms as a kind of jihad. Meanwhile in her study on Islamic Feminists, Margot Badran also spoke of a new kind of "gender jihadists." Coinciding with the advent of new forms of technology, these gender jihadists advocate the return of Muslim women to a purer and therewith more authentic Islamic way of life.[67]

In an anthology concerned with non-violent movements of civil unrest in the Middle East, Maria Stephan put various forms of civic striving under the rubric of a "civilian jihad," a term that she derived from the Iraqi intellectual Khalid Kishtainy.[68] In Turkey, both religious militarists and religious pacifists apply the semantics of jihad. While the government of President Erdoğan describes military service as "the most sacred national duty" based on the dual obligation to the state and the Islamic requirement of jihad,[69] Turkish conscientious objectors proclaim their religiously inspired rejection of national military services as their personal form of moral jihad.[70] In the context of the discourse about Muslim immigrants to Europe, Tariq Ramadan called European Muslims to fight a jihad for trust. According to Ramadan, this genuine jihad for trust aims at achieving "self-respect and respect for others: for everyone, Muslim and non-Muslims."[71] The Muslim environmentalist group

"Clean Medina" in Birmingham, United Kingdom, called for an "international jihad on trash."[72] The Pakistani Sufi rock musician Salman Ahmad has been fighting a "Rock & Roll jihad," and Faraz Khan, a spokesman for the tiny Northern Canadian Muslim community of White Horse, described the summertime in Canada's arctic Yukon territory as a "real jihad."[73] In a recent scholarly article, to name a last example, the author aimed to explicate "the possibility of retrieving at the very least the spirit, if not the term, of jihad for the purposes of peacebuilding."[74] In an apologetic vein, socially and religiously engaged Muslims have redefined jihad in multiple ways in order "to reclaim the concept of 'jihad' and to invest it with other meanings different to those imposed by the Mullahs and militants."[75]

Against this background, the dispute between Christopher Melchert and Asma Afsaruddin with which I began this chapter comes to seem rather futile. In their own application of the term jihad, contemporary Muslims do not really care about any "historically correct" understanding of this Islamic institution. Although drawing historical lines, these activists do so randomly and at their own discretion. Not surprisingly, jihadist groups emphasize the military notion of jihad and link their understanding of it to prophetical and imperial traditions of warfare. Muslim civic action groups, instead, propagate and invoke the tradition of greater jihad in their aspirations of achieving societal change. Looking at contemporary social practices, both sides make justified borrowings from Islamic history. In this sense, these invocations of jihad are perfect examples for understanding Islam as a discursive tradition as proposed by Talal Asad.[76] The question about the "true meaning" of jihad, however, is not a scholarly question of Islamic studies but a matter of Islamic theology. From this perspective, Melchert's criticism of Afsaruddin—to a certain extent—falls back on himself. "True Islam" is defined by the consent of the believers and not by academic scholarship.

In this chapter, by taking the example of the classical Islamic institution of jihad, my aim has been to further support the two intertwined theses of my book concerning the hegemonic nature of the Islamic discourse of modernity and the internal fragmentation of this discourse in contemporary Islamic thought and practice. The latter, the increasing fragmentation of this hegemonic idea, corresponds with an observation made by Ibrahim M. Abu-Rabi', the editor of a companion to contemporary Islamic thought. Similar to my own argumentation in this chapter, he has emphasized the puzzling plurality that exists in the today's interpretation of Islamic religious traditions.⁷⁷ In particular the dissemination of modern print technologies and the spread of mass education has facilitated a significant break with the authoritative interpretation of Islamic sources by the religious establishment, leading to a fragmentation of religious authority through new forms of social, religious, and political activism.⁷⁸ From this perspective, the technological innovations of the twentieth century have contributed strongly to the hegemonic rise of the Islamic discourse of modernity.

Although there has never been a single and therefore ultimately decisive religious authority in Islamic history, the specific modern situation is characterized by the degree and scope to which the very meaning and purpose of Islamic religious traditions have been globally contested.⁷⁹ Islam as a discursive tradition meanwhile serves as a means for the justification of numerous Muslim projects of modernity. It is the references to Islam that make them authentic. The modern understandings of jihad are a significant case in point for this increasing plurality of the interpretation of Islamic traditions that take their point of departure in Islamic modernist thought of the nineteenth century. The multiple voices of Islamic modernities have been further documented and critically discussed in an ever-growing number of academic books that also inform current public debate about the "true nature of Islam."⁸⁰ Yet again, this true nature is given by the continuously unfolding reality of Muslim thought and practices. The case of jihad further supports this assumption, and the findings of this chapter lead me directly to the conclusions of my book.

Notes

1. This chapter draws partly on a previous article that I published in *TEMENOS—Nordic Journal of Comparative Religion*. I would like to thank the journal for allowing me to use some parts of the article for this chapter. Jung, Dietrich. 2016. Understanding the Multiple Voices of Islamic Modernities: The Case of Jihad. *TEMENOS* 52 (1): 61–85.
2. For a translation of the *fatwa*: Lewis, Geoffrey. 1975. The Ottoman Proclamation of Jihad in 1914. *The Islamic Quarterly* 19 (3 and 4): 157–163.
3. While this origin of the Ottoman–German Jihad in Berlin has remained the dominant storyline, it has also been disputed, and there are good arguments for

identifying its "genuine roots" as being in the empire itself. However, this is not the place to discuss this issue in more detail. See: Aksakal, Mustafa. 2011. Holy War Made in Germany? Ottoman Origins of the 1914 Jihad. *War in History* 18 (2): 184–199.

4. Hurgronje, Christiaan Snouck. 1915. The Holy War Made in Germany. In *Verspreide Geschriften, Deel III: Geschriften Betreffende Arabie en Turkije*. Bonn und Leipzig: Kurt Schroeder [1923], first published in *De Gids*, 1915, 274.
5. Ibid. 265–266.
6. Ibid. 283.
7. Becker, Carl-Heinrich. 1915. Die Kriegsdiskussion über den heiligen Krieg. In *Islamstudien: Vom Werden und Wesen der islamischen Welt*. Hildesheim: Georg Olms Verlagsbuchhandlung [reprint 1932], 288.
8. Jung, Dietrich. 2014. The "Ottoman–German Jihad": Lessons for the Contemporary "Area Studies" Controversy. *British Journal of Middle Eastern Studies* 41 (3): 247–265, 253.
9. Cf. Cobb, Paul M. 2003. Book Review of Jihad. The Origin of Holy War in Islam. *Journal of Near Eastern Studies* 62 (3): 222–223, 223.
10. Melchert, Christopher. 2015. Reviewed Work(s): Striving in the Path of God: Jihad and Martyrdom in Islamic thought by Asma Afsaruddin. *Review of Middle East Studies* 49 (2): 175–178, 175.
11. Afsaruddin, Asma. 2013. *Striving in the Path of God: Jihad and Martyrdom in Islamic Thought*. Oxford: Oxford Scholarship Online.
12. Afsaruddin, Asma. 2015. Interpreting Jihad: Asma Afsaruddin Responds to Christopher Melchert. *Review of Middle East Studies* 50 (2): 228–230, 228.
13. Ibid. 229.
14. Melchert 2015, 176.
15. Ibid. 178.
16. In principle, I am sympathetic with Afsaruddin's argument that we should go beyond narrow juridical interpretations of jihad. This applies in particular when looking at the contemporary usage of the concept. On this position, I will elaborate more in the conclusion to this chapter.
17. Hourani, Albert. 1962. *Arabic Thought in the Liberal Age, 1798–1939*. Cambridge: Cambridge University Press, 228–229.
18. Shakib Arslan was a leading figure in the Islamic reform movement who was fully engaged in Arab nationalist politics. In particular from his exile in Geneva, the descendent of a princely Druze family from Lebanon lobbied for the Arab nationalist cause. He was a close associate of Rashid Rida and provided the readers of

the journal *al-manār* with essential information about "Western religious, social and political ideas." Ryad, Umar. 2009. *Islamic Reformism and Christianity: A Critical Reading of the Works of Muhammad Rashid Rida and His Associates (1898–1935)*. Leiden: Brill, 43.

19. Sedgwick, Mark. 2010. *Muhammad Abduh*. Oxford: One World, 24; Makdisi, Ussama. 2008. *Artillery of Heaven: American Missionaries and the Failed Conversion of the Middle East*. Ithaca: Cornell University Press, 131.
20. Meyer, John W. and Ronald L. Jepperson. 2000. The Cultural Construction of Social Agency. *Sociological Theory* 18 (1): 100–120, 111.
21. Boli, John, and George M. Thomas. 1997. World Culture in the World Polity: A Century of International Non-Governmental organizations. *American Sociological Review* 62 (2): 171–190, 172.
22. Drori, Gili S., John W. Meyer, and Hokyu Hwang. 2006. Introduction. In *Globalization and Organization, World Society and Organizational Change*. Edited by Gili S. Drori, John W. Meyer, and Hokyu Hewang. Oxford: Oxford University Press, 1–22, 12.
23. Zemmin, Florian. 2021. The Modern Prophet: Radhid Rida's Construction of Muhammad as Religious and Social Reformer. In *The Presence of the Prophet in Early Modern and Contemporary Islam Series: Volume 2: Heirs of the Prophet: Authority and Power in Early Modern and Contemporary Islam*. Edited by Rachida Chih, David Jordan and Stefan Reichmuth. Leiden: Brill, 349–369, 358.
24. I consider this empirical argument as a fundamental critique of the cultural bias that characterizes the work of the Stanford School. Throughout their publications, the various authors of the school suggest perceiving the rising world culture as a product of the Christian culture of Europe and North America. The Stanford School applies a basic idea of classical modernization theory in locating the temporal and spatial origin of the structures of global culture exclusively in the so-called West. From the perspective of social emergence presented in Chapter Two, I would argue for a much more global evolution of these patterns and use the Islamic Reform Movement as one of its historical examples.
25. Meyer and Jepperson 2000, 101.
26. Ibid. 106–108.
27. Drori, Meyer and Hwang 2006, 1.
28. Meyer and Jepperson 2000, 111.
29. Meyer, John W., John Boli, George Thomas and Francisco O. Ramirez. 1997. World Society and the Nation-State. *American Journal of Sociology* 103 (1): 144–181, 167–168.

30. Cf. ibid. 167.
31. Meyer, John W. 2010. World Society, Institutional Theories, and the Actor. *Annual Review of Sociology* 36 (1): 1–20, 10–12.
32. These examples are taken from the standard dictionary: Wehr, Hans. 1985. *Arabisches Wörterbuch für die Schriftsprache der Gegenwart*. Arabisch–Deutsch, 5th edition. Wiesbaden: Otto Harrasowitz.
33. I briefly discussed Ibn Rushd's role in the Arabic golden age of science in chapter six.
34. Cf. Dutton, Yasin. 1994. The Introduction to Ibn Rushd's Bidāyat al-Mujtahid. *Islamic Law and Society* 1 (2): 188–205.
35. Al-Khalili, Jim. 2011. *The House of Wisdom: How Arabic Science Saved Ancient Knowledge and Gave Us the Renaissance*. New York: Penguin Press, 200.
36. Ibn Rushd, Muhammad A. 1966. *Bidāyat al-mujtahid wa nihāyat al-muqtaṣid* (transl. "The Distinguished Jurist Primer"). Vol. 1. Cairo: Maktaba al-Kuliyyat al-Azhariyye, 390–418; See also: Peters, Rudolph. 1977. *Jihad in Medieval and Modern Islam*. Leiden: Brill, 9–25.
37. Bonner, Michael. 2006. *Jihad in Islamic History: Doctrines and Practice*. Princeton and Oxford: Princeton University Press, 20.
38. Firestone, Reuven. 1999. *JIHAD: The Origin of Holy War in Islam*. Oxford: Oxford University Press, 47.
39. Noth, Albrecht. 1966. *Heiliger Krieg und heiliger Kampf in Islam und Christentum: Beiträge zur Vorgeschichte und Geschichte der Kreuzzüge*. Bonn: Ludwig Rohrscheid Verlag, 66–87.
40. El Fadl, Khaled Abou. 1999. The Rules of Killing in War: An Inquiry into Classical Sources. *The Muslim World* LXXXIX (2): 144–157.
41. From the perspective of an historian, Albrecht Noth already discussed here jihad in its non-legal dimension as it is the topic of Asma Afsaruddin's book.
42. Noth 1966, 50.
43. Peters 1977, 113.
44. Firestone 1999, 64.
45. Taking the example of Sudan under the rule of Omar al-Bashir (1993–2019), Rüdiger Seesemann, however, showed that justification for military campaigns happened with the support of Sufi orders and in a fusion of the two different understandings of jihad. Seesemann, Rüdiger. 2006. Between Sufism and Islamism: The Tijaniyya and Islamist Rule in Sudan. *Interdisciplinary Journal of Middle Eastern Studies* XV: 23–57.
46. Noth 1966, 59; and Sedgwick, Mark. 2000. *Sufism: The Essentials*. Cairo: American University of Cairo Press, 18.

47. Cook, David. 2005. *Understanding Jihad*. Berkeley: University of California Press, 35–37.
48. Ibrahim, Haslina. 1999. *Free Will and Predestination: A Comparative Study of the Views of Abu al-Assan Al-Ash'ari and Muhammad 'Abduh*. Unpublished MA thesis, Kulliya of Islamic Revealed Knowledge and Human Sciences. Kuala Lumpur: Islamic International University Malaysia, 71.
49. Cf. Sedgwick 2010, 54.
50. See: Peters, Rudolph. 1979. *Islam and Colonialism: The Doctrine of Jihad in Modern History*. The Hague, Paris and New York: Mouton; Faulkner, Neil. 2021. *Empire and Jihad: The Anglo-Arab Wars of 1870–1920*. New Haven and London: Yale University Press.
51. Malešević, Siniša. 2010. *The Sociology of War and Violence*. Cambridge: Cambridge University Press, 10.
52. Ibid. 11.
53. Krämer, Gudrun. 2010. *Hasan al-Banna*. London: Oneworld, 100.
54. Mitchell. Richard P. 1969. *The Society of the Muslim Brothers*. London: Oxford University Press, 207.
55. Commins, David. 2005. Hasan al-Banna (1906–1949). In *Pioneers of Islamic Revival*. Edited by Ali Rahnema. London: zed books, 125–153.
56. Cook 2005, 100; Nasr, Seyyed Vali Reza. 2005. Mawdudi and the Jamma'at-I Islami: The Origins, Theory and Practice of Islamic Revivalism. *Pioneers of Islamic Revival*. Edited by Ali Rahnema. London: zed books, 98–124.
57. Moten, Rashid. 2003. *Revolution to Revolution: Jamaat-e-Islami in the Politics of Pakistan*. Karachi: Royal Book Company, 27.
58. For this argument regarding modern *jāhiliyya*, see also my references to Sayyid Qutb in the theoretical elaborations of Chapter Two.
59. The Islamist ideology of Sayyid Qutb has been the topic of numerous studies; in this paragraph I rely on the works of Khatab, Sayed. 2006. *The Power of Sovereignty: The Political and Ideological Philosophy of Sayyid Qutb*. London and New York: Routledge; Musallam, Adnan A. 2005. *From Secularism to Jihad: Sayyid Qutb and the Foundations of Radical Islam*. Westport and London: Praeger; Shepard William E. 1996. *Sayyid Qutb and Islamic Activism: A Translation and Critical Analysis of Social Justice in Islam*. Leiden: Brill.
60. Heghammer, Thomas. 2020. *The Caravan: Abdallah Azzam and the Rise of Global Jihad*. Cambridge: Cambridge University Press. McGregor, Andrew. "Jihad and the Rifle Alone": Abdullah Azzam and the Islamist Revolution. *The Journal of Conflict Studies* 22 (2): 92–113.
61. Cf. Klausen, Jytte. 2015. Tweeting the Jihad: Social Media Networks of Western

Foreign Fighters in Syria and Iraq. *Studies in Conflict & Terrorism* 38 (1): 1–22.

62. Rahman, Azly. 2015. *Controlled Chaos: Essays on Malaysia's New Politics beyond Mahathirism and the Multimedia Super Corridor*. Petaling Jaya: Strategic Information and Research Development Centre, 33.

63. Sloane-White, Patricia. 2017. *Corporate Islam: Sharia and the Modern Workplace*. Cambridge: Cambridge University Press, 56.

64. Ibid. 77.

65. Deeb, Lara. 2006. *An Enchanted Modern: Gender and Public Piety in Shi'i Lebanon*. Princeton: Princeton University Press.

66. Ibid. 128.

67. Badran, Margot. 2005. Between Secular and Islamic Feminism. *Journal of Middle East Women's Studies* 1 (1): 6–28.

68. Stephan, Maria S. 2009. *Civilian Jihad: Non-Violent Struggle, Democratization, and Governance in the Middle East*. London and New York: Palgrave.

69. Kemerli, Pinar. 2015. Religious Militarism and Islamist Conscientious Objection in Turkey. *International Journal of Middle East Studies* 47: 281–301, 287.

70. Ibid. 282.

71. Ramadan, Tariq. 2010. *What I Believe*. Oxford: Oxford University Press, 114.

72. Saniotis, Arthur. 2012. Muslims and Ecology: Fostering Islamic Environmental Ethics. *Contemporary Islam* 6: 155–171, 164.

73. Ahmad, Salman. 2010. *Rock & Roll Jihad: A Muslim Rock Star's Revolution*. New York: Free Press; Stasyszyn, Roxanne. 2012. The Yukon's Muslim Community: Accepted and Accepting. *Yukon News*, September 28.

74. Sheikh, Naveed. S. 2015. Reclaiming Jihad as a Strategy of Conflict Transformation. *Peace Review* 27 (3): 288–295, 289.

75. Noor, Farish A. 2001. The Evolution of "Jihad" in Islamist Political Discourse: How a Plastic Concept became Harder. *Social Science Research Council*, at: www.ssrc.org/sept11/essays/noor.htm.

76. I discussed Talal Asad's concept briefly in Chapter One.

77. Abu-Rabi', Ibrahim M. 2006. Editor's Introduction. In *The Blackwell Companion to Contemporary Islamic Thought*. Edited by Ibrahim M. Abu-Rabi'. Oxford: Blackwell, 1–20.

78. I briefly described the role of these media in the formation of modern subjectivities with reference to the work of the German sociologist Andreas Reckwitz in Chapter Seven. For a discussion about new media in Muslim contexts, see Eickelman, Dale F. and Jon W. Anderson (eds.). 1999. *New Media in the Muslim*

World: The Emerging Public Sphere. Bloomington and Indianapolis: Indiana University Press; Robinson, Francis. 1993. Technology and Religious Change: Islam and the Impact of Print. *Modern Asian Studies* 27 (1): 229–251.

79. Mandaville, Peter. 2007. *Global Political Islam*. London and New York: Routledge.
80. Behloul, Samuel M., Susanne Leuenberger and Andreas Tunger-Zanetti. (eds.). 2013. *Debating Islam: Negotiating Religion, Europe, and the Self*. Bielefeld: Transcript. cooke, miriam and Bruce Lawrence (eds.). 2005. *Muslim Networks from Hajj to Hip Hop*. Chapel Hill: University of North Carolina Press; Euben, Roxanne and Muhammad Qasim Yaman (eds.). 2009. *Princeton Readings in Islamist Thought: Texts and Contexts from al-Banna to Bin Laden*. Princeton: Princeton University Press; Hunter, Shireen. (ed.). 2009. *Reformist Voices of Islam: Mediating Islam and Modernity*. Armonk and London: M. E. Shape; Kamrava, Mehran. 2007. *New Voices of Islam: Rethinking Politics and Modernity—A Reader*. Berkeley and Los Angeles: University of California Press, Kurzman, Charles. (ed.). 2002. *Modernist Islam. 1840–1940: A Sourcebook*. Oxford: Oxford University Press.

CONCLUSIONS: THE MOSAIC OF ISLAMIC MODERNITIES

In the introduction to this book, I promised to discuss questions about Islam *in* modernity from a specific perspective of social theory. In Chapter Two, I presented this perspective in the form of a theoretical and heuristic framework, as well as a conceptual and analytical one. It goes without saying that my approach to social theory is subjective and to a large extent the result of the trajectory my academic socialization has taken. In each chapter, I tried to make the readers familiar with some of the biographical elements which have played a role in my scholarly work. In terms of social theory, the most important element is my education in the German university system. I accessed the world of social theory first via German authors, among whom the most important were Norbert Elias, Jürgen Habermas, Immanuel Kant, Niklas Luhmann, Karl Marx, Georg Simmel, and Max Weber. Only later in my career did I add various non-German social theorists such as Émile Durkheim, Shmuel Eisenstadt, Anthony Giddens, Michel Foucault, and Charles Taylor. Looking back, however, I would say that Max Weber's work has registered the most lasting influence on my social thought.

Already in my first semester at Hamburg University, I read some of Max Weber's essays from the *Protestant Ethic*. His writings immediately attracted me, and they virtually changed my—at this point—rather naive worldview. Reading Max Weber made it clear to me that I had to learn a new language in order to view the world from the perspective of social science. The conceptual language of social theory forms a different world to the vernacular of everyday talk, and while often using the very same terms, there is a difference in their meaning. To be sure, common-sense understandings and scientific interpretations of the world are interrelated. For Alfred Schütz, this interrelationship constituted the decisive difference between the natural and the social sciences. He defined everyday life as a highly complex social construct to which the social sciences always refer. The social world necessarily has a particular meaning, it has social relevance and is therefore both preselected and pre-interpreted by a set of commonly shared "abstractions, generalizations, formalizations and idealizations."[1] In echoing the methodological position of Max Weber, Schütz defined the "world of everyday life" as a "universe of significance."[2] It is the task of social theory to methodologically analyze and critically reflect on this social universe of significance. Doing precisely that, I started to learn from Weber's *Protestant Ethic*. Yet this does not mean I follow Weber in all respects. On the contrary, this book has also been an attempt to refute one of his core theses about European exceptionalism.

In the introduction to the *Protestant Ethic*—actually written in 1920, about fifteen years after the essays themselves—Weber makes a strong argument for European exceptionalism.[3] He begins this introduction with the statement that a specific kind of cultural phenomena with universal significance could only have appeared in Western civilization.[4] This statement is then followed by a point-by-point explanation of what is meant by it. Beginning with science, Weber moves on to the arts and then the organization of politics before ending with capitalism, the "most fateful force in our modern life."[5] In all these societal realms—in my own terminology, functionally differentiated modern subsystems—we recognize cultural features which, according to Weber, in their specifically modern forms are only known in the Occident. Weber then goes into more detail about the nature of modern capitalism before ending in the peculiarities of Western rationalism. While attributing the economic conditions a core role in the development of this peculiar kind of rationalism, at the same time Weber points to several types of "practical rational conduct" that equally contributed to the rise of Western culture. Given the crucial historical importance of magical and religious forces in the past, Weber tells us, his collected essays take up the role of these forces in shaping the modern world. More precisely: "In this case we are dealing with the connection of the spirit of modern economic life with the rational ethics of ascetic Protestantism."⁶ From the retrospective vista of 1920, Weber leads his readers from the statement of European exceptionalism step by step to the essential question at the heart of his essays in *The Protestant Ethic and the Spirit of Capitalism*, the role of a specific kind of religious rationalization in the evolution of modern capitalism.⁷

In this introduction, originally written for the *Economic Ethics of the World Religions*, Max Weber strongly advocates the exceptional birth of the modern in Europe. It is against this kind of classical narrative of European exceptionalism that scholars of global history such as Bayly, Conrad, and Osterhammel have directed their critique. They replace this history of the origin, spread, and diffusion of modernity from its European core with a new emphasis on patterns of global interdependence and connectedness. Global historians have advocated a new narrative of the historical entanglement of cultures in the rise of modern society. It has been one purpose of this book to support this narrative from a decisively sociological perspective. In considering modern society as world society, in Chapter Two I presented the overarching theoretical and analytical framework of this perspective. Modernity, as a social structure should not be seen as a product of the so-called West but as resulting from a process of socio-cultural emergence. In the metatheoretical framework of social emergence, questions about the temporal and spatial origins of modernity become obsolete. Similar to Karl Jaspers' civilizational thesis of an axial age, the rise of the modern age can be seen as a long period of emerging elements of modernity in different cultures and regions of the world.⁸

I described my theoretical perspective in sufficient detail in Chapter Two, so there is no reason to repeat it here. The six empirical chapters, then, had the task of underpinning this theoretical approach and the two core arguments of this book. First, I have argued that we can observe emerging elements of modernity in Islamic history prior to the imperial impact of the West. In most of the six empirical chapters I presented historical evidence for this precolonial rise of patterns of modernity in boundary negotiations between religion (Islam) and other realms of functionally differentiated communications such as economics, politics, and science. In this way, I turn Max Weber's research program upside down. While Weber was looking for cultural differences to the Occidental experience, in my comparison I was looking for similarities based on a macrosociological concept of modernity that I derive from Modern Systems Theory. In all these social boundary negotiations I could find traces of specifically modern patterns of communication, so-called preadaptive advances to the functionally separated and self-referential systems of modern social systems. Long before the impact of the West, we can already discern in Islamic history specific logics of communication in negotiating the boundaries of different realms of social life—at least if we apply the anachronistic lenses of a kind of contemporary social theory as I do it in this book.[9]

My second argument has related to the discussion about an "Islamic resurgence" or revival in modern times. Rejecting these two concepts as an inadequate description of the historical role of Islam in contemporary Muslim life, I suggested interpreting this role through the concept of an Islamic discourse of modernity and the various Islamic projects of modernity this discourse has generated during the past two centuries. The six case studies, therefore, also serve as descriptions of some of these different projects of modernity, which I label, according to Eisenstadt's conceptual terms, as "multiple Islamic modernities." However, in contradistinction to Eisenstadt I stress the multiplicity of modern projects within Islam and not between different civilizational complexes. The empirical chapters of my book analyze some elements of this mosaic of modern projects within Islam through the lenses of intense boundary demarcations between the emergent macrostructures of functionally divided subsystems of world society. Thereby, the references to Islamic traditions aim at bestowing these projects of modernity with modern authenticity.

Generally speaking, this book challenges the thesis of European "modern" exceptionalism so forcefully proposed by Max Weber, in particular when it comes to the "scientification" of this thesis as in the linear and axiomatic propositions of classical modernization theories in the 1950s and 1960s.[10] The above two arguments had precisely this task of disproving the thesis of European exceptionalism from a sociological perspective. In this way, this book has also aimed to contribute to the sociological debate surrounding the contingency of modernity. This debate questions the teleological assumption of a quasi, almost necessary, evolution of the modern world in European history. In particular Chapter Three on the Ottoman Empire and the sections about the golden ages of Arabic science and Arab economy in Chapters Six and Seven should be seen as contributions to this debate. However, in applying theories of emergence,

I have tried to also move beyond this debate—wherein the notion that modernity arose in Europe, albeit as a contingent result of historical developments, remains the mainstream position.[11] Consequently, this book allocates Islamic projects of modernity a firm representation in world society. All chapters present arguments for closing the futile debate about Islam and modernity. Islam is *in* modernity. Let us move on to questions about the multiple ways in which Muslims have constructed different projects of Islamic modernities. Let us examine the contemporary mosaic of Islamic modernities. More precisely, I am advocating further research into the historical path along which the idea of specifically Islamic modernities became hegemonic in Muslim negotiations about modern social orders and about collective and individual identity construction. In which ways have Muslims claimed modern authenticity based on references to Islamic traditions in pursuing their modernizing social projects?

The empirical chapters in this book have given initial answers to this question. Together, they deliver some pieces of the mosaic with which the Islamic discourse of modernity confronts us. While the macrosociological elements of social theory provide a language of observation for this kind of research, the investigation in concrete projects of modernity takes place at lower levels of social analysis. I understand the multiplicity of concrete Islamic projects of modernity as social constructions with references to modernity's macrostructures, but these references occur in utterly contingent rather than systematic ways. It is at the levels of social actorhood and institution building that we can observe the many ways in which collective and individual actors construct historically diverse modern semantics based on the syntax of modernity. In this book, the bureaucrats of the Tanzimat, the Young Ottomans, Muhammad Abduh, Mustafa Kemal Atatürk, Hasan al-Banna, Said Nursi, Seyyed Hossein Nasr, the scholars and students at IIUM, the Malaysian government, Islamic banks, producers of halal goods, and Muslim volunteers and entrepreneurs in Egyptian youth organizations have served me as cases. They all have been deeply involved in those social constructions that together make up the Islamic discourse of modernity. They all refer to Islam as a "discursive tradition"—to apply Talal Asad's terminology once more. The references to this tradition bestow them with authenticity and legitimacy in pursuing their otherwise rather diverse social projects. Let me stress this argument once more with a final example.

In the introduction, I criticized Wael Hallaq's book on the Islamic state. More precisely, I rejected his exclusivist argument of considering the modern state as a mere European invention without any roots in the historical experience of Muslim peoples. I think some of the previous chapters have already proven this assumption to be historically wrong. Applying concepts of historical sociology, in Islamic history we can find indigenous paths to modern state formation. Hallaq takes his point of departure in the fact that Islamist movements consider the modern state as an instrument for shaping a true Islamic social order. The "implementation" of the shariʿa by the means of the state, so runs their argument, will establish this Islamic order.[12] Yet examples such as the Islamic Republic of Iran are for Hallaq proof of the failure of this political strategy. In Iran, according to him, the Islamist state apparatus has factually "subordinated and disfigured" the norms of Islamic governance.[13] Following Hallaq, the impossibility of the Islamic state is due to a fundamental incompatibility of the modern state with true shariʿa governance. As a European form of governance, the modern state is completely foreign to traditional Muslim culture and not even compatible with the most "basic requirements of Islamic governance."[14] These basic requirements Hallaq finds in classical Islamic jurisprudence (*fiqh*). Several scholars criticized Hallaq for his narrow and essentialist perspective on the Islamic state, which is based on the informal legal understanding of classical Islamic law until the nineteenth century. In short, Hallaq treats Islamic law as being synonymous with *fiqh*.[15] Yet, what is actually Islamic in those contemporary states that claim political authority as Islamic states? This question remains utterly open in Hallaq's historical and philosophical deliberations.

From my own point of view, the normatively guided question about the compatibility or incompatibility of the shariʿa with modern state governance misses the point. Rather than investigating the concrete (Islamic) practices of contemporary state-builders, Hallaq has written a treatise against modernity as such. For him, the state incarnates all the vices of modernity. The state is, as the subtitle of his book indicates, the epitome of modernity's moral predicament. Islam and the shariʿa serve him thereby as the antithesis of the morally intact harmony of premodern times. Like Seyyed Hossein Nasr, Wael Hallaq presents us with a critique of modernity from a holistic traditionalist perspective. Yet, while Nasr's major target is the field of modern science,

Hallaq puts politics and the modern state at the center of his anti-modernist critique. The positions of Nasr and Hallaq relate more broadly to the intellectual stream of neo-traditionalism in Islam. In Chapter Six, I showed how Seyyed Hossein Nasr stood in relation to the Traditionalist movement of René Guénon. According to my knowledge, Wael Hallaq is not a part of this anti-modernist network, but he apparently shares some of the propositions of neo-Traditionalist thought.[16] In particular, his almost "mystical" veneration of premodern Islamic culture and his advocation of a trans-historical meaning of the shariʿa appear to me similar to the neo-Traditionalist understanding of traditional Islam as an "uninterrupted transmission of Islamic knowledge."[17] Critical of liberal and Islamist projects of modernity, neo-Traditionalist thinkers nevertheless share major traits of modern thought.[18] With respect to the *Impossible State*, Andrew March rightly argued that Hallaq's imagination of a premodern Islamic social harmony ironically reflects the modern norms of "equality, social justice, privacy and the rule of law."[19]

The Islamic state, however, is not only a social imaginary. It is also a concrete, modern political project in which state authorities draw on Islam as a discursive tradition. In the move toward political independence, postcolonial political elites have often tried to bolster their political legitimacy by reverting to the symbolic sources of Islam. In declaring Islam as the state religion, allying themselves with the religious establishment, or elevating the shariʿa to a constitutionally defined source of law, Muslim regimes were a part of the Islamic discourse of modernity once launched by Islamic modernists in the nineteenth century. How should the postcolonial state relate to religion? In which ways do Islamic traditions serve as a source for modern postcolonial authenticity and political legitimacy? These became highly contested questions of the boundary negotiations between religion and politics in the newly independent Muslim states. Hallaq's book, unfortunately, hardly relates to any of them. Projects of Islamic states, however, are an essential part of the Islamic discourse of modernity. In these state-building projects, the modern state appears in an Islamic garb. I will briefly discuss three very different examples of postcolonial states: the Islamic Republic of Iran, Saudi Arabia, and the Federation of Malaysia. While the national political ideologies of all three states draw on the semantics of Islamic states, they employ this in utterly different ways. They are excellent cases for analyzing the contextual differences among the state-driven

Islamic projects of political modernity that have appeared in postcolonial state formation.

The Islamic Republic of Iran is a hybrid political system combining republican constitutional provisions with institutional elements of the political theory of Ayatollah Khomeini (1902–89) on the rule of the Islamic jurisprudent (*vilāyat-i faqīh*).[20] This fundamental dualism is reflected in the fact that state power in Iran builds on two kinds of sovereignty. On the one hand, the Islamic Republic invokes the sovereignty of the Iranian nation and known electoral processes, as well as the formal separation of executive, juridical and legislative powers. On the other hand, it derives its religious legitimacy from the "sovereignty of God," on which Khomeini's religio-political concepts rest.[21] The latter is important with respect to article 110 of the constitution, which stipulates the powers of the Islamic supreme leadership. The implementation of political decisions by the executive, for instance, needs the consent of the Supreme Leader. His powers further include appointing the country's highest judge and the leadership of the army and the Revolutionary Guards. In addition, he has the power to dismiss the popularly elected president. Finally, the religious leader controls the legislature via the "Guardian Council," whose members are appointed by him and who are responsible for checking parliamentary legislative initiatives for their compatibility with Islamic norms.

The political theory of Ayatollah Khomeini ties in with the classic doctrine of the Shiite Imamate, but revolutionizes it insofar as it replaces the passive expectation of salvation associated with the hope for the return of the Twelfth Imam with a kind of modern political activism.[22] In his theory of the *vilāyat-i faqīh*, Khomeini combined general aspects of Islamic modernism with components of Shiite Islamic traditions.[23] To some extent, his theory of Islamic governance corresponds to the ideas of Sunni Islamist modernists, such as those represented by Hasan al-Banna and the Muslim Brotherhood. This concerns in particular the normative foundations of Islamic governance in Islamic law and the idea that the shari'a can provide an institutional foundation for an authentically modern Islamic order. The specifically Shiite elements in Khomeini's political theory, however, are evident in articles two and five of the Iranian constitution. The second article establishes the political order of the country, among other things, in the belief in one God, the Shiite Imamate, and the incessant holy struggle of the Shiite legal scholars. Article five of the constitution then declares that "in the absence of the Lord of Time," the most exemplary of all jurists will be appointed the leader of the community. As Islamic governance means the rule of divine laws, Khomeini consequently assigns political leadership to the Islamic legal scholars (*fuqahā*, sing. *faqīh*). Their spiritual leader is therefore best suited to take over the supreme rule of the Islamic state during the period of the occultation of the Twelfth Imam.[24]

The political theory of Khomeini and the Islamic Republic of Iran underpin Eisenstadt's assumption that religious traditions may play a significant role in the shaping of modern political projects. Yet the Iranian Republic is far from being a blueprint for an Islamic state. This becomes clear when looking at the foundations of Islamic governance in Saudi Arabia. In sharp contrast to Iran, the political system of Saudi Arabia is a monarchy based on dynastic and religious sources of legitimacy.[25] Its official government website defines Saudi Arabia as an Arab and Islamic state whose constitution is the Qur'an and the sunna. The Saudi King is the head of state and acting prime minister. To some extent, he combines executive, legislative, and juridical power. In his executive function, the king is assisted by a council of ministers. Furthermore, the king presides over the juridical system, which in both criminal law and civil cases dispenses justice according to the stipulations of Islamic law.[26] Thus in formal terms the shari'a is the ultimate foundation of the Saudi state.[27] Islamic governance in Saudi Arabia follows the classical political theory of *siyasa shari'yya*. This theory goes back to the Hanbali scholar Ibn Taymiyya (1263–1328 CE), according to whom the legitimacy of the Islamic ruler ultimately rests on the authority of God and therewith on the sovereignty of Islamic law. Fully employing Islamic law, therefore, is the duty of the Saudi King. This religious obligation of the king is closely monitored by the Islamic jurisprudents of the country. The Saudi *'ulama'* supervise the application of Islamic law and its adjustment to the practices in a modern national state. In substance, the Islamic character of the Saudi state rests on this intertwined relationship and the related continuous social bargain between the ruling family and the Saudi jurisprudents.[28]

This peculiar relationship between rulers and *'ulama'* in Saudi Arabia has been historically constructed in the course of the country's modern state formation process since the eighteenth century. Following the Islamic reformist traditions of *'iṣlāḥ* and *tajdīd*, the Hanbali scholar Muhammad Abd al-

Wahhab (1703–92) launched a purist reform movement solely based on the Qur'an and the Prophetic traditions.[29] In spreading his reform ideas, Abd al-Wahhab joined forces with the military power of Muhammad bin Saud (1710–65) and his son Abd al-Aziz I (1765–1803). Since the eighteenth century, this religio-political alignment of the Al Saud family with "Wahhabi" scholars has been able to monopolize the means of physical force and gain control over large parts of the Arabian Peninsula in a series of military struggles against regional forces and those of the Ottoman Empire.[30] In a historically complex process during and after the First World War—involving the Hashemite ruler of the Hijaz, Sharif Husayn (1853–1931), and British colonial forces—Ibn Saud prevailed and eventually received recognition as King of the Hijaz and the Najd from Great Britain in 1927.[31] In 1932, he proclaimed the Kingdom of Saudi Arabia to be a modern national state. The contours of Saudi Arabia as an Islamic state, therefore, are the historical result of the close cooperation of political and religious leaders on the Arabian Peninsula in a colonial setting.

The context of British colonialism also shaped modern politics in Malaysia in various ways pertaining to its governmental system, ethnic-religious composition, and the role of Islam. Malaysia is a federal state combining 13 regional states and three federal territories.[32] The federation was declared on February 1, 1948 and revoked the British inauguration of the Malayan Union of April 1946. In a situation of fierce class conflicts, economic hardship, and ethnic violence, the British proposal of a centralized state had faced the strong opposition of Malayan forces.[33] In the design of its political institutions, however, the country resembles the institutional setting of Great Britain. Malaysia is a constitutional monarchy with an elected central government modeled on the bicameral parliamentarian system of Westminster. The position of the monarch is mainly representative and rotates among the nine sultans of the regional Malayan states. The executive power ultimately rests with the prime minister and the council of ministers of the federal government, whereas legislative power is with the parliament. While article three of the constitution defines Islam as the religion of the federation, article 11 grants the right to practice other religions. However, paragraph four of article 11 restricts the propagation of other religions among Muslims. In addition, article 121 assigns Islamic law an equal role to civil law in matters concerning Muslims. Furthermore, most

Malayan regional states consider apostasy of Islam as a punishable offense.³⁴ Consequently, the constitution remains somehow ambiguous when it comes to the relationship between Islam and state.³⁵

The Islamic character of the Malayan Peninsula goes back to precolonial times, and Malayan anticolonial nationalism was already impregnated with references to the country's Islamic traditions.³⁶ This historical heritage entered the constitution in article 160. Under the heading "Interpretations," this article defines a Malay as "a person who professes the religion of Islam," closely connecting religion and ethnicity. The Islamization of Malaysian politics, however, really picked up speed under the first premiership of Mahathir Mohamad (1981–2003). In Chapters Six and Seven, I already showed the ways in which the Malaysian government has instrumentalized Islam to provide a means of propagating nationalist politics in the realms of education and economics. For Prime Minister Mahathir, Islam was both a developmental tool and a strategic instrument in combating the internal Islamic opposition against his rule. Moreover, under his leadership, Islamic discourse developed into a major means of identity construction for the Malayan middle class. In international politics, the prime minister employed Islamic rhetoric in his strong advocation of "Asian values" vis-á-vis the West.³⁷ Molded by the historical experience of British colonialism and the Japanese occupation (1942–45), he employed references to Islam to validate his "rather anti-Western orientation."³⁸ In late 2001, then, Mahathir declared Malaysia to be an Islamic state.³⁹ The consequences of these policies of Islamization have threatened more pluralist conceptions of national identity in Malaysia, increasingly articulating nationhood in exclusivist ethno-religious terms.⁴⁰ At the same time, the ruling elite's hope to control the Islamist opposition backfired. Mahathir's policies "inflated the Islamic discourse in the country," and the government has been confronted with the dismissal of its Islamization policies by Islamist civil society groups and orthodox *'ulama'*.⁴¹

The Islamic Republic of Iran, Saudi Arabia, and the Federation of Malaysia constitute very different examples of what an Islamic state is or can be. They combine constitutional, dynastic, republican, monarchical, and parliamentarian features of rule with Shiite and Sunni Islamic traditions. They do so by being firmly based on the institutional model of the modern national state as this was defined by Max Weber: They claim both the legitimate monopoly of physical force and sovereign political authority over a certain territory and its people. In this way, they are historically contingent institutional manifestations of Islamic states, different from the mere ideological state in the thought of Ala al-Mawdudi briefly touched upon in Chapter Eight of this book. It is precisely these institutionalized forms of an Islamic state that Wael Hallaq rejects from a normative position in his *Impossible State*. Empirically, however, Islamic states exist; and they do so in various forms. My sketchy comparison of Iran, Saudi Arabia, and Malaysia has been intended to make the argument that the Islamic state is an empirical possibility. These states represent examples of the different ways in which modern political elites have constructed modes of governance for which they claim a form of religious legitimacy. Yet in this process, they combine Islamic traditions with the modern model of the national state and some of its features of legal authority. In short, these states are perfect examples for historically specific modern political projects that draw from and reinforce once again the Islamic discourse of modernity.

In his introduction to the *Princeton Encyclopedia of Islamic Political Thought*, the editor argues that Islamic political thought "must be understood from within." The realms of religion and state are, according to him, intimately intertwined; Islam represents "a vibrant integration of the secular and the sacred in obedience to God and his Prophet."[42] In this way, he argues for a kind of Islamic exceptionalism that mimics Max Weber's exclusivist contention about Europe outlined at the beginning of this concluding chapter. He represents a scholarly trend which the sociologist Rogers Brubaker defined as "methodological Islamism,"[43] a tendency to declare religion the independent variable in researching Islamic history and Muslim social practices. The case studies in this book are a treatise against this trend. They present analytical insights into the rise of a historically specific discourse of Islamic modernity to relative hegemony toward the end of the twentieth century. This historical process led to an "objectivation of Islam" as a religious system through an interplay of self- and other-identification among Muslims and non-Muslims, as well as among Muslims themselves.[44] We cannot understand this objectivation of Islam and its role in the discourse of modernity from within. The mosaic of Islamic modernities is an integral part of world society. We must instead analyze the Islamic discourse of modernity as a process of historical entanglement, as an instance of global history, as a specific but historically contingent signature of modern times. The purpose of this book has been to put forward theoretical and empirical arguments for this insight.

Notes

1. Schuetz, Alfred. 1953. Common-Sense and Scientific Interpretation of Human Action. *Philosophy and Phenomenological Research* 14 (1): 1–38, 3–8.
2. Ibid. 7.
3. Originally, Max Weber published his essays on Protestantism in *Archiv für Sozialwissenschaften* during the years 1904–5. The so-called "introduction" to these essays, however, he actually wrote as a preface to his essays *Wirtschaftsethik der Weltreligionen* in the year 1920. This is apparent on p. xxxix of the introduction. Here Weber writes that, besides two older essays in the beginning, he presents the reader a survey of the relationship of the most important religions to economic life. One of his biographers, Dirk Kaesler, considered this short preface to the *Economic Ethics of the World Religions* to be the pinnacle of all his scholarship. However, he strongly criticized Talcott Parsons, who used the text as the introduction to the *Protestant Ethic* in his translation of 1930. In this way, according to Kaesler, Parsons' translation caused a number of misinterpretations of the essays in the anglophone world. Kaesler, Dirk. 2014. *Max Weber: Eine Biographie*. Munich: C. H. Beck, 833.
4. Weber, Max. 2005. *The Protestant Ethic and the Spirit of Capitalism*. Translated by Talcott Parsons. With an Introduction by Anthony Giddens. London and New York: Routledge, xxiix.
5. Ibid. xxxi.
6. Ibid. xxxix.
7. There is no room here for a more detailed discussion of Weber's thesis, which has often been utterly misinterpreted. This applies in particular to interpretations according to which Weber had claimed to find the origin of capitalism in Protestantism.
8. I do not consider perspectives of emergence and entanglement as mutually exclusive. Features of modernity may have developed independently at different places while being institutionalized through the historical entanglement of social actors.
9. My specifically theoretical perspective, however, also corroborates the work of other scholars who pursue a similar research agenda to mine, though in different ways. A good example is Rushain Abbasi, who argues convincingly against the "popular understanding" of an Islamic culture in which Muslims have never been able to distinguish between the religious and secular spheres of life.

Abbasi, Rushain. 2020. Did Premodern Muslims Distinguish the Religious and Secular? The *Dīn-Dunyā* Binary in Medieval Islamic Thought. *Journal of Islamic Studies* 31 (2): 185–225, 185; Abbasi, Rushain. 2021. Islam and the Invention of Religion: A Study of Medieval Muslim Discourses on *Dīn*. *Studia Islamica* 116: 1–106. For another discussion of the conceptual usefulness of terms such as religion, civilization, and secularization in Islamic contexts, see: Krämer, Gudrun. 2021. *Religion, Culture, and the Secular: The Case of Islam*. Working Paper Series of the CASHSS "Multiple Secularities—Beyond the West, Beyond Modernities," 23. University of Leipzig, Germany.

10. I have my doubts as to whether Max Weber would ever have endorsed such a scientification of his interpretative sociology. He himself did not have strong truth claims regarding his findings and even warned in his introduction against exaggerating the importance of his investigations. Based on the relative scarcity of his sources, Weber emphasized the "provisional character" of his studies. Weber 2005, xi–xii

11. Cf. Knöbl, Wolfgang. 2007. *Die Kontingenz der Moderne: Wege in Europa, Asien und Amerika*. Frankfurt am Main and New York: Campus, 11.

12. I presented an example of this line of thought in Chapter Five through the case of the Muslim Brotherhood.

13. Hallaq, Wael B. 2013. *The Impossible State: Islam, Politics, and Modernity's Moral Predicament*. New York: Columbia University Press, x–xi and 2.

14. Ibid. 156.

15. Fahmy, Khaled. 2018. *In Quest of Justice: Islamic Law and Forensic Medicine in Modern Egypt*. Berkeley: University of California Press, 26. See also: Hussin, Iza, Nathan J. Brown and Neguin Yavari. 2014. Review Symposium: The Impossible State. *Perspectives on Politics* 12 (2): 461–467; and the review essay: March, Andrew F. 2015. What Can the Islamic Past Teach Us about Secular Modernity? *Political Theory* 43 (6): 838–849.

16. In a later book publication, Hallaq also refers directly to the intellectual thought of Guénon: Hallaq, Wael. 2018. *Restating Orientalism: A Critique of Modern Knowledge*. New York: Columbia University Press.

17. Sedgwick, Mark. 2020. The Modernity of Neo-Traditionalist Islam. In *Muslim Subjectivities in Global Modernity: Islamic Traditions and the Construction of Modern Muslim Identities*. Edited by Dietrich Jung and Kirstine Sinclair. Leiden: Brill, 121–146, 131.

18. Ibid. 139.

19. March 2015, 842.

20. I rely here on the translation of the Constitution of the Islamic Republic of Iran, adopted in November 1979, published in: Tellenbach, Silvia. 1985. *Untersuchungen zur Verfassung der Islamischen Republik Iran vom 15. November 1979.* Berlin: Klaus Schwarz Verlag.
21. Zubaida, Sami. 1997. Is Iran an Islamic State? In *Political Islam.* Edited by Joel Beinin and Joe Storck. London: I. B. Tauris, 103–122, 105.
22. Sheikoleslami, Ali Reza. 1986. From Religious Accommodation to Religious Revolution: The Transformation of Shi'ism in Iran. In *The State, Religion, and Ethnic Politics: Afghanistan, Iran, and Pakistan.* Edited by Ali Banuazizi and Myron Weiner. Syracuse, NY: Syracuse University Press, 227–256, 249.
23. Regarding the intellectual background for Khomeini's construction of the *vilāyat-i faqīh* in his exile in Iraq, see: Scharbrodt, Oliver. 2021. Khomeini and Muhammad al-Shirazi: Revisiting the Origins of the "Guardianship of the Jurisconsult" (*vilāyat-i faqīh*). *Die Welt des Islams* 61: 9–38.
24. Khomeini, Ruhollah. 1981. *Islam and Revolution: Writings and Declarations of Imam Khomeini.* Berkeley: Mizan Press, 27–80.
25. Thereby the dynastic legitimacy is closely linked to the tribal structures and customary norms of the region; Al-Atawneh, Muhammad. 2009. Is Saudi Arabia a Theocracy? Religion and Governance in Contemporary Saudi Arabia. *Middle Eastern Studies* 45 (5): 721–737, 726.
26. Quoted according to the official homepage of "The Embassy of the Kingdom of Saudi Arabia" in Washington, DC: https://www.saudiembassy.net/legal-and-judicial-structure-0; accessed: August 1, 2022.
27. In contrast to Iran, Saudi Arabia does not have an official constitution. However, there exist an increasing number of so-called "bylaws" or "basic laws" of government which deal with general guidelines for the government and Saudi citizens; cf. Al-Fahad, Abdulaziz. 2005. Ornamental Constitutionalism: The Saudi Basic Law of Governance. *Yale Journal of International Law* 30 (2): 376–396.
28. An excellent analysis of the functioning of this bargain is provided by the as-yet unpublished PhD thesis: Krell, Dominik. 2021. *Islamic Law in Saudi Arabia: Concepts, Practices and Developments.* Fakultät für Rechtswissenschaft, University of Hamburg, Germany.
29. Haj, Samira. 2002. Reordering Islamic Orthodoxy: Muhammad ibn Abdul Wahab. *The Muslim World* 92 (3–4): 333–370; Haj, Samira. 2009. *Reconfiguring Islamic Tradition: Reform, Rationality, and Modernity.* Stanford: Stanford University Press.
30. Due to this linkage with the reform ideas of Muhammad Abdul Wahhab,

external observers named the interpretation of Islam in Saudi Arabia as "Wahhabism."
31. For a brief description of this process, see: Rogan, Eugene. 2009. *The Arabs: A History*. London Penguin Books, 218–227.
32. In my description of the political system of Malaysia, I rely on the government publication: *Laws of Malaysia: Federal Constitution of 31st August 1957*, reintroduced as *Constitution of Malaysia* on 16th September 1963.
33. Andaya, Barbara Watson and Leonard Y. Andaya. 2017. *A History of Malaysia*. Third Edition. London: Palgrave Macmillan, 271–273.
34. There is no room here to deal with the complex role of Islamic law and sharia courts in Malaysia. More detailed information is offered by: Trakic, Adnan and Hanifah Haydar Ali Tajuddin (eds.). 2021. *Islamic Law in Malaysia: The Challenges of Implementation*. Singapore: Springer.
35. Wain, Barry. 2010. *Malaysian Maverick: Mahathir Mohamad in Turbulent Times*. New York: Palgrave, 2018.
36. Liow. Joseph Chinyong. 2016. *Religion and Nationalism in Southeast Asia*. Cambridge: Cambridge University Press, 137. However, it is important to mention that Malaysia, despite the anticolonial rhetoric in the country, has continued to remain a member of the British Commonwealth.
37. Maszlee, Malik. 2017. *Foundations of Islamic Governance: A Southeast Asian Perspective*. London and New York: Routledge, 43–44; Wain 2009, Chapter Nine.
38. Khalid, Khadijah Md. 2011. Malaysia's Foreign Policy under Najib: A Comparison with Mahathir. *Asian Survey* 51 (3): 429–452, 430.
39. Wain 2009, 218.
40. Liow 2016, 135.
41. Noor, Farish. A. 2009. Reformist Muslim Thinkers in Malaysia: Engaging with Power to Uplift the *Umma*? In *Reformist Voices of Islam: Mediating Islam and Modernity*. Edited by Shireen T. Hunter. Armonk, New York, and London: M. E. Sharpe, 208–226, 216.
42. Bowering, Gerhard (ed.). 2013. *The Princeton Encyclopedia of Islamic Political Thought*. Princeton and Oxford: Princeton University Press, viii. The book comprises more than 200 entries by contributors who are something of a who's-who of Islamic studies. I am quite sure that many of these contributors would hardly endorse the editor's essentialist argumentation at the beginning of the book.
43. Brubaker, Rogers. 2013. Categories of Analysis and Categories of Practice:

A Note on the Study of Muslims in European Countries of Immigration. *Ethnic and Racial Studies* 36 (1): 1–8.
44. Ibid. 3. The concept of an "objectivation" of Islam was put forward by: Eickelman, Dale F. and James Piscatori. 1997. *Muslim Politics*. Delhi: Oxford University Press.

BIBLIOGRAPHY

Abbasi, Rushain. 2020. Did Premodern Muslims Distinguish the Religious and Secular? The *Dīn-Dunyā* Binary in Medieval Islamic Thought. *Journal of Islamic Studies* 31 (2): 185–225.

Abbasi, Rushain. 2021. Islam and the Invention of Religion: A Study of Medieval Muslim Discourses on *Dīn*. *Studia Islamica* 116: 1–106.

Abaza, Mona. 2002. *Debates on Islam and Knowledge in Malaysia and Egypt: Shifting Worlds*. London: Routledge.

Abaza, Mona. 2006. *Changing Consumer Cultures of Modern Egypt: Cairo's Urban Reshaping*. Leiden: Brill.

Abdel Halim, Mahmoud. 2013. *Al-ikhwān al-muslimīn, aḥdāth ṣanaʿat al-tārīkh, ruʾyā min al-dākhil* (The Muslim Brotherhood, Events that Shaped their History, a View from Inside). Vol. I–III. Alexandria: Dār al-Daʿwa.

Abdel Aziz, Jumʿah Amin (ed.) 2006. *Min turāth al-imām al-Banna: Al- daʿwa wa al- ḥukūmāt wa al-hayʾāt (From the Heritage of Imam al-Banna: Missions, Governments and Institutions)*. Port Said: dār al-tawzīʿ wa al-nashr al-islāmiyyah.

Abduh, Muhammad. 2006. *Al-aʿmāl al-kāmila lī al-imām al-shaykh Muhammad ʿAbduh, ṭabʿa al-thāniyya, al-juzʾ al-thālith* (The Collected Works of the Imam Sheikh Muhammad Abduh, second edition, third volume). Cairo: dār al-shurūq.

Abou el-Haj, Rifaat Ali. 1991. *Formation of the Modern State: The Ottoman Empire Sixteenth to Eighteenth Centuries*. Albany: SUNY Press.

Abu-Rabi`, Ibrahim M. 2006. Editor's Introduction. In *The Blackwell Companion to Contemporary Islamic Thought*. Edited by Ibrahim M. Abu-Rabi`. Oxford: Blackwell, 1–20.

Adams. Charles. C. 1933. *Islam and Modernism in Egypt: A Study of the Modern Reform Movement Inaugurated by Muhammad Abduh*. London: Oxford University Press.

Adorno, Theodor W. 2000. *Introduction to Sociology*. Edited by Christoph Gödde and translated by Edmund Jephcott. Cambridge: Polity Press.

Afsaruddin, Asma. 2013. *Striving in the Path of God: Jihad and Martyrdom in Islamic Thought*. Oxford: Oxford Scholarship Online.

Afsaruddin, Asma. 2015. *Contemporary Issues in Islam*. Edinburgh: Edinburgh University Press.

Afsaruddin, Asma. 2015. Interpreting Jihad: Asma Afsaruddin Responds to Christopher Melchert. *Review of Middle East Studies* 50 (2): 228–230.

Agai, Bekim. 2017. The Religious Significance of Science and Natural Science in the Writings of Bediuzzaman Said Nursi. In *Ein traditioneller Gelehrter stellt sich der Moderne: Said Nursi 1876–1960*. Edited by Martin Riexinger und Bülent Ucar. Osnabrück: V&R unipress, 121–143.

Ahmad, Feroz. 1993. *The Making of Modern Turkey*. London: Routledge.

Ahmad, Feroz. 2014. *The Young Turks and the Ottoman Nationalities: Armenians, Greeks, Albanians, Jews, and Arabs, 1908–1918*. Salt Lake City: The University of Utah Press.

Ahmad, Salman. 2010. *Rock & Roll Jihad: A Muslim Rock Star's Revolution*. New York: Free Press.

Aksakal, Mustafa. 2011. Holy War Made in Germany? Ottoman Origins of the 1914 Jihad. *War in History* 18 (2): 184–199.

Al-Atawneh, Muhammad. 2009. Is Saudi Arabia a Theocracy? Religion and Governance in Contemporary Saudi Arabia. *Middle Eastern Studies* 45 (5): 721–737.

Al-Azm, Sadik J. 1981. Orientalism and Orientalism in Reverse. *Khamsin* 8: 5–26.

Al-Azmeh. Aziz. 1996. *Islams and Modernities*. Second Edition. London: Verso.

Al-Banna, Hasan 2004. *Majmu'at rasā'il al-imām al-shahīd Hasan al-Banna* (The Collection of the Tracts of the Martyr Imam Hasan al-Banna). Beirut: Al-Islamiyyah.

Al-Banna, Hasan. 2011. *Mushkilatunā fī ḍaw' al-niẓām al-islamī (niẓām al-hukm)* (Our Problem in the Light of the Islamic System (the System of Governance)). Cairo: Muasasat Iqraa.

Al-Banna, Hasan. 2013. *Mudhakirāt al-daʿwa wal-dāʿiyya* (Memoirs of the Mission and the Missionary). Cairo: Dār al-kalimah.

Al-Banna, Jamal. 2009. *Khiṭābāt Hasan al-Banna al-Shāb ilā Abīh* (Letters from the young Hasan al-Banna to his father). Cairo: Halā lil-Nashr wal-Tawzīʿ.

Al-Fahad, Abdulaziz. 2005. Ornamental Constitutionalism. The Saudi Basic Law of Governance. *Yale Journal of International Law* 30 (2): 376–396.

Albert, Gert. 2013. Figuration und Emergenz. Zur Ontologie und Methodologie des Ansatzes von Norbert Elias. *Kölner Zeitschrift für Soziologie und Sozialpsychologie* 65 (1): 193–222.

Algar, Hamid. 1979. Said Nursi and the Risala-i Nur: An Aspect of Islam in Contemporary Turkey. In *Islamic Perspectives: Studies in Honour of Mawlana Sayyid Abul Ala Mawdudi*. Edited by Khurshid Ahmad and Zafar Ishaq Ansari. London and Jeddah: The Islamic Foundation, 313–334.

Alici, D. M. 1996. The Role of Culture, History and Language in Turkish National Identity Building: An Overemphasis on Central Asian Roots. *Central Asian Survey* 15 (2): 217–231.

Al-Khalili, Jim. 2011. *The House of Wisdom: How Arabic Science Saved Ancient Knowledge and Gave Us the Renaissance*. New York: Penguin Press.

Al-Qaradawi, Yusuf. 2001. *The Lawful and the Prohibited in Islam*. Translated by: Kamal El-Hebawy, M. Moinuddin Siddiqui and Syed Shukry. Reprint of the Malaysian Student's Edition. Kuala Lumpur: Islamic Book Trust.

Al-Rasheed, Madawi, Carool Kersten and Marat Shterin (eds.). 2015. *Demystifying the Caliphate: Historical Memory and Contemporary Contexts*. Oxford: Oxford University Press.

Aminrazavi, Mehdi. 2001. Philosophia Perennis and Scienctia Sacra in a Postmodern World. In *The Philosophy of Seyyed Hossein Nasr*. Edited by Lewis Edwin Hahn et al. Peru, Illinois: Open Court Publishers, 551–562.

Andaya, Barbara Watson and Leonard Y. Andaya. 2017. *A History of Malaysia*. Third Edition. London: Palgrave Macmillan.

Anders, Andreas. 2012. *Theorien der Macht zur Einführung*. Hamburg: Junius.

Andrews, Walter G. and Mehmet Kalpaklı. 2004. *The Age of Beloveds: Love and the Beloved in Early-Modern Ottoman and European Culture and Society*. Durham, NC and London: Duke University Press.

Anjum, Ovamir. 2007. Islam as a Discursive Tradition: Talal Asad and His Interlocutors. *Comparative Studies of South Asia, Africa and the Middle East* 27 (3): 656–672.

ʿArafāt, ʿAlāʾ al-Dīn. 2001. *Al-alaqāt al-maṣriyya al-faransiyya min al-taʿāwun ilā al-tawāṭū* 1906–1923 (Egyptian–French Relations from Cooperation to Agreement 1906–1923). Cairo: Al-Arabi.

Aristoteles. 1958. *Politik*. Übersetzt und mit erklärenden Anmerkungen und Registern versehen von Eugen Rolfes. Hamburg: Felix Meiner.

Arnason, Johan P. 2003. *Civilizations in Dispute: Historical Questions and Theoretical Traditions*. Leiden: Brill.

Asad, Talal. 1986. *The Idea of an Anthropology of Islam*. Washington, DC: Center for Contemporary Arab Studies, Georgetown University.

Asad, Talal. 1993. *Genealogies of Religion: Discipline and Reasons of Power in Christianity and Islam*. Baltimore, MD: Johns Hopkins University Press.

Asad, Talal. 2003. *Formations of the Secular: Christianity, Islam, Modernity*. Stanford: Stanford University Press.

Atia, Mona. 2012. "A Way to Paradise": Pious Neoliberalism, Islam, and Faith-Based Development. *Annals of the Association of American Geographers* 102 (4): 808–827.

Awad, Najib G. 2016. "Understanding the Other From-Within": The Muslim Near East in the Eyes of Duncan Black Macdonald. *The Muslim World* 106: 523–538.

Aydin, Cemil. 2007. *The Politics of Anti-Westernism in Asia: Visions of World Order in Pan-Islamic and Pan-Asian Thought*. New York: Columbia University Press.

Badran, Margot. 2005. Between Secular and Islamic Feminism. *Journal of Middle East Women's Studies* 1 (1): 6–28.

Baldwin, David A. 2016. *Power and International Relations: A Conceptual Approach*. Princeton: Princeton University Press.

Bamyeh, Mohammed A. 2019. *Lifeworlds of Islam: The Pragmatics of a Religion*. New York: Oxford University Press.

Bangstad, Sindre. 2009. Contesting Secularism/s. Secularism and Islam in the Work of Talal Asad. *Anthropological Theory* 9 (2): 188–208.

Bano, Masooda. 2022. Islamic Authority and Centres of Knowledge Production in Europe. *Journal of Muslims in Europe* 11: 1–16.

Barkey, Karen. 2008. *Empire of Difference: The Ottomans in Comparative Perspective*. Cambridge: Cambridge University Press.

Baron, Beth. 2014. *The Orphan Scandal: Christian Missionaries and the Rise of The Muslim Brotherhood*. Stanford: Stanford University Press.

Baumann, Zygmunt. 2007. *Liquid Times: Living in an Age of Uncertainty*. Cambridge: Cambridge University Press.

Bayat, Asef. 2007. *Making Islam Democratic: Social Movements and the Post-Islamist Turn*. Stanford: Stanford University Press.

Bayly, Christopher A. 2004. *The Birth of the Modern World 1780–1914*. London: Blackwell Publishing.
Bayly, C. A. 2016. Indian and Arabic Thought in the Liberal Age. In *Arabic Thought Beyond the Liberal Age: Towards an Intellectual History of the Nahda*. Edited by Jens Hansen and Max Weiss. Cambridge: Cambridge University Press Cambridge: Cambridge University Press, 325–350.
Beck, Ulrich. 1992. *Risk Society: Towards a New Modernity*. London: Sage.
Beck, Ulrich and Nathan Sznaider. 2006. Unpacking Cosmopolitanism for the Social Sciences: A Research Agenda. *British Journal of Sociology* 57 (1): 1–23.
Becker, Carl-Heinrich. 1915. Die Kriegsdiskussion über den heiligen Krieg. In *Islamstudien: Vom Werden und Wesen der islamischen Welt*. Hildesheim: Georg Olms Verlagsbuchhandlung [reprint 1932], 281–304.
Becker, Carl-Heinrich. 1910. Der Islam als Problem. *Der Islam* 1 (1): 1–21.
Behloul, Samuel M., Susanne Leuenberger and Andreas Tunger-Zanetti (eds.). 2013. *Debating Islam: Negotiating Religion, Europe, and the Self*. Bielefeld: Transcript.
Bendix, Regina. 1997. *In Search of Authenticity: The Formation of Folklore Studies*. Madison: University of Wisconsin Press.
Ben-Zaken, Avner. 2004. The Heavens of the Sky and the Heavens of the Heart: The Ottoman Cultural Context for the Introduction of Post-Copernican Astronomy. *British Journal of the History of Science* 37 (1): 1–28.
Bergunder, Michael. 2020. Umkämpfte Historisierung. Die Zwillingsgeburt von "Religion" und "Esoterik" in der zweiten Hälfte des 19. Jahrhunderts und das Programm einer globalen Religionsgeschichte. In *Wissen um Religion: Erkenntnis—Interesse. Epistemologie und Episteme in Religionswissenschaft und interkultureller Theologie*. Leipzig: Evangelische Verlagsanstalt, 47–132.
Berkes, Niyazi. 1964. *The Development of Secularism in Turkey*. Montreal: McGill University Press.
Beyer, Peter. 2006. *Religions in Global Society*. London: Routledge.
Birand, Mehmet A. 1991. *Shirts of Steel: An Anatomy of the Turkish Armed Forces*. London: I. B. Tauris.
Blank, Steve. 2013. Why the Lean Start-Up Changes Everything. A Faster, Smarter Methodology for Launching Companies May Make Business Plans Obsolete. *Harvard Business Review* 91 (5): 63–72.
Boehmer, Elleke and Steven Matthews. 2011. Modernism and Colonialism. In *The Cambridge Companion to Modernism*. Edited by Michael Levenson. Cambridge: Cambridge University Press, 284–300.

Boli, John and George M. Thomas. 1997. World Culture in the World Polity: A Century of International Non-Governmental Organizations. *American Sociological Review* 62 (2): 171–190

Bonner, Michael. 2006. *Jihad in Islamic History: Doctrines and Practice*. Princeton and Oxford: Princeton University Press.

Bouquet, Olivier. 2015. Is it Time to Stop Speaking about Ottoman Modernisation? In *Order and Compromise: Government Parctices in Turkey from the Late Ottoman Empire to the Early 21st Century*. Edited by Aymes, Marc, Benjamin Gourisse and Élise Massicard. Leiden: Brill, 45–67.

Bowering, Gerhard (ed.). 2013. *The Princeton Encyclopedia of Islamic Political Thought*. Princeton and Oxford: Princeton University Press.

Bøel, Marianne. 2017. Halal-dating som ungdomskultur. Forhandlinger om ekteskaps—og samlivsprakiser blant norsk ungdom med mulimsk bakgrunn. *Prismet Forskning* 68 (1–2): 9–26.

Brahimi, Mohamed Amine and Houssem Ben Lazreg. 2021. Post-Islamism and Intellectual Production: A Bibliometric Analysis of the Evolution of Contemporary Islamic Thought. *Religions* 12 (49): 1–25.

Brekke, Torkel. 2012. *Prophecy and Protest in an Age of Globalization*. Cambridge: Cambridge University Press.

Bröckling, Ulrich, Susanne Krasmann and Thomas Lemke (eds.). 2007. *Governmentality: Current Issues and Future Challenges*. London: Routledge.

Brown, Carl. 2000. *Religion and State: The Muslim Approach to Politics*. New York: Columbia University Press.

Brubaker, Rogers. 2013. Categories of Analysis and Categories of Practice: A Note on the Study of Muslims in European Countries of Immigration. *Ethnic and Racial Studies* 36 (1): 1–8.

Büssow, Johann. 2015. Re-Imagining Islam in the Period of the First Modern Globalization: Muhammad Abduh and His Theology of Unity. In *A Global Middle East: Modernity, Materiality and Culture in the Modern Age, 1880–1940*. Edited by Liat Kozma et. al. London: I. B. Tauris, 273–320.

Büssow, Johann. 2017. Muhammad Abduh: The Theology of Unity (Egypt, 1898). In *Religious Dynamics under the Impact of Imperialism and Globalisation: A Source Book*. Edited by Björn Bentlage et al. Leiden: Brill, 141–159.

Burhanudin, Jajat. 2005. Aspiring for Islamic Reform: Southeast Asian Requests for Fatwās in al-Manār. *Islamic Law and Society* 12 (1): 9–26.

Buskens, Léon and Annemarie van Sandwijk (eds.). 2016. *Islamic Studies in the Twenty-First Century: Transformations and Continuities*. Amsterdam: Amsterdam University Press.

Buzan, Barry. 2014. *An Introduction to the English School of International Relations: The Societal Approach.* Cambridge: Polity.

Çağatay, Neşet. 1970. Ribā and Interest Concept and Banking in the Ottoman Empire. *Studia Islamica* 32: 53–68.

Casanova, José. 2006. Secularization Revisited: A Reply to Talal Asad. In *Powers of the Secular Modern: Talal Asad and His Interlocutors.* Edited by David Scott and Charles Hirschkind. Stanford: Stanford University Press, 12–30.

Celik, Gürkan, Johan Leman and Karel Steenbrink (eds.). 2015. *Gülen-Inspired Hizmet in Europe: The Western Journey of a Turkish Muslim Movement.* Brussels: P. I. E. Peter Lang.

Çevik, Neslihan. *Muslimism in Turkey and Beyond: Religion in the Modern World.* New York: Palgrave.

Chapra, Umer M. 2000. Is it Necessary to Have Islamic Economics? *The Journal of Socio-Economics* 29: 21–37.

Choi, David Y. and Edmund R. Gray. 2008. Socially Responsible Entrepreneurs: What do They do to Create and Build Their Companies? *Business Horizons* 51: 341–352.

Citarella, Armand O. 1968. Patterns in Medieval Trade: The Commerce of Amalfi Before the Crusades. *The Journal of Econcomic History* 28 (4): 531–555.

Clark, Janine A. 2004. *Islam, Charity, and Activism: Middle-Class Networks and Social Welfare in Egypt, Jordan, and Yemen.* Bloomington and Indianapolis: Indiana University Press.

Clayton, Philip. 2006. Conceptual Foundations of Emergence Theory. In *The Re-Emergence of Emergence: The Emergentist Hypothesis from Science to Religion.* Edited by Philip Clayton and Paul Davies. Oxford: Oxford University Press, 1–31.

Cleveland, William L. 1971. *The Making of an Arab Nationalist: Ottomanism and Arabism in the Life and Thought of Sati al-Husri.* Princeton: Princeton University Press.

Cleveland, William L. 1985. *Islam against the West: Shakib Arslan and the Campaign for Islamic Nationalism.* London: Al Saqi Books.

Cobb, Paul M. 2003. Book Review of "Jihad". The Origin of Holy War in Islam. *Journal of Near Eastern Studies* 62 (3): 222–223.

Colish, Marcia L. 2006. Avicenna's Theory of Efficient Causation and Its Influence on St. Thomas Aquinas. In *Studies in Scholasticism.* Aldershot and Burlington: Ashgate, Variorum.

Commins, David. 2005. Hasan al-Banna (1906–1949). In *Pioneers of Islamic Revival.* Edited by Ali Rahnema. London: zed books, 125–153.

Conrad, Sebastian. 2016. *What is Global History?* Princeton: Princeton University Press.

Cook, David. 2005. *Understanding Jihad.* Berkeley: University of California Press.

cooke, miriam and Bruce Lawrence (eds.). 2005. *Muslim Networks from Hajj to Hip Hop.* Chapel Hill: University of North Carolina Press.

Coruh, Hakan. 2019. The Qur'an and Interpretation in the Classical Modernism: Tafsircentric Approach of Muhammad 'Abduh. *Australian Journal of Islamic Studies* 4 (2): 1–21.

Coulson, N. J. 1965. Reviewed Work(s): An Introduction to Islamic Law by Joseph Schacht. *The International and Comparative Law Quarterly* 14 (1): 336–338.

Dallal, Ahmad. 1993. The Origins and Objectives of Islamic Revivalist Thought, 1750–1850. *Journal of the American Oriental Society* 113 (3): 341–359.

Dallal, Ahmad. 1999. Science, Medicine, and Technology. In *The Oxford History of Islam.* Edited by John Esposito. Oxford: Oxford University Press, 155–214.

Dallal, Ahmad. 2000. Appropriating the Past: Twentieth-Century Reconstruction of Pre-Modern Islamic Thought. *Islamic Law and Society* 7 (1): 325–358.

Dallal, Ahmad. 2010. *Islam, Science, and the Challenge of History.* Yale: Yale University Press.

Daniel, Norman. 1960. *Islam and the West: The Making of an Image.* Edinburgh: Edinburgh University Press.

Deeb, Lara. 2006. *An Enchanted Modern: Gender and Public Piety in Shi'i Lebanon.* Princeton: Princeton University Press.

Deringil, Selim. 1998. *The Well-Protected Domains: Ideology and the Legitimation of Power in the Ottoman Empire, 1876–1909.* London: I. B. Tauris.

Di-Capua, Yoav. 2015. Nahda: The Arab Project of Enlightenment. In *The Companion to Modern Arab Culture.* Edited by Dwight F. Reynolds. Cambridge: Cambridge University Press, 54–74.

Doğan, Mehmet Ali and Heather J. Sharkey (eds.). 2011. *American Missionaries and the Middle East: Foundational Encounters.* Salt Lake City: University of Utah Press.

Drori, Gili S., John W. Meyer, Francisco Ramirez and Evan Schofer. 2003. *Science in the Modern World Polity: Institutionalization and Globalization.* Stanford: Stanford University Press.

Drori, Gili S., John W. Meyer, and Hokyu Hwang. 2006. Introduction. In *Globalization and organization, World Society and Organizational Change.* Edited by Gili S. Drori, John W. Meyer, and Hokyu Hwang. Oxford: Oxford University Press, 1–22.

Duderija, Adis (ed.). 2014. *Maqāṣid al-Sharī'a and Contemporary Reformist Muslim Thought*. London: Routledge.

Duffy, Andrew and Ginnette Ng Hui Xian. 2021. Edible Communities: How Singapore Creates a Nation of Consumers for Consumption. *Journal of Consumer Culture* 21 (4): 782–799.

Duiguid, Stephen. 1973. The Politics of Unity: Hamidian Policy in Eastern Anatolia. *Middle East Studies* 9 (2): 139–155.

Durkheim, Émile. 1964. *The Division of Labor*. New York: The Free Press.

Dutton, Yasin. 1994. The Introduction to Ibn Rushd's "Bidāyat al-Mujtahid". *Islamic Law and Society* 1 (2): 188–205.

Eickelman Dale F. and James Piscatori. 1997. *Muslim Politics*. Delhi: Oxford University Press.

Eickelman, Dale F. and Jon W. Anderson (eds.). 1999. *New Media in the Muslim World: The Emerging Public Sphere*. Bloomington and Indianapolis: Indiana University Press.

Eisenstadt, Shmuel N. 2000. Multiple Modernities. *Daedalus* 129 (1): 1–29.

Eisenstadt, Shmuel N. 2000. The Reconstruction of Religious Arenas in the Framework of "Multiple Modernities". *Millennium: Journal of International Studies* 29 (3): 591–611.

Eisenstadt, Shmuel N. 2001. The Civilizational Dimension of Modernity: Modernity as a Distinct Civilization. *International Sociology* 16 (3): 320–340.

El Fadl, Khaled Abou. 1999. The Rules of Killing in War: An Inquiry into Classical Sources. *The Muslim World* LXXXIX (2): 144–157.

El-Hani, Charbel N. 2002. On the Reality of Emergents. *Principa* 6 (1): 51–87.

Elias, Norbert. 1994. *The Civilizing Process: The History of Manners and State Formation and Civilization*. Oxford: Basil Blackwell.

El-Rouayheb, Khaled. 2015. *Islamic Intellectual History in the Seventeenth Century: Scholarly Currents in the Ottoman Empire and the Maghreb*. Cambridge: Cambridge University Press.

El-Wereny, Mahmud. 2018. Reichweite und Instrumente islamrechtlicher Normfindung: Yūsuf al-Qaraḍāwīs *iğtihād*-Konzept. *Die Welt des Islams* 58 (1): 65–100.

Elshakry, Marwa. 2008. Knowledge in Motion. The Cultural Politics of Modern Science Translations in Arabic. *ISIS* 99 (4): 701–730.

Elshakry, Marwa. 2010. When Science Became Western: Historiographical Reflections. *ISIS* 101 (1): 98–109.

Elshakry, Marwa. 2013. *Reading Darwin in Arabic, 1860–1950*. Chicago: University of Chicago Press.

Emmeche, Claus, Simon Køppe and Frederik Stjernfelt. 1997. Explaining Emergence: Towards an Ontology of Levels. *Journal for General Philosophy of Science* 28: 83–119.

Erginbaş, Vefa. 2019. Introduction. In *Ottoman Sunnism: New Perspectives*. Edited by Vefa Erginbaş. Edinburgh: Edinburgh University Press, 1–11.

Euben, Roxanne L. 1999. *Enemy in the Mirror: Islamic Fundamentalism and the Limits of Modern Rationalism*. Princeton: Princeton University Press.

Euben, Roxanne and Muhammad Qasim Yaman (eds.). 2009. *Princeton Readings in Islamist Thought: Texts and Contexts from al-Banna to Bin Laden*. Princeton: Princeton University Press.

Fadil, Nadia and Fernando, Myanthi. 2015. Rediscovering the 'Everyday' Muslim: Notes on an Anthropological Divide. *HAU: Journal of Ethnographic Theory* 5 (2): 59–88.

Fahmy, Khaled. 2018. *In Quest of Justice: Islamic Law and Forensic Medicine in Modern Egypt*. Oakland: University of California Press.

Farquhar, Michael. 2017. *Circuits of Faith: Migration, Education, and the Wahhabi Mission*. Stanford: Stanford University Press.

Faroqhi, Suraiya. 2010. *Subjects of the Sultan: Culture and Daily Life in the Ottoman Empire*. London: I. B. Tauris.

Faulkner, Neil. 2021. *Empire and Jihad: The Anglo–Arab Wars of 1870–1920*. New Haven and London Yale University Press.

Firestone, Reuven. 1999. *JIHAD: The Origin of Holy War in Islam*. Oxford: Oxford University Press.

Fischer, Johan. 2008. *Proper Islamic Consumption: Shopping Among the Malays in Modern Malaysia*. Copenhagen: NIAS Press.

Fischer, Johan. 2011. *The Halal Frontier: Muslim Consumers in a Globalized Market*. New York: Palgrave Macmillan.

Fitzgerald, Timothy. 2007. Introduction. In *Religion and the Secular: Historical and Colonial Formations*. London: Acumen.

Fitzgerald, Timothy. 2007. *Discourse on Civility and Barbarity: A Critical History of Religion and Related Categories*. Oxford: Oxford University Press.

Fontaine, Laurence. 2014. *Le marché: Historie et usages d'une conquete sociale*. Paris: Gallimard.

Fortna, Benjamin C. 2012. The Ottoman Empire and After. From a State of "Nations" to "Nation-states". In *State-Nationalisms in the Ottoman Empire: Greece and Turkey: Orthodox and Muslims, 1830–1845*. Edited by Benjamin C. Fortna, Stefanos Katsikas, Dimitris Kamouzis, and Paraskevas Konortas. London: Routledge, 1–12.

Fosset, Karelyn. 2013. What Makes a Sex Shop Halal? *Foreign Policy*. October 23rd.
Foucault, Michel. 1977. *Discipline and Punish: The Birth of the Prison*. London: Penguin.
Foucault, Michel. 1980. About the Beginning of the Hermeneutics of the Self. In *Religion and Culture by Michel Foucault*. Edited by Jeremy R. Carrette. Manchester: Manchester University Press.
Foucault, Michel. 1984. What is Enlightenment. In *The Foucault Reader*. Edited by Paul Rabinow. Pantheon Books: New York, 32–51.
Foucault, Michel. 1989. *Archaeology of Knowledge*. London: Routledge.
Foucault, Michel. 1994. *The Order of Things*. London: Routledge.
Freely, John. 2009. *Aladdin's Lamp: How Greek Science Came to Europe Through the Islamic World*. New York: Alfred A. Knopf.
Frye, R. N. (ed.). 1956. *Islam and the West*. S-Gravenhage: Mouton.
Geaves, Ron. 2010. *Islam Today*. London: Continuum.
Geertz, Clifford. 1973. *The Interpretation of Culture: Selected Essays*. New York: Basic Books.
Gershoni, Israel. 1999. Egyptian Liberalism in an Age of "Crisis of Orientation": Al-Risala's Reaction to Fascism and Nazism, 1933–39. *International Journal of Middle East Studies* 31: 551–576.
Getachew, Adom. 2016. Universalism After the Post-Colonial Turn: Interpreting the Haitian Revolution. *Political Theory* 44 (6): 1–25.
Ghazzal, Amal. 2016. "Illiberal" Thought in the Liberal Age. Yusuf al-Nabhani (1849–1932), Dream Stories and Sufi Polemics against the Modern Era. In *Arabic Thought Beyond the Liberal Age: Towards an Intellectual History of the Nahda*. Edited by Jens Hansen and Max Weiss. Cambridge: Cambridge University Press, 214–233.
Ghulam, Nabi Saqeb. 2000. Some Reflections on Islamization of Education Since 1977 Makkah Conference: Accomplishments, Failures and Tasks Ahead. *Intellectual Discourse* 8 (1): 45–68.
Gibb, Sir Hamilton and Harold Bowen. 1950. *Islamic Society and the West: A Study of the Impact of Western Civilization on Moslem Culture in the Near East*. London, New York and Toronto: Oxford University Press.
Giddens, Anthony. 1991. *The Consequences of Modernity*. Stanford: Stanford University Press.
Gökarıksel, Banu and Anna J. Secor. 2009. New Transnational Geographies of Islamism, Capitalism and Subjectivity: The Veiling-fashion Industry in Turkey. *Area* 41 (1): 6–18.

Göle, Nilüfer. 1997. Secularism and Islamism in Turkey: The Making of Elites and Counter-Elites. *Middle East Journal* 51 (1): 46–58.

Goitein, S. D. 1960. The Documents of the Cairo Geniza as a Source for Mediterranean Social History. *Journal of the American Oriental Society* 80 (2): 91–100.

Goffmann, Daniel. 2002. *The Ottoman Empire and Early Modern Europe*. Cambridge: Cambridge University Press.

Goldstein, Jeffrey. 1999. Emergence as a Construct: History and Issues. *Emergence* 1 (1): 49–72.

Goldziher, Ignaz. 1978. *Tagebuch*. Edited by Alexander Schreiber. Leiden: Brill.

Goodman, L. E. 1986. Review of Arabic Thought in the Liberal Age, 1798–1939. *The International History Review* 8 (1): 107–111.

Gran, Peter. 1979. *Islamic Roots of Capitalism: Egypt, 1760–1840*. Austin and London: University of Texas Press.

Gräf, Bettina and Jakob Skovgaard-Petersen (eds.). 2009. *The Global Mufti: The Phenomenon of Yusuf al-Qaradawi*. London: Hurst.

Griffel, Frank. 2015. What do We Mean by "Salafi"? Connecting Muḥammad ʿAbduh with Egypt's Nūr Party in Islam's Contemporary Intellectual History. *Die Welt des Islams* 55: 186–220.

Griffel, Frank (ed.). 2016. *Islam and Rationality: The Impact of al-Ghazālī. Papers Collected on His 900th Anniversary*. Vol. 2. Leiden: Brill.

Günther, Sebastian. 2016. Bildung und Ethik im Islam. In *Islam. Einheit und Vielfalt einer Weltreligion*. Edited by Rainer Brunner. Stuttgart: Kohlhammer, 210–236.

Gürpinar, Doğan. 2013. *Ottoman/Turkish Visions of the Nation, 1860–1950*. New York: Palgrave Macmillan.

Guizot, François. 1828. *Cours d'histoire modern—Histoire général de la civilisation en Europe*. Paris: Pichon et Didier.

Habermas, Jürgen. 1962. *Strukturwandel der Öffentlichkeit*. Neuauflage 1990. Frankfurt am Main: Suhrkamp.

Habermas, Jürgen. 1980. Die Moderne—ein unvollendetes Projekt. In *Die Moderne— ein unvollendetes Projekt: Philosophisch-politische Aufsätze 1977–1990*. Leipzig: Reclam, 32–55.

Habermas, Jürgen. 1981. *Theorie des kommunikativen Handelns*. Zwei Bände. Frankfurt am Main: Suhrkamp.

Habermas, Jürgen. 2005. *Zwischen Naturalismus und Religion: Philosophische Aufsätze*. Frankfurt am Main: Suhrkamp.

Habermas, Jürgen and Niklas Luhmann. 1971. *Theorie der Gesellschaft oder Sozialtechnologie—was leistet die Systemforschung?* Frankfurt am Main: Suhrkamp.

Habib, Irfan S. and Dhruv, Raina. 2004. *Domesticating Modern Science and Culture in Colonial India*. New Delhi: Tulika Books.

Haddad, Mahmoud. 1997. Arab Religious Nationalism in the Colonial Era: Rereading Rashid Rida's Ideas on the Caliphate. *Journal of the American Oriental Society* 117 (2): 253–266.

Haddad, Yvonne. 2005. Muhammad Abduh: Pioneer of Islamic Reform. In *Pioneers of Islamic Revival*. New edition. Edited by Ali Rahnema. London: zed books, 30–63.

Hafez, Sherine. 2011. *An Islam of Her Own: Reconsidering Religion and Secularism in Women's Islamic Movements*. New York and London: New York University Press

Haj, Samira. 2002. Reordering Islamic Orthodoxy: Muhammad ibn Abdul Wahab. *The Muslim World* 92 (3–4): 333–370.

Haj, Samira. 2009. *Reconfiguring Islamic Tradition: Reform, Rationality, and Modernity*. Stanford: Stanford University Press.

Halevi, Leor. 2019. *Modern Things on Trial: Islam's Global and Material Reformation in the Age of Rida, 1865–1935*. New York: Columbia University Press.

Hallaq, Wael B. 2013. *The Impossible State: Islam, Politics, and Modernity's Moral Predicament*. New York: Columbia University Press.

Hallaq, Wael. 2018. *Restating Orientalism: A Critique of Modern Knowledge*. New York: Columbia University Press.

Hanafi, Sari. 2021. From Streaming to Mainstreaming "Islamization of Knowledge": The Case of the International Islamic University of Malaysia. *American Journal of Islam and Society* 38 (1–2): 101–135.

Hanioğlu, Şükrü M. 2005. Blueprints for a Future Society: Late Ottoman Materialists on Science, Religion, and Art. In *Late Ottoman Society: The Intellectual Legacy*. Edited by Elisabeth Özdalga. London: Routledge, 28–116.

Hanioğlu, Şükrü M. 2011. *Atatürk: An Intellectual Biography*. Princeton: Princeton University Press.

Hanna, Nelly. 2011. *Artisan Entrepreneurs in Cairo and Early-Modern Capitalism (1600–1800)*. Syracuse, NY: Syracuse University Press.

Hansen, Jens and Max Weiss. 2016. Introduction. Language, Mind, Freedom and Time: The Modern Arab Intellectual Tradition in Four Words. In *Arabic Thought Beyond the Liberal Age: Towards an Intellectual History of the Nahda*. Edited by Jens Hansen and Max Weiss. Cambridge: Cambridge University Press, 1–37.

Hasan, Farah. 2021. Keep it Halal! A Smartphone Ethnography of Muslim Dating. *Journal of Religion, Media and Digital Culture* 10: 135–154.

Hashim, Rosnani. 2004. *Educational Dualism in Malaysia: Implications for Theory and Practice*. Second Edition. Kuala Lumpur: The Other Press.

Hattemer, Richard. 1997. *Atatürk und die türkische Reformpolitik im Siegel der ägyptischen Presse*. Berlin: Klaus Schwarz Verlag.

Hattemer, Richard. 1999. Atatürk and the Reforms in Turkey as Reflected in the Egyptian Press. *Journal of Islamic Studies* 11 (1): 21–42.

Heck, Gene W. 2006. *Charlemagne, Muhammad, and the Arab Roots of Capitalism*. Berlin and New York: Walter de Gruyter.

Heghammer, Thomas. 2020. *The Caravan: Abdallah Azzam and the Rise of Global Jihad*. Cambridge: Cambridge University Press.

Heidemann, Stefan. 2010. Numismatics. In *The New Cambridge History of Islam: Volume I: The Formation of the Islamic World, Sixth to Eleventh Centuries*. Edited by Chase Robinson. Cambridge: Cambridge University Press, 648–663.

Heintz, Bettina and Tobias Werron. 2011. Wie ist Globalisierung Möglich? Zur Entstehung globaler Vergleichshorizonte am Beispiel von Wissenschaft und Sport. *Kölner Zeitschrift für Soziologie und Sozialpsychologie* 63: 359–394.

Hennis, Wilhelm. 1987. *Max Webers Fragestellung*. Studien zur Biographie des Werks. Tübingen: Mohr/Siebeck.

Heper, Metin. 1981. Islam, Polity and Society in Turkey: A Middle Eastern Perspective. *Middle East Journal* 35 (3): 346–363.

Heper, Metin. 1998. *İsmet İnönü: The Making of a Turkish Statesman*. Leiden: Brill.

Herrera, Linda. 2010. Young Egyptians' Quest for Jobs and Justice. In *Being Young and Being Muslim: New Cultural Politics in the Global South and North*. Edited by Linda Herrera and Asef Bayat. Oxford: Oxford University Press, 127–143.

Hildebrandt, Thomas 2002. Waren Jamāl Ad-Dīn Al-Afgānī und Muhammad 'Abduh Neo-Mu'ataziliten? *Die Welt des Islams* 42 (2): 207–262.

Hirschkind, Charles. 2006. *The Ethical Soundscape: Cassette-Sermons and Islamic Counterpublics*. New York: Columbia University Press.

Hitti, Philip K. (ed.). 1962. *Islam and the West: A Historical Cultural Survey*. Princeton: Princeton University Press.

Hobsbawm, Ernest and Terence O. Ranger (eds.). 1992. *The Invention of Tradition*. Cambridge: Cambridge University Press.

Holland, W. J. D. 1965. Review: An Introduction to Islamic Law by Joseph Schacht. *Journal of African Law* 9 (3): 187–188.

Honneth, Axel. 2004. Considerations on Alessandro Ferrara's Reflective Authenticity, *Philosophy & Social Criticism* 30 (1): 11–15.

Hopwood, Derek. 1998. Introduction: The Culture of Modernity in Islam and the Middle East. In *Islam and Modernity: Muslim Intellectuals Respond*. Edited by John Cooper, Ronald Nettler and Mohamed Mahmoud. London: I. B. Tauris, 1–9.
Hourani, Albert. 1957. The Changing Face of the Fertile Crescent in the XVIIIth Century. *Studia Islamica* 8: 89–122.
Hourani, Albert. 1962. *Arabic Thought in the Liberal Age, 1798–1939*. Cambridge: Cambridge University Press.
Hourani, Albert. 1972. Review of the Cambridge History of Islam. *The English Historical Review* 87: 348–357.
Hourani, Albert. 1992. *Die Geschichte der arabischen Völker*. Frankfurt am Main: Fischer.
Huff, Toby. 2011. *Intellectual Curiosity and the Scientific Revolution: A Global Perspective*. Cambridge: Cambridge University Press.
Hunter, Shireen (ed.). 2009. *Reformist Voices of Islam: Mediating Islam and Modernity*. Armonk and London: M. E. Sharpe.
Hurewitz, Jacob C. 1956. *Diplomacy in the Near and Middle East: A Documentary Record: 1535–1914*. Princeton: D. van Nostrand Company.
Hurgronje, Christian Snouck. 1915. The Holy War Made in Germany. In *Verspreide Geschriften, Deel III: Geschriften Betreffende Arabie en Turkije*. Bonn und Leipzig: Kurt Schroeder [1923]. First published in *De Gids*.
Hussain, Khurram. 2020. *Islam as Critique: Sayyid Ahmad Khan and the Challenge of Modernity*. London: Bloomsbury.
Hussin, Iza, Nathan J. Brown and Neguin Yavari. 2014. Review Symposium: The Impossible State. *Perspectives on Politics* 12 (2): 461–467.
Ibn Rushd, Muhammad A. 1966. *Bidāyat al-mujtahid wa nihāyat al-muqtaṣid* (transl. "The Distinguished Jurist Primer") (Vol. 1). Cairo: Maktaba al-Kuliyyat al-Azhariyye.
Ibrahim, Haslina. 1999. *Free Will and Predestination: A Comparative Study of the Views of Abu al-Assan Al-Ash'ari and Muhammad 'Abduh*. Unpublished MA thesis, Kulliyah of Islamic Revealed Knowledge and Human Sciences. Kuala Lumpur: Islamic International University Malaysia.
İhsanoğlu, Ekmeleddin, Kostas Chatzis, and Efthymios Nicolaidis (eds.). 2003. *Multicultural Science in the Ottoman Empire*. Turnhout: Brepols.
İhsanoğlu, Ekmeleddin. 2004. *Science, Technology and Learning in the Ottoman Empire*. Aldershot: Ashgate.
İnalcık, Halil. 1964. Turkey. The Nature of Traditional Society. In *Political*

Modernization in Japan and Turkey. Edited by Robert E. Ward and Dankward A. Rustow. Princeton: Princeton University Press, 42–63.

Jaspers, Carl. 1956. *Vom Ursprung und Ziel der Geschichte*. Frankfurt am Main und Hamburg: Fischer.

Jeltoft, Nadia. 2011. Lived Islam: Religious Identity with Non-organized Muslim Minorities. *Ethnic and Racial Studies* 34 (7): 1134–1151.

Johansen, Barber. 1967. *Muhammad Husain Haikal: Europa und der Orient im Weltbild eines ägyptischen Liberalen*. Beirut: Orient-Institut der Deutschen Morgenländischen Gesellschaft.

Jorga, Nicolae. 1990. *Geschichte des Osmanischen Reiches*. Vol. 5. Darmstadt: Wissenschaftliche Buchgesellschaft.

Jouili, Jeanette S. 2015. *Pious Practice and Secular Constraints: Women in the Islamic Revival in Europe*. Stanford: Stanford University Press

Jung, Dietrich. 2006. "Secularism": A Key to Turkish Politics. *Intellectual Discourse* 14 (2): 129–154.

Jung, Dietrich. 2010. The Origin of Difference: Edward Said, Michel Foucault and the Modern Image of Islam. In *Islam in the Eyes of the West*. Edited by Tareq Y. Ismael and Andrew Rippin. London: Routledge, 15–31.

Jung, Dietrich. 2011. *Orientalists, Islamists and the Global Public Sphere: A Genealogy of the Modern Essentialist Image of Islam*. Sheffield: Equinox.

Jung, Dietrich. 2012. Islamic Reform and the Global Public Sphere: Muhammad Abduh and Islamic Modernity. In *The Middle East and Globalization: Encounters and Horizons*. Edited by Stephan Stetter. London: Palgrave Macmillan, 153–170.

Jung, Dietrich. 2013. Islamic Studies and Religious Reform. Ignaz Goldziher—A Crossroads of Judaism. Christianity and Islam. *Islam—Journal of the History and Culture of the Middle East* 90 (1): 106–126.

Jung, Dietrich. 2014. "The Ottoman–German Jihad": Lessons for the Contemporary "Area Studies" Controversy. *British Journal of Middle Eastern Studies* 41 (3): 247–265.

Jung, Dietrich. 2016. Understanding the Multiple Voices of Islamic Modernities: The Case of Jihad. *TEMENOS* 52 (1): 61–85.

Jung, Dietrich. 2016. Sociology, Protestant Theology, and the Concept of Modern Religion: William Robertson Smith and the "Scientification" of Religion. *Journal of Religion in Europe* 8 (3–4): 335–364.

Jung, Dietrich. 2017. *Muslim History and Social Theory: A Global Sociology of Modernity*. Cham: Palgrave Macmillan.

Jung, Dietrich. 2017. War and State in the Middle East: Reassessing Charles Tilly in a Regional Context. In *Does War Make States? Critical Investigations of Charles Tilly's Historical Sociology*. Edited by Lars Bo Kaspersen and Jeppe Strandberg. Cambridge: Cambridge University Press, 221–242.

Jung, Dietrich. 2018. The Multiple Faces of Mustafa Kemal Atatürk: Authority, Iconography, and Subjectivity in Modern Turkey. In *Reframing Authority: The Role of Media and Materiality*. Edited by Laura Feldt and Christian Høgel. Sheffield: Equinox, 207–228.

Jung, Dietrich. 2020. "Modernization in the Name of God": Christian Missionaries, Global Modernity, and the Formation of Modern Subjectivities in the Middle East. In *Middle East Christianity: Local Practices, World Societal Entanglements*. Edited by Stephan Stetter and Mitra Moussa Nabo. Cham: Palgrave Macmillan, 69–90.

Jung, Dietrich. 2021. *Der Islam in der Globalen Moderne: Soziologische Theorie und die Vielfalt islamischer Modernitäten*. Wiesbaden: Springer VS.

Jung, Dietrich. 2022. *"Abu Hamid al-Ghazali and Niklas Luhmann: Boundary Negotiations between Religion and Science in the Abbasid Empire."* Working Paper Series of the CASHSS "Multiple Secularities—Beyond the West, Beyond Modernities" 26. Leipzig University.

Jung, Dietrich and Wolfango Piccoli. 2001. *Turkey at the Crossroads: Ottoman Legacies and a Greater Middle East*. London: zed books.

Jung, Dietrich and Kirstine Sinclair. 2015. Multiple Modernities, Modern Subjectivities and Social Order: Unity and Difference in the Rise of Islamic Modernities. *Thesis Eleven* 130 (1): 22–42.

Jung, Dietrich and Kirstine Sinclair. 2020. Religious Governmentality: The Case of Hizb ut-Tahrir. *TEMENOS: Nordic Journal of Comparative Religion* 56 (1): 95–117.

Jung, Dietrich, Marie Juul Petersen and Sara Lei Sparre. 2014. *Politics of Modern Muslim Subjectivities: Islam, Youth, and Social Activism in the Middle East*. New York: Palgrave.

Jung, Dietrich and Ahmed Abu El Zalaf. 2022. Islamic Politics of Imagination: The Case of the Muslim Brotherhood. In *Debating Imaginal Politics: Dialogues with Chiara Bottici*. Edited by Suzi Adams and Jeremy C. A. Smith. Lanham, Maryland: Rowman & Littlefield, 121–142.

Kaesler, Dirk. 2014. *Max Weber: Eine Biographie*. Munich: C. H. Beck.

Kamrava, Mehran. 2007. *New Voices of Islam: Rethinking Politics and Modernity—A Reader*. Berkeley: University of California Press.

Kant, Immanuel. 1783. Beantwortung der Frage: Was ist Aufklärung. In: *Gesammelte*

Werke, Band 9: Schriften zur Anthropologie, Geschichtsphilosophie, Politik und Pädagogik, Erster Teil. Darmstadt: Wissenschaftliche Buchgesellschaft, 53–61.

Karpat, Kemal H. 1972. The Transformation of the Ottoman State, 1779–1908. *International Journal of Middle East Studies* 3: 243–281.

Kateman, Ammeke. 2019. *Muhammad 'Abduh and His Interlocutors: Conceptualizing Religion in a Globalizing* World. Leiden: Brill.

Kaufmann, Stuart A. 1993. *The Origins of Order: Self-Organization and Selection in Evolution*. Oxford: Oxford University Press.

Kaviraj. Sudipta. 2005. An Outline of a Revisionist Theory of Modernity. *European Journal of Sociology* 46 (3): 497–526.

Kayali, Hasan. 1997. *Arabs and Young Turks: Ottomanism, Arabism, and Islamism in the Ottoman Empire, 1908–1918*. Berkeley: University of California Press.

Keddi, Nikki R. 1972. *Sayyid Jamal ad-Din al-Afghani: A Political Biography*. Berkeley: University of California Press.

Keddi, Nikki. 2005. Sayyid Jamal al-Din al-Afghani. In *Pioneers of Islamic Revival*. New edition. Edited by Ali Rahnema. London: zed books, 11–29.

Kedourie. Elie. 1966. *Afghani and Abduh: An Essay on Religious Unbelief and Political Activism in Modern Islam*. London: Frank Cass.

Keim, Wiebeke. 2016. Islamization of Knowledge—Symptom of the Failed Internationalization of the Social Sciences? *Méthod(e)s: African Review of Social Sciences Methodology* 2 (1–2): 127–154.

Kemerli, Pinar. 2015. Religious Militarism and Islamist Conscientious Objection in Turkey. *International Journal of Middle East Studies* 47: 281–301.

Kerr, Malcom. 1980. Orientalism—Book Review. *International Journal of Middle East Studies* 12: 544–547.

Kersten Carool. 2011. *Cosmopolitans and Heretics: New Muslim Intellectuals and the Study of Islam*. London: Hurst.

Kersten, Carool. 2016. *Islam in Indonesia: The Contest for Society, Ideas and Values*. Oxford: Oxford Scholarship.

Kersten, Carool. 2017. *A History of Islam in Indonesia: Unity in Diversity*. Edinburgh: Edinburgh University Press.

Khalid, Khadijah Md. 2011. Malaysia's Foreign Policy under Najib: A Comparison with Mahathir. *Asian Survey* 51 (3): 429–452.

Khatab, Sayed. 2006. *The Power of Sovereignty: The Political and Ideological Philosophy of Sayyid Qutb*. London: Routledge.

Khomeini, Ruhollah. 1981. *Islam and Revolution: Writings and Declarations of Imam Khomeini*. Berkeley: Mizan Press.

Kjaer Poul 2006. Systems in Context. On the Outcome of the Habermas/Luhmann-Debate. *Ancilla Iuris* 66: 66–77.

Klausen, Jytte. 2015. Tweeting the Jihad: Social Media Networks of Western Foreign Fighters in Syria and Iraq. *Studies in Conflict & Terrorism* 38 (1): 1–22.

Knöbl, Wolfgang. 2007. *Die Kontingenz der Moderne: Wege in Europa, Asien und Amerika*. Frankfurt am Main and New York: Campus.

Krämer, Gudrun. 2010. *Hasan al-Banna*. London: Oneworld Publications.

Krämer, Gudrun. 2021. *Religion, Culture, and the Secular: The Case of Islam*. Working Paper Series of the CASHSS "Multiple Secularities—Beyond the West, Beyond Modernities", 23. University of Leipzig, Germany.

Kraince, Richard G. 2009. Reforming Islamic Education in Malaysia. Doctrine or Dialogue? In *Making Modern Muslims: The Politics of Islamic Education in Southeast Asia*. Edited by Robert W. Hefner. Honolulu: University of Hawai'i Press, 106–140.

Krawietz, Birgit. 2002. Cut and Paste in Legal Rules: Designing Islamic Norms with Talfiq. *Die Welt des Islams* 42 (1): 3–40.

Krell, Dominik. 2021. *Islamic Law in Saudi Arabia: Concepts, Practices and Developments*. Fakultät für Rechtswissenschaft (unpublished PhD dissertation). University of Hamburg, Germany.

Kristijánsdóttir, Dagný and Gudrídur Símonardottír. 2014. The Suspected Victim of the Turkish Abductions in the 17th Century. In *The Post-Colonial North Atlantic: Iceland, Greenland and the Faroe Islands*. Edited by Lill-Ann Körber and Ebbe Volquardsen. Berlin: Nordeuropa-Institut, 142–162.

Krstić, Tijana 2021. Historicizing Sunni Islam in the Ottoman Empire, c. 1450–c. 1750. In *Historicizing Sunni Islam in the Ottoman Empire, c. 1450–c. 1750*. Edited by Tijana Krstić and Derin Terzioğlu. 2021. Leiden: Brill, 1–30.

Krücken, Georg and Gili S. Drori (eds.). 2009. *World Society: The Writings of John W. Meyer*. Oxford: Oxford University Press.

Küçük, Harun B. 2012. *Early Enlightenment in Istanbul*. PhD Dissertation. San Diego: University of California.

Küçük, Harun B. 2017. Early Modern Ottoman Science: A New Materialist Framework. *Journal of Early Modern History* 21: 407–419.

Küng, Hans. 2010. *Projekt Weltethos*. Munich: Piper.

Kuhn, Thomas S. 1970. *The Structure of Scientific Revolutions*. Second Edition, Enlarged. Chicago: University of Chicago Press.

Kuppinger, Petra. 2015. *Faithfully Urban: Pious Muslims in a German City*. New York: Berghahn Books.

Kuran, Timur. 1995. Islamic Economics and the Islamic Subeconomy. *Journal of Economic Perspectives* 9 (4): 155–173.

Kuran, Timur. 2004. *Islam and Mamon: The Economic Predicaments of Islamism*. Princeton: Princeton University Press.

Kurzman, Charles (ed.). 2002. *Modernist Islam: 1840–1940: A Sourcebook*. Oxford: Oxford University Press.

Kushner, David. 1977. *The Rise of Turkish Nationalism*. London: Frank Cass.

Laffan, Michael. 2002. *Islamic Nationhood and Colonial Indonesia: The Umma Below the Winds*. London: Routledge.

Laffan, Michael. 2011. *The Making of Indonesian Islam: Orientalism and the Narration of a Sufi Past*. Princeton: Princeton University Press.

Lawrence, Bruce B. 2010. Afterword: Competing Genealogies of Muslim Cosmopolitism. In *Rethinking Islamic Studies: From Orientalism to Cosmopolitanism*. Edited by Carl W. Ernst and Richard C. Martin. Columbia: The University of South Carolina Press, 302–323.

Leaman, Oliver. 1999. *A Brief Introduction to Islamic Philosophy*. Cambridge: Polity Press.

Lelyveld, David. 1996. *Aligarh's First Generation: Muslim Solidarity in British India*. New Delhi: Oxford University Press.

Lewis, Bernard. 1961. *The Emergence of Modern Turkey*. Oxford: Oxford University Press.

Lewis, Geoffrey. 1975. The Ottoman Proclamation of Jihad in 1914. *The Islamic Quarterly* 19 (3 and 4): 157–163.

Lieber, Alfred E. 1968. Eastern Business Practices and Medieval European Commerce. *The Economic History Review* 21 (2): 230–243.

Lindholm, Charles. 2008. *Culture and Authenticity*. Oxford: Blackwell Publishing.

Liow. Joseph Chinyong. 2016. *Religion and Nationalism in Southeast Asia*. Cambridge: Cambridge University Press.

Livingston, John W. 1995. Muhammad Abduh on Science. *The Muslim World* 85 (3–4): 215–234.

Livingston, John W. 2017. *The Rise of Science in Islam and the West: From Shared Heritage to Parting of the Ways, 8th to 19th Centuries*. London: Routledge.

Lockman, Zachary. 2004. *Contending Visions of the Middle East: The History and Politics of Orientalism*. Cambridge: Cambridge University Press.

Lohlker, Rüdiger. 2008. *Islam: Eine Ideengeschichte*. Vienna: Facultas.

Loimeier, Roman. 2003. Patterns and Peculiarities of Islamic Reform in Africa. *Journal of Religion in Africa*. 33 (August): 237–262.

Lombard, Maurice. 1992. *Blütezeit des Islam: Eine Wirtschafts- und Kulturgeschichte des 8.—11. Jahrhunderts*. Frankfurt am Main: Fischer.
Luhmann, Niklas 1970: Funktion und Kausalität. In *Soziologische Aufklärung: Aufsätze zur Theorie sozialer Systeme*. Vol. 1. Opladen: Westdeutscher Verlag: 9–30.
Luhmann, Niklas. 1981. Handlungstheorie und Systemtheorie. In *Soziologische Aufklärung 3. Soziales System, Gesellschaft, Organisation*. Opladen: Westdeutscher Verlag.
Luhmann, Niklas. 1986. *Ökologische Kommunikation: Kann die moderne Gesellschaft sich auf ökologische Gefährdungen einstellen?* Opladen: Westdeutscher Verlag.
Luhmann, Niklas. 1987. *Soziale Systeme: Grundriss einer allgemeinen Theorie*. Frankfurt am Main: Suhrkamp.
Luhmann, Niklas. 1990. The World Society as a Social System. In *Essays on Self-Reference*. New York: Columbia University Press.
Luhmann, Niklas. 1992. *Die Wissenschaft der Gesellschaft*. Frankfurt am Main: Suhrkamp.
Luhmann, Niklas. 1998. *Die Gesellschaft der Gesellschaft*. Zwei Bände. Frankfurt am Main: Suhrkamp.
Luhmann, Niklas. 1999. *Die Kunst der Gesellschaft*. Frankfurt am Main: Suhrkamp.
Luhmann, Niklas. 2002. *Die Religion der Gesellschaft*. Frankfurt am Main: Suhrkamp.
Luhmann, Niklas. 2008. *Die Moral der Gesellschaft*. Frankfurt am Main: Suhrkamp.
Luhmann, Niklas. 2017. *Einführung in die Systemtheorie*. Heidelberg: Carl Ayer Verlag.
Lukes, Steven. 2004. *Power: A Radical View*. London: Red Globe Press.
Lyons, Jonathan. 2009. *The House of Wisdom: How the Arabs Transformed Western Civilization*. New York: Bloomsbury Press.
McCarthy, Richard J. 1980. *Freedom and Fulfillment: An Annotated Translation of Al-Ghazālī's Al-Munqidh Min Al-Dalāl and Other Relevant Works of Al-Ghazālī*. Woodbridge: Twayne Publishers.
McCutcheon, Russel T. 1997. *Manufacturing Religion: The Discourse on Sui Generis Religion and the Politics of Nostalgia*. Oxford and New York: Oxford University Press.
MacDonald, Duncan B. 1906. The Problems of Muhammadanism. In *Arts and Science: Universal Exposition, St. Louis, 1904, Vol. 2: History of Politics and Economics, History of Law, History of Religion*. Edited by H. J. Rogers. Boston: Houghton, Mifflin & Company, 518–536.
Macfie, A. L. 1994. *Atatürk*. London: Longman.

McGregor, Andrew. "Jihad and the Rifle Alone": Abdullah Azzam and the Islamist Revolution. *The Journal of Conflict Studies* 22 (2): 92–113.

McGuire, Meredith B. 2008. *Lived Religion: Faith and Practice in Everyday Life*. Oxford: Oxford University Press.

McMeekin, Sean. 2015. *The Ottoman Endgame: War Revolution and the Making of the Modern Middle East*. London: Penguin Books.

Mahmood, Saba. 2005. *Politics of Piety: The Islamic Revival and the Feminist Subject*. Princeton: Princeton University Press.

Mahmood, Saba. 2016. *Religious Difference in a Secular Age: A Minority Report*. Princeton: Princeton University Press.

Mahner, Martin and Bunge, Mario. 2001. *Scientific Realism: Selected Essays of Mario Bunge*. Amherst: Prometheus Books.

Makdisi, Ussama. 2008. *Artillery of Heaven: American Missionaries and the Failed Conversion of the Middle East*. Ithaca: Cornell University Press.

Malešević, Siniša. 2010. *The Sociology of War and Violence*. Cambridge: Cambridge University Press.

Malik, Jamal. 2020. *Islam in South Asia: Revised, Enlarged and Updated Second Edition*. Leiden: Brill.

Mandaville, Peter. 2007. *Global Political Islam*. London: Routledge.

March, Andrew F. 2015. What Can the Islamic Past Teach Us about Secular Modernity? *Political Theory* 43 (6): 838–849.

Mardin, Şerif 1962. *The Genesis of Young Ottoman Thought: A Study in the Modernization of Turkish Political Ideas*. Princeton: Princeton University Press.

Mardin, Şerif. 1969. Power, Civil Society and Culture in the Ottoman Empire. *Comparative Studies in Society and History* 11 (1): 258–281.

Mardin, Şerif. 1971. Ideology and Religion in the Turkish Revolution. *International Journal of Middle East Studies* 2: 197–211.

Mardin, Şerif. 1989. *Religion and Social Change in Modern Turkey: The Case of Bediüzzaman Said Nursi*. Albany: SUNY Press.

Marsont, Afaf Lutfi al-Sayyid. 2007. *A History of Egypt: From the Arab Conquest to the Present*. Cambridge: Cambridge University Press.

Marx, Karl. 1974. *Grundrisse der Politischen Ökonomie* (MEW 13). Berlin: Diez Verlag.

Marx, Karl. 1976. A Contribution to the Critique of Political Economy. In *Collected Works*. Volume 29. Ondon: Lawrence and Wishart, 257–420.

Masud, Muhammad K., Salvatore, Armando, and van Bruinessen, Martin (eds.). 2009. *Islam and Modernity: Key Issues and Debates*. Edinburgh: Edinburgh University Press.

Masuzawa, Tomoko. 2005. *The Invention of World Religions*. Chicago and London: University of Chicago Press.

Matar, Nabil. 1998. *Islam in Britain 1558–1685*. Cambridge: Cambridge University Press.

Matar, Nabil. 2009. *Europe Through Arab Eyes 1578–1727*. New York: Columbia University Press.

Maturana Humberto R. and Varela, Francisco J. 1980. *Autopoiesis and Cognition: The Realization of the Living*. Dordrecht. D. Reidel.

Matuz, Josef. 1985. *Das Osmanische Reich: Grundlinien seiner Geschichte*. Darmstadt: Wissenschaftliche Buchgesellschaft.

Maussen, Marcel, Veit Bader and Annelies Moors (eds.). 2011. *Colonial and Post-Colonial Governance of Islam: Continuities and Ruptures*. Amsterdam: Amsterdam University Press.

Mazher, Hussain et al. 2022. Rise of Muslim Modernist Discourse in the Nineteenth Century India: A Thematic. *Multicultural Education* 8 (1): 211–217.

Maszlee, Malik. 2017. *Foundations of Islamic Governance: A Southeast Asian Perspective*. London: Routledge.

Melchert, Christopher. 2015. Reviewed Work(s): Striving in the Path of God: Jihad and Martyrdom in Islamic thought by Asma Afsaruddin. *Review of Middle East Studies* 49 (2): 175–178.

Menemencioğlu, Nermin. 1967. Namik Kemal Abroad: A Centenary. *Middle Eastern Studies* 4 (1): 29–49.

Messick, Brinkley. 1993. *The Calligraphic State: Textual Domination and History in a Muslim Society*. Berkeley: University of California Press.

Metcalf, Barbara. 2002. *"Traditionalist" Islamic Activism: Deoband, Tablighis, and Talibs*. Leiden: ISIM Papers.

Metcalf, Barbara. 2014. *Islamic Revival in British India: Deoband, 1860–1900*. Princeton: Princeton University Press.

Mex-Jørgensen, Line. 2020. Imaginaries of the Good Life from the Egyptian Revolution in 2011: Pride and Agency. In *Muslim Subjectivities in Global Modernity: Islamic Traditions and the Construction of Modern Muslim Identities*. Edited by Dietrich Jung and Kirstine Sinclair. Leiden: Brill, 216–237.

Meyer, John W. 2010. World Society, Institutional Theories, and the Actor. *Annual Review of Sociology* 36 (1): 1–20.

Meyer, John W., John Boli, George Thomas and Francisco O. Ramirez. 1997. World Society and the Nation-State. *American Journal of Sociology* 103 (1): 144–181.

Meyer, John W. and Ronald L. Jepperson. 2000. The Cultural Construction of Social Agency. *Sociological Theory* 18 (1): 100–120.

Mitchell. Richard P. 1969. *The Society of the Muslim Brothers*. London: Oxford University Press.

Mittermaier, Amira. 2019. *Giving to God: Islamic Charity in Revolutionary Times*. Oakland: University of California Press.

Moaddel, Mansoor. 2001. Conditions for Ideological Production: The Origins of Islamic Modernism in India, Egypt, and Iran. *Theory and Society* 30 (5): 669–731.

Mongia, Padmini. 1996. *Contemporary Postcolonial Theory: A Reader*. London: Arnold.

Moosa, Ebrahim. 2015. *What is a Madrasa?* Edinburgh: Edinburgh University Press.

Mota, Aurea and Gerard Delanty. 2015. Eisenstadt, Brazil and the Multiple Modernities Framework: Revisions and Reconsiderations. *Journal of Classical Sociology* 15 (1): 39–57.

Moten, Abdul Rashid. 1998. Book Review: The Islamization of Science: Four Muslim Positions Developing an Islamic Modernity. *Intellectual Discourse* 6 (1): 88–98.

Moten, Rashid. 2003. *Revolution to Revolution: Jamaat-e-Islami in the Politics of Pakistan*. Karachi: Royal Book Company.

Müller, Rudolf. 1977. *Geld und Geist: Zur Entstehungsgeschichte von Identitätsbewußtsein und Rationalität seit der Antike*. Frankfurt am Main and New York: Campus.

Münch, Richard. 1992. *Die Struktur der Moderne: Grundmuster und differenzielle Gestaltung des institutionellen Aufbaus der modernen Gesellschaften*. Frankfurt am Main: Suhrkamp.

Münch, Richard. 2009. Die Weltgesellschaft im Spannungsfeld von funktionaler, stratifikatorischer und segmentärer Differenzierung. In *Inklusion und Exklusion: Analysen zur Sozialstruktur und sozialen Ungleichheit*. Edited by Rudolf Stichweh and Paul Windolf. Wiesbaden: VS Verlag für Sozialwissenschaften, 283–298.

Musallam, Adnan A. 2005. *From Secularism to Jihad: Sayyid Qutb and the Foundations of Radical Islam*. Westport and London: Praeger.

Nafi, Basheer M. 2004. The Rise of Islamic Reformist Thought and its Challenge to Traditional Islam. In *Islamic Thought in the Twentieth Century*. Edited by Suha Taji-Farouki and Basheer M. Nafi. London: I. B. Tauris, 28–60.

Nash, Geoffrey. 2022. *Religion, Orientalism and Modernity: Mahdi Movements of Iran and South Asia*. Edinburgh: Edinburgh University Press.

Nash, Geoffrey, Kathleen Kerr-Koch and Sarah E. Hackett. 2013. Introduction.

In *Postcolonialism and Islam: Theory, Literature, Culture, Society and Film.* Edited by Geoffrey Nash, Kathleen Kerr-Koch and Sarah E. Hackett. London: Routledge, 1–14.

Nasr, Seyyed Hossein. 1975. *Islam and the Plight of Modern Man.* London: Longman.

Nasr, Seyyed Hossein. 1979. Decadence, Deviation and Renaissance in the Context of Contemporary Islam. In *Islamic Perspectives: Studies in Honour of Mawlānā Sayyid Abul Al'ā Mawdūdī.* Edited by Kurshid Ahmad and Zarfar Ishaq Ansari. London: The Islamic Foundation, 35–42.

Nasr, Seyyed Hossein. 1987. *Science and Civilization in Islam.* Second Edition. Cambridge: The Islamic Text Society.

Nasr, Seyyed Hossein. 1993. *The Need for a Sacred Science.* Richmond: Curzon Press.

Nasr, Seyyed Hossein. 2001. Intellectual Autobiography of Seyyed Hossein Nasr. In *The Philosophy of Seyyed Hossein Nasr.* Edited by Lewis Edwin Hahn et al. Peru, Illinois: Open Court Publishers, 1–86.

Nasr, Seyyed Vali Reza. 2005. Mawdudi and the Jamma'at-I Islami: The Origins, Theory and Practice of Islamic Revivalism. In *Pioneers of Islamic Revival.* Edited by Ali Rahnema. London: zed books, 98–124.

Nongbri, Brent. 2013. *Before Religion: A History of a Modern Concept.* New Haven and London: Yale University Press.

Noor, Farish A. 2001. The Evolution of "Jihad" in Islamist Political Discourse: How a Plastic Concept Became Harder. Social Science Research Council, at: www.ssrc.org/sept11/essays/noor.htm.

Noor, Farish. A. 2009. Reformist Muslim Thinkers in Malaysia: Engaging with Power to Uplift the *Umma*? In *Reformist Voices of Islam: Mediating Islam and Modernity.* Edited by Shireen T. Hunter. Armonk, New York, and London: M. E. Sharpe, 208–226.

Noth, Albrecht. 1966. *Heiliger Krieg und heiliger Kampf in Islam und Christentum: Beiträge zur Vorgeschichte und Geschichte der Kreuzzüge.* Bonn: Ludwig Rohrscheid Verlag.

Nursi, Said. *1996. The Words: On the Nature and Purposes of Man, Life, and All Things.* Istanbul: Sözler.

Nursi, Said. 1997. *Letters 1928–1932.* Istanbul: Sözler.

Østebø, Terje (ed.). 2021. *Routledge Handbook of Islam in Africa.* London: Routledge.

Osterhammel, Jürgen. 2009. *Die Verwandlung der Welt: Eine Geschichte des 19. Jahrhunderts.* Munich C. H. Beck.

Ovamir, Anjum. 2007. Islam as a Discursive Tradition: Talal Asad and His

Interlocutors. *Comparative Studies of South Asia, Africa and the Middle East* 21 (3): 656–672.
Pahl, Jon. 2019. *Fethullah Gülen: A Life of Hizmet: Why a Muslim Schollar in Pennsylvania Matters to the World*. Clifton, NJ: Blue Dome Press.
Parla, Taha. 1998. Mercantile Militarism in Turkey: 1960–1998. *New Perspectives on Turkey* 19: 29–52.
Pedersen, Gry Hvass. 2020. *Modernity, Islamic Tradition and Higher Education: Visions of Modern Muslim Selfhoods among Contemporary Students at Islamic Universities in Asia*. PhD Thesis. Odense: University of Southern Denmark.
Peters, Rudolph. 1977. *Jihad in Mediaeval and Modern Islam*. Leiden: Brill.
Peters, Rudolph. 1979. *Islam and Colonialism: The Doctrine of Jihad in Modern History*. The Hague, Paris, and New York: Mouton.
Peters, Rudolph. 1989. Erneuerungsbewegungen im Islam vom 18. Bis zum 20. Jahrhundert und die Rolle des Islam in der neueren Geschichte: Antikolonialismus und Nationalismus. In *Der Islam in der Gegenwart*. Edited by Werner Ende and Udo Steinbach. Munich: C. H. Beck, 90–127.
Peterson, Mark Allen. 2011. *Connected in Cairo: Growing up Cosmopolitan in the Modern Middle East*. Bloomington and Indianapolis: Indiania University Press.
Philipp, Thomas. 2016. From Rule of Law to Constitutionalism. The Ottoman Context of Arab Political Thought. In *Arabic Thought Beyond the Liberal Age: Towards and Intellectual History of the Nahda*. Edited by Jens Hanssen and Max Weiss. Cambridge: Cambridge University Press, 142–166.
Philstrom, Sami. 2002. The Re-Emergence of the Emergence Debate. *Principa* 6 (1): 133–181.
Poya, Abbas and Maurus Reinkowski (eds.). 2015. *Das Unbehagen in der Islamwissenschaft: Ein klassisches Fach im Scheinwerferlicht der Politik und der Medien*. Bielefeld: Transcript.
Presley, John R. and John G. Sessions. 1994. Islamic Economics: The Emergence of a New Paradigm. *The Economic Journal* 104 (424): 584–596.
Ragab, Ahmed. 2017. Making History: Identity, Progress and the Modern-Science Archive. *Journal of Early Modern History* 21: 433–444.
Rahman, Azly. 2015. *Controlled Chaos: Essays on Malaysia's New Politics beyond Mahathirism and the Multimedia Super Corridor*. Petaling Jaya: Strategic Information and Research Development Centre.
Rahman, Fazlur. 1964. Ribā and Interest. *Islamic Studies* 3 (1): 1–43.
Ramadan, Tariq. 2010. *What I Believe*. Oxford: Oxford University Press.
Randeria, Shalini. 2002. Entangled Histories of Uneven Modernities: Civil Society,

Caste Solidarities and Legal Pluralism in Post-Colonial India. In *Unravelling Ties—From Social Cohesion to New Practices of Connectedness*. Edited by Yehuda Elkana, Ivan Kratev, Eísio Macamo, and Shalini Randeria. Frankfurt am Main: Campus, 284–311.

Reckwitz, Andreas. 2006. *Das hybride Subjekt: Eine Theorie der Subjektkulturen von der bürgerlichen Moderne zur Postmoderne*. Weilerwist: Velbrück Wissenschaft.

Rehman, Aamir A. 2010. *Gulf Capital & Islamic Finance: The Rise of the New Global Players*. New York: McGraw Hill.

Reid, Donald M. 1982. Arabic Thought in the Liberal Age Twenty Years after. *International Journal of Middle East Studies* 14: 541–557.

Reinkowski, Maurus. 2005. Gewohnheitsrecht im multinationalen Staat: Die Osmanen und der albanische Kanun. In *Rechtspluralismus in der islamischen Welt: Gewohnheistrecht zwischen Staat und Gesellschaft*. Edited by Michael Kemper and Maurus Reinkowski. Berlin: Walter de Gryther: 121–142.

Riesebrodt, Martin. 1990. *Fundamentalismus als patriarchale Protestbewegung: Amerikanische Protestanten (1910-28) und iranische Schiiten (1961-79) im Vergleich*. Tübingen: Mohr Siebeck.

Riexinger, Martin. 2010. Islamic Opposition to the Darwinian Theory of Evolution. In *Handbook of Religion and the Authority of Science*. Leiden: Brill, 483–510.

Riexinger, Martin. 2016. *Al-Ghazālī's* "Demarcation of Science". A Commonplace Apology in the Muslim Reception of Modern Science—and Its Limitations. In *Islam and Rationality: The Impact of al-Ghazālī: Papers Collected on His 900th Anniversary*. Vol. 2. Edited by Frank Griffel. Leiden: Brill, 283–309.

Riexinger, Martin 2017. Freiheit und Moderne im Denken Said Nursis und seiner Schüler. In *Ein traditioneller Gelehrter stellt sich der Moderne: Said Nursi 1876-1960*. Edited by Martin Riexinger und Bülent Ucar. Osnabrück: V&R unipress: 63–73.

Riexinger, Martin. 2017. Die Diskussion über die Evolutionstheorie in der islamischen Welt. *Nova Acta Leopoldina* 414: 179–200.

Riexinger, Martin. 2020. Evolution, the Purpose of Life and the Order of Society. How a Nurcu Connects Worldview and Normativity in Pseudo-Biographical Narratives. *Marburg Journal of Religion* 22 (2): 1–19.

Robinson, Francis. 1993. Technology and Religious Change: Islam and the Impact of Print. *Modern Asian Studies* 27 (1): 229–251.

Robinson, Francis. 2000. *Islam and Muslim History in South Asia*. New Delhi: Oxford University Press.

Robinson, Francis. 2008. Islamic Reform and Modernities in South Asia. *Modern Asian Studies* 42 (2–3): 259–281.

Rock, Aron. 2010. Amr Khaled: From Da'wa to Political and Religious Leadership. *British Journal of Middle Eastern Studies* 37 (1): 15–37.

Rock-Singer, Aron. 2021. The Sunni Islamic Revival. In *The Oxford Handbook of the Sociology of the Middle East*. Edited by Armando Salvatore, Sari Hanafi, and Kieko Obuse (online publication).

Rodinson, Maxime. 1966. *Islam et capitalisme*. Paris: Seuil.

Rodinson, Maxime. 1974. The Western Image and Western Studies of Islam. In *The Legacy of Islam*. Edited by Joseph Schacht and C. E. Bosworth. Oxford: Clarendon Press, 9–72.

Rodinson, Maxime. 1986. *Islam und Kapitalismus: Mit einer Einleitung von Bassam Tibi*. Frankfurt am Main: Suhrkamp.

Rogan, Eugene. 2009. *The Arabs: A History*. London: Penguin Books.

Rosa, Hartmut. 2014. Historischer Fortschritt oder leere Progression? Das Fortschreiten der Moderne als kulturelles Versprechen und als struktureller Zwang. In *Moderne und Religion: Kontroversen um Modernität und Säkularisierung*. Edited by Ulrich Willems, Detlev Pollack, H. Basu, Thomas Gutmann und U. Spohn. Bielefeld: Transcript, 117–141.

Rudnyckyj, Daromir. 2009. Spiritual Economies. Islam and Neoliberalism in Contemporary Indonesia. *Cultural Anthropology* 24 (1): 104–141.

Ryad, Umar. 2009. *Islamic Reformism and Christianity: A Critical Reading of the Works of Muhammad Rashid Rida and His Associates (1898–1935)*. Leiden: Brill.

Ryzova, Lucie. 2014. *The Age of Efendiyya: Passages to Modernity in National-Colonial Egypt*. Oxford: Oxford University Press.

Said, Edward W. 1978. *Orientalism*. New York: Vintage.

Saikia, Yasmin and M. Raisur Rahman. 2019. *The Cambridge Companion to Sayyid Ahmad Khan*. Cambridge: Cambridge University Press.

Sajdi, Dana (ed.). 2007. *Ottoman Tulips, Ottoman Coffee: Leisure and Lifestyle in the Eighteenth Century*. London: I. B. Tauris.

Sajdi, Dana. 2013. *The Barber of Damascus: Nouveau Literacy in the Eighteenth-Century Ottoman Levant*. Stanford: Stanford University Press.

Saliba, George. 2002. Greek Astronomy and the Medieval Arabic Tradition. *American Scientist* 90 (4): 360–367.

Saliba, George. 2007. *Islamic Science and the Making of the European Renaissance*. Cambridge: Cambridge University Press.

Sallah, Asmahan. 2015. Islamic Modernism and Discourse on Reason as a Reconciliatory Argument between Islam and Western Enlightenment. *International Journal of Islamic Thought* 7: 11–24.

Salvatore, Armando. 1997. *Islam and the Political Discourse of Modernity*. Reading: Ithaca Press.

Salvatore, Armando. 2016. *The Sociology of Islam: Knowledge, Power and Civility*. Oxford: Wiley-Blackwell.

Salzmann, Ariel. 2004. *Tocqueville in the Ottoman Empire: Rival Paths to the Modern State*. Leiden: Brill.

Sandıkcı, Özlem. 2018. Religion and the Marketplace: Constructing the 'New' Muslim Consumer. *Religion* 48 (3): 453–473.

Saniotis, Arthur. 2012. Muslims and Ecology: Fostering Islamic Environmental Ethics. *Contemporary Islam* 6: 155–171.

Sarton, George. 1927. *Introduction to the History of Science: Volume I. From Homer to Omar Khayyam*. Baltimore: The Williams & Wilkins Company.

Sarton, George. 1932. *Introduction to the History of Science: Volume II. From Rabbi Ben Ezra to Roger Bacon*. Baltimore: The Williams & Wilkins Company.

Sawyer, Keith. 2001. Emergence in Sociology: Contemporary Philosophy of Mind and Some Implications for Sociological Theory. *American Journal of Sociology* 107 (3): 551–585.

Schacht, Joseph. 1964. *An Introduction to Islamic Law*. Oxford: Oxford University Press.

Schacht, Joseph. 1979. Ḥiyal. In *The Encyclopaedia of Islam*. New Edition. Volume III. Leiden: Brill, 510–513.

Schacht, Joseph. 1995. Ribā. In *Encyclopaedia of Islam*. New Edition. Volume VIII. Leiden: Brill, 391–393.

Scharbrodt, Oliver. 2007. The Salafiyya and Sufism: *Muḥammad 'Abduh* and His *Risālat al-Wāridāt* (Treatise on Mystical Inspirations). *Bulletin of SOAS* 70 (1): 89–115.

Scharbrodt, Oliver. 2008. *Islam and the Baha'i Faith: A Comparative study of Muhammad 'Abduh and 'Abdul-Baha 'Abbas*. London: Routledge.

Scharbrodt, Oliver. 2021. Khomeini and Muhammad al-Shīrāzī: Revisiting the Origins of the "Guardianship of the Jurisconsult" (*wilāyat al-faqīh*). *Die Welt des Islams* 61: 9–38.

Schatzki, Theodore R. 2002. *The Site of the Social: A Philosophical Account of the Constitution of Social Life and Change*. University Park: Pennsylvania State University Press.

Scheuner, Ulrich. 1975. Staatsräson und religiöse Einheit des Staates. Zur Religionspolitik in Deutschland im Zeitalter der Glaubensspaltung. In *Staatsräson: Studien zur Geschichte eines politischen Begriffes*. Edited by Roman Schnur. Berlin: Duncker and Humboldt, 363–405.

Schielke, Samuli. 2010. Second Thoughts about the Anthropology of Islam, or How to Make Sense of Grand Schemes in Everyday Life. *Working Papers*, No. 2, Zentrum Moderner Orient, Berlin.

Schimank Uwe. 2005. *Differenzierung und Integration der modernen Gesellschaft: Beiträge zur akteurzentrierten Differenzierungstheorie*. Wiesbaden: VS Verlag.

Schilling, Hans. 1992. *Religion, Political Culture and the Emergence of Early Modern Society: Essays in German and Dutch History*. Leiden: Brill.

Schneider, Wolfgang L. 2011. Religion und funktionale Differenzierung. In: *Soziale Differenzierung: Handlungstheoretische Zugänge in der Diskussion*. Edited by Thomas Schwinn, Clemens Kroneberg, and Jens Greve. Wiesbaden: VS Verlag, 181–210.

Schuetz, Alfred. 1953. Common-Sense and Scientific Interpretation of Human Action. *Philosophy and Phenomenological Research*. 14 (1): 1–38.

Schwab, Raymond. 1950. *La renaissance orientale*. Paris: Payot.

Seesemann, Rüdiger. 2006. Between Sufism and Islamism: The Tijaniyya and Islamist Rule in Sudan. *Interdisciplinary Journal of Middle Eastern Studies* XV: 23–57.

Sedgwick, Mark. 2000. *Sufism: The Essentials*. Cairo: American University of Cairo.

Sedgwick, Mark. 2004. *Against the Modern World: Traditionalism and the Secret Intellectual History of the Twentieth Century*. Oxford: Oxford University Press.

Sedgwick, Mark. 2010. *Muhammad Abduh*. London: Oneworld Publications.

Sedgwick, Mark. 2020. The Modernity of Neo-Traditionalist Islam. In *Muslim Subjectivities in Global Modernity: Islamic Traditions and the Construction of Modern Muslim Identities*. Edited by Dietrich Jung and Kirstine Sinclair. Leiden: Brill, 121–146.

Sedra, Paul. 2011. *From Mission to Modernity: Evangelicals, Reformers and Education in Nineteenth-Century Egypt*. London: I. B. Tauris.

Seyhun, Ahmet. 2021 (ed.). *Competing Ideologies in the Late Ottoman Empire and Early Turkish Republic: Selected Writings of Islamist, Turkist, and Western Intellectuals*. London: I. B. Tauris.

Shahab, Ahmed. 2016. *What is Islam? The Importance of Being Islamic*. Princeton: Princeton University Press.

Shehata, Dina. 2014. Youth Movements and the 25 January Revolution. In *Arab Spring in Egypt: Revolution and Beyond*. Edited by Bahgat Korany and

Rabab El-Mahdi. Cairo and New York: American University of Cairo Press, 105–124.

Sheikh, Naveed. S. 2015. Reclaiming Jihad as a Strategy of Conflict Transformation. *Peace Review* 27 (3): 288–295.

Sheikoleslami, Ali Reza. 1986. From Religious Accommodation to Religious Revolution: The Transformation of Shi'ism in Iran. In *The State, Religion, and Ethnic Politics: Afghanistan, Iran, and Pakistan*. Edited by Ali Banuazizi and Myron Weiner. Syracuse, NY: Syracuse University Press, 227–256.

Shepard William E. 1996. *Sayyid Qutb and Islamic Activism: A Translation and Critical Analysis of Social Justice in Islam*. Leiden: Brill.

Shirazi, Faegheh. 2016. *Brand Islam: The Marketing and Commodification of Piety*. Austin: University of Texas Press.

Şiviloğlu, Murat R. 2018. *The Emergence of Public Opinion: State and Society in the Late Ottoman Empire*. Cambridge: Cambridge University Press.

Simmel, Georg. 1989. *Philosophie des Geldes*. Frankfurt am Main: Suhrkamp.

Sinclair, Kirstine. 2016. "Liberal Arts are an Islamic Idea": Subjectivity Formation at Islamic Universities in the West. *Review of Middle East Studies* 50 (1): 38–47.

Sinclair, Kirstine. 2017. Er klinisk psykologi brugbart, sheikh? En undersøgelse af subjektivitetsformation på islamiske universiteter i vesten. *Tidsskrift for islamforskning* 11 (1): 83–98.

Singer, Amy. 1999. Review of State and Provincial Society in the Ottoman Empire: Mosul, 1540–1834 by Dina Rizk Khoury. *International Journal of Middle East Studies* 31 (2): 300–303.

Sivasundaram, Sujit. 2010. Sciences and the Global: On Methods, Questions, and Theory. *ISIS* 101 (1): 146–158.

Skovgaard-Petersen, Jakob. 1997. *Defining Islam for the Egyptian State: Muftis and Fatwas of the Dār al-Iftā*. Leiden: Brill.

Sloane-White, Patricia. 2017. *Corporate Islam: Sharia and the Modern Workplace*. Cambridge: Cambridge University Press.

Soares, Benjamin and Filippo Osella. 2009. Islam, Politics, Anthropology. *The Journal of the Royal Anthropological Institute* 15: 1–23.

Southern. R. W. 1962. *Western Views of Islam in the Middle Ages*. Cambridge, MA: Harvard University Press.

Sparre, Sara Lei. 2018. Experimenting with Alternative Futures in Cairo: Young Muslim Volunteers between God and the Nation. *Identities: Global Studies in Culture and Power* 25 (2): 158–175.

Spivak, G. C. 1985. Subaltern Studies: Deconstructing Historiography. In *Subaltern*

Studies IV: Writings on South Asian History and Society. Edited by R. Guha and G. C. Spivak. Oxford: Oxford University Press, 330–363.

Springborg, Robert. 2018. *Egypt*. Cambridge: Polity Press.

Stasyszyn, Roxanne. 2012. The Yukon's Muslim Community: Accepted and Accepting. *Yukon News*, September 28th.

Stausberg, Michael. 2010. Distinctions, Differentiations, Ontology, and Non-humans in Theories of Religion. *Method and Theory in the Study of Religion* 22: 354–374.

Stauth, Georg. 1993. *Islam und westlicher Rationalismus: Der Beitrag des Orientalismus zur Entstehung der Soziologie*. Frankfurt am Main: Campus.

Stauth, Georg. 2000. *Islamische Kultur und moderne Gesellschaft*. Bielefeld: Transcript.

Stenberg, Leif. 1996. *The Islamization of Science: Four Muslim Positions Developing an Islamic Modernity*. Lund: Lund Studies in History of Religions, University of Lund.

Stephan, Achim: Eine kurze Einführung in die Vielfalt und Geschichte emergentistischen Denkens. In: *Blinde Emergenz? Interdisziplinäre Beiträge zu Fragen kultureller Evolution* Edited by Thomas Wägenbaur. Heidelberg: Synchron Wissenschaftsverlag der Autoren.

Stephan, Maria S. 2009. *Civilian Jihad: Non-Violent Struggle, Democratization, and Governance in the Middle East*. London: Palgrave.

Stichweh, Rudolf and Paul Windolf (eds.) *Inklusion und Exklusion: Analysen zur Sozialstruktur und sozialen Ungleichheit*. Wiesbaden: VS Verlag für Sozialwissenschaften.

Stirling, Paul. 1958. Religious Change in Republican Turkey. *Middle East Journal* 12 (4): 395–408.

Tauber, Eliezer. 1989. Rashid Rida as Pan-Arabist before World-War I. *The Muslim World* 85 (2): 102–112.

Taylor, Charles. 1991. *The Ethics of Authenticity*. Cambridge, MA: Harvard University Press.

Tayob, Abdulkader. 2018. Decolonizing the Study of Religions: Muslim Intellectuals and the Enlightenment Project of Religious Studies. *Journal of the Study of Religion* 31 (2): 7–35.

Tayob, Abdulkader. 2021. Reform in the Discourse of Islam and the Making of Muslim Subjects. In *Handbook of Islam in Africa*. Edited by Terje Østebø. London: Routledge, 223–235.

Tee, Caroline and David Shankland. 2013. Said Nursi's Notion of "Sacred Science": Its Function and Application in Hizmet High School Education. *Sociology of Islam* 1: 209–32.

Tellenbach, Silvia. 1985. *Untersuchungen zur Verfassung der Islamischen Republik Iran vom 15. November 1979*. Berlin: Klaus Schwarz Verlag.

Terpe, Sylvia. 2020. Working with Max Weber's "Spheres of Life": An Actor-centred Approach. *Journal of Classical Sociology* 20 (1): 22–42.

Terzan, Levent. 2005. The Problems of Religious Modernity. *AJSS* 33 (3): 506–528.

Theodossopoulos, Dimitrios. 2013. Laying Claim to Authenticity: Five Anthropological Dilemmas. *Anthropological Quarterly* 86 (2): 337–360.

Therborn, Göran. 2003. Entangled Modernities. *European Journal of Social Theory* 6: 293–305.

Thomassen, Bjørn. 2010. Anthropology, Multiple Modernities and the Axial Age Debate. *Anthropological Theory* 10 (4): 321–342.

Thorn, Gary. 2000. *End of Empires: European Decolonisation 1919–80*. London: Hodder & Stoughton.

Tibawi, A. L. 1963. *English-Speaking Orientalists: A Critique of Their Approach to Islam and Arab Nationalism*. London: Islamic Cultural Center.

Tieman, Marco. 2018. Measuring Corporate Halal Reputation. A Corporate Halal Reputation Index and Research Propositions. *Journal of Islamic Marketing* 11 (3): 591–601.

Tilly, Charles. 1990. *Coercion, Capital, and European States, AD 990–1990*. Oxford: Basil Blackwell.

Todorof, Maria. 2018. *Shariah*-compliant FinTech in the Banking Industry. *ERA Forum* 19 (1): 1–17.

Topal, Alp Eren. 2021. Political Reforms as Religious Revival: Conceptual Foundations of *Tanzimat*. *Oriente Moderno* 101: 153–180.

Trakic, Adnan and Tajuddin, Hanifah Haydar (eds.). 2021. *Islamic Law in Malaysia: The Challenges of Implementation*. Singapore: Springer.

Tripp, Charles. 2006. *Islam and the Moral Economy: The Challenge of Capitalism*. Cambridge: Cambridge University Press.

Trivedi, Raj Kumar. 1981. Mustafa Kemal and the Indian Khilafat Movement (to 1924). *Proceedings of the Indian History Congress* 42: 458–467.

Troll, Christian, W. 1978. *Sayyid Ahmad Khan: A Reinterpretation of Muslim Theology*. New Delhi: Vikas Publishing House.

Tuma, Elias H. 1965. Early Arab Economic Policies (1st/7th–4th/10th Centuries). *Islamic Studies* 4 (1): 1–23.

Turner, Bryan S. and Kamaludeen Mohamed Nasir (eds.). 2013. *The Sociology of Islam: Collected Essays of Bryan S. Turner*. Farnham: Ashgate.

Turner, Colin and Hasan Horkuc. 2009. *Said Nursi: Makers of Islamic Civilization*. London: I. B. Tauris.

Tyrell, Hartmann. 1978. Anfragen an die Theorie der gesellschaftlichen Differenzierung. *Zeitschrift für Soziologie* 7 (2): 175–193.

Umer, Zaituna Y. 1974. Introduction. In *Major-General G.F.I. Graham, The Life and Work of Sir Syed Ahmed Khan*. Karachi: Oxford University Press, v–xvii.

Usher, Abbott Payson. 1934. The Origins of Banking: The Primitive Bank of Deposit, 1200–1600. *The Economic History Review* 4 (4): 399–428.

Vahdat, Farzin. 2013. *Islamic Ethos and the Specter of Modernity*. London: Anthem Press.

Vahide, Şükran. 1999.The Life and Times of Bediuzzaman Said Nursi. *The Muslim World* LXXXIX (3–4): 208–244.

Vahide, Şükran. 2011. *Beduizzaman Said Nursi: Author of the Risale-I Nur*. Kuala Lumpur: Islamic Book Trust.

Vanderstraeten Raf. 2002. Parsons, Luhmann and the Theme of Double Contingency. *Journal of Classical Sociology* 2 (1): 77–92.

Vicini, Fabio. 2020. "Worship is Not Everything:" Volunteering and Muslim Life in Modern Turkey. In *Muslim Subjectivities in Global Modernity: Islamic Traditions and the Construction of Modern Muslim Identities*. Edited by Dietrich Jung and Kirstine Sinclair. Leiden: Brill, 97–120.

Viskovatoff, Alex. 1999. Foundations of Niklas Luhmann's Theory of Social Systems. *Philosophy of the Social Sciences* 29 (4): 481–516.

Voll, John. 1979. The Sudanese Mahdi. Frontier Fundamentalist. *International Journal of Middle East Studies* 20: 145–166.

Volpi, Frédéric. 2010. *Political Islam Observed*. London: Hurst.

Wägenbaur, Thomas. 2000. Emergenz der Kommunikation. In *Blinde Emergenz? Interdisziplinäre Beiträge zu Fragen kultureller Evolution*. Edited by Thomas Wägebaur. Heidelberg: Synchron Wissenschaftsverlag der Autoren, 121–141.

Wagner, Peter. 1994. *A Sociology of Modernity: Liberty and Discipline*. London: Routledge.

Wagner, Peter. 2001. *Theorizing Modernity: Inescapability and Attainability in Social Theory*. London: Sage Publications.

Wagner, Peter. 2008. *Modernity as Experience and Interpretation: A New Sociology of Modernity*. Cambridge: Cambridge University Press.

Wagner, Peter. 2010. Successive Modernities and the Idea of Progress: A First Attempt. *Distinktion* 11 (2): 9–24.

Wain, Barry. 2010. *Malaysian Maverick: Mahathir Mohamad in Turbulent Times*. New York: Palgrave.
Wakin, Jeanette. 1993. Muḍāraba. In *The Encyclopaedia of Islam*. New Edition. Vol. VII. Leiden: Brill, 284–285.
Walby, Sylvia. 2007. Complexity Theory, System Theory, and Multiple Intersecting Social Inequalities. *Philosophy of the Social Sciences* 37 (4): 449–470.
Watt, Montgomery. 1972. *The Influence of Islam on Medieval Europe*. Edinburgh: Edinburgh University Press.
Weber, Max. 1904. 'Objectivity' in Social Science and Social Polity. In *Max Weber: The Methodology of the Social Sciences*. Edited by Edward A. Shils and Henry A. Finch. New York: The Free Press [1949], 50–112.
Weber, Max. 1919 [1991]. Science as a Vocation. In: *From Max Weber: Essays in Sociology*. London: Routledge.
Weber, Max. 1920 [1984]. Vorbemerkungen zu den Gesammelten Aufsätzen der Religionssoziologie. In *Die Protestantische Ethik I. Eine Aufsatzsammlung*. Edited by J. Winckelmann. Gütersloh: Mohn, 9–26.
Weber, Max. 1920. *Gesammelte Aufsätze zur Religionssoziologie*. Vol. I. Tübingen: UTB [1988].
Weber, Max. 1922. *Gesammelte Aufsätze zur Wissenschaftslehre*. Tübingen: UTB [1988].
Weber, Max. 1968. *Economy and Society: An Outline of Interpretive Sociology*. Edited by Guenther Roth and Claus Wittich. Volume I. New York: Bedminister Press.
Weber, Max. 1972. *Wirtschaft und Gesellschaft: Grundriß der verstehenden Soziologie*. Studienausgabe. Tübingen: Mohr.
Weber, Max. 1991. *From Max Weber: Essays in Sociology*. Edited by H. H. Gerth and C. W. Mills. London: Routledge.
Weber, Max. 2005. *The Protestant Ethic and the Spirit of Capitalism*. Translated by Talcott Parsons. With an Introduction by Anthony Giddens. London: Routledge.
Wehler, Hans-Ulrich. 1989. *Deutsche Gesellschaftsgeschichte: Band 1: Vom Feudalismus des Alten Reiches bis zur defensiven Modernisierung der Reformära 1700–1815*. Munich: C. H. Beck.
Wehr, Hans. 1985. *Arabisches Wörterbuch für die Schriftsprache der Gegenwart. Arabisch-Deutsch* (5. Auflage). Wiesbaden: Otto Harrasowitz.
Weismann, Itzshak. 2015. Framing a Modern Umma: The Muslim Brothers' Evolving Project of Da'wa. *Sociology of Islam* 3: 146–169.

Weismann, Itzchak. 2017. A Perverted Balance: Modern Salafism between Reform and Jihad. *Die Welt des Islams* 57: 33–66.

West, John B. 2008. Ibn al-Nafis, the Pulmonary Circulation, and the Islamic Golden Age. *Journal of Applied Physiology* 105: 1877–1880.

Wickham, Carrie Rosefsky. 2002. *Mobilizing Islam: Religion, Activism, and Political Change in Egypt*. New York: Columbia University Press.

Wigen, Einar. 2018. *State of Translation: Turkey in Interlingual Relations*. Ann Arbor: University of Michigan Press.

Wigen, Einar. 2018. Post-Ottoman Studies. An Area Studies that Never Was. In *Building Bridges to Turkish: Essays in Honour of Bernt Brendemoen*. Wiesbaden: Harrassowitz, 313–321.

Wise, Lindsay. 2003. *"Words from the Heart": New Forms of Islamic Preaching in Egypt*. MPhil. Thesis, Oxford University.

Wise, Lindsay. 2006. *Amr Khaled versus Usulf Al Qaradawi: The Danish Cartoon Controversy and the Clash of Two Islamic TV Titans*. https://www.ikhwanweb.com/article.php?id=4529. Accessed: May 4, 2022.

Wishnitzer, Avner. 2015. *Reading Clock, Alla Turca: Time and Society in the Late Ottoman Empire*. Chicago: University of Chicago Press.

Wohlrab-Sahr, Monika and Marian Burchardt. 2012. Multiple Secularities: Toward a Cultural Sociology of Secular Modernities. *Comparative Sociology* 11: 875–909.

Wood, Simon. 2019. Reforming Muslim Politics. Rashid Rida's Visions of Caliphate and Muslim Independence. *Journal of Religion & Society* (Supplement 18): 63–78.

Xiong, Jia and Zhang Chaozhi. 2020. "Halal tourism": Is it the Same Trend in Non-Islamic Destinations with Islamic Destination? *Asia Pacific Journal of Tourism Research* 25 (2): 189–204.

Yavuz, Hakan M. 2013. *Toward an Islamic Enlightenment: The Gülen Movement*. Oxford: Oxford University Press.

Yılmaz, Yasir. 2019. Confessionalization or a Quest for Order? A Comparative Look at Religion and State in the Seventeenth-century Ottoman, Russian and Habsburg Empires. In *Ottoman Sunnism: New Perspectives*. Edited by Vefa Erginbaş. Edinburgh: Edinburgh University Press, 90–120.

Yoksamon Jeaheng, Amr Al-Ansi and Heesup Han. 2019. Halal-friendly Hotels: Impact of Halal-Friendly Attributes on Guest Purchase Behaviors in the Thailand Hotel Industry. *Journal of Travel & Tourism Marketing* 26 (6): 729–746.

Young, R. J. C. 2003. *Postcolonialism: A Very Short Introduction*. Oxford: Oxford University Press.

Yuhanis, Abdul Aziz and Nyen Vui Chok. 2013. The Role of Halal Awareness, Halal Certification, and Marketing Components in Determining Halal Purchase Intention among Non-Muslims in Malaysia: A Structural Equation Modeling Approach. *Journal of International Food & Agribusiness Marketing* 25 (1): 1–23.

Zaki, Muhammad Shawqi. 1954. *Al-ikhwān al-muslimīn fī al-mujtamaʿ al-miṣrī* (The Muslim Brotherhood in the Egyptian Society). Cairo: Dār al-ʿahd al-Jadīd.

Zalaf, Ahmed Abou El. 2019. Det specielle apparat hos det Muslimiske Broderskab. *Babylon—Nordisk Tidskrift for Midtøstenstudier* 17 (1): 8–17.

Zalaf, Ahmed Abou El. 2022. The Special Apparatus (*al-Nizam al-Khass*): The Rise of Nationalist Militancy in the Ranks of the Egyptian Muslim Brotherhood. *Religions* 13 (77): 1–18.

Zalaf, Ahmed Abou El. 2023. *The Muslim Brotherhood and State Repression in Egypt: A History of Secrecy and Militancy in an Islamist Organization*. London: Bloomsbury.

Zemmin, Florian. 2019. Validating Secularity in Islam: The Sociological Perspective of the Muslim Intellectual Fariq al-ʿAzm (1865–1925). *Historical Social Research/Historische Sozialforschung* 44 (3): 74–100.

Zemmin, Florian. 2020. *Modernity in Islamic Tradition: The Concept of "Society" in the Journal al-Manar (Cairo 1898–1940)*. Berlin and Boston: Walter de Gruyter.

Zemmin, Florian. 2021. The Modern Prophet: Radhid Rida's Construction of Muhammad as Religious and Social Reformer. In *The Presence of the Prophet in Early Modern and Contemporary Islam Series: Volume 2: Heirs of the Prophet: Authority and Power in Early Modern and Contemporary Islam*. Edited by Rachida Chih, David Jordan and Stefan Reichmuth. Leiden: Brill, 349–369.

Zenciri, Gizem. 2020. Markets of Islam: Performative Charity and the Muslim Middle Classes in Turkey. *Journal of Cultural Economy* 13 (5): 610–625.

Zubaida, Sami. 1997. Is Iran and Islamic State? In *Political Islam*. Edited by Joel Beinin and Joe Storck. London: I. B. Tauris, 103–122.

Zürcher, Jan Erik. 1993. *Turkey: A Modern History*. Reprint 1998. London: I. B. Tauris.

Zürcher, Jan Erik. 2012. In the Name of the Father, the Teacher, and the Hero: The Atatürk Personality Cult in Turkey. In *Political Leadership, Nation and Charisma*. Edited by Vivian Ibrahim and Margret Wunsch. London: Routledge, 129–142.

INDEX

Abbasi, Rushain, 270n9
Abbasid Caliphate, 164–5
Abd al-Aziz I, 267
Abd al-Wahhab, Muhammad, 266–7
Abdel-Ghani, Mona, 213
Abduh, Muhammad, 5, 41–2, 101–2, 207, 262
  and education, 160, 168
  and jihad, 243–4
  and liberalism, 103
  and modernity, 110–14, 115, 116, 129–30
  and reform movement, 105, 107, 108, 109
  and science, 182
  and traditions, 237
Abdülhamit II, Sultan, 74, 83, 86–8, 91, 108, 169
  and Atatürk, 142, 150n47
Abdülmecit, Sultan, 84
Abou el-Haj, Rifaat, 79–80, 81
absolutist states, 75, 76, 82

Abu Bakr, Caliph, 138
Abu-Rabi', Ibrahim M., 250–1
Abu Sulayman, Abdul Hamid, 177
activism, 199, 210–11, 212–16, 235–8, 249
'adāla (justice), 236, 246–7
al-Afghani, Jamal al-Din, 105, 107–8, 110–11, 113, 114, 169
  and jihad, 243, 244
Afghanistan, 3, 248
Afsaruddin, Asma
  Contemporary Issues in Islam, 16
  Striving in the Path of God, 234, 242, 250
Agai, Bekim, 170
Ahmad, Feroz
  The Making of Modern Turkey, 72
Ahmad, Salman, 250
Ahmad Khan, Sayyid, 5, 105, 106, 157, 181, 185n18
  and science, 158–9, 160, 167, 168, 182

Ahmadiyya, 100
Ahmed, Shahab, 17
Ali, Muhammad, 107
Aligarh Muslim University, 157–8, 159, 181
Amalfi (Italy), 201
Amer, Entisar, 2
American Muslims, 16
Aminrazavi, Mehdi, 175
Ankara (Turkey), 128–9
anthropology, 17, 20–5
Aquinas, Thomas, 162, 163
Arab nationalism, 19
Arab Renaissance, 49, 64n78
Arab Spring, 212
Arabian Peninsula, 267
Arab–Israeli wars, 3
Aristotle
  Politika, 200
Arnason, Johan, 49
Arslan, Shakib, 151n52, 235, 252n18
Asad, Talal, 16, 42, 111–12, 250
  Formations of the Secular, 23–5
  and tradition, 50, 262
'aṣāla (authenticity), 49–50
Atatürk, Mustafa Kemal, 8n13, 72, 139–45, 170, 262
  and Islam, 151n52, 153n59
  and Kemalism, 133–4, 146
  and mausoleum, 129
  and secularism, 131–2
Atia, Mona, 214
al-Attas, Syed Muhammad Nagib, 177
authenticity, 3–4, 5, 49–50
authoritarianism, 3
autonomy, 54
autopoiesis, 40, 43, 45, 56, 147, 199–200

Averroes *see* Ibn Rushd
Avicenna *see* Ibn Sina (Avicenna)
Axial Age Theory, 48–9, 51, 52
al-Azm, Sadik, 99
al-Azmeh, Aziz, 49
Azzam, Abdallah, 247–8

Babism, 100
Badran, Margot, 249
Baghdad, 165
Bahaism, 100
Balkans, 79
Bamyeh, Mohammed A.
  Lifeworlds of Islam, 15–16
banking, 205–7, 249, 262
al-Banna, Hasan, 99, 131–2, 135–9, 146, 262
  and governance, 265
  and jihad, 244, 245
  and science, 182
  and Turkey, 140–1
Barkey, Karen, 81, 89
  Empire of Difference, 78
Bayat, Asef, 210–11
Bayly, Christopher, 165
  The Birth of the Modern World, 34, 6–7, 139
Beck, Ulrich, 7n3
Becker, Carl-Heinrich, 232, 233, 234, 241, 247
Berkes, Niyazi
  The Development of Secularism in Turkey, 72
Beyer, Peter, 112
  Religions in Global Society, 41, 42
Bin Laden, Osama, 248
Bin Saud, Muhammad, 267

al-Biruni, Abu Rayhan, 163, 164, 173, 175, 183
boundary negotiations, 6, 56, 57, 58, 104–5, 260–1
   and Ottoman Empire, 90
   and science, 166
   and the state, 264
bourgeoisie, 133, 134
Britain *see* Great Britain
Brubaker, Rogers, 269
Bucaille, Maurice, 182
Buddhism, 41, 48, 176
Butler, Judith, 21

Cairo, 2, 20–1, 135, 136
Canada, 250
capitalism, 80–1, 199, 201–2, 217, 259, 260
Casanova, José, 62n46
Chapra, Umer, 197–8
Christianity, 41, 48, 176, 236
   and science, 167, 185n19
Çiller, Tansu, 153n70
Colonial and Post-Colonial Governance of Islam, 20
colonialism, 58, 244, 245, 267, 268; *see also* decolonization; postcolonialism
commerce *see* trade
Committee of Union and Progress (CUP), 142, 169, 232
communication, 43, 45, 53–4, 56–7, 86, 261
   and Luhmann, 34, 38, 40–1, 46
confessionalization, 82–3
Confucianism, 48
Conrad, Sebastian, 4

constitutive interdependence, 53–4, 55
consumerism, 4, 17
Coomaraswamy, Ananda K., 173
creationism, 171
Crimean War, 85
Cromer, Lord, 110
culture, 80, 133

Al-Dahiyya, 21
Dar al-Ulum (Cairo), 135, 136
decolonization, 18, 89
Deeb, Lara, 249
   An Enchanted Modern, 21–2
democracy, 47–8
Deringil, Selim, 87
differentation, 38–41, 42–3, 46, 54–5, 75
double contingency, 60n20
downward causation, 53–4
dress codes, 2
Duguid, Stephen, 86
Durkheim, Émile, 38, 130, 258
   De la division du travail social (The Division of Labor), 44

economics, 4, 7, 58, 196–9, 204–5, 216–19
   and communication, 56
   and finance, 205–7
   and halal market, 208–9
   and Islamic reform movement, 57
   and Malaysia, 207–8, 209–10
   and Middle East, 80–1
   and money, 199–201
   and premodern Islam, 201–4
   and the state, 76

and Weber, 259–60
see also entrepreneurship
education, 4, 85, 86–7, 88, 160–3; *see also* universities
efendis, 132–3, 134, 136
Egypt, 8n13, 25, 145, 146, 137–8
   and capitalism, 81
   and economics, 204
   and efendis, 132–3, 134, 136
   and Salafism, 107–9
   and secularism, 24
   and trade, 201
   and Turkey, 140–1, 151n52
   and universities, 177
   and youth organizations, 199, 212–16, 218, 262
   see also Abduh, Muhammad; Cairo; Muslim Brotherhood
Eisenstadt, Shmuel, 115, 217, 258
   and multiple modernities, 6, 16, 25, 36, 37, 47–51, 261
el-Guindy, Khaled, 213
Elias, Nobert, 74, 81, 86, 258
   Der Prozess der Zivilisation (The Civilizing Process), 45–6, 53–4, 76–7, 78
Elshakry, Marwa, 167
emergence theories, 51–5, 57
Enlightenment, 34–5, 36, 54
entangled modernities, 102–4
entrepreneurship, 4, 7, 199, 211–12
   and Egypt, 81, 262
   and youth organizations, 215–16, 218
environment, 34
Erbakan, Necmettin, 145, 153n70
Erdoğan, Recep Tayyip, 145, 153n71, 172, 249

ethics, 21, 45
ethnography, 20–5
Europe, 16–17, 20, 99, 113–14
   and exceptionalism, 259–60, 261–2
   and Ottoman Empire, 80, 85
   and statehood, 75, 76, 77, 82–3
   see also colonialism; France; Germany; Great Britain; Italy
evolution, 171

al-Farabi, Abu Nasr, 175
al-Faruqi, Ismail Raji, 177, 182
fatwa (juridical opinion), 232
feminism, 16, 21
finance, 205–7, 216, 249
fiqh see jurisprudence
Firestone, Reuven, 241
First World Conference of Muslim Education, 160, 168, 176–7, 182
First World War, 6, 88, 142, 151n52, 232–4
Fisher, Johan, 216
Fitzgerald, Timothy, 42
Foucault, Michel, 18, 19, 21, 45–6, 258
   and panopticon, 143–4
   and power, 64n85
   and technology, 212
France, 22, 76, 79, 106–7
functionalism, 38–41, 42–3, 46, 54–5, 75–6

Galal, Isam al-Din, 136
Geaves, Ron
   Islam Today, 16–17
Gehlen, Arnold, 40
gender, 16, 17; *see also* women
Genoa, Republic of, 89

Germany, 22, 232–4, 247, 258
al-Ghazali, Abu Hamid, 166, 167, 175, 183, 184
  Deliverance from Error, 164
  and jihad, 242, 244
Giddens, Anthony, 258
global public sphere, 103–4
Gökalp, Ziya, 153n59
Goldziher, Ignaz, 13, 108
Göle, Nilüfer, 16
governance, 20
  and Iran, 265–6
  and Malaysia, 267–8
  and Saudi Arabia, 266–7
Gran, Peter, 80–1, 217
Great Britain, 16–17, 137–8, 249–50, 267
Guénon, René, 173, 174, 175, 264
Guizot, François
  History of Civilization in Europe, 113–14
Gülen, Fetullah, 171–2, 176
Gulf Cooperation Council (GCC), 198

Habermas, Jürgen, 7n3, 103, 258
  Theorie des kommunikativen Handelns (Theory of Communicative Action), 34–5
Habsburg Empire, 88, 89
Hafez, 100
Haj, Samira, 103
ḥākimiyya (sovereignty), 246–7
halal market, 205, 207, 208–9, 216, 229n147, 262
Hallaq, Wael, 4, 5, 263–4
  Impossible State, 269

Hammer-Purgstall, Joseph von, 100
Hanna, Nelly, 81, 204, 217
ḥarām (forbidden), 207
Hatt-i Hümayun, 85
Hatt-i Sherif, 84, 85
Hennis, Wilhelm, 44
higher education *see* universities
Hinduism, 41, 48, 176
Hirschkind, Charles, 2
Hizbullah, 21
Hizmet movement, 172
holy war *see* jihad
Honneth, Axel, 49
Hosni, Mustafa, 213
Hourani, Albert, 14, 17, 79, 129–30, 235–6
  Arabic Thought in the Liberal Age, 101–2, 103, 105, 133
human agency, 34–5
Hurgronje, Christiaan Snouck, 232, 233, 234, 241, 247
Husayn, Sharif, 267
al-Husri, Sati, 151n52
Husserl, Edmund, 40

Ibn al-Nafis
  Commentary on Anatomy in Avicenna's Canon, 166
Ibn Rushd, 163–4, 167, 175, 183
  and jihad, 239, 240, 241
Ibn Saud, King, 137, 267
Ibn Sina (Avicenna), 162, 164, 167, 173, 175, 183
  Canon of Medicine, 163
Ibn Taymiyya, 266
IIUM *see* International Islamic University Malaysia

'ilm (modern science), 167–8
immigration *see* migration
India, 106, 151n52, 165, 198; *see also*
    Aligarh Muslim University
individualism, 43–6, 52, 53, 54
Indonesia, 109
inflation, 196, 197
İnönü, İsmet, 8n13, 129, 144, 152n56
interest-based lending *see* usury
interfaith dialogue, 16, 17
International Islamic University
    Malaysia (IIUM), 160, 168–9,
    177–81, 183, 262
Iqbal, Muhammad, 151n52
Iran, 3, 99, 173, 263, 264–6, 268–9
Islam, 13–20, 20–3, 48, 49–50
    and Abduh, 41–2, 129–30
    and activism, 210–11
    and economics, 80–1, 197–9, 204–5,
        207–8, 209–10, 216–19
    and essentialist image, 98–100
    and finance, 205–7
    and halal market, 208–9
    and Iran, 265–6
    and knowledge, 168–81, 181–4
    and Malaysia, 267–8
    and modernity, 1–2, 3–4, 5–6, 25–7,
        269–70
    and money, 200–1
    and multiple modernities, 261, 262
    and Ottoman Empire, 73, 74, 78, 80
    and Saudi Arabia, 266–7
    and science, 157, 158–60, 163–8
    and secularism, 23–5
    and the state, 263–5, 268–9
    and Turkey, 128–9, 140–1, 144, 145,
        146, 151n52
    see also Islamic reform movement;
        jihad; Muslim Brotherhood;
        precolonial Islam; shari'a; Shiite
        Islam; Sunni Islam
Islamic Caliphate, 87, 130–1, 136, 140,
    151n52
Islamic reform movement, 5, 56, 57–9,
    100–2, 105–10
    and Abduh, 110–16
    and activism, 212–16
    and jihad, 235–6
    see also Tanzimat
Islamic University of Medina (IUM),
    177
Italy, 89, 201–2

jahada (effort/endeavor), 238, 240
jāhiliyya ("ignorance"), 246–7
Jamaat-i Islami, 246
Jamjoon, Sheikh Ahmed, 168
Janissaries, 84
Jaspers, Karl
    Vom Ursprung und Ziel der
        Geschichte (The Origin and Goal of
        History), 48–9, 51, 52
Jeltoft, Nadia, 25
jihad, 7, 14, 18, 242–7
    and contemporary understandings,
        247–51
    and interpretations, 231–2, 234–5
    and Ottoman Empire, 232–4
    and premodern legal tradition,
        239–42
    and social actorhood, 235–8
Jordan, 197, 214, 218
Jouli, Jeanette, 22
Judaism, 41, 48, 176

jurisprudence (*fiqh*), 13, 15, 17, 177, 263
  and economics, 205, 206, 216–17
  and jihad, 234, 238–41, 242, 244, 247–8
Justice and Development Party (AKP), 145

Kant, Immanuel, 258
  Beantwortung der Frage: Was ist Aufklärung? (Answer to the Question: What is Enlightenment?), 54
Kateman, Ammeke, 111, 113
Kazzem, Tahia, 2
Kemal, Namık, 5, 100, 105, 106–7, 131, 182
Kemalism, 116, 133–4, 140–5, 145, 191n103
Khaled, Amr, 213–14, 215, 227n128
al-Khalili, Jim
  House of Wisdom, 163
Khan, Faraz, 250
al-Khatib, Muhib al-Din, 136
Khilafat movement, 151n52
Khomeini, Ayatollah, 265–6
Kishtainy, Khalid, 249
kitāb al-ḥiyal literature, 202, 216–17, 223n72
knowledge, 6, 104, 168–81; *see also* science
Krämer, Gudrun, 136
Küçük, Harun, 80
Kuhn, Thomas
  The Structure of Scientific Revolutions, 17–18, 19
Küng, Hans, 7n3

Kuran, Timur, 198, 216
Kyrgyzstan, 98–9

labour, 196–7
language, 46–7, 55–6
law *see* jurisprudence; legislation; shari'a
Lebanon, 21, 249
legislation, 81
Lewis, Bernard
  The Emergence of Modern Turkey, 72
liberalism, 22, 24, 101, 103–4, 133
Libya, 205
Lohlker, Rüdiger
  Islam: Eine Ideengeschichte (Islam: A History of Ideas), 15, 16
Luhmann, Niklas, 38–41, 42–3, 60n20, 64n85, 258
  Ökologische Kommunikation (Ecological Communication), 34–5, 36
  and organization membership, 146–7
  and politics, 74, 76, 77–8
  and society, 43, 45, 46, 48, 52, 54–5, 56
  see also Modern Systems Theory
Lyons, Jonathan, 164

McCutcheon, Russel, 42
MacDonald, Duncan Black, 98, 99
Maghraoui, Abdeslam, 3
Mahathir Mohamad, 181, 218, 268
mahdi movements, 100, 104
Mahmood, Saba, 24
  Politics of Piety, 20–1
Mahmud II, Sultan, 84

Malaysia, 205, 207–8, 209–10, 218, 219, 262, 264–5
  and governance, 267–9
  and jihad, 248–9
  see also International Islamic University Malaysia (IIUM)
Malešević, Siniša, 245
al-Mamun, Caliph, 165
al-manār (The Lighthouse), 109
al-Mansur, Abu Jafar, 165
March, Andrew
  Impossible State, 264
Mardin, Şerif
  The Genesis of Young Ottoman Thought, 72–3
Marx, Karl, 200–1, 203, 258
Masoud, Moez, 213
materialism, 57, 134, 171, 191n103, 198
Maturana, Humberto, 40
al-Mawdudi, Abu Ala, 99, 174, 182, 198, 219n3, 269
  Jihad in Islam (*al-jihād fi-l-islām*), 246
Mecca, 14; *see also* First World Conference of Muslim Education
media, 15, 17, 213, 248
medicine, 166
Medina, 14, 177
Mehmet V, Sultan, 232
Mehmet VI, Sultan, 142
Melchert, Christopher, 234, 250
Menderes, Adnan, 144, 170
Meyer, John, 160, 161, 236
Middle East *see* Egypt; Iran; Jordan; Lebanon; Saudi Arabia; Turkey; United Arab Emirates; Yemen
Midhat Pasha, 86

migration, 3, 17, 18, 249
militancy *see* jihad
minorities, 13, 14, 15, 16–17, 24, 81–2
Modern Systems Theory, 6, 25, 34–5, 38–43, 54, 261
  and economics, 198, 199–200
  and Islam, 57–8
  and politics, 75
  and science, 160–3, 182
modernity, 4–5, 24–7, 260–1, 263–4
  and Abduh, 129–30
  and activism, 210–11
  and Atatürk, 139–45
  and authenticity, 58–9
  and boundary negotiations, 104–5
  and economics, 198–9
  and Egypt, 132–3
  and entangled, 102–4
  and evolution, 51–5
  and Islam, 1–2, 3–4, 5–6, 269–70
  and jihad, 235–8, 242–7
  and language, 46–7, 55–6
  and Luhmann, 38–41
  and Muslim Brotherhood, 136–9
  and organization membership, 146–7
  and Ottoman Empire, 72–4, 78–80, 84–5
  and piety, 21–3
  and pluralistic, 211–12
  and reform movement, 57, 105–10
  and science, 159–60, 161–2, 167–8, 181–2
  and society, 34–7
  and Weber, 44–5
  and youth organizations, 212–16
  see also Islamic reform movement; multiple modernities

monarchy, 266, 267
money, 199–201, 202–4, 222n44
Moon, Alexander, 186n34
morality, 4, 39, 205
Moten, Abdul Rashid, 182
Mubarak, Hosni, 146, 212
muḍāraba, 206, 216
Muhammad, Prophet, 13, 14, 17, 175, 237, 240–1
Müller, Max, 130
multiple modernities, 6, 16, 25, 36, 47–51, 261, 262
Münch, Richard, 56
Mursi, Muhammad, 145
Muslim Brotherhood, 5, 8n13, 116, 237–8
 and al-Banna, 131–2, 135–7, 138–9, 146
 and jihad, 244–5, 246
 and mission (*da'wa*), 149n26
 and politics, 145, 147, 265
Muslimism, 229n148
Muslims *see* Islam

nahḍa (Renaissance), 49, 64n78
al-Nahhas, Mustafa, 140–1
Nash, Geoffrey, 100
Nasr, Muhammad Hamed Abul, 137
Nasr, Seyyed Hossein, 160, 168, 172–6, 182, 262, 263–4
al-Nasser, Gamal Abd, 2, 177, 246
nation states, 5, 6, 58, 74–8; *see also* statehood
nationalism, 36–7, 137–8, 244, 268
 and Turkey, 88, 141, 142, 151n52, 152n56
natural sciences, 15, 163, 170

New Economic Policy (NEP), 180–1
new media, 15, 17
Noth, Albrecht, 241
Nurcu movement, 171, 176

Oppenheimer, Robert, 173
orientalism, 13–14, 15, 18–19, 31n54, 99–100, 174
Osella, Filippo, 24
Osterhammel, Jürgen, 4, 41, 102, 115
Ottoman Empire, 5, 6, 58, 140, 142
 and economics, 204
 and jihad, 232–4, 247
 and modernization, 25, 72–4
 and Saudi Arabia, 267
 and science, 166–7
 and state formation, 78–83, 89–90
 and Sunnitization, 90–1
 see also Tanzimat

Pahl, Jon, 171–2
Pakistan, 205, 246
Paret, Rudi, 13
Paris Peace Conference (1919–20), 137
Paris Peace Congress (1856), 85
Parsons, Talcott, 38, 39, 60n20
Patey, Luke, 157
peace, 16, 85, 137
Pedersen, Gry Hvass, 179, 180
physical force, 76–8, 81–3, 84, 267, 269
 and jihad, 239–40, 248
 and Ottoman Empire, 86, 90
Piccoli, Wolfango, 71
piety, 14–15, 20–3, 25
pluralism, 17, 23, 211–12
politics, 4, 15, 40, 74–8, 259
 and Eisenstadt, 47–8, 49

and Iran, 265–6
and Malaysia, 180–1, 267–8
and Ottoman Empire, 82
and Saudi Arabia, 266–7
and Turkey, 143–4, 145–6, 153n70–1
polytheism, 45, 57
postcolonialism, 20, 31n54
precolonial Islam, 5, 260–1, 268
and economics, 201–4, 217
and jihad, 239–42
Prophet *see* Muhammad, Prophet
Prussia, 89
public sphere, 103–4

al-Qaida, 248
al-Qaradawi, Yusuf, 224n84
The Lawful and the Prohibited in Islam, 207
Qur'an, 13, 116, 177
and economics, 202–3, 204
and jihad, 240
and science, 158, 170, 171–2, 175, 176
Qutb, Sayyid, 57, 99, 246–7

Rahman, Azly, 248–9
Rahman, Fazlur, 203
Ramadan, Tariq, 249
rationality, 6, 259
al-Raziq, Ali Abd, 130–1
al-Raziq, Mustafa Abd, 130
reason (*'aql*), 112
Reckwitz, Andreas, 131, 132–3, 134, 146, 211–12
Rehman, Aamir
Gulf Capital & Islamic Finance, 216

religion, 17, 40–3, 45, 56–7
and Abduh, 112–14, 116
and Eisenstadt, 47, 48, 49, 50
and revivalism, 36–7
and science, 160–1
and state formation, 82–3
see also Christianity; Buddhism; Hinduism; Islam; Judaism
Resala Association for Charity, 214, 215
ribā (usury), 200, 202–4, 205–6, 243
Rida, Rashid, 105, 108–10, 130, 151n52, 182
and al-Banna, 136, 137
The Revelation of Muhammad (*al-waḥī al-muḥammadī*), 237
risālat al-tawḥīd (The Theology of Unity) (Abduh), 111–14, 115, 116
Rodinson, Maxime, 80, 217
Rosa, Hartmut, 35, 48
Russell, Bertrand, 173
Ryzova, Lucie
The Age of Efendiyya, 132, 134, 136

Sadat, Anwar El, 146
Safavid Empire, 91
Said, Edward, 27
Orientalism, 18–19, 23, 99–100
Said Nursi, Bediüzzaman, 160, 168, 169–72, 176, 182, 183, 262
Salafism, 107–9, 121n42
Saliba, George, 165–6
Salvatore, Armando, 26–7
Salzmann, Ariel, 82
Sanders, Liman von, 142
al-Sarakhsi, Ahmad, 14, 204
Sardar, Ziauddin, 182

Sarton, George, 173
  Introduction to the History of Science, 163–4
Saudi Arabia, 3, 177, 205, 264–5, 266–7, 268–9
Sawyer, Keith, 53
Schacht, Joseph, 13
  Introduction to Islamic Law, 98, 99, 110
Scharbrodt, Oliver, 115
Schuon, Fritjhof, 173, 175
Schütz, Alfred, 259
science, 4, 6, 19, 58, 170–1
  and Arabic golden age, 163–8, 186n21
  and botany, 186n34
  and Islam, 57, 157, 158–60, 181–4
  and Modern Systems Theory, 40, 160–3
  and Nasr, 173, 174–5
  and religion, 112
  and Weber, 259, 261
secularism, 3, 6, 23–5, 62n46
  and Ottoman Empire, 85
  and piety, 21, 22
  and Turkey, 8n13, 129, 131–2, 139–45
Selim III, Sultan, 84
September 11 attacks, 231
Serjeant, Robert Bertram, 13
shari'a, 15, 16, 98, 99, 110, 243
  and al-Banna, 136–7
  and economics, 202–3, 205, 206–7, 210, 218, 219
  and Hallaq, 263, 264
  and Iran, 265
  and Ottoman Empire, 81

and Saudi Arabia, 266
and tourism, 209
Shiite Islam, 21–2, 91, 265
Shirazi, Faegheh, 207, 216
Shirazi, Sadr al-Din, 173
shura (representative council), 243
Simmel, Georg, 258
  Philosophy of Money, 201
Sinan, Mimar, 129
al-Sisi, Abdel Fattah, 2, 145, 146
slavery, 80
Sloane-White, Patricia, 207, 208, 209, 216
Soares, Benjamin, 24
social actorhood, 58, 235–8, 244, 249
social theory, 4, 6, 27, 34, 258–60
society, 34–7, 38–41, 43–6, 47–8, 52–4
  and organized, 133, 134
  see also world society
sociology, 17, 26
Soviet Union, 3, 248
Stanford School of Sociological Institutionalism, 160–1, 236–7, 253n24
statehood, 6, 75–8, 263–5, 268–9
  and Iran, 265–6
  and Ottoman Empire, 78–83, 85–6, 88–90
  and Saudi Arabia, 266–7
Stauth, Georg, 26
Stenberg, Leif, 182
Stephan, Maria, 249
strong emergence, 52–3
Sufism, 15, 242, 254n45
Suhrawardi, 173
Sultaniyya (Beirut), 112
Sunni Islam, 82, 83, 90–1, 265

Tahir Pasha, 169
Tahtawi, Rifaat, 107
talfīq, 207
Tanzimat, 50, 73, 74, 79, 102, 262
   and history, 84–9
Taoism, 176
taqlīd (blind imitation), 116
tawḥīd (unity), 113–14, 174
taxation, 76, 81–2, 85, 86
Taylor, Charles, 104, 258
Tayob, Abdulkader, 111–12, 113
technology, 182
terrorism, 17, 231
Terzan, Levent, 171
theology (*kalām*), 177
Tilly, Charles, 74, 76–7, 78, 81, 89
tourism, 205, 209
trade, 78, 198, 201–4
   and Ottoman Empire, 80, 82, 85, 86
Traditionalism, 160, 172–3, 174, 175–6, 182, 264
traditions, 5, 17, 49, 50, 239–41
Tripp, Charles, 209, 216
"Tulip Age," 79
Turkey, 8n13, 71–2, 73–4, 99, 169–71
   and AKP, 145–6
   and Atatürk, 131, 139–45
   and economics, 197
   and jihad, 249
   and Kemalism, 133–4
   and Khilafat movement, 151n52
   and nationalism, 88
   and secularism, 131–2
   see also Ankara; Ottoman Empire
Turner, Bryan, 26

'ulama' (religious learned), 242, 266, 268
ulema, 73, 83, 84, 87
Umer, Zaituna, 158
Unbehagen in der Islamwissenschaft, Das (The Malaise in Islamic Studies), 19
United Arab Emirates (UAE), 196
United States of America (USA), 16, 172–4, 176, 216, 229n141
universities, 6, 161–3, 169, 176–7; *see also* Aligarh Muslim University; International Islamic University Malaysia (IIUM)
usury, 200, 202–4, 205–6

Vahdat, Farzin, 50
vilāyat-i faqīh (rule of the Islamic jurisprudent), 265
violence, 17
Viskovatoff, Alex, 46–7
Voll, John, 110
Volpi, Frédéric, 13–14
voluntarism, 214–16, 262

Wagner, Peter, 103, 131, 133, 146, 211–12
Wahhabism, 267
war, 16; *see also* First World War
Weber, Max, 6, 44–7, 57, 64n85, 184, 201
   The Protestant Ethic and the Spirit of Capitalism, 258–60, 261, 269, 270n3
   and statehood, 74, 77, 78
Wellhausen, Julius, 13
Wensinck, Jan Arent, 13

West, the, 4, 16–17, 19, 24, 161; *see also* Europe; United States of America
Westphalia, Peace of, 83
Wiener, Norbert, 173
Wigan, Einar, 90
Wishnitzer, Avner, 86
women, 14, 20–3, 143, 227n128, 249
world of Islam (*dār al-islām*), 15–16
world society, 2, 4–5, 6, 36–7, 48–9, 56
  and jihad, 236–8
  and politics, 75

Yemen, 99, 205
Young Ottoman movement, 72–3, 85–6, 88, 89, 91, 262; *see also* Kemal, Namık
Young Turk Revolution, 72, 73, 169
youth organizations, 212–16, 218
Yusuf, Hamza, 216, 219

Zaghlul, Saad, 108, 137
zakat (alms-giving), 205, 243

EU representative:
Easy Access System Europe
Mustamäe tee 50, 10621 Tallinn, Estonia
Gpsr.requests@easproject.com

www.ingramcontent.com/pod-product-compliance
Lightning Source LLC
Chambersburg PA
CBHW052056300426
44117CB00013B/2159